KERI

Fighting Back

Kat Ward

Dedication

Being a teenager isn't easy. Even kids who are growing up in happy, loving households have all manner of problems in adolescence. For those kids who have been abused, raped, bullied, mistreated or neglected it is a thousand times worse. This volume is dedicated to all teenagers everywhere. Especially those who suffer at the hands of those who should understand, love and protect them.

Prologue

In book one of Keri – The Early Years – I related events up to the age of fourteen. I began with my very earliest memories when I could have been only about two or three years old. I think most people do not recall such early life. For me, the recall is not only vivid, it is traumatic. That Mother never wanted me is very clear, even before Nana (my maternal grandmother) told me about how Mother had married my father against Grandfather's wishes and how the marriage broke down very quickly. I never met my real father to my knowledge. If I ever did, I cannot remember it.

Mother married again. Unfortunately, the man who became my step-father began to use me for his own sexual gratification when I was around four or five years old. Along with the constant psychological and emotional abuse I endured from Mother, who claimed that by the very act of breathing and being alive I had ruined her life, I also suffered physical violence from both of them. Book one relates many of these abuses in graphic detail.

I rarely made friends during childhood. Children seemed to know instinctively that I should be avoided at all costs. Looking back now, I am glad that no-one else became embroiled in my family situation. Perhaps being unpopular saved some strangers from similar abuses to my own. Of course, teenagers are different to younger children – and not just in their attitudes and the way they look. I did make friends more easily as a teenager as will become clear in this volume. As an adult survivor now, I can see that most of my friend choices were decidedly suspect. Still, by the time I reached adolescence, I was prepared to take whatever I could get, good or bad.

At the end of the first volume, I had just met a Social Worker who visited the house. Of course, this lady had already spoken to Mother at some length and had swallowed the lies, hook, line and sinker. I tried to stick up for myself, but I knew, even as I railed and shouted, I was already beaten.

1. Farewell Friends – Back To School

As it turned out, I didn't get the hiding I expected. The Social Worker stayed for quite some time. I had a very good idea of what Mother must be saying about me ... and an even better idea of how her words would be received. Feelings of impotent rage consumed me; why these so-called child-care experts would neither listen to, nor believe me was a mystery.

When I heard the front door close, I crossed the room and watched the Social Worker walk to her car. The storm had eased to a persistent light rain; I noticed the lady used an umbrella just to cross from the cottage door to her car, parked as it was, in the lane outside Mrs. Meadowes' gate.

"Stupid old cow!" I muttered to myself.

I went back to my bed and sat, braced for the storm I anticipated when Mother came up the stairs to thrash and berate me. After about half an hour, I opened the door and peered down. I could hear the clacking of typewriter keys coming from Mother's room.

I crept down the stairs, avoiding the steps which I knew to creak. The door to Mother's room was closed, so I hurried to the kitchen, where Tammy greeted me enthusiastically. I made a cup of tea and sat at the table, staring through the window at the raindrops. Adrenaline, which had been keeping me on edge and alert, completely drained away and I felt morose and full of confusion and despair.

I saw Mother leave the house via the front door; she quickly got into her car and reversed out of the drive. I supposed she'd return to work, although she could have been going to collect Russell from school. Taking advantage of her absence, I rummaged in the cupboards for something to eat but found nothing that required no preparation or cooking. Sighing, I settled for a piece of bread and butter.

When I'd eaten, I cleaned up the crumbs and took Tammy upstairs with me. There was nothing to do but read or play patience. I thought about Mam and wondered what the gypsies were doing; I felt willing to bet they were engaged in some interesting activity.

Likewise, Benjamin and his parents would be busy at the farm; Sylvia too, would probably be baking or cleaning. I felt like the only person in the world with nothing more interesting to do than sit alone in my room with a book I'd already read and a pack of worn-out playing cards.

Overwhelmed with boredom, I dozed off to sleep with the dog lying beside me on the bed. Angry voices jolted me awake; I had no idea how long I'd been sleeping. Tammy whined, her eyes wide with anxiety. My bedroom door stood open and I could hear what was being said.

"... why you can't just leave it!" That was Terry's voice.

"Oh, you'd like that, wouldn't you? Then you could do whatever you want with her and turn her into some common little tart like ... like ... your sister!" Mother's tone dripped venom.

"Aunty Jenny isn't a tart, Mum! She's really nice! Why would you say she's a tart?" Clearly, Russell was present in the room downstairs. Mother must have collected him from school after all.

"Shut up, Russell. It's nothing to do with you. Go and play or something." Mother modified her tone slightly.

"Don't tell him to shut up! You're an evil cow, Milly. Russell, take yourself round to see Kevin and don't interrupt."

"But, Dad! I want to watch ..."

"Yea, I know, go round Kevin's to watch it. Go on. Here's some money. If it stops raining later you can get yourself some chips."

"He can watch it here! Go in the lounge and don't put your feet on the furniture. You stupid man, it's pouring with rain, he's hardly going outside to play in the rain!"

"Oh, I see. So it's fine for her to be out in the rain, but not him, is that what you're saying now? Anyway, a bit of rain never hurt anyone; and I told him to go to Kevin's. Don't change the subject. You think these bloody people are completely stupid don't you? You just had to get them involved ..."

"How dare you! She *is* stupid! I told her to walk the damned dog, not wander about in the rain. Even I thought she'd got more sense than that!"

"Why? You've got no fucking sense! You're so busy trying to make out that everything is fine and rosy to these fucking do-gooders ... and blaming everything that goes wrong on her. If you were a halfway decent wife, there'd never have been any problems. You're not even a decent mother! You and your snooty, stupid airs and graces, pretending you're better than me, when all the time you're out screwing that posh, opinionated arsehole! I've had it up to here with you. If you hadn't filled me full of crap in the first place, things might have been different. You made all this happen; she'd probably be normal if it wasn't for you! You just had to get those damned social workers poking their noses in! Now they'll be all over the fucking place asking questions and wanting to know everything about all of us! What are you gonna do when they discover you're not the perfect wife and mother after all? They will ... and if they don't, I think I'll fucking tell them myself!"

"Dad ... can I just go in the lounge? Don't argue, please."

"No. Get round to Kevin's or somewhere else. You shouldn't be stuck in the middle of this. She'll be manipulating you next. Go on, get out of here."

"Russell! Stay where you are and do as I told you. You're not going anywhere."

I heard the sounds of a scuffle and Russell cried out, "Let go, Mum! You're hurting me! I'll go! I'll go round to Kevin's"

"No, you won't! You'll go in the lounge and watch television as I told you to do!" Mother screeched.

"Get off him! You're a raving maniac, you are! He's just a kid and I'm not having you start your evil ways on my son."

There was another scuffle and then rapid, running footsteps up the stairs. I sat up as Russell appeared in my doorway.

"What have you done now?" Russell snarled at me. "It's always your fault when they fight. What did you do?"

Russell was red in the face, but I noticed him trembling as he stood in the doorway, glaring at me.

"She told lies about me again," I mumbled. "I refused to listen to any more rubbish when the social worker came, that's all. I wouldn't speak to her."

"If you were just normal, like everyone else, we wouldn't need a social worker here anyway. Mum's right. It is your fault that everything is always horrible and everyone's unhappy! I hate you!"

Russell turned and went to his own bedroom. He slammed the door. Mother and Terry continued to roar insults at one another downstairs. I hugged Tammy close to me and wished desperately that I could be anywhere else but there. I tried not to listen to what was being said, but I couldn't help hearing as the shouting grew even louder.

"... would I even want to consider sleeping with you! You're not even clean! You stink like a midden!"

"So what? It's sweat, from bloody hard work! You wouldn't know anything about that, would you, Lady Muck? I might make a fucking effort if I had anything to look forward to!"

"I wouldn't touch you with a ten-foot barge-pole, you ... you ... pervert!"

I jumped up and closed my bedroom door before flinging myself on the bed and covering my head with the pillow. I felt Tammy crawl as close to me as she could get.

The pillow muffled the shouting somewhat, although it made it difficult to breathe properly. I lay with the dog, wondering which of my 'parents' would rush upstairs to thrash me when the argument ended.

After about half an hour, during which the shouts continued, interspersed with a few heavy thumps, I heard the unmistakeable sound of the front door slamming. I moved the pillow away and listened intently. I heard the sound of Mother's car moving over the gravel of the drive.

A feeling of relief that Mother had left the house combined with apprehension as to what Terry might do. I wanted the toilet, but didn't dare go downstairs in case Terry started shouting at me. I crossed my legs and hugged Tammy. I must have sat like that for well over half an hour before my bedroom door opened and Terry looked in at me.

"Get your coat and stuff; I'm taking you and Russell to the club. We'll get fish and chips on the way. Hurry up."

On the way to the club, Russell asked Terry, "Dad, where's Mum?"

"She said she was going to her mother's place, but that's unlikely. She's probably staying with ... a friend or something."

"You mean Riley Douglas, don't you?" asked Russell.

"That's enough of that. It's none of your business." Terry replied.

No-one mentioned Mother again. Not that evening at the club, during which time Russell and I enjoyed ourselves immensely; not the following day or the day after that. It was almost as if Mother had ceased to exist.

I spent the next couple of days visiting with Mam, Sylvia and Benjamin. I had a wonderful time. I helped on the farm, laughing and joking with Mr. and Mrs. Jones as well as Benjamin whilst they chattered like Jays doing all the farm chores and readying everything for Benjamin's return to school. It was worlds away from my own life, but I slipped into it and felt privileged to be accepted as a part of it all.

In Sylvia's kitchen, I prepared pounds and pounds of fruit and vegetables for jam and pickles as I listened to all the village gossip, of which Sylvia always had an endless supply. She said she'd miss me when I went back to school and this made me feel happy and sad all at once. I hugged her frequently.

At the gypsy camp I ran across the heather with Mia and our dogs bounded joyfully around us; Benjamin didn't visit the gypsies with me as he was too busy at home. I sat on the steps of Mam's wagon and listened to the old gypsy woman speak about so many things. I probably learned more about nature and the ways of the gypsy folk in two days than most people could learn in a whole lifetime. Mam's gentle wisdom settled around me like a cloak and I felt loved, warm and safe. I never had time to feel bored ... or unhappy.

On the Friday evening, after dinner, Terry sat at the table whilst I washed the dishes.

"Have you er ... packed your trunk thing yet?" he asked.

"No. I don't know where everything is. Mummy always does my packing," I replied.

"Well, you'll be doing your own packing tonight. I'm taking you back to school early tomorrow morning. I'll go and have a look in her room and see if I can find everything. You must know what you should have?"

"I think my new uniform is hanging in Mummy's wardrobe ... some of my clothes are in my room, but I don't know where everything else is."

"Well, I suppose there must be a list or something somewhere. That's probably in her room too. I'll go and have a look."

I can honestly say that was the first time I missed Mother at all. I wondered what would happen if I arrived at school with the wrong things. Nothing much could happen, I supposed. If I'd forgotten anything vitally important, I could get the school to telephone, or I could even write to Terry and ask him to send whatever it was by post.

Terry found the list and it was quite easy to pack the trunk and the small suitcase. I put several things in that were not on the list, but Terry didn't even check, so he never knew about them. Several girls took a good deal more mufti clothes than the specified amount. So long as I had all the uniform - most of which Terry found stacked up in Mother's room - there could be no real problem.

Russell went round to Sylvia's house before I left. He barely said goodbye to me; this might have been because he missed Mother a lot more than I did and he blamed me for her absence.

Terry let me have the car window open on the journey to school, so I didn't feel as sick as usual by the time we arrived. There were not many vehicles in the courtyard; we'd arrived much earlier than ever before.

Sister Violet came to greet me as I stepped from the car. Terry got out and manhandled the trunk and suitcase out of the boot.

"I hope it's all right if I cut and run," Terry remarked. "Only I have to be back in Norwich by half past ten and I'm cutting it fine already."

"Yes, yes, that's fine," replied the nun, smiling. "Keri knows her way about. We'll manage the trunk between us, won't we, child?"

Terry leaned inside the car and opened the glove-box. He took out an envelope, which he handed to Sister Violet.

"I think that's all as it should be. There's stamps and forty quid pocket money in there. I have to go now. See you soon, Keri. Behave yourself!"

Without so much as a hug or a wave, Terry got back into the car and started the engine. Sister Violet and I watched as he expertly turned the car around and sped off along the drive toward the main gate.

"Did you have a nice holiday, Keri?" Sister Violet asked as we hefted the trunk between us. "I must say, you're looking very well. You certainly look a lot better than when I last saw you."

"Yes, thanks," I mumbled. I knew I couldn't mention Mam or the gypsies to the nuns; they'd be shocked to learn that I was mixing with such people.

We progressed toward the main stairs. I saw several girls I knew. Most greeted me in passing with a nod or a cheery 'Hello'. The place smelled of floor polish and steaming vegetables. My stomach growled.

Sister Violet laughed. "Let's get this to your new dorm and then you can unpack. It sounds to me as if you're hungry. No-one else has arrived yet from the group in your room, so you'll get first choice of bed. Won't that be nice?"

I selected a bed near the window and placed my suitcase on the bed next to it, effectively reserving it for my one friend, Sarah. It didn't take me long to unpack everything and put it all away with Sister Violet's help. We dragged the trunk out onto the long landing. Later, all trunks would be taken down to one of the annexes for storage.

I raced down the main stairs to the refectory. Several girls were sitting with their families, drinking tea and eating cakes, biscuits and other treats. I helped myself to a mug of tea and an individual pack of biscuits and sat down at a table near the long window. It occurred to me I might also manage to get first choice of desk in the classroom, but since I could see no-one from my year group, I took my time and enjoyed the snack.

I went back to my dormitory to collect my pens, books and stationery then made my way to the other building. I found a nun in the school block and asked which would be my classroom for the year. She directed me to a room next to the science laboratory. I hurried straight to the back of the class and chose two desks, one for me and one for Sarah. I placed my pens and pencils inside the desk and left my books, equally divided between the two, on top. Then, having nothing much else to do, I returned to the dormitory.

When I got there, I immediately noticed all my belongings strewn on a completely different bed. Confused, I went to the drawers of the bed I'd chosen and opened them. Inside, neatly laid out, were someone else's clothes. I checked the name tape on a blouse. Veronica!

No-one was about; fuming with outrage, I removed all Veronica's things from both wardrobe and drawers, tossing them as carelessly onto an empty bed as she had tossed mine. Then I replaced everything just as I had originally arranged them. I sat on my chosen bed and looked out the window.

After about half an hour, Veronica entered the room with Amanda. I had never got along particularly well with either girl, although we had never really crossed swords.

Veronica glared at me. "Look at all my things!" she exclaimed. "You've thrown all my things out and taken my bed!"

"No." I replied, as calmly as I could manage. "I was here first and I had already put all my things away. I've only done the same to you as you did to me."

"Just look at the mess!" yelled Veronica. "I never did. I was here first and I chose that bed. I'm telling Matron what you've done."

I bristled. "Tell Matron then, it won't make any difference. I was here first and Sister Violet was right here with me when I chose this bed. She helped me to unpack, actually."

"Well, that's my bed and I'm having it back. Amanda, help me to move all her stuff."

Amanda hesitated. She'd never been unpleasant to me and I could see the doubt in her expression. "Leave it, Veronica. Come down the other end and have the bed opposite mine. That's near a window too."

"No, I'm having the bed I chose," Veronica insisted.

At that moment, the twins arrived with Sister Violet and another nun helping them with their trunks. Veronica barely greeted the twins before she launched into her complaints about me to Sister Violet, who folded her hands inside her baggy sleeves and listened intently.

The twins manoeuvred themselves around the indignant Veronica and selected beds next to one another further down the room.

"... and that's what she did to my things!" finished Veronica, indicating the clothing and belongings piled, higgledy-piggledy on the bed near the door.

I folded my arms and said nothing, but I watched Sister Violet from under a deep frown.

"Now, Veronica. Keri *was* here first and I helped her to unpack. That is the bed she chose. You'll have to choose another." Sister Violet turned to me. "You shouldn't have taken all Veronica's things and thrown them about like that, Keri. If there was a problem, you should have come to find me. Now, I want you to help Veronica sort and fold her clothes up, do you understand?"

"But, Sister! She did it to my things. They were screwed up all over the place when I came back to the dormitory! I only did the same to her as she did to me."

"I understand, Keri. Even so, two wrongs don't make a right, do they? Now, you get to keep the bed you chose and Veronica must select another. It won't hurt you to help her sort her things out. After all, I helped you, didn't I?"

I nodded. I glanced at Veronica who stood, staring at the nun in disbelief. Amanda was helping the twins unpack, the three of them chattering gaily about their holidays.

Sister Violet smiled. "Right then. That's all settled. Come along girls, we don't want any disagreements right at the start of term. You get on with putting Veronica's things away and I'll be back in a little while." She turned and glided away along the corridor.

"I'll get you back for this!" hissed Veronica. "You see if I don't."

"Shall I help you fold your clothes?" I asked, sweetly.

"No. I don't want you near anything of mine; you smell and you've probably got fleas or something. Leave me alone." Veronica turned away and snatched up a great armful of clothes which she dropped on a bed next to one of the twins.

I shrugged and left the room. It occurred to me that it might be a good idea to go to the school block and sit at the desk I'd selected. Veronica usually sat at the back of the room and I had a good idea she'd happily move my things in the classroom as well, if she had the opportunity. If I were seated at the desk, with all my books on top and other belongings inside, she could hardly say anything at all.

That was the beginning of a long-running enmity between me and Veronica. It lasted for the rest of the time I was at All Hallows. She did get me back for thwarting her - several times; she certainly never let me forget that, in her opinion, I was not as important as her. Since she was a very popular girl, the bad feeling between us spread until most of the girls in my year either ignored me completely or made catty remarks just within hearing at every possible opportunity. So much for standing up for myself!

2. Differences and Uncertainty

Surprisingly, at first I settled back into school life, almost as if there had been no holiday. It was a relief to have a structured day, filled with things which had to be done and expectations as to how to behave. I certainly had no time to feel bored.

As I sat in the convent chapel on that first Sunday, with Father Godwin preaching his sermon, my thoughts drifted. It occurred to me I had barely thought about either the school, the girls or God during the whole eleven week holiday. I wondered if that was 'normal'. This led on to me pondering why it should be that I seemed to drift through my own life, almost like a shadow; I had no purpose. If I tried my hardest to please everyone the result was no different than if I'd been as naughty as could be. I recalled the horrible hospital examination, the dismissal of my disclosures that my step-father raped me and the way both the child psychiatrist and social worker seemed to believe everything Mother said about me, whilst totally ignoring anything I said to them.

I studied the other girls around me. Mostly, they looked bored, as if they couldn't wait for the service to end when they could rush back to the school for a hearty breakfast. One or two were actually paying attention to the words Father Godwin spoke so passionately. Catherine in particular looked happy and attentive; her eyes shone and she had a faint smile on her lips. It must have been nice to be Catherine; her parents loved her, she was pretty, friendly and clever. I curled my lip in a sneer of brief envy, which I regretted almost at once. Catherine couldn't help being loved and she was far too nice to dislike for something as petty as jealousy.

Sarah sat beside me fiddling with the buttons on her jacket. She nudged me slightly and in barely more than a whisper she said, "I feel sick. Shall I just get up and go out?"

I glanced toward the door. No-one else had left the service that morning. I didn't want to sit alone, but the prospect of having Sarah vomit so close to me made my stomach twist with anxiety. "Yes," I whispered. "Matron might come out, but otherwise, no-one will take any notice. Don't be sick in here whatever you do!"

Sarah picked her way between other girls and fled outside. For a few seconds, I contemplated following her. For once, I didn't actually feel nauseated myself, but I felt as if I were betraying my only friend by not going with her. I caught Matron's eye and she frowned, dispelling my charitable ideas immediately.

Although I felt happy enough during lessons because I threw myself into the school work with every bit of energy I could muster, it was a different matter in the dormitory and common room. For a start, it quickly became apparent that I was the only girl in my year group who had not been away for a holiday. Most girls had gone abroad - some for several weeks; others had been away to destinations in this country. I had not even been to stay with Nana, although there had been a week of day trips to Sheringham, where Nana spent her holiday with Great Aunty Ellen and Great Uncle John. I did not wish to recall that period as it had included one of the worst beatings of my life thus far.

All I could do was to maintain an apparently bored silence as I listened to other girls' tales of foreign lands and people, or of anecdotes about themselves and their families during the holiday period. Both Sarah and Catherine asked me about my holiday and seemed concerned when I mumbled that my family were far too busy to spend time away. I could not be drawn by anyone to tell anything of my holiday period at all. How could I tell them that I spent long hours alone or with gypsies? I began to feel out of place again and withdrew into myself.

Several times, I recalled Mam's twinkling, dark eyes and her warm little hands. I longed for the old gypsy woman's company and advice. She would know what I should say and do. In many ways, I felt angry with myself for being too fearful to mention her. I felt proud of the way the gypsies had accepted me, yet I felt I couldn't mention them as they and their way of life would in no way be accepted by my peers or the nuns and staff.

Sister Stephanie noticed how quiet and withdrawn I had become. She drew me aside after a particularly hard game of hockey, during which Veronica had whacked at my ankle - apparently by accident. It hurt.

"Keri, is everything well with you, child? You don't seem to have the same er ... vitality that you used to have."

I must have looked alarmed because the novice went on, "No, no, don't be worried. You're not in any trouble. I'm just concerned for you. Is everything all right at home? Are you having problems with the work this term? Or perhaps something else is troubling you?"

"I'm all right, Sister. It's just ..."

"Come and see me when you've changed out of your gym clothes, Keri. We can have a little chat." Sister Stephanie smiled and patted my shoulder before turning to one of the other girls with a cheery comment.

I liked Sister Stephanie. In fact, the previous year I had spent long periods worrying and fretting about the pretty young nun. It seemed a dreadful waste for her to spend her life shut up in a convent. I'd raised numerous objections to her continuing in her apparent vocation as a nun. In fact, on one occasion, I'd called her a coward - too afraid to face real life. The fact that she could still speak to me amazed me.

I changed quickly and made my way to the classroom where Sister Stephanie would teach her next lesson. I found the young novice marking books and hesitated for fear of disturbing her. She looked up at me.

"Come in, child. Sit by me here and tell me, what is worrying you?"

I sat down and stared at my hands for a few minutes before looking up into Sister Stephanie's clear, blue eyes.

"There's nothing much, really ... it's all so silly ... but ..."

Sister Stephanie waited in silence whilst I collected my thoughts.

"Well, the first thing that's bothering me is that I'm the only girl in my year group who didn't go away on holiday with her family. I feel stupid and as if I'm not as good as the rest of them."

"I didn't go away on a holiday either," replied Sister Stephanie.

"Well, you wouldn't. I don't expect you're allowed to go away on holiday!"

"Where would you have liked to have gone, Keri?"

This question stumped me for a moment. I hadn't given it any thought at all. I'd listened to other girls talking about swimming, snorkelling, riding and a whole host of other activities. In fact, none had really appealed to me much. What made me feel so envious had little to do with the things they'd done or the places they'd been, but the closeness they had with their families. In the end, I gave the only answer I could have given.

"I'd have liked to spend the summer with Nana."

Sister Stephanie smiled. "Not in Switzerland or Monte Carlo?"

I shook my head.

"Well, I'm sure you'll have other holidays with your Nana, Keri. I'm also sure that's not the only thing which is troubling you. If you really don't want to talk about it, I understand, but sometimes, a trouble shared is a trouble halved. Do you know what I mean?"

"It's not that I don't want to talk about things, Sister. The thing is I've tried talking about it, lots of times. Have you ever had people disbelieve you when you're telling the truth?"

Sister Stephanie sighed. "I think it's a thing which happens to most people occasionally, Keri. Have the girls been unpleasant to you?"

"Not really. I got on the wrong side of Veronica on the first day back because I chose the bed she wanted. She threw all my stuff out of the cupboards and drawers and tried to claim she'd been there first. Sister Violet knew I was there first though because she helped me unpack. Veronica's never liked me much anyway. No, it's not the girls."

"Well, Keri, I cannot force you to talk to me, of course. If you feel you can't speak to me, perhaps you'd like to talk to someone else about it, whatever it is? How about Father Godwin?"

"No!" I cried. "I'm sorry, Sister. I didn't mean to shout. Honestly, I'll be all right. I'll try to be more cheerful and everything. It doesn't matter at all, really."

I stood up and looked at the seated novice. "Thank you for asking," I added. "It makes me happy that you care about me."

Before Sister Stephanie could reply, I fled. As I ran through the corridors and out into the autumn sunshine, my heart beat painfully against my ribs; I'd come too close to revealing my real life, purely because I liked Sister Stephanie. From past experience, I knew if I trusted a teacher with my tales about my horrible family, it led to more trouble. I headed toward the refectory, where I knew there would be warm soup and thick slices of brown bread waiting; my appetite had fled, but I would eat anyway. I tried not to let myself think what might have happened if I'd told Sister Stephanie about my family, what had happened in the holidays and that my only friends were a farmer's wife and son, a village widow, an old gypsy and a timid, cowed dog.

I recalled the bracelet Penelope had given me that I'd handed in to the Bursar the previous term. Doctor Stewart accused me of stealing it. I wondered if she'd contacted Penelope and confirmed the bracelet as truly mine. If she had, then I would be allowed to have it back. When I'd finished my soup, I trotted along to the Bursar's office.

The Bursar peered over his horn-rimmed spectacles at me. "Your bracelet? Why, child, it's not here. I sent it by post to your mother as soon as I received her telephone call. Did she not tell you and return it to you?"

Rage swept over me. Clearly, Dr. Stewart had contacted Penelope and told Mother that the bracelet was mine. I wanted to stamp my foot or scream, but the Bursar hadn't known that Mother would keep the bracelet from me. I swallowed my fury and said, between clenched teeth, "She must have forgotten. I'm sorry I troubled you."

I sat alone on the steps of the school block, seething with suppressed anger until the bell rang to indicate the second period of lessons beginning. It was such a small thing, but the more I thought about it, the more I hated Mother. Why she wouldn't allow me to have pretty clothes like other girls my age, or my own jewellery and hair ornaments was a mystery.

I paid little attention during the next lesson; Miss Walker told me off more than once. I barely acknowledged her. I stared at the other girls in the classroom and thought all kinds of unpleasant, jealous things about every one of them.

At lunch time, I quickly finished my chores and hurried to the dormitory to find my letter-writing case. I wrote a long, impassioned letter to Penelope, explaining everything; how I had been unfairly accused of stealing the bracelet and further, how Mother had received it by post but not returned it to me. Satisfied, I placed a stamp on the envelope and put the letter in the posting box outside the Bursar's office.

When lessons finished for the day and I had time to myself, I sat in the Common Room to write more letters. I wrote to Great Uncle John and told him how I had been beaten so badly I had to be locked in my room where no-one could see me - because he'd told Mother off for picking on me without cause. I also said she was sleeping with Riley Douglas but blaming the family problems on me. I could have told him about Terry and the rapes and abuse; I don't know why I didn't. I think perhaps I only told Great Uncle John what I knew for certain he would believe because he'd seen the evidence with his own eyes.

I began a letter to Nana. Mam advised me to speak to Nana the same way as I spoke to her. I tried to tell Nana about my life, but it just didn't seem right, writing it all down. I knew my words would hurt her and she might even disbelieve me. It was a risk I felt I couldn't take. I tore the writing paper up and started again.

After several more false starts, I had a single page letter to Nana which simply told her I had arrived safely back at school, the weather continued warm for autumn and that I missed her. As an afterthought, I added a post script in which I said I hoped Mother was enjoying her stay.

As the days passed and I had no word from home or Nana, I worried constantly about the cats and Tammy. I knew Terry hated the cats and only tolerated the dog; without Mother, I wondered if he would feed them and whether Tammy would be taken for walks. The worry kept me from sleeping well and soon I had dark circles under my eyes and felt distinctly ill tempered.

Staff members were busy arranging a gymkhana event to raise funds for something or other that the school required. Most girls had their own horses, which were to be brought to the school by parents; some had more than one. It seemed, once again, I was the only girl different from everyone else. I'd never ridden on horseback at all. In fact, the only horses I'd ever been close to were those which Aunty Maisie and I fed when I was very small and those had been cart-horses. I felt left out and isolated. Even Sarah had a horse to ride. Of course, I pretended indifference to the whole affair, but several times over the period of planning, I noticed Sister Stephanie and Sister Violet watching me intently.

I took to running around the perimeter of the upper playing field, just for something to do which involved no-one else and which may tire me out. To some degree, this worked well; I was exhausted most of the time, but I still couldn't sleep at night.

In lessons, although I tried as hard as I could, my concentration wavered and I made silly errors, particularly in math. This enraged Sister Mathilda; my denseness became quite a source of entertainment for the class. The diminutive nun stood beside me, often armed with a ruler which she smacked down on the edge of the desk repeatedly as she tried to emphasize a point. With each crack of wood upon wood, I flinched. I looked up at the furious nun and wondered if the day might come when she would beat me with the ruler instead of the edge of the desk.

One day, about three weeks into the term, which had thus far, been quite miserable for me, Father Godwin found me sitting alone under a tree on the bank near the school block in the pouring rain. He studied me in silence for a few moments, tapping his teeth with a fingernail.

"Come with me, my child. You can't sit here in the rain all alone."

I scrambled to my feet and hung my head. "I'm all right, Father. I was just thinking, that's all."

"Yes, I realise that. The problem is, child, you've done nothing but think since you've been back at school. Sister Stephanie tried to talk to you about your problems, but you said something cryptic and refused to be drawn. You cannot continue like this. Come along to the chapel with me, at least it's relatively warm and out of the rain. You don't want to catch a chill."

I followed Father Godwin to the chapel. Two nuns were attending to flowers and candles, but they departed quickly when they saw me with the priest. Father Godwin ushered me toward the ornate, wooden confessional. I tried to protest, but there was little point.

"Now, I'm pretty certain that whatever is bothering you is not necessarily a sin, but you definitely need to talk to somebody, child, if I'm any judge. Remember, whatever you say in the confessional is entirely confidential. It can go no further and you may find it helps to ease your mind. In you go. I will be with you directly."

I sat in the gloom and stared at my hands folded in my lap. It had never occurred to me to speak to Father Godwin in the confessional. It should have done, because we had been told, as a group, plenty of times that whatever was said during confession would remain absolutely confidential. Even so, I didn't want Father Godwin to brand me a liar. Would he believe me if I told him everything? I took a deep, jagged breath and waited.

When Father Godwin sat down on the other side of the panel in the confessional booth, I automatically intoned, "Bless me, Father, for I have sinned." I cannot now recall how I began my 'confession'; I can only say it took a very long time indeed for me to tell Father Godwin everything. I heard the bell in the distance, summoning me to my next lesson, but since Father Godwin ignored it, so also did I.

When I had done with relating the incidents of sex abuse, rape and beatings, I continued with Mother's hatred and disapproval - how I could do nothing right in her eyes. I told Father Godwin that neither the child psychiatrist nor the social worker believed me; how the hospital doctor dismissed my tale out of hand, and how, through it all, Mother sat crying and telling lies about me. I related the incidents I knew of when Terry killed or abused the cats - how he dislocated Tammy's shoulder when the dog tried to defend me as he thrashed me. I added that my mother was either staying with Nana or with Riley Douglas - with whom it seemed she was having a love affair. I couldn't stop worrying about Tammy if Mother were not at home to ensure Terry didn't hurt her. I finished by telling the priest that I felt the only places I ever fitted in at all were either with Nana or the old gypsy woman, Mam.

"Child ... I need your permission to speak with the Bishop about what you have told me," Father Godwin almost whispered. "These are very serious matters and you need help, urgently."

"You said this was confidential, Father!" I exclaimed.

"It is, child, it is. I need to speak to the Bishop and the Authorities in order to help you but ..."

"No. They won't believe me," I insisted. "No-one ever believes me. You don't believe me either, do you?"

"No-one who heard you speak so could fail to believe you, Keri, my child. It is because I know what you've said is true that I feel we must seek other help."

"When I told the teacher at Thorpe House, she told the Head and the Head told Mother. I know how it goes. Then I got taken to see Dr. Stewart - but not until after Mother had already spoken to her and filled her full of lies. The same would happen again, I know it. You promised you wouldn't tell anyone, Father. Your Bishop couldn't make it stop. God has never made it stop. If you tell anyone, you'll be in trouble, won't you?"

"Yes, indeed I would. But what if I were to come with you to see this ... Dr. Stewart? Without your Mother? I'm sure the school can make the appropriate arrangements. Or I could come with you to the police station ..."

At this, I actually laughed. "Father, the police wouldn't believe me either! Who will believe a girl who is apparently so naughty she's been expelled from school? A girl who has to go and see a child psychiatrist regularly because her Mother says she is a wicked and violent liar? No. I trusted you and now you want to turn on me as well. Just tell me what to do to make it all stop and I'll do it ... so long as I don't have to tell anyone else, because I'm sick of being called a liar, trouble-maker and slut." Tears trickled down my cheeks as I spoke and I suppressed a sob.

"Very well. As you wish, child. Just promise me that, should you need to talk, you'll come and speak with me again. You don't need to speak to anyone else until you're ready."

I sniffed. "All right. Shall I go and do penance now, Father? I know that I'm wicked because I've wished my parents would die and I've been jealous of the other girls because they're happy and have nice families."

Father Godwin drew in a sharp breath. "My child, I think just one 'Hail Mary' and a few moments of communion with the Lord are the only penance I can possibly give you."

I left the confessional and knelt near the front of the chapel. I looked up at the marvellous sculpture of Christ but my tears blurred the detail. I'm afraid to say that although I said the Hail Mary and stayed quietly on my knees for several minutes, there was no sincerity there. If anything, I felt even bleaker inside than I had before speaking with Father Godwin.

If there was a God, either he was too big to notice someone as small as me or He simply didn't care. I thought about the ant I'd seen when I watched the patch of ground as Mam instructed me. The ant had been struggling to carry the body of another ant. Several times, it put the body down, ran about, apparently without purpose, before returning to pick up the body and continue. I could have intervened - but I didn't know what help the ant needed. I didn't know where it was taking the body or why. Perhaps that was the problem with God too? I wondered if I should pray ... then I thought of the ant again. If it had stopped to pray, I would neither have heard nor understood what it wanted; I wouldn't even have recognized that it was praying! No, I thought to myself. There could be no help from God - if He existed - any more than there could be help from anyone else.

I left the Chapel and wandered slowly toward the school block. As I started up the steps, the bell rang for lunch. I stopped and waited for girls to pour from the building in a chattering horde. They flowed past me entirely unheeding on their way to the refectory.

When most of the girls had passed me, I hurried toward the science laboratory, where I should have been studying Physics in the lesson I missed whilst in the confessional.

Sister Mathilda was busy tidying away books from the lesson.

"Sister ..."

"Ah. There you are, Keri. Why did you miss my lesson?"

"Sorry, Sister. I was with Father Godwin in the Chapel."

"I see. Well, I'm sure you can look at someone else's work to catch up on the work you missed. There is prep to be completed before the next lesson, too."

"Yes, Sister, I will. Er ..."

Sister Mathilda stood in the middle of the laboratory with her arms filled with books. "Is there something else?"

"Yes. Please, Sister, could you telephone my home and find out if my dog is all right? I'm really worried about her."

Sister Mathilda put the books down on a bench and studied me. "Would you like to telephone for yourself, Keri? I could arrange that, if you wish."

Although I didn't relish the prospect of speaking to either Terry or Russell, I supposed it would be better than worrying. I nodded my head.

"Very well. Come to the staff room after supper and I'll take you into the office to make the call. There would be no-one at home during the day so there is no point in attempting to call immediately."

I thanked the tiny nun and rushed to the refectory for lunch. I felt relieved but also nervous. So long as I could reassure myself about Tammy, I would be able to cope with everything else.

3. Shattered

I knew my home telephone number, but because of my inexperience with telephones, I needed Sister Mathilda to help with dialling the call. She handed me the receiver and said, "There. It's ringing."

"Swanton Abbot three-eight-three," Mother's voice.

I nearly dropped the telephone with surprise. "Hello? Who is this?" Mother sounded irritated.

"Er ... hello, Mummy, it's me."

"What are you doing using a telephone? Where are you? You should be safe at school! If I find out ..."

"I am at school, Mummy," I interrupted. "They let me 'phone you."

"Why?" Mother sounded suspicious.

"Well ... I haven't heard from you ... or Nana and ..."

"Nana's here; she's fine. Now, what do you want?"

"I ... er ... I'm glad you're home again, Mummy. I was worried about the cats and Tammy."

"They're none of your business, so why should you 'worry' about them? I suppose you're using them as an excuse to draw attention to yourself. If you must know, nearly all the cats are dead. I'm trying to nurse Kipling now. She's the last one."

Tears sprang to my eyes and I spluttered, through a lump in my throat, "What? D ... d ... dead? Did he kill them?"

Mother snorted derisively. "Don't be so stupid! They all caught that awful Feline Enteritis disease and have suffered days of agony. Is there anything else? I'm very busy with the cat, you know ... and they may have let you use the 'phone but I hope you realise that I shall be charged for this call?"

31

"My bracelet. The one Penelope gave me. The Bursar says he posted it to you. Can you send it to me, please?"

"No. I threw it away. Now, go and get on with some school work!"

In truth, I had expected no less. I practically ignored the news. I wanted Mother to talk to me now that I knew the poor cats had died and Kipling was desperately ill.

"Wait! Please, Mummy, how is Tammy? Does she miss me?"

There was a pause. For a few seconds, I thought perhaps Mother had hung up.

"She's gone."

"Gone?" I echoed, my heart sinking. "Gone where?"

"She ... er ... it wasn't fair for her to be stuck in the house all day alone whilst we were all out. She's ... er ... gone ... to live on a farm. Now, I need to get back to Kipling ..."

"What, the farm in Swanton Abbot?" My heart lifted somewhat. Perhaps if Tammy had gone to live with Farmer Jones she would be happy. She loved spending time with Shep and was intelligent enough for the farmer to train her.

"No, another ... er ... farm. Anyway, why all the questions? It's nothing to do with you. I hope you're getting on with your school work and not causing any trouble. Now, get off the phone. I might need to call the vet in a moment."

"Mummy!" I cried out. Sister Mathilda sat close by, reading a book. She looked up at me.

"Mummy, please don't go yet. Can I say hello to Nana, please?"

"No. She's busy. I'll write to you when I have the time. This pointless call is costing me money. Goodbye."

The line went dead. I stared at the receiver for a few seconds before replacing it. Tears spilled down my cheeks and I sank onto a nearby chair.

Sister Mathilda put her book down and approached me. She placed a hand on my arm and said, very gently, "Oh dear, poor child. Bad news?"

I nodded as I covered my face with both hands and began to sob. Sister Mathilda patted my arm several times, then wrapped her arms around my shoulders and hugged me tightly.

"Do you want to talk about it, child?"

"Sister!" I sobbed. "Tammy's been sent away to a strange farm and all the cats are dead, except one! I'll never see them again!"

For nearly half an hour, I sat in the office with Sister Mathilda. I could not control the gulping sobs which shook my whole body. A great tide of grief overwhelmed me.

At length, Sister Mathilda led me up the stairs toward Matron's office. We passed several girls; all of them stared at me. Once inside the office, I sank into an armchair and continued to weep as Sister Mathilda quietly explained to Matron that I'd made a telephone call and received bad news.

I spent the rest of the evening, until bed time with Matron in her office. She gave me a cup of cocoa and sat talking to me. She seemed to understand my connection with animals, particularly Tammy. She told me about the dog she'd had as a child.

Eventually, my tears stopped and were replaced with a headache. Matron gave me half a glass of water with soluble aspirin in it. I drank the bitter fluid with a shudder.

That night, sleep eluded me for a long time. I curled in my bed and hugged Lambie close, listening to the sounds of the other girls sleeping. Moonlight shone through a crack in the curtains and fell in a pale streak across the bedspread. I fancied I saw the shadow of a large dog standing between the window and the bed. Tears slid from my eyes once more.

"Oh, Tammy," I breathed. "I so hope you'll be happy. I hope they'll be kind to you on the farm and you'll find another dog like Shep to be friends with. I shall miss you so much - you were my closest friend."

I felt different within myself as the weeks passed. Somehow, it seemed a part of me had inexplicably become lost and wandered away. Although I did everything expected of me to the best of my ability, a great deal of my ability had fled. Mostly, the staff were kind and treated me with tolerance and understanding.

Plans for the gymkhana continued. I attempted to join in, but I knew virtually nothing about horses or competition rules. Sarah confided in me about her own reservations concerning her riding ability. Apparently, she had not ridden on horseback for several years and would be using a borrowed horse. She greatly feared making a fool of herself. I could offer nothing by way of advice. I simply told Sarah that I'd never ridden on horseback at all.

Sister Violet approached me a few days before the gymkhana, which was to be held in a nearby field on the last day of the half term.

"Keri, it has come to my attention that you have no horse to ride at the gymkhana," she began.

I shook my head. "I don't know how to ride, Sister. Even if I had a horse, I'd probably fall off it."

"Well, that's a very defeatist attitude, Keri. I always thought you were braver than that and would give almost anything a try. It's just ... well, I have been speaking with one of the parents and they could bring an extra horse, so you wouldn't feel left out. Would you like that?"

"I haven't got a riding hat, Sister, or any jodhpurs. It's all right, really. I'll just watch."

"Well, hats and jodhpurs are about in plenty. Matron has quite a store of clothing which girls have grown out of and given to the school. I'm almost certain both can be found for you if you'd like to try."

I felt pressured. I didn't want to take part in the gymkhana; it was not the kind of activity I'd ever had any interest in. However, it was clear that Sister Violet had gone to a great deal of trouble on my behalf.

"All right," I agreed, "I'll have a go."

Sister Violet beamed and hurried away.

At bed time, when I entered the dormitory after my bath, I noticed several girls sitting with Veronica on her bed. They stopped speaking as I came into the room and stared at me. I ignored them all. I had no idea what they were talking about in relation to me, but it was pretty obvious I had been the subject of their conversation. I kept my back to them all as I got into bed; I didn't want any of them to see my burning red cheeks.

Half term and the day of the gymkhana approached all too fast. I packed my weekend case carelessly. I didn't want to go home. Neither did I want to take part in the gymkhana, but there was no backing out now.

I stared at the few letters I'd received. I didn't want to leave them behind, but on the other hand, I couldn't risk taking them home with me in case Mother found them. The one from Penelope expressed outrage that Mother should have taken the bracelet away and promised to buy me an even prettier bracelet the very next time we saw one another. Great Uncle John's letter was long and mentioned several of the things I'd told him. One paragraph said I should let him know as soon as Terry or Mother became violent again and he would go straight to the Police. The two letters from Nana were quite short and contained nothing I would object to Mother seeing. I put them in my case and tucked the letters from Penelope and Great Uncle John underneath the mattress. The beds had all been stripped bare for half-term laundry. I could retrieve the letters when I re-made the bed after half term.

A party atmosphere filled the school that day. No one wore school uniform; girls trotted about in jodhpurs and smart jackets - including me. Matron found everything I needed in her clothing store. In fact, Matron said I could keep the clothes if I wanted to.

I didn't want to. The jodhpurs felt tight and uncomfortable and I was pretty sure I looked utterly ridiculous. The neck of the blouse pressed against my throat uncomfortably and the jacket seemed too short, although it looked pretty much the same as everyone else's.

Parents began arriving at about mid-morning. Girls ran to greet their families, laughing and chattering gleefully. The lane held an almost continuous procession of horse-boxes pulled by large vehicles.

I sat in the Common Room staring out the window. I wondered if it would be Mother or Terry who came to collect me - and what they'd make of all the activity and horses.

Veronica stuck her head round the door. "Keri! Come on! The horses are here!"

I glanced back at the girl I disliked. "I can see that," I replied.

Veronica scowled. "Well, come on then. You're so rude and ungrateful. My father went to a great deal of trouble to bring an extra horse. He had to use the large, double box."

I stared at Veronica. "You're the person who's lending me a horse?"

"Yes, of course, now hurry up."

I scrambled out of the armchair and hurried after Veronica. She didn't speak as we jogged down to the field, for which I was grateful. Now I understood what she had been talking to other girls about. I truly wished it could have been anyone but Veronica that loaned me a horse. For a start, the enmity between us had only grown stronger throughout the half term. There had been numerous small incidents in which Veronica had been able to make me feel everything from unimportant to totally isolated. Secondly, I knew Veronica was an accomplished horsewoman and had won several competitions with her beloved horse. A sick feeling of dread mounted within me as we drew closer to the crowded field.

Veronica's father was an enormous man who sported a magnificent curled moustache. He wore a tweed jacket and a strange shaped, brown hat which had curious flaps fastened on the top of it. He greeted me with a wide grin which showed all his teeth.

"Ah! So you're the gel without a horse, eh, what? We'll soon have you up and riding, don't-yer-know. Easy as falling off a log."

Veronica's mother was stunning. Although she wore slacks and a tailored jacket with a silken scarf pinned at her neck, she oozed elegance. Her blonde hair was swept back from her face in a neat chignon; her make-up was perfect. She inclined her head toward me and murmured, "Hello."

Part of the field had been marked off with a temporary fence. Within it, a series of 'jumps' had been erected using brightly coloured, striped poles. A few girls were already on horseback, trotting their mounts around in circles, looking at the obstacles.

Close to where the horse-boxes were gathered, a small stream ran. Beyond the stream, rose a low hill. I noticed several girls at the top of the hill, some on horseback.

I watched as Veronica led a brown and white pony toward me. It had one blue eye and one brown eye. It seemed huge. I automatically backed away a little.

Veronica's father laughed loudly. "Now then, gel, don't ever be letting the animal see you're worried. Be firm and confident at all times. Marty's all right, he's an old softie. Come along; let's get you up in the saddle."

Marty looked over his shoulder as I scrambled awkwardly up onto his back. I recalled my brief attempt to ride the gypsy horse, when Mia and Benjamin persuaded me to sit on it and Mia led it round in a circle. There had been no saddle then. This was far worse. The leather seat felt hard and uncomfortable, the stirrups wobbled on leather straps and the reins felt strange in my hands.

Veronica's father held Marty steady whilst Veronica mounted her own beautiful, chestnut mare. Every time Marty shifted his feet, I felt a wave of panic. I didn't feel at all safe. In fact, I wanted to jump down and run all the way back to the school, but I didn't dare. I swallowed hard and tried to pay attention to the instructions Veronica's father gave me.

After about half an hour, during which time, Veronica's father showed me how to hold the reins properly and how to sit with my back straight, Veronica announced she would lead Marty and I should hang on to the edge of the saddle.

"If you don't even get used to him walking, you'll never manage even the simplest thing," she remarked.

I clung to the saddle and tried to grip the horse with my knees as Veronica led Marty first, round in a long circle, then off, across the stream and up the hill, to where a group of girls were sitting on their horses watching the proceedings in the field below.

One or two of the girls greeted me as we approached. I tried to grin, but it must have looked more like a snarl; terror had a firm grip on me.

At the brow of the hill, Veronica suddenly tossed me the reins and said, "Here. He'll wait quietly now. You may as well look as if you're in control. Honestly, you're useless. I didn't really believe you when you said you'd never ridden before. What on earth do you do with yourself?"

I shrugged. Marty shifted his feet and I clung to the saddle again.

"Do you know what I think?" Veronica suddenly said, in an overloud voice. "I think you're not one of us at all, Keri. I think you're probably some poor little kid from a crummy council estate that's been taken on here for charity. That's why you don't fit in."

"What? No, I'm not!"

"Well, how else are we to explain everything? You don't have holidays, you don't ride or swim or seem to do anything at all. You haven't a clue how to behave in company and your clothes ... well ... what more need I say?"

Ginny interrupted Veronica. "I say, that's a bit much. She's not from a council estate. Her mother is in the same business as my father - swimming pools."

"Well, the business isn't doing very well then!" Veronica retorted. "Have you seen her mother?"

I hung my head. Next to Veronica's mother, mine looked positively scruffy. I hated Mother, but even so, it was quite another thing to listen to someone who didn't even know her make unpleasant remarks about her.

"Actually, the business is doing rather well," I remarked, trying to keep the embarrassment out of my voice.

"Leave it, Veronica," said one of the other girls. "Let's not argue and spoil a lovely day. We'll all be going home in a couple of hours."

"Why should I leave it?" demanded Veronica. "I should have been having a lovely day today. After all, the gymkhana was my idea and my father has paid for most of it! Now I've got to spend the day trailing around with her. She hasn't got a clue, look at her!"

My cheeks burned with shame and I felt tears prickling at the corners of my eyes. I tried to turn away, but this was not easy sitting on a horse I didn't know how to control.

I'm not actually sure what caused Marty to bolt. He suddenly tossed his head and began to run back down the hill. I slipped around on the saddle, lost the reins completely and flung myself forward to put my arms around the horse's neck. Marty didn't like that at all. He tossed his head and kicked his legs. I screamed for help - right by Marty's laid back ears. He bucked and kicked again and shook his head, trying to dislodge me.

When he came to the stream, Marty stopped dead. I continued. Over his head I tumbled and into the water, where I landed on my back with an almighty splash. I gasped and flailed my arms as the water went over my face. Unconcerned and relieved of his nervous passenger, Marty trotted through the stream, treading heavily on one of my hands as he passed. I screamed; water ran into my mouth and I sat up, coughing, retching and spluttering. I couldn't get my breath and in my panic, I wet myself. I doubt if anyone noticed; after all I was sitting in the stream and the horse had stirred up silt and detritus with his passage.

Matron fussed around me in the infirmary. She bandaged my bruised hand and scolded me for being silly and irresponsible. I didn't reply. Veronica's words were ringing in my ears still and I felt deeply humiliated and ashamed.

When I'd changed out of the soaked clothes, I went to the empty Common Room and sat in an armchair staring at the floor. Matron had instructed me to go directly back to the gymkhana and not to get into any more trouble. I couldn't bear the thought of going back among all those people. Everyone had seen me fall off a horse which was apparently docile enough for a ten year old to ride.

I sat, doing nothing at all for a couple of hours. When I heard the sounds of girls coming back to the school, I hurried to the dormitory to collect my suitcase. I had no idea where I should wait or whether Mother had arrived.

I entered the dormitory and saw Veronica standing in the middle of the room with several girls around her. She was relating the incident of my fall again; they were all laughing uproariously. No one noticed me.

I swallowed a lump in my throat and took a couple of steps backward so as to be hidden behind the door.

"Well, as far as I'm concerned, it serves her right. She shouldn't have gone whining to Sister Violet saying she'd got no horse to ride! She's spent the whole of this term so far, trying to get me into trouble. Even right at the start, she took my bed! Do you know, she threw all my things out of the cupboards and drawers and then got Sister Violet to back her up! Just wait 'till after half term, I'll teach her that I'm not going to put up with any more of her nonsense. She's nothing but common scum!"

Rage took hold of me. I had not approached Sister Violet at all; it had been the other way around. I'd wanted nothing to do with the gymkhana, much less Veronica or her hateful horses. As for the bed incident ... it was true enough. I had thrown her clothes out of the drawers and cupboards, but only after she'd done the same to me. I rushed into the room and barged between the girls to face Veronica.

"I never asked Sister Violet for anything. *She* persuaded *me*! If I'd had any idea that it would be *your* horse she wanted me to ride, I'd have refused! And I'm *not* common scum!"

I drew my hand back and slapped Veronica's face with all the force I could muster. "You're just a stuck-up cow! You've no idea about me or my family or the life I have to live. You're far too wrapped up in your precious horses, foreign holidays and being snooty, thinking you're better than everyone else!"

Veronica staggered under the blow. "Oh!" she cried and sat down heavily on the edge of the nearest bed.

There was shocked silence. My body began to shake uncontrollably. I felt nauseated. I bitterly regretted what I'd just done, but it was too late.

"I'm sorry I hit you," I muttered.

Tears trickled down Veronica's cheeks. My hand had left a large, red mark. In fact, every finger was visible on her pale skin. She looked up at me.

"You'll pay for this!" she exclaimed. "My father won't tolerate this. He'll call the police and have you thrown in jail."

"Good," I replied. "At least in jail I won't have to listen to snooty people who think they're better than me."

I turned, snatched up my suitcase and marched out of the dormitory into the corridor with tears of dismay and fury blurring my vision.

There was no sign of Mother or Terry in the courtyard, so I retreated to the Common Room once more. The nausea and shaking disappeared and was replaced by a familiar, sick sense of dread. I felt no surprise when a nun came and summoned me to the Head's study. My feet dragged as I followed her.

Outside the study, Mother stood with her lips pressed into a thin line. Her ice blue eyes glittered with suppressed fury. A few feet away, Veronica's father stood with his hands in his trouser pockets. He frowned when he saw me.

I remember little of the interview save that it was extremely unpleasant. The Head was dismayed. She tried to coax me into explaining myself, but words would not come. I felt far too fearful of how Mother might react. Veronica's father was outraged and made several furious threats about withdrawing both Veronica and his financial support from the school. As for Mother ... I had no idea of what she must be feeling because she wouldn't look at me. She sat tight lipped and frowning. I do not recall Mother saying anything at all. I do remember the Head telling me that assault and violence of any kind were completely unacceptable and that there were other ways of dealing with anger and frustration. The interview ended with Miss Forster solemnly shaking my hand and wishing me the very best of luck in life.

Sister Violet helped me to collect all my belongings from around the school. She barely spoke, other than to ask the whereabouts of certain belongings. Another nun brought my trunk from the annexe.

All the girls had left for half term. The dormitory echoed because all the bedding and curtains had gone to the laundry. I packed everything into the trunk on my own. I felt completely numb and empty. Everything had happened so quickly and I had been the instrument which destroyed my one sanctuary. I had never felt more alone.

I sat on the edge of what had been my bed and stared out the window for the last time, trying to commit the school to memory. Yet again, my actions had caused my life to change direction. I knew there would be trouble at home but I couldn't focus on that at all. I sat, alone and despairing until a nun came to help me carry the trunk down the stairs for the last time.

I completely forgot about the letters from Great Uncle John and Penelope hidden under the mattress. They must have been found. Whether they were sent to Mother or destroyed, I'll never know.

4. Lost

Mother didn't speak to me or look at me on the journey home. I sat in the passenger seat of the little, three-wheeled car and stared at the bare trees, their leafless branches stark against an iron grey sky. They looked how I felt - stripped naked and without hope.

I couldn't cry. Even though I knew I would never see All Hallows again nor feel the warmth and acceptance of the school as a whole. I knew also that I'd never see Sarah again; I wondered if she'd miss me. It had all happened so fast.

For many years, Mother told teachers, social workers and anyone who would listen that I attacked her and Russell physically - to explain away her attitude toward me. It wasn't true. In fact, I'd never hit anyone until I slapped Veronica. I reflected upon what I'd done. I had no idea why I attacked the girl. She was spiteful and some of the things she'd said were unforgivable, but to attack and hit her ... why on earth would I do such a thing?

When we reached Swanton Abbot, Mother slowed the car to a crawl. She glanced at me before she spoke. "I don't know how I'm ever going to live this down," she grated. "It will be obvious to everyone that you've been expelled - again. I'm not messing about any more. You can go to the school in North Walsham, although you'll not get much of an education in some crummy state school full of common ruffians. I don't expect you care about that though, do you?"

"She said I came from a common, council estate family and that we're too poor for you to dress nicely or for me to have pretty things," I mumbled.

Mother stopped the car in the middle of the street and stared at me, incredulous. "She said what?" she demanded.

I repeated what I'd just said.

"Why the ... of all the ... *right*! I'm not putting up with that kind of nonsense. You stupid little cow! Why didn't you say that when we were with that dreadful man in front of the Headmistress? You just sat there staring at them all as if you'd never seen people before! When the Head asked you why you thought you could go round hitting people, you should have damned well said why you did it!"

"Why?" I asked. "None of you would believe me if I had. You're always telling people that I go round attacking everyone when I never have. Now that I have, you're angry with me. I suppose it's all right for you to thrash and beat me but it seems you're the only one who thinks so! They'll never take me back there now. Why couldn't we just be like other families and be nice?"

Mother started the car again and drove to the cottage where she pulled onto the drive. Her face was red with anger. I sat very still in the hope that she might simply go inside and leave me alone in the car. I didn't want to go into the cottage because I knew Tammy would not be there to greet me.

"Get out of the car and get indoors. I'm going to telephone that bloody convent and give them a piece of my mind."

"Mummy ... please don't."

"Why shouldn't I?" Mother snarled. "Unless you're lying again. That would be a novelty, wouldn't it? I want to see what they've got to say about it. I'm not having things like that said about me!"

My heart sank still further, although I hadn't realised that was possible. So Mother intended to make a fuss now that we were away from the convent. I had a very good idea that Veronica would deny saying anything about me at all. I thought about the incident. There had been several girls present. In fact, none of them had known I was listening until I barged into the room and screamed at Veronica. However, they'd all heard what Veronica said. In fact, some of them had heard other things she'd said whilst at the gymkhana as well.

Resigned, I made no protest as Mother propelled me through the front door ahead of her. The house seemed eerily empty. I glanced at the window sill in the sitting room where Kipling, the cat used to sit. A small vase of flowers stood there now.

Mother went straight to the telephone. I wanted to go to my room, but I dared not walk away in case mother had questions for me, so

I sat down on an armchair and listened as Mother announced herself and waited to be transferred to the Head.

"Good afternoon, Miss Forster. I felt the need to ring you because I have got to the bottom of the incident which required me to remove my daughter from the school." Mother's tone was pleasant enough, but I could see by her expression that she was making an effort not to lose her temper as she listened to what Miss Forster said.

"That's as maybe," Mother said, "But sometimes there is extreme provocation, which I believe is the case in this instance."

I couldn't hear what Miss Forster was saying to Mother, but the scowl on Mother's face told me it was nothing good.

"Well, she's right here with me. She can tell you herself."

Mother handed the receiver to me and said, "Go on. Tell her what that stuck up little cow said to you. All of it, mind. There's no point just telling her half of it."

I put the receiver to my ear and fought down panic. "Hello?"

"Good afternoon, Keri. Your mother seems to think there is something you need to tell me." Miss Forster sounded as reasonable as ever.

"Yes." I hesitated.

"What is it, dear?"

"Well ... Veronica has been mean to me since the start of term. I chose the bed she wanted and she threw all my belongings out of the wardrobes and cupboards and took it."

"Sister Violet did mention the incident to me, dear. But that was right at the start of term, wasn't it? I'm sure that's not a reason for your behaviour now, is it? Sister Violet also told me she made great efforts to reconcile the two of you by arranging with Veronica's parents for you to borrow a horse today."

"But I didn't want a horse!" I blurted. "I don't know how to ride and Veronica said I was useless and spoiling her day because she had to stay with me!"

"Yes, Keri. I'm sure that was very hurtful for you, but you can't go about hitting people because ..."

"I didn't! She made the horse run off with me and I fell off and got hurt ... and wet. She laughed. Everybody laughed. It was later, in the dorm. She said ..."

"Keri, I can understand you were somewhat embarrassed by falling off, but Matron says you weren't seriously hurt. I think ..."

"She said my mother is scruffy and that I'm just common scum! She said I live on a council estate and don't know how to act in company, she said ..."

Miss Forster's tone became more forceful, "Keri, I'm sure there were things said. There usually are, in any argument. I understand that you and Veronica had words. I have to insist though, that striking another girl is the point in question. Veronica may well have upset you, dear, but she didn't attack you, did she? I'm very sorry, but the decision has been made. I wish you the very best of luck in life. I'm quite sure that whatever you decide to do, you'll do it very well."

I couldn't speak any more. I had known the call would be futile before Mother made it. I handed the telephone receiver back to Mother and sank back into the armchair.

I paid no attention to the rest of the conversation, other than to note Mother's rising temper. It was all just pointless arguing as far as I could see.

"Go and make some tea," Mother snapped, as she hung up. "I may as well have been talking to a brick wall. Why couldn't you have just ignored the stupid girl?"

I wandered into the empty kitchen. Tammy's basket, food and water dishes had gone, of course. Tears sprang to my eyes as I recalled the enthusiastic greeting the dog always gave me. She didn't care if I was common or didn't dress as nicely as everyone else. I had to exercise tremendous self-control not to sit down and sob - which is what I wanted to do.

When I took Mother the mug of tea, she scowled at me. "I'll have to waste time getting you into another school now," she grumbled. "And another bloody uniform too!"

"Can I go upstairs?" I asked.

"Yes. Get out of my sight."

When I reached my bedroom, it looked bare and different. The bed was not made up and every trace of me had been removed. I opened a few drawers in the chest. They were all empty. The few items I'd left on the pin-board had also gone. I sat down on the ottoman and stared out the window, unsure if I should make up the bed and too fearful to go down again and ask Mother to help me with my trunk.

I saw Martin come down the village street and go into his house. Mrs. Meadowes came out of her gate and hobbled up the road with a shopping basket on her arm. Several young children raced out of a gate and chased one another past the cottage, laughing and squealing as they went. I felt like a stranger again. There'd be nothing for me to do and probably only Sylvia to visit - if that. The gypsies had moved on, so I would be unable to visit Mam and draw comfort there. Benjamin had returned to his boarding school and although I knew Mrs. Jones would welcome me, a visit to the farm meant seeing Shep ... which would remind me I no longer had Tammy. My stomach knotted at the thought of Tammy. The big dog had loved me unconditionally and been a comfort and companion through the worst of times. Alone in my bare room, I let the tears flow at last.

It was dark when Terry and Russell came in. They'd been to a football match in Norwich. I wandered down the stairs when I heard them laughing and joking. Terry took of his green and yellow striped scarf and threw it over the back of an armchair.

"All right?" he said to me.

"No," I replied. "I got expelled."

Terry paused and stared at me. "Bloody hell!" he said, at length. "That's all we need! She'll be impossible to live with now. I suppose she's going through the 'phone book looking for another fancy school for you now. Where is she?"

"Mummy's in the lounge, I think," I said. It struck me as rather odd that Terry seemed neither angry nor disappointed in me. His only concern was that my expulsion would make Mother difficult. "I've got to go to the school in North Walsham, Mummy said."

"What, the Secondary Modern?" Terry asked.

I nodded.

"They'll soon sort you out," Russell interrupted. "Nobody at that school will put up with you and your snootiness. I bet you'll get a hiding or two!"

"Shut up, Russell," Terry said in an absent-minded tone.

"Well, they won't!" Russell exclaimed. "Everyone round here thinks she's too posh and snooty anyway."

Terry ignored Russell and went to the lounge. Russell flung his coat on top of Terry's football scarf and sat down on an armchair.

"So, what'd you do?" he asked.

"I smacked a girl's face," I replied.

"Cor! Did you knock her down?"

"Sort of."

"I wish I'd seen it," Russell grinned. "Was she snotty and snooty like you?"

"Worse than me. She said we're common scum and live on a council estate."

"Ha! So you thumped her. That's so funny!" Russell began to laugh.

I heard raised voices from behind the closed lounge door.

Russell stopped laughing and stood up. "They'll argue about it now," he said as he went toward the kitchen. "She'll moan and groan and Dad'll probably tell her she's a stuck up cow and then she'll scream insults at him and then ..."

The door opened and Terry came out. "Come on, Keri. Better get that trunk out of her car. She wants to go and see her friend now."

The sarcasm in Terry's tone didn't surprise me. I knew full well he meant that Mother intended to visit Riley Douglas. I followed Terry out the front door to Mother's little car.

"Maybe you'll get to live a normal life if you go to an ordinary school," Terry said, conversationally as we hefted the trunk between us. "Make a few mates locally and get a boyfriend. Do all the usual teenage stuff."

"Russell says everyone hates me," I replied.

"He's just soft in the head. He ain't got a clue. You got on all right when you came to the Club with me, didn't you? When she's gone, we can go over to the Club, me, you and Russell. We don't have to sit here being miserable all evening."

"Aren't you cross with me?" I asked.

"Cross? What for?" Terry replied.

"I got expelled."

"Well ... you didn't really do anything, though, did you? Your mum says you clonked some snotty bitch round the ear-hole."

"I did," I agreed as we lugged the trunk up the stairs. "She said I was common scum and that we came from a council estate."

Terry gave a bark of laughter. "Nothing wrong with that. I come from a council estate. It's better than being born with a bloody silver spoon in your mouth. I'm as common as they come and I'm proud of it."

Terry left me alone in the bedroom to unpack the trunk while he went back to collect the suitcase. I opened the heavy lid and began to sort through the clothing and belongings, which I had not packed neatly.

"When she's buggered off, we'll go and get fish and chips and then go on to the Club. That Dave will be pleased to see you. He's done nothing but talk about you recently." Terry tossed the suitcase on the bed.

"All right," I agreed. "Shall I make my bed now?"

Terry grinned. "Well, you'll have a cold and uncomfortable night if you don't." He left the room, rubbing his hands together and chuckling.

I found clean sheets in the airing cupboard, which was in my room. Blankets and eiderdowns were stored in the ottoman. As I made the bed, I heard more raised voices downstairs, followed by the sound of the front door slamming. I went to the window and watched Mother clamber into her three-wheeled car, start the engine and drive off.

I'd hardly finished unpacking before Terry called me downstairs. He looked me up and down.

"Haven't you got anything better to wear than that?" he asked, indicating my knee-length, pleated skirt and plain blouse.

"What's wrong with it?" I asked.

"Well. You look about forty instead of nearly fifteen. Maybe once you get to an ordinary school you'll start dressing for your age."

"Mummy buys my clothes."

"Yeah, and it shows. She's got about as much taste and fashion awareness as a turnip!"

I raced back to my room, tears prickling at my eyes. Terry had never mentioned my clothes before. In fact, the only people who had ever really commented on what I wore were girls at the convent - mainly Veronica. I knew I'd never be able to persuade Mother to buy me fashionable things. I rummaged through my clothing and selected a different skirt and a prettier blouse, although both were still frumpy.

I dragged the clothes on, leaving the discarded clothing in a heap on the floor. I rolled up the sleeves of the blouse and left the top button undone, leaving the neck open a little. The skirt presented different problems. I tried to roll the waistband over and over to make the hemline higher, but this just resulted in a big bulk around my middle which showed, even if I left the blouse un-tucked. Frustrated, I stamped my foot. There was nothing for it, but I'd have to wear the clothes as they were.

No-one at the Club remarked on my clothes or dress-sense, although in all honesty, I felt frumpy and self-conscious all evening. As Terry predicted, Dave attached himself to me and seemed genuinely pleased to see me. We played cards and darts and during the evening, I forgot some of my troubles. Dave knew a great many jokes and I laughed a lot.

We stopped very late at the Club. I sat in the huge lounge bar and watched Match of the Day with all the men and boys. Dave expressed surprise that I enjoyed watching football.

"I used to play football a bit," I said. "Before we moved here, I mean."

"Really, actually play it?" Dave asked, intrigued. "I bet you were a striker, eh? Score lots of goals, did you?"

"No. No goals at all. I played *in* goal actually."

"Ah. Right. I might have known. They always put the fat kid or the girl in goal, just to make up the numbers."

"Actually, I was quite a good Keeper," I retorted.

"Yea, I bet you were," Dave teased. "One day, I'll get you out on the field behind the club and you can show me!"

That was the first time I'd ever managed to watch the football programme right through. I decided I liked Tottenham Hotspur and would support them. I kept the thought to myself though. Most people in the Club supported Norwich City, but my memories of living in Norwich were too cruel and I couldn't find any enthusiasm for the football team. Since I'd been happiest in Chingford with Nana, and Chingford was on the London outskirts, a London club seemed like the right choice for me. There are stranger ways of choosing a team to support I suppose.

On the way home, Terry asked me, "So you like football then?"

"Yes, but don't tell Mummy. She'll be furious."

"Yea, she would. You can watch Match of the Day with me and Russell next time when we're at home, if you like."

"Thanks, I will."

"Aw! Dad! She'll spoil it if you let her watch it with us!" Russell interrupted.

"Don't be daft, Russell. She can watch it, if she likes football."

Russell subsided and scowled at me. Terry seemed to be searching for things to talk about.

"So; what music do you like, then?"

I shrugged. "I don't know."

"It's like trying to talk to a bloody wall! Ain't you got any interests?"

I shrugged again. "I like drawing ... and writing. I suppose I like music, but I only hear whatever Mummy has on the radio. I liked 'T-Rex' when I heard them."

"And is that it?"

Russell began to chuckle. "She's been shut up in that convent place too long. I bet it's all church music ... la, la, la, 'holy this' and 'holy that' and all that God twaddle!"

Terry laughed too. I felt somehow belittled, but I tried to grin and appear as if their mirth didn't bother me.

Mother's car was parked on the driveway when we got home. My heart sank. I felt sure there would be another row as soon as we went inside. I went to put the kettle on as Terry went into the lounge. Russell stood in the doorway between the kitchen and the sitting room.

To make conversation as I set the cups out, I said to Russell. "I really miss Tammy. I hope she's happy at that farm."

"What are you on about now?" Russell sneered. "Is that where you think they go? To a big farm in the sky? What? are all the little doggies and moggies laying about up there with steaks to eat and no limit to the amount of shit they can produce?"

I stood stock still, a cup dangling from my hand. It felt as if my heart had stuttered and now beat with an erratic rhythm. "What?"

Russell shifted his feet and looked over his shoulder.

"Nothing," he mumbled. "It doesn't matter."

I put the cup down with a shaky hand. "Mummy said Tammy went to live on a farm because it wasn't fair to leave her here alone all day when no-one was here. Is that true?"

Russell stared at me. He looked distinctly uncomfortable.

"Russell! Tell me! Is it true?"

He shook his head and glanced over his shoulder again. "You're so thick. You'll believe any shit she comes out with, won't you? No, it's not true. Dad was giving her a hiding and the bloody mutt went to bite him, so he kicked its flea-bitten head in! She went raving mental and went and got that Martin bloke and he went mental too and went and got some old bloke with a gun. Nana was here and got all hysterical and everything. It was ..."

I didn't hear the rest of what Russell said. My legs turned to jelly and I sank to the floor. A loud, wailing, screech came from somewhere. I couldn't see through the mist of tears and dizziness. The noise went on and on and on.

5. Aftermath and Starting Again

According to Russell, watching me being dragged up the stairs by Terry, who hauled on one limp arm as I continued to "wail and screech like a banshee" was great entertainment. I listened as Russell expanded on what he'd already told me.

"Mum fetched you such a ding round the head, but you didn't shut up, not even then. It was so funny watching them both panic. They thought the police would come again if they didn't shut you up." He giggled and clutched at his ribs.

"What do you mean, the police would come again?"

"Oh, it was only that fat, nosey, local plod. He squared up to Dad and threatened to have him done, it was great! He even tried to get Mum to make a statement, but she wouldn't. She told him it was all an accident and that the stupid dog had attacked for no reason at all. She had a bloody nose and that, but the copper couldn't prove nothing, so he had to go. Nana got all shitty too, but Dad said he'd ding her one if she didn't shut up and mind her own business."

I gasped in horror. "He actually threatened Nana?"

"Yup. It's all bloody Martin's fault. He shouldn't've gone and told the copper. Dad went and had a big row with Sylvia about that and all. I'm not allowed to go round there any more now. Still, it don't matter. Me and Kevin still go up the plant'n - so does Martin. He can't help being a bit soft. He's simple. Sylvia told me. He still keeps crying on and off about the bloody dog."

My stomach knotted at mention of Tammy, my lovely, dead dog. Poor Martin. He might have been huge and strong, but he was little more than a young child in his head. I knew how tormented he would be and could well imagine Sylvia's fury about it.

"I bet you didn't cry over poor Tammy," I snarled.

"I nearly did, but Dad would've leathered me if I had. It was pretty gross, there was all ..."

"Shut up! I don't *want* to know all the horrible, grisly details."

Russell looked surprised. "But you liked the dog!"

"Yes, I loved her. You wouldn't know about love. That's why I don't want to hear any more details. It makes me sick that you can still even look at Da ... I mean Terry. Don't you even care that he hurt Mum and threatened Nana?"

Russell paused and stared at me. "What? You think Mum should be allowed to get away with all the stuff she says to him and he shouldn't thrash her for it?"

"Yes. I don't think Mum should do all the things she does or say the things she says either, but it can't be right for a man to beat up a woman, or threaten a tiny old lady - or kill a defenceless animal."

Russell shrugged. "Someone's got to keep them in line. Anyway, the dog was hardly 'defenceless'. It's teeth were massive. Remember when she bit Mum before?"

"I'm not ever likely to forget! If you remember, there was violence then as well. There's always so much of it here. At All Hallows it was quiet and peaceful and nobody beat up or thrashed anyone."

Russell roared with laughter. "No-one except you!"

He was right. I'd ruined everything and now all I had to look forward to was another new school and endless time with Mother and Terry. I tried to change the subject.

"Why aren't you allowed round to Sylvia's anymore? Did Sylvia say that?"

"No. Dad says she's a busy-body and a trouble-maker. He won't let Mum go round there any more either. He says he'll know if she has. It's all right though, she doesn't like Mum anyway; she told me."

"What? Have you been round there then?"

"No. I'm staying on the right side of Dad 'till he calms down and forgets about it. I saw her up the village when me and Kev were getting sweets from the Post Office."

56

I made a mental note to visit Sylvia just as soon as I could. No-one had told me not to go there; even if they had, I wouldn't take any notice. In many ways, I think I'd made up my mind to try and goad both Mother and Terry into killing me, if I could. There didn't seem to be any reason to remain alive.

I was able to see Sylvia the very next day. Both Mother and Terry went off to work, leaving me alone in the cottage. They made no mention of not going anywhere, although Mother locked the back door and took the key with her. I knew, without being told, that if I went out, I'd have to go via the front door and then would be unable to get back inside. I did it anyway.

When I knocked on Sylvia's door, she only opened it a crack so she could peer out to see who was knocking. When she saw me, she opened the door wider and practically dragged me over the threshold. Once the door was closed, Sylvia enfolded me in a tight hug.

"Ooooh! You give me quoite a turn, seein' you standin' there. Oi never thought Oi'd see you again, girl!" Sylvia stepped back and looked at me. "Oi s'pose they dunt know you're 'ere then?"

I shook my head. For some reason, tears filled my eyes.

"Never moind now, don't you cry, Keri. Come on and we'll have a noice cuppa tea."

I followed Sylvia into her kitchen. Martin sat at the table whittling at a piece of wood with a small pen-knife. He looked up at me. He tried to smile, but dismay overcame me as his eyes filled with tears also.

"Oi'm sorry. 'Bout yer dog, Oi means. Oi did try, but ..."

Sylvia patted Martin's shoulder. "Now, now, lad," she said. "Keri knows it weren't your fault and she knows you done all you could. Let's all 'av a noice cuppa."

Martin nodded dolefully and returned to his whittling. I sat down beside him.

"What are you making, Martin?"

Without a word, Martin held out the piece of wood. I gasped. Although unfinished, it was a perfect replica of Tammy, about ten inches long. Already, the dog's expression showed. A stray tear trickled down my cheek.

"It's beautiful, Martin. I ..."

"You dint know he done carving, did you, Keri?" Sylvia interrupted. She put the teapot on the table. "He's quoite clever loike that. He's done all sorts o' stuff. He said next year, when them gypsies come, he's gonna try and do a carving of Mam. That'll be a thing to see now, won't it?"

Somehow, I knew Sylvia meant that I shouldn't speak of Tammy or the traumatic events in front of Martin. I gulped and sniffed to get control of myself.

"Mam done came 'ere and read 'is fortune for 'im afore she left," said Sylvia. "She said he'm gonna do roight well in life. She said he was an 'old soul' and has got plenty to teach us all. Ent that roight, Martin?"

Martin nodded. He folded the half carved dog into a piece of leather and pocketed the little knife. I watched as he carefully swept away the little splinters and pieces of wood with his hands. Then he went to the tall cupboard and took out a dustpan and brush. He knelt and patiently swept every scrap and shaving from the floor.

"Oi'm goin' up tha plant'n now Mam," he rumbled.

"Yes, son. You do that. You keeps an Oi on them lads and make sure them don't get into no trouble. Off you go now."

When Martin had gone, I looked at Sylvia. In just a few weeks she seemed older, somehow.

"Are you all right, Sylvia?"

"Oi'll be foine, Keri. Oi'm just a bit tired is all. Martin ent bin sleepin' too well since ... well, you know." She paused and looked thoughtful for a moment or two. "Mam was 'ere, loike Oi said.

She said Oi gotta 'elp you iffen Oi can. She dint need to tell me that, 'cos Oi would've done it anyway. She said to tell you to 'member the ant, whatever that means."

I nodded. I knew full well what Mam meant with her cryptic message. In short, I should help myself as much as I could and let others who were willing, help me too.

"So; you've decided to leave that convent place then?" Sylvia poured the tea.

"I didn't decide, Sylvia. I was expelled."

Sylvia put the teapot down and stared at me. "Expelled? Whatever for? Ooooh, that mother of yours is a lying toe rag, so she is! She told Missus Meadowes she decided you gotta go to tha local school so's you can make some friends!"

I gaped. I had no idea when Mother had seen Mrs. Meadowes, although I had spent most of the previous day in my bedroom, sleeping off a headache induced by my hysteria the night before.

"No. I was expelled, Sylvia. One of the girls was picking on me right at the start of term. It was awful because everyone liked her. I hit her!"

"Oh my! Oi bet that dint go down well at all. You shouldn't go hittin' folks, Keri."

"I know. I don't even know why I did it. She was yelling about me being common and scruffy and she told everyone that I came from some crummy council estate and was too poor to be able to afford nice clothes and things."

Sylvia nodded. "With a mother loike yours, Oi can well see why that would upset you. But us council estate folks ent all bad, are we? Oi mean, this is a council house. Oi dunt reckon it's that crummy. And Oi s'pose Oi'm a bit common, but Oi ent bad."

I laughed. "You're wonderful, Sylvia!"

I was pleased to see her blush as she batted her hand in front of her face in a gesture of embarrassment. "Aw! Bless you, Keri."

I stayed with Sylvia for a couple of hours, drinking strong tea and chatting. She admitted she sent Martin to get the policeman because she felt Terry might be arrested, if not Mother too. She'd been dismayed when all he did was warn Terry about his behaviour. Since Mother made no complaint and Terry claimed the dog attacked for no reason and he was just defending himself, there wasn't enough evidence to go ahead with a report.

When I explained to Sylvia that Mother had locked the back door and taken the key with her, she stood up and went to a drawer in her kitchen dresser. She rummaged about for a few moments and produced a key, which she handed to me.

"Oi 'ad this cut after Mam came 'ere," she explained. "It were her oidea. It weren't difficult to get it done. Your 'orrible mother still give me the key every day ... roight up until that evenin' with the dog. Oi had a copy made. Oi ent actually troid it to see iffen it works, but it should do. You can let yourself in and out whenever you wants now you got that. Just don't ever let them know you got it, see?"

I grinned at Sylvia. Dear Mam; the old gypsy was a canny soul. It seemed she'd thought of almost everything. I wondered if she'd 'seen' that I would be expelled from school.

During the conversation with Sylvia that morning, I learned that Terry had buried my beloved dog in the back garden. It had been Old Tom who rushed to the house with his gun to relieve the poor animal of its suffering after Martin barged into the pub screaming for help.

"'E ent welcome in the Jolly Farmer's - your step-dad. Reckon iffen 'e wants a drink, it'd 'av to be the Wheatsheaf, but even then ..."

I interrupted. "He goes to a club in Norwich, Sylvia. He takes me sometimes, too."

Sylvia looked concerned. "Be careful, Keri. You don't know what kind of thing he'll get you mixed up in."

"Oh, it's all right, Sylvia. Lots of men take their children. I've even made a couple of friends."

"Hmmm. Even so, you just look out, young lady."

When I left Sylvia's house, I went straight to the back garden of the cottage. It didn't take long to find the low mound which marked my dog's resting place. I sat quietly beside it, remembering the dog's exuberant play and curiosity as we walked. I let the tears trickle down my face and drip off my chin. It wasn't fair at all. Poor Tammy, she never had a chance against my horrible family.

My thoughts turned back to myself. It seemed anything I loved or cared about was taken from me. I began to form a plan in my head. If I never showed any interest in anything, then the things I liked could not easily be identified and so could neither be refused nor removed. I only had to be like that whilst at home. If I were at school or say, with Nana, I could be myself. My thoughts drifted to Nana. She would be so disappointed in me for being expelled; I wasn't even sure I could face her.

When it began to rain, I let myself into the cottage, locked the door behind me and hid the key under a plant pot on the kitchen windowsill. I knew if I hid it anywhere in my bedroom, Mother would find it during one of her regular searches.

I went to my room and looked about. The room seemed so bare, no longer mine. I set about trying to make it more suitable to my taste. I'd lifted a few magazines from the school Common Room. Several of them had pin up pages. I found a great picture of Marc Bolan from the group T-Rex, which I carefully pinned to the board on my bedroom wall. After more searching, I found several pictures, all of 'heavy metal rockers' - long haired, wild looking young men. I added these to the board and grinned to myself. A definite improvement!

Half-term passed so quickly, yet I did nothing and went nowhere. Each day followed the one before with a kind of monotonous feeling of dread. Mother largely ignored me; she hardly nagged at all and never entered my bedroom once. I automatically washed dishes after meals and made sure I did everything else which would normally be expected of me.

Russell seemed to spend all his time out with friends or at various activities. Terry spoke to me as if nothing bad had ever happened. He came in from work in the evenings, changed his clothes and after the evening meal, either went to his club, spent time in the garage tinkering with his motor bike or sat in the lounge watching television.

I existed in a kind of limbo. No-one had mentioned a new school or anything else in relation to me. It felt like I was a ghost, drifting around the cottage during the day with not so much as a cat to talk to and shut in my bedroom at night. I think, had it not been for my illicit visits to Sylvia, I might have faded away altogether.

On the Friday evening, Mother returned from work carrying several carrier bags from large stores in Norwich. She tossed them down on a chair in the sitting room and informed me, in a flat, disinterested tone, that they contained my new school uniform, which had apparently cost her more than she cared to waste on me.

"Which school am I going to, Mummy?"

"That horrible, common Secondary Modern in North Walsham, just as I said you would. I've tried giving you a good education and doing right by you, but it's got me nowhere at all. You'll always be awful and a complete waste of time and effort. There's nothing good about you at all. You're ugly, scrawny and skinny; you're clearly stupid as well. No sane person would behave the way you do."

I bit my lip. Any reply might cause Mother to fly into a rage. I stood in the middle of the sitting room, unsure whether to take the bags to my room or wait until Mother handed them to me.

"Well! You could at least try them on!"

I opened the first bag. It contained two long, grey, pleated skirts. I lifted one out and held it up.

"Hurry up!" Mother urged. "I'm going out this evening and I haven't got time for your dilly-dallying. If it's too small, which I doubt, I'll have to take it back tomorrow. If it's too big, we can use a safety pin to tighten the waist and you'll just have to grow into it."

I slipped out of my skirt and stepped into the school skirt. It was clearly much too big around the waist. It hung well below my knees too.

"Well, as I said, you'll just have to use safety pins to hold it up," Mother scolded. "Why can't you be a normal size? I have to buy bigger to get the length because you're too tall."

"Mummy, it's too long!"

"No, it isn't. The length is just fine. I'm not having any daughter of mine flashing her thighs about like all those common little tarts I see walking about in Norwich and everywhere else!"

I didn't dare protest any further. With my heart sinking, I knew I would have to attend a new school looking as dowdy and old-fashioned as Mother could make me. The other bags contained white blouses, also too big and baggy for me, a horrible, itchy blazer and a tie. I nearly choked saying 'thank you' to Mother. It felt terrible having to be polite to her about such a dreadful collection of clothing.

Mother dug out the old school satchel that I had used whilst at Thorpe House School. She told me to make sure I put all my pens and pencils into it so I had everything I would need for school.

On Monday, at around eight in the morning, Mother shoved me out the door of the cottage and told me to go to the crossroads by the Jolly Farmers. Apparently, a school bus collected students from the village there. She gave me fifty pence, which was to cover the bus fare there and back. Apparently, she had already paid for my school meals in advance.

I hesitated on the drive for a few seconds. I felt ugly and vulnerable. As I stood there, two girls passed the cottage chatting animatedly. They both wore similar blazers to the one I had on. However, there any similarity to me ended. Both girls had very short, straight skirts on, grown up tights and high heeled shoes. Their blouses were tight across well developed breasts and had ties fastened in a way I had never seen before, with a huge, loose knot and short, stubby ends. Their hair was carefully back-combed and set in modern styles and I was pretty sure I noticed make-up on their faces.

I glanced over my shoulder and noticed Mother standing in the window of the sitting room with her hands on her hips, glaring at me. She made a dismissive gesture with her hand and turned away. I gulped and set off up the village street, my feet feeling heavy in the flat, lace-up shoes I had lately worn for outdoor wear at All Hallows.

As I approached the crowd of young people waiting at the crossroads, a loud gale of laughter greeted me. I suppose they could have all been laughing at some joke or other, but deep down, I knew I was the subject of their mirth.

Only one person stood slightly apart from the main group; a boy of around thirteen. He had a satchel similar to mine, which he carried with the strap over his body, like a newspaper boy's bag. He had thick, horn-rimmed spectacles on, a tie fastened in the same way as my own and a blazer obviously a couple of sizes too large for him.

I edged my way closer to the group and stood silently, next to that boy. He kept his eyes cast downward and did not speak or give any indication that he knew I was there.

During the ten minute wait for the bus, when several other young people arrived, I overheard remarks; snatches of conversation with derogatory words in them like 'posh', 'stupid' and 'soon cut her down to size'. I knew they were talking about me.

I waited until everyone had got onto the bus in front of me before stepping onto the single step to board. The vehicle was full. The only available seat was next to the bespectacled boy. I ignored hoots of laughter and sat down. More than anything, I wanted to fling off the dreadful clothes and run for miles without ever looking back.

6. Ordinary School: Extraordinary Girl

When the bus pulled in to a final stop right outside the school, in the town of North Walsham, I waited until everyone else had alighted before leaving my seat. I really didn't want to become enmeshed in the stream of laughing, chattering teenagers, most of whom completely ignored me. I noticed the bespectacled boy did the same. Perhaps he felt similarly.

As I stood up, I said, "My name is Keri."

The boy glanced at me, but turned away without replying. I tried again.

"I'm new. I don't know where to go. Could you show me, please?"

"No. Leave me alone," he pushed past me and got off the bus.

I stood there, in the empty bus, staring after the boy in astonishment.

"Come on, luv, 'urry up! Oi got a toimetable ta keep!"

I glanced at the driver. He was middle aged, with a big, red face.

"Sorry," I mumbled as I descended the single step.

There were, quite literally, hundreds of students milling about on the pavement, on the wide yard and round the general area of the school. I saw a group of girls leaning against the railing nearby, smoking cigarettes and screaming with laughter. They all wore very short skirts and had fancy hairstyles. I noticed some of them wore knee high, shiny, patent boots. The others wore fashionable, high-heeled shoes. Every one of them had eye-shadow, mascara and lipstick on.

As I stared, a couple of older teenage boys approached. Both had long hair. One wore no tie and his shirt was open almost to his waist. I could see he was very slender and tanned. A large, gold medallion swung against his chest.

"G'is a fag," he said to the girls.

All of them proffered cigarette packets. He could have had ten or twelve 'fags' if he'd taken one from each of them. They offered their cigarettes to the other boy, but he declined.

"Don't try getting me started on them things," he joked. "I wouldn't be able to run far if I started smoking!"

I eased my way through the crowd and entered the wide gateway with its huge, iron gates propped open. I had absolutely no idea where I should go, what class I would be in or where it was. Conscious of people staring at me, I made my way to the main building, looking for some kind of sign.

I had to walk past a large group of boys who stood, laughing and joking near the door. Even though they all wore blazers, shirts and ties, they looked scruffy and unkempt. Some had the lapels of their blazers turned up; all had ties with huge, loose knots and most had their shirt tails hanging out over the waistbands of their trousers. As I passed, their conversation ceased. I knew they were staring at me.

"Bloody hell!" exclaimed one of them, "She looks about forty! You reckon she's the new French teacher or just some poor cow that's travelled in time?"

I felt my cheeks and neck turning red with humiliation and quickened my step in order to get away from them.

Inside, the walls were painted 'Institional Green', a sickly, dull shade. I glanced around. More students hurried past, some jostling me in their haste to get wherever they were going. No-one spoke, although several stared at me as if they'd never seen such a specimen before. I saw a sign which read 'Reception' on a door with a frosted glass panel in it. With difficulty, I pushed through the throng and tapped, timidly, on the glass.

Whilst I waited for someone to open the door, a bell rang, long and loud. The throng of teenagers became a little more 'busy' but no-one really seemed in any hurry to get anywhere. I pressed myself against the wall to allow a large group of children younger than me to pass. I noticed that even these girls wore quite short skirts and ties with the large, loose knot. I felt so incredibly different; ugly, out of place and lost. Tears prickled my eyelids and I hung my head, blinking furiously. It certainly wouldn't do to be seen crying!

A harassed-looking woman with iron-grey hair pulled back from her face and fastened in a tight bun approached the door. She glared at me.

"What are you doing here?" she demanded. "You should be on your way to your class by now!"

The corridor seemed to have magically emptied of people. I felt even more exposed, pressed against the wall with this woman blocking my escape.

"I ... I'm new," I stammered. "I ... I don't know where to go."

The woman reached forward and opened the door. "Right, follow me."

I followed her into the reception office, leaving the door open behind me.

"What's your name?" the woman asked, without looking at me.

I told her. She shuffled through some paperwork on her desk, eventually lifting a single sheet of paper, which she studied.

"Right. Expelled from two schools before this; a trouble-maker and a thief with violent tendencies. You'll fit right in here then. Come on, you'd better come and see the Head."

My jaw dropped. How easily I had been labelled! I wondered what the woman meant by the expression 'you'll fit right in here'. I followed her out of the room and along the now silent corridor to another door which had a wooden plate screwed to it which read, 'Headmaster'.

The woman knocked and opened the door, without waiting for a summons to enter. She turned and beckoned to me. "Come on, girl. I haven't got all day and neither has the Head."

I sidled through the doorway and stood very still with my hands folded in front of me as I had been taught to stand at All Hallows.

I watched as the woman leaned across the desk and spoke to a large, heavy-jowled man who had a balding head with hair combed over the bare patch in wispy strands. He wore a brown, corduroy jacket. I couldn't hear what she said, but I noticed her pointing things out on the piece of paper she'd brought from her own office.

When the woman straightened up and turned around, she frowned at me. "I'll get one of the Prefects to come by and collect you from here in a few minutes. They can show you to your class and point out anything important as well."

She swept from the room, closing the door behind her. I kept my eyes fixed on the man as he read the sheet of paper the woman had given him. Eventually, he put the paper down and looked up at me.

"Quite the little fire-cracker, aren't you?" he said, sarcastically.

I couldn't think of a reply which seemed appropriate, so I kept my silence.

"Well, this is a large school. You won't be anything special here, girl. I'm quite sure we have a great many kids who are more efficient thieves, fighters and trouble-makers than you. There're too many of your type about these days, kids who think they can do whatever they like and get away with it. I've no doubt I'll be seeing you again and frequently. Not that it will make much difference. I suppose you've decided already the way you intend to behave and there is little point in my lecturing you. Just like all the others, you'll take no notice and it will make no difference at all."

He glanced back down at the piece of paper. "Your school meals are all paid up till the end of term. That makes a change, I suppose. Now, go and wait outside the office for the Prefect. I sincerely hope I won't have cause to speak to you again, but I doubt it very much."

He opened a drawer in his desk and shoved the piece of paper inside. I felt unsure as to whether he'd dismissed me or not. I shuffled my feet a little.

The Head looked up. "Get a move on, girl! I'm a busy man!" he roared.

I jumped and quickly turned to the door. I fumbled with the handle in my haste to get away, but at last, I stood in the empty corridor, my heart pounding inside my chest. It seemed these people were not prepared to give me a chance at all. They'd made up their minds about me already. From the little the Head had said, I gathered that there were several students at the school who behaved even worse than me! My knees trembled and I tried to fight back tears yet again. I did not succeed.

A tall girl wearing a skirt so short it was hardly more than a belt and with her hair tied up in bunches high on the sides of her head approached me. She wore several strings of beads which dangled to her waist and her blouse was open at the neck, revealing a deep cleavage. The huge knotted tie stuck out across her large bosom, its stubby ends no more than three inches long. She was chewing gum.

"You Keri?" she asked in a bored tone.

I nodded.

She looked me up and down with distaste written all over her face. "Bloody hell, you look like you stepped out of the Ark! D'ya always look like that?"

I hung my head and found no reply.

"C'mon, I gotta take you to your class and show you round." The girl set off, back the way she'd come. I trailed along behind her, noticing the way she swung her hips as she walked in her high-heeled, platform shoes.

The girl stuck out a hand to the left. "Girls toilets."

And a little further along the corridor, again to the left, "Girls cloakroom. Don't leave anything in there, it'll get nicked."

Several times, the girl pointed at doors with numbers on them and made a single word statement like 'Geography' or 'French'. I knew I'd never remember the location of everything. I followed her up a wide staircase with a cream-painted, straight, steel banister. And down again. We went outside, via a different, double-door to the one I'd entered earlier. The girl stood still and pointed at various buildings.

"Science rooms, sports hall, canteen - don't eat the food, it's rough as hell, main hall ... that's it. Right. Apparently, you're supposed to be in Math now. That was room 6A; upstairs. Think you can find your way back there?"

I nodded, although I knew I had no chance of finding my way back through the maze of corridors.

"Right then. See ya." The girl spat her used gum on the concrete, unwrapped another stick, which she folded into her mouth before tossing the wrapper carelessly to the ground. She walked off without a backward glance leaving me standing, feeling so exposed and small on the edge of the large, concrete 'playground'.

I gulped and swallowed. Before finding my class, I really needed to find a toilet. I turned and went back through the double doors, where I hesitated, wondering which way I should take to find the girls' toilets I'd been shown. My need became more urgent as I hurried along the corridor and I began to fear I might have an accident if I didn't find my way back there soon.

Fortunately, I did find the toilets. Having relieved myself, I stuck my head out the door and looked up and down the corridor. I hated the subject of mathematics and had been the despair of poor Sister Mathilda, who tried to drum the facts into me by every method she could think of – without success. I felt I'd been humiliated and intimidated enough for one day. I wondered if I could avoid going to the maths class altogether. Surely, if I stayed in the toilets until the bell rang for break ... it occurred to me that I wouldn't know where to go next. Without the benefit of having seen others who were in my class I wouldn't even be able to simply follow everyone else to the next class. I realised I would have to find the math class after all.

I did find room 6A upstairs after several wrong turns to find the stairs themselves. I knocked at the door. It opened abruptly. I looked up into the frowning face of an extremely tall, straight backed man.

"Is this the maths class, please? I think I'm supposed to be in here."

"Indeed!" exclaimed the man, "And why have you arrived so late to this lesson? No lies, now. I won't tolerate lies."

"I ... I'm new. I had to go and see the Head and then ..."

"I see. Well, there's an empty desk down there at the front. Get to it quickly and quietly. I'll find you a book."

I slipped past the man and walked to the front of the room. Several of the class members stopped their writing to look up at me.

"Get back to work!" yelled the man. "Anyone coming into this room is my concern, not yours!"

I sat down at the desk the man indicated. He strode to a cupboard in the corner and after a few moments, returned with a textbook and an exercise book, which he tossed onto the desk in front of me.

"Page sixty-three. Since you missed part of the lesson, you will not have time to complete the class work in this period. I shall expect you to finish it for homework and present it to me in the staff-room first thing in the morning. Understand?"

I drew the text book toward me and nodded, miserably.

"I assume you have a name?" the man said, coldly.

"Keri," I replied.

I stared at the math problems in front of me. They looked relatively easy; certainly, by comparison to what I had been unsuccessfully studying at the Convent, they were easy. I set to work.

It seemed such a short period of time had passed when the bell rang to indicate the end of the lesson. No-one moved from their seat; the stern teacher stood by his desk and surveyed the class.

"It's about time we had some effort in this class," he began. "The standard of work is atrocious. Bring your books and leave them here on my desk. Anyone who has done less than they should can look forward to an after-school detention tomorrow."

Chairs scraped as many students left their seats. I sat, still holding my pen, whilst pretty girls and trendy boys filed past me to deposit their books on the desk at the front. No-one spoke until they got out into the corridor. I could hear shrill comments from girls and raucous laughter. I put my pen away and stood up.

"Bring that work to the staff-room first thing tomorrow morning," the teacher reminded me.

I scuttled out of the room and hurried after a group of girls. I didn't dare approach them or try to talk to them, but I needed to keep them in sight so I could follow them to the next classroom. Although one of the girls turned round and looked me up and down, none of them spoke to me.

When we emerged into the large concrete 'playground', the girls hurried straight across it toward a long, low building. I trailed behind, at what I hoped was a discreet distance. Once or twice I nearly lost sight of them as groups of older girls or crowds of boys crossed between me and the girls I followed.

When the girls disappeared behind the building, I crept forward, keeping close to the wall. I could hear them speaking and laughing together. As I hesitated, a plume of cigarette smoke drifted from the side of the building. So, they were smoking. I knew I couldn't go any further. I didn't want to make any enemies, so I stood, leaning on the wall my side of the building and watched the general chaos and hubbub of the morning break.

I saw the bespectacled boy from the bus. He sat on a bench beneath one of the school-block windows. No-one went near him. As I watched, he opened his satchel and took out a banana. My own stomach growled at the sight of the boy eating and I wondered how long it would be until lunch-time and whether the food in the school canteen was as bad as the senior girl who showed me round had said it was.

A group of younger boys were kicking a battered old leather football about. Virtually everyone else stood about in groups both large and small. Even so, there didn't seem to me, to be many people in the playground. I wondered where the rest of the students were. Perhaps there was a place to sit indoors. I thought I would have to investigate the possibility, but not until I had positively identified a few people that I could trail to get to my classes.

A large group of boys sauntered past me and disappeared behind the low building. I heard screams of laughter from the girls and a few ribald comments from the boys. Once again, I felt frumpy and out of place. I didn't want to remain standing there in full view of everyone, but since those girls were the only ones I recognised, I had no alternative. I shifted my weight onto the other foot and stared at the ground.

I happened to look up just as the football flew toward me. I had no time to dodge or move away and it hit me square in the face. The impact snapped my head back to bang against the pebble-dashed wall of the building I leant against.

I heard a few people laughing through the ringing in my ears. It took me a few moments to realise my nose was bleeding badly and the back of my head felt sore and damp too. I staggered slightly and felt in my pocket for a handkerchief. The playground swung around me and my knees buckled. I sank down into a squatting position and tried to hold the handkerchief to my face, but somehow, my arms didn't want to move.

"You'd best go get Miss," I heard a boy's voice coming from close by. "I think she's really hurt."

"Blimey!" said another voice, "Look at all the blood. Must've caught her right on her beak!"

I waved my free hand, trying to indicate that they should go away and leave me alone, but more voices joined the others. I looked up.

I had been surrounded by kids of all ages. They appeared hazy, as if there was a fog between them and me. No-one came any closer; they simply stood in a semi-circle and stared, talking loudly between themselves.

As the fog began to clear and feeling came back into my arms and legs, along with pins and needles, the crowd parted and a small, neatly dressed woman approached me. She bent down and laid a hand on my shoulder.

"Oh dear," she said. "That's an awful lot of blood. I think we'd better take you to the First Aid room. Come along, girl. Up you get. Can you walk?"

Still dazed, I nodded and tried to stand. A combination of dizziness and blood trickling down the back of my throat caused me to retch loudly.

"Urgh! Get back! She's gonna puke!" yelled a girl.

The lady turned and said something in a stern tone of voice before grasping my arm to steady me.

I allowed myself to be led across the playground toward the double doors. I heard a lot of chatter as I passed between the gathered hordes of kids.

"Yea, she's new."

"Poor cow, why didn't she duck or move?"

"She's probably retarded or something. Maybe she's a spastic!"

Roars of laughter.

"Well she's dressed like one."

"Where's she from?"

There were more but I became more engrossed in trying to stem the stream of blood with my already sodden handkerchief. My head ached and nausea gnawed in the pit of my stomach. I spat out a mouthful of blood just outside the door.

The lady led me to a stark, tiled room and told me to sit down. She handed me a bunch of green, paper towels and told me to hold them under my nose whilst she sought a bowl. Apparently, she had sent someone for the school nurse, who had taken a coffee break.

When the nurse arrived, she listened to what the lady told her and clicked her tongue in annoyance. She put her hand on my forehead and looked at my face and the blood streaming from both nostrils.

"D'ya often get nosebleeds, luv?"

I nodded; this caused more blood to splatter onto my drenched blouse.

"Bit stupid really, standing right by where them lads were playing football, wasn't it?"

I made no reply. All I could focus on was the fact that I now had no idea where my next class would be. I couldn't have spoken anyway.

"It's all right, Eve, I'll see to her. If I'm any judge, this'll need to be cauterized, but I'll see if I can stop it bleeding. Just alert the staff-room that I might need someone to drive her to the hospital, will you?

My heart sank. My nose had been cauterized before and it was an extremely painful procedure. Tears began to leak from the corners of my eyes.

The nurse squatted down in front of me. "D'you hurt anywhere else, luv?"

I pointed to the back of my head, which felt distinctly wet now. The nurse stood up and leaned over me.

"Gawd! You're bleeding there and all! Right, I'll just clean that up and have a look at it. Let me give you a cold towel to put over the bridge of your nose first though."

The cold cloth made no difference whatsoever; blood continued to flow, bright red and sticky, into the bowl I held on my lap. The nurse cleaned the back of my head with an antiseptic solution which stung.

"There're quite a few little cuts here," she murmured. "I think most of them are just superficial, but you'll definitely need stitches in one of them. Right. You'll have to go to the hospital, luv. This is more than I can deal with here. There's no sign that your nose is going to stop bleeding any time soon. Have you had it cauterized before?"

I found my voice. "Yes. It's horrible. I don't want to go to hospital."

"Well, I'm afraid what you want and what you're gonna get are worlds apart, luv. It's my responsibility and I say you have to go."

She went to the door of the little room and stuck her head out into the corridor. She must have seen someone because I could hear her giving instructions for a member of staff to come to the First Aid room to collect me and take me to the hospital in Norwich.

A short, stout man wearing a tweed waistcoat and creased brown trousers eventually arrived. He listened as the nurse explained what needed to be done. His pudgy hands took hold of one of my arms and the nurse took the other as they led me to the car park. I carried the grisly bowl of blood between my own hands.

The man chattered about mundane things such as weather as he drove. I barely listened. My heart thudded in my chest. I'd heard the nurse tell him she would telephone my mother and let her know that I was going to hospital. Mother would be furious; I had no doubt of that.

I recall very little of the actual hospital procedure, except that one particular doctor questioned me closely as to how I'd come by my injuries. The teacher remained only until Mother arrived. He gave her a brief account of what had happened and left without saying goodbye to me.

When I eventually got to go home with Mother, it was completely dark. Once again, my nose was packed with yards of gauze and I had to breathe through my mouth. I knew I would have to return to the hospital in four days time to have the gauze removed and that in the meantime, I would be unable to attend school. The hospital gave Mother another bottle of the foul, orange coloured medicine to administer to me. I now knew it was an Iron tonic, given because of the volume of blood I'd lost. I knew it would give me diarrhoea too.

All the way home, Mother kept up a litany of my failings. Apparently, I had contrived to get myself injured simply so that I could be lazy and stay off school. She intended to get work for me to complete at home, so I needn't think I could laze around all day doing nothing. My ruined blouse would have to be soaked in cold water and then thoroughly scrubbed to remove the blood-stains; she wasn't going to buy more blouses, I'd have to make do with the ones she'd already got me. She droned on and on throughout the journey. In fact, it seemed to me, she hardly even paused to draw breath, my faults were so numerous.

I let her words pass unremarked. I knew there would be no point to defending myself. In many ways, I felt relief that I could stay at home for the week, despite the discomfort in my nose. Then it occurred to me that I would need to go through the whole 'being new at school' process again the following week. I still had no idea of my timetable or where the classrooms were.

7. Caught In A Trap!

Terry was surprisingly sympathetic to my injury. Several times, he patted me on the back and made comments such as "That's such a painful thing, a ball in the face. It's happened to me loads of times."

Mother was tight-lipped about the whole affair. She appeared to be convinced that I had deliberately got in the way in order to have time off school. She made constant acid comments about my being thick and becoming ever more so because I 'kept missing so much school'.

Eventually, I snapped a reply. "What do you mean, 'keep missing school'? I've never missed any school, except when I was ill."

Mother sneered at me. "Oh, yes. The mysterious illness; for all I know, that was just put on too."

I gaped. Fortunately, Terry interrupted before I could reply and cause a full blown argument.

"I'm off to the club later. Do you want to come along?"

In all honesty, even despite how bad my face looked with its nasal packing, I would have preferred to be anywhere but stuck at home with Mother. I opened my mouth to reply, but Mother answered instead.

"No she does not want to go to your horrible, common club. For God's sake, man, look at her! She can't go out looking like that! Whatever will people think?"

Terry shrugged and ignored Mother. "Well? How about it?"

I shook my head. Mother was right, I looked dreadful. I didn't want anyone at the club to see me looking that way.

Mother began to scold at Terry for ignoring her. I left them to it and wandered up to my bedroom. I heard their voices becoming louder and more agitated. They seemed to argue over just about anything, but clearly, I was their favourite subject. I thought about Nana and wished I could go and stay with her.

The doorbell interrupted the argument between Mother and Terry. I crept to the door of my room and peeped out. I saw Mother go to the front door at the foot of the stairs and open it part way.

After a brief conversation, Mother stepped aside and pointed up the stairs. "Well. All right. Just for a little while. She's up there, but you can't stay long as we'll be having our meal in an hour or so."

A girl with long, brown hair braided into a plait stepped past Mother and looked up.

I didn't know her. In fact, she didn't even look vaguely familiar. She smiled at me and began to walk up the stairs. She carried a large bag which looked quite heavy.

I stepped aside as the girl got closer and indicated she should come into my room. As she closed the door behind herself, I waited for her to speak.

"I'm Janice," she said.

"Hello, Janice," I replied. I couldn't think of anything else to say.

"Mr. Winters asked me to bring you some work to do while you're away from school." She put the bag down on my bed. "He never usually does that if someone's away. Are you very badly behind?"

"I don't know," I replied. "I only started at the school today, then I somehow managed to get in the way of a football," I indicated my swollen, packed nose.

"Ouch! I bet that really hurt. I got hit in the back last summer with a football; that stung for ages."

I took in the girl's neat appearance. She must be a couple of years older than me. She wore a skirt which, whilst short, could not be described in the same way as other girls I'd seen in the same uniform. She wore tights and black shoes which had a medium sized heel. Her blouse was buttoned to the neck, but the tie still had the large, loose knot I'd seen in others. She wore make-up too, but nothing like as much as other girls; just a hint of eye-shadow and mascara and a touch of pale lipstick. I saw her looking around my room.

"Oh," she began. "You like Donny Osmond and David Cassidy! I do too. Aren't they just wonderful?"

I followed her gaze. To my absolute and utter horror, I noticed the pictures I had carefully placed on my wall board, of long-haired, heavy metal bands and Marc Bolan of T-Rex had gone. In their place were two centrefold portraits. Both were of young men with collar length hair. One looked rather goofy and the other decidedly effeminate. I had to exercise extreme self-control not to curl my lips into a snarl.

"Er ... yes?" I hazarded, whilst making a mental note to tear the pictures down and rip them into tiny pieces as soon as Janice left.

"I hope they're on Top-of-The-Pops this week," Janice continued. "I love Top-of-The-Pops, don't you?"

I turned toward the bag of books. "I've never really seen much of it," I mumbled.

"Really? Oh, my goodness! Why ever not? I thought everyone watched Top-of-The-Pops!"

"Um ... my mother doesn't like it," I mumbled.

Janice giggled. "Neither does mine, much. Dad's all right, but Mum grumbles and always tells me to turn the volume down a bit. Of course, I don't take any notice, who does?"

I saw her looking around the rest of my bare room. Apart from the horrible pictures on the board, there was nothing to indicate the room belonged to a teenage girl.

"My, aren't you a tidy person!"

I nodded, miserably. I felt very uncomfortable with this girl in my room. I simply wanted her to leave but could not think of a way to tell her so without being offensive.

"Do you live in the village?" I asked, on impulse.

"Yes, I live at The Wheatsheaf pub. I think I've seen you outside once or twice when Mum is making chips."

Again, I nodded. I had been there on a couple of occasions, when Terry had given me money and told me to get chips from the pub.

"It's my birthday next week," Janice tried again. "I'm having a disco at the hall in North Walsham. You can come if you like."

"Thanks," I muttered. My insides quivered. How could I possibly go to a disco? I had nothing at all suitable to wear and had never been to such a thing before. Anyway, I was pretty sure Mother wouldn't let me.

"I've got to go now," Janice turned and went to the door. "I'll tell your mum about my disco party and where it is. It starts at seven. I hope you get better soon and your nose stops hurting. I'm so sorry you had a bad first day. If I'd known, I would have shown you around and kept you out of the way of flying footballs."

"Thanks. A girl did show me round but I don't know her name. Anyway, I forgot practically all of it almost immediately. I got lost trying to find the math lesson."

"Oh dear. Did you have to go late to Mr. Watson's lesson?"

I didn't know the maths teacher's name, but assumed she referred to the stern man whose class I'd entered. I nodded.

"I wouldn't have wanted to be in your shoes for that! Was he very angry?"

"No, he just told me to finish the work and take it to the staff room tomorrow morning. I'm not going to school tomorrow, so I can't take it. I haven't done it anyway."

Janice hesitated in the doorway. "Oh, you should do the work. He gets very cross if people don't do the work. Why don't I call by in the morning and collect your book? I can hand it in for you and explain that you won't be in for a while because of your injury?"

"But ... you live at the other end of the village! Won't you miss the bus?"

"It's all right," I don't go on the bus. My dad takes me in the car. He works in North Walsham. I'll get him to stop here and I'll pick up your book. You may as well try to get on Watson's good side - not that he's really got one."

"All right," I replied. "I'll do the work and have the book ready for tomorrow morning. Thanks for bringing me the books."

"Oh, that's all right. You just try to get well quickly. I'll see you next week at my disco if I don't see you before. Bye."

"Bye."

I watched Janice trot down the stairs. She tapped on the door to the sitting room and when Mother called out, she went in. I heard faint voices talking for a while, although I couldn't hear what was being said. The front door opened and closed.

With nothing better to do, I looked at the pile of books. Every single subject had a book and tucked just inside the cover, a hand-written page with instructions as to what 'work' I should do. I skim-read every one of them. These tasks would be easy!

In fact, by the time Mother called me down for the evening meal, I had already completed all the history work and most of the geography. I had covered everything already during my time at All Hallows, so had been able to write a great deal.

"What have you been doing up there?" Mother snapped.

"Janice brought me school work," I replied. "I've been doing some of it."

"A likely story!" Mother glared at me. "I'll check, so there's no point lying!"

Privately, I wondered what else Mother might think I could do in a room which held little but school books, a bed, a chest of clothes and two pictures of horrible pop stars.

"Why did you take my pictures down?" I asked.

"What? You ask me why I took them down. I might have known I'd need to tell you. No decent girl would put those kinds of pictures up anyway! Long-haired louts with guitars. They're dressed obscenely, none of them can sing a note; all they do is make a horrible racket. I won't have those kinds of pictures in my house, do you hear? Where did you get them from anyway?"

"Out of magazines," I mumbled.

Mother paused with a fork-full of food half-way to her mouth. "What magazines? Where did you get magazines from? No lies now. I suppose you've been stealing again?"

"They gave them to me at The Child Guidance Clinic," I lied. "I haven't stolen anything! What's wrong with me liking things that other girls like?"

"It's because you don't like the things other girls like that I'm concerned!" Mother roared, flinging her fork down. "Why can't you be normal?"

"Because *you* won't let me!" I screamed. I stood up suddenly. The chair I vacated fell over behind me. "You dress me like an old woman, you won't let me have make-up or jewellery or anything pretty and fashionable! I look stupid and they all laugh at me! And you don't care!"

I felt pressure in my head and nose. The packing caused the loss of all resonance in my voice. I staggered a little as I stepped over the chair.

"I hate you!" I yelled.

Terry grinned widely. I vaguely noticed his expression before I turned and stormed back to my room. In the sitting room, I could hear Mother shouting at Terry.

"How can you just sit there and let her speak to me like that? Why didn't you stop her?"

I didn't hear what Terry replied. I ran into my room, hot tears trickling down my cheeks and the packing in my nose hurting. I flung myself onto the bed and swept the books to the floor. I could not understand why Mother always had to be so hateful to me. I'd done nothing wrong that I could see.

I turned onto my back and wiped my eyes with the corner of the bedspread. I noticed the pictures of Donny Osmond and David Cassidy grinning at me from the wall-board. In a flash, I jumped up, tore the glossy pictures down and ripped them into hundreds of tiny pieces.

Downstairs, I could hear shouting and a lot of banging about. Knowing I must be the subject of the argument once again, I found myself sincerely hoping Terry would give Mother a good thumping. I heard the back door slam. Seconds later, the engine of Mother's horrible little three-wheeled car started and I heard it pull out of the gravelled driveway and accelerate off up the village street.

I waited for about ten minutes before I opened my bedroom door and peered down the stairs. Everything was quiet. I crept down and went into the sitting room, where the remains of the meal still lay on the table. Through the closed door of the lounge, I could hear the television. I sat down and began to eat my meal, which had gone cold.

When I'd eaten as much as I could I cleared the plates and dishes away and began the washing up in the kitchen. I resolutely refused to look into the corner of the kitchen where Tammy's basket used to be. I missed my dog so terribly. If I kept my back turned, I could almost feel her presence; I scrubbed the dishes and imagined the dog's big, brown eyes watching my every move. It was silly, but it comforted me.

Russell appeared in the kitchen. "Oh. You're in here. Dad wants a cup of tea then he's taking us to the club."

I dried my hands and put the kettle on. "I'll make his tea, but I can't go to the club. Look at my face!"

Russell studied me for a while then he shrugged. "It's not that bad. Anyway, anyone who'd got a wet football in the face would look pretty crap. Did it hurt?"

"I can't actually remember," I replied as I set two mugs out on the worktop. "I saw stars, I know that. I had to have stitches in the back of my head, too. I'm not supposed to get them wet, so I won't be able to wash my hair until they've been taken out."

"Cor!" exclaimed Russell. "Let me have a look!"

I bent my head so that he could see. "You're lucky," he said, after inspecting the two stitched wounds, "You've got an extra week off school."

"Yes. An extra week to be bored to death in."

I handed Russell a mug full of tea. "Here. Take that to D ... him. I'm going back upstairs."

I took up my mug of tea and went back to my bedroom.

About fifteen minutes later, Terry opened my bedroom door and peered at me. "Come on, get ready. We're going to the club in a minute," he said.

I hung my head. "I can't go to the club," I replied. "I look awful and anyway, I'm sick of going everywhere looking so old-fashioned and ugly. I don't want people to see me."

To my astonishment, Terry sat down on the end of my bed. "Really, you don't look that bad," he said. "It could have been worse. No-one will think badly of you. How about I take you into Norwich on Saturday and get you some fashionable clothes to wear? That girl who came round earlier invited you to her party. You'll have to get something trendy to wear for that anyway."

I looked up. "What? You mean I'll be allowed to go?"

"I don't see why not. It's about time you started going out a bit."

"Mummy won't let me," I began.

"Fuck her!" Terry exclaimed. "She's got her head stuck so far up her own snooty arse she can't see anything! You'll do what I say and leave me to deal with the old bitch, right?"

In fact, I had a wonderful time at the club. Dave wasn't the only person to express concern. Several people made quite a fuss of me. One lady, somebody's wife, hugged me and told me not to worry; soon I'd be right as rain.

It was very pleasant to be the focus of so much kind attention. When, later in the evening, I complained to Dave that I had a headache, he went off and fetched his dad, who solemnly handed me a small, foil strip enclosing two round shapes.

"Drop them in a little water and wait for them to dissolve, Luv. That'll sort your head out."

"What is it?" I asked, suspiciously.

"Only Disprin, Luv. I 'ent got owt stronger 'n that."

I vaguely recalled Nana having given me Disprin in the past. I stared at the foil strip. Sure enough, there was the word, 'Disprin' and the sword trademark. I thanked both Dave and his father and dropped the tablets into half a glass of water Dave held out for me.

On the way home, Terry glanced at me before speaking. "We'll get up and go shopping early on Saturday. The old bitch is stopping out on Friday night. You can go and stop round at Dave's whilst me and Russell go to the match. Give you a chance to try everything on and make sure it looks all right. Trevor says that's OK. His missus won't mind."

"All right," I agreed. I felt pleased and full of anticipation.

In fact, I felt so excited I found it difficult to sleep all the nights of that long week. I couldn't wait for Saturday. The discomfort of the nasal packing didn't help, but it was anticipation more than anything else which kept me from sleep. I kept thinking about all the lovely clothes I might get; then I worried about being unable to wash my hair for a week; then I considered shoes - or rather, lack of them. It was probably close to four in the morning before I finally fell into a fitful sleep nearly every night of that long week.

I did all the work required of me in the books which Janice brought me. In fact, I wrote a great deal and in certain subjects, I did detailed drawings and diagrams too. Mother glanced through the work several times, but despite her waspish attitude and stern expression, she didn't find any faults that she could complain about.

The English teacher had set several essay subjects, all of which I wrote on. Only later did I realise she'd only expected me to choose two.

On Friday morning, Mother took me to the hospital clinic, where the packing was removed from my nose. Again, I gagged, not least because as it was withdrawn, I became aware of the smell! The stitches were removed from my scalp and the nurse said I could safely wash my hair.

Mother drove me home and told me to make sure I'd finished all my set school work. She added that I should do the vacuuming and other housework because she had a weekend conference she had to attend. Mother did not come in with me. She told me she'd see me Sunday night and drove off, leaving me standing on the drive holding the front door key.

I did do the housework, but not to help Mother. I needed something to while away the time. I also took a long, hot bath and washed my hair. By the time Russell and Terry came home, I felt so excited I could barely contain myself.

Once again, after a hurried supper, Terry took us both to the club. I spent all evening explaining to Dave about all the clothes I would likely get the next day. He grinned at me and told me he looked forward to seeing them. We played pool and darts as before and Dave put his arm around me and gave me a quick hug when we left.

On Saturday morning, I was bleary-eyed and felt distinctly sleep-deprived, but I didn't care. I ate the cooked breakfast Terry prepared and listened as Russell and Terry discussed the football match they were going to watch. I would have liked to go with them, but in view of the fact that Terry would be buying me nice clothes, I didn't dare ask. Besides, I liked Dave and thought it would be fun to spend some time with him at his home.

Terry didn't even give me time enough to wash the breakfast things and clear the kitchen before he announced it was time to leave. Russell sat in the front passenger seat. I opened the rear window a little and tried to plan what I might ask for as I settled in the back seat. A shorter, straight school skirt without pleats for one thing! I had no idea how much Terry intended to spend, but I also had very little idea of the prices of clothes. The only place Mother had ever taken me to buy clothing had been Debenhams or Jarrolds, both rather up-market department stores.

The first place Terry took me to was the large market. He went straight to a stall where colourful clothing hung on rails under a striped awning. It seemed he knew the lady who ran the stall. I looked along the rails as Terry and the woman chatted. I found a short dress made of some shiny, silky material. It had blue and green swirls, no sleeves and a rounded neckline. I lifted the hanger off the rail to look at it more closely.

"What size are you, Luv?" the lady asked me, breaking off her conversation with Terry.

I shrugged. I had no idea of my size.

"I've got a tape measure here somewhere," the lady added, rummaging in the pouch of her apron. "We'll find out, shall we?"

I stood still whilst she measured my chest, waist and hips. She turned to Terry. "How old did you say she is? She's awful thin, Terry."

"Fifteen in a few months," Terry replied with a grin. "She barely eats anything, although old Misery Guts makes sure she only gives her stuff that she doesn't like, so no wonder."

The woman clicked her tongue. "I dunno why you ever married her! She's always been such a cow. You'd have been all right with me, you know!" she nudged Terry and winked at him. They both laughed.

The lady took the dress from my unresisting fingers. "That'd drown you, Luv," she said, kindly. "Anyway, it's meant for an older woman with more ... er ... you know," she patted her own bosom. I felt myself go red. Not for the first time, I wondered why I hadn't developed any breasts and felt intensely embarrassed about the lack of them.

"Aw ... don't get worried, Luv! It's right fashionable to be thin just now! There's lots of girls would give their eye teeth to be thin like you. Come on, have a look along here and see if there's anything you like." She indicated another rail. I began going through the clothes. There was a huge variety; skirts, dresses and tops, even a few jackets.

"Dad, I'm bored. Can I go down to the comic stall?" Russell whined.

Terry fished in his pocket and pulled out a very large wad of notes. He peeled a ten pound note from the wad and handed it to Russell.

"Yeah. Here y'are. If you can't find us here in a bit, I'll be taking her down to Dorothy Perkins and that Tammy Girl shop. Then we'll go and get some chips before I take her round to Trevor's all right?"

Russell snatched the note and grinned. "Thanks, Dad!" He darted off, between the stalls.

I wondered where Terry had got so much money from, but I didn't dwell upon it. I'd found two dresses I really liked. One was black and mauve with a large, gaudy buckle around a false belt. The other was sky-blue and black. I lifted them and showed them to Terry.

"Yea, they'll do, if you like them," Terry barely glanced at the dresses. He continued talking to the woman, who took the dresses off their hangers and folded them before placing them in a striped bag.

"Don't forget, she's gonna need underwear and all!" the woman reminded Terry as he bade her farewell.

The rest of the shopping trip passed too quickly for me. Terry took me to both the stores he'd mentioned and bought me 'skinny rib jumpers' with low, scooped necks, two short, black skirts to wear for school and several other very short skirts. In another store, he handed me over to a lady, who took me into a fitting room to 'measure my bust' properly. I left that shop very red in the face bearing a bag containing three 'AA' cup 'training bras' and a number of pairs of coloured tights. Terry also purchased a pair of shiny, black patent boots with cube heels and a pair of strappy, platform shoes for me.

Russell found us as we emerged from the shoe shop. I wondered how he felt so comfortable wandering around the city centre on his own, but I held my tongue, deciding it better not to say anything to him which may cause a problem.

We sat in the car eating chips. The many bags and parcels Terry had bought were piled high on the back seat next to me. Not once had Terry queried the price of anything or refused to let me have anything I particularly liked. This was such a novelty for me and I revelled in being able to have anything fashionable that I wanted. I couldn't wait to try on all my new clothes.

"Right," said Terry, screwing up his chip paper. "I'll take you round to Trevor's now. You can try on all that stuff. Make sure you keep the tickets because I'll have to go change them if they don't fit right. At least we know the shoes fit. I'll be back to collect you at about half five. I'm gonna keep all your new stuff in my bedroom, all right? The old bitch never goes in there, so she won't be able to get them to rip them up or throw them away. Those school skirts you'll have to wear under that horrible rag she makes you wear. Then, when you get up the road, you can take the big, long one off and stuff it in your bag till home-time."

I grinned and nodded vigorously. I loved the idea of deceiving Mother.

"I'll get hold of some make-up for you after the match. You'll have to keep that in my bedroom and all. You'll soon be fitting right in with all the others. Right. Let's go."

When we arrived outside Trevor's house, Terry put the parking brake on and turned in his seat to look at me. "Go on," he urged.

"Get your bags of stuff and go to the door. Behave yourself. Do as you're told and mind your manners. I'll see you later."

I scrambled from the car and collected the many bags and boxes. The door of the semi-detached house opened. I saw Trevor wave to Terry. He wore old, baggy trousers held up over his string vest with tatty braces. I giggled as I stumbled to the door. I could just imagine what Mother would say if she saw him.

Terry pulled away, giving another wave and a cheery grin. I dropped several of the bags and waved back. I couldn't wait to show Dave all my new clothes. The Consul sped away.

"All right, lass?" Trevor asked as he helped me pick up what I'd dropped. "Looks like you've been on a shopping spree of a lifetime! Come on indoors. Dave 'ent back from his football for an hour or so and the missus is off out shopping. She won't be back for hours yet."

He held the front door open. I had to duck beneath his outstretched arm to enter a narrow hallway, tastefully decorated.

"You and me can be all alone," Trevor added as he closed the door behind me. "We're gonna have a lot of fun, we are."

8. Learning To Be A Good Girl

Trevor told me to leave my shopping bags in the wide hallway and showed me into a pleasant room decorated in a much more modern way than the cottage in Swanton Abbot. I sat on a deep, plush, blue settee which appeared relatively new and gazed around the room.

"How about something to drink, luv?" Trevor asked.

I nodded. Even though I'd seen Trevor many times at the club, I felt inexplicably shy and didn't know what to say. I watched him as he went to the corner of the room where there was a mini-bar.

"What's your poison then, girl?"

"Sorry?"

"What d'you want to drink? I got all the usual stuff - whisky, vodka, gin. I think there're still a few beers in the fridge too."

Confused, I shook my head. "I'm only fourteen; I'm not allowed to drink those things. Could I have a cup of tea, please?"

Trevor turned and winked at me. "Who's to know what you have while you're here, eh? I ain't tellin' anyone. Go on. Have a proper drink."

I hesitated. I honestly had no idea of what the drinks were or even if I'd like them. Worse, I wondered what Mother would say if she knew. I resolutely shook my head.

"No, thanks; just a cup of tea, please."

Trevor grinned at me. "Right then, if you're sure. A cup of tea. With lots of sugar in it, I expect?"

"No. No sugar at all, thanks, I don't like it."

Trevor left the room and went off down the hallway. I sat on the edge of the blue settee and looked around the room. There were several shelves on the wall which held photographs in frames. I noticed a wedding photograph of what must have been a much slimmer and younger Trevor. Next to it stood a picture of a chubby baby holding a teddy. That must be Dave.

On the mantelpiece over the gas fire were many delicate works of fine porcelain; ladies in frilly dresses and with old-fashioned bonnets. The detail in these was fantastic and I stood up to get a closer look.

Trevor came back and placed a mat on the low coffee table and a steaming mug of strong tea on the mat.

"You like those, do you, girl? The missus collects them. They cost a bomb, they do. I try to get her one every year at Christmas."

"Yes. They're beautiful. Thank you for the tea." I sat down again and lifted the mug.

"Right." Trevor sat down in an armchair near the wide window where lace curtains hung flanked by long, blue velvet drapes. "You gonna try on some of them clothes what your dad bought you, then?"

I bit back a remark about Terry not being my 'dad'. I glanced across to the open doorway.

"Yes. Is there somewhere I can change?"

"Aw ... you'll be all right in 'ere. No-one can see you through them," Trevor waved a hand at the lace curtains.

I swallowed hard and put my cup down. I certainly didn't want to try the clothes on here in front of him.

"I ... er ... actually, it's all right. I'll try them on when I get home, thanks." I mumbled.

"Aw. Come on, luv. Your dad wanted you to try 'em here. He said, didn't he? Don't worry about me. I won't look ... well, not until you want me to. Go on, have some fun."

I suddenly felt afraid. I recalled the night at the fair when I had first seen Trevor with Terry. I hadn't liked the appraising look he'd given me then. He was looking at me like that again now. I glanced toward the open doorway into the hall.

"C'mon, luv, you don't need to get all coy. You know what I want and how to do it. Your dad said ..."

"He's not my dad!" I spoke between clenched teeth.

Trevor grinned. "Well, that's probably just as well, ain't it? Otherwise it would be incest and that's really mucky stuff."

I stood up and edged toward the hall door.

"No good you going out there, luv," Trevor waved a key at me. "I won't hurt you, if that's what you're afraid of. Look, leave that cuppa and have a proper drink. You'll feel a lot better for it."

He stood up and went to the mini-bar. I stood in the doorway and watched as he poured some clear liquid into a tall glass. He opened a small, covered bucket and scooped out some ice, which he dropped into the glass.

"I'll put some Coke in it for you."

Trevor topped the glass up using most of the contents of a bottle of Coke. He held it out to me.

"Get that down your neck, luv. Go on. Then you can try on all them lovely clothes for me."

I shook my head.

Trevor put the glass down on the bar-top and looked at me. "Now. What do you suppose will happen when your dad gets back and I tell him you wouldn't co-operate?"

My legs began to shake.

"He's not gonna be too pleased about that, now, is he? I reckon as how he might be really angry with you. He'll take all them clothes away for sure and, well ... I dunno exactly what he does to punish you, but punish you he surely will."

My heart thumped against my ribs and a knot formed in the pit of my stomach. I had a very good idea of what Terry might do if Trevor told him I'd refused his advances. Very slowly, I approached the bar and lifted the drink. I stared at it for a few moments, and then gulped it down in about four swallows. I set the glass back on the bar top; the ice chinked around the sides of the glass.

"There ya go. I'll fix ya another one and you can drink that more slowly."

I retreated to the settee and sank down onto it. I felt sick and afraid. I knew there was no escape. There was nothing I'd be able to do which wouldn't result in at the very least, a beating from Terry, possibly much, much worse. When Trevor appeared at my side and held out another long drink, I accepted it.

I sipped at the cool liquid as Trevor went to the hallway and brought the shopping bags into the room. The drink only tasted of Coke, which wasn't too bad; I wondered what the clear liquid was.

Trevor lifted some of the clothes out of the bags and placed them next to me on the settee. One of the short black skirts lay on top of the pile. Trevor pointed at it.

"That's a right sweet little skirt. Try that on first."

I drained the glass, set it on the low table next to my half consumed cup of tea and snatched up the skirt.

"Want me to help you get undressed?"

I shook my head. I stood up and undid the zipper on my ugly skirt. I let the skirt fall to the floor and stepped out of it. As I lifted the little black skirt, Trevor reached down to the floor between the wall and the chair he was sitting in. He produced a camera.

Aware of the camera pointing at me, I pulled on the short skirt and fastened the zipper. It was actually very short indeed. I tugged at the hem, but the skirt remained where it was - revealing my skinny, white thighs.

"Turn around and bend over, luv."

I felt ever so slightly dizzy, but somehow, the request did not seem so terrible. I complied, resting my hands on the arm of the settee.

"Oooh! Now that's pretty!"

"Hey, how about you take off that blouse thing and put on one of them bras?"

I stood up and fumbled with the buttons of my blouse, keeping my back to Trevor. My cheeks were burning red, I knew. I slipped the blouse over my shoulders revealing the childish vest I wore beneath.

"Oh, lose the vest, darlin'. That ain't pretty at all!"

I rummaged amongst the clothes and found one of the training bras Terry had bought me. It only took seconds to lift the hated vest over my head and loop the bra straps over my arms. I fumbled with my hands behind me, to find the hook for the bra.

I jumped violently when I felt Trevor's hands on my own. I hadn't been aware that he'd left his seat. He fastened the bra for me and turned me around to face him.

"There now. You sit down there and I'll get you another drink."

I sat, crossing my arms over the thin strips of lace covering my flat chest, trying with my thin arms, to hide as much of my bare flesh as possible. Trevor handed me another glass full to the brim.

"See? I ain't hurt ya, have I?"

I shook my head. Trevor sat down again. He had a small glass with a golden brown liquid in it. He sipped at this and placed it on the small table.

"Right. Let's get some more pictures, luv. Lean back on that settee like a good girl and open your legs so I can see your knickers eh?"

I complied, but I moved in a stiff and jerky fashion. I did not want to do this; only fear of what Terry might do to me stopped me from screaming and trying to escape.

"That's lovely! Now, just put your hand between your legs and move your knickers aside a bit. Great! Yea, that's just great. Can you get your fingers inside yourself a bit and wiggle them about?"

"What?"

"You know, like you do to make yourself feel good?"

"I don't know what you mean!"

Trevor lowered the camera and stared at me. "What, you don't get your fingers in there and fiddle about till it feels good? That's mad! You should try it."

He reached down and tugged my knickers aside. "Go on, luv. You just do that and I'll be happy. Rub your hand up and down over it first so it gets nice and hot, then you can push your fingers inside. I'll get some great pictures."

I did rub my hand up and down - I'd had plenty of training from Terry when I was much younger in doing that. However, I could not bring myself to do as Trevor asked. I thought it disgusting. Why would I want to put my fingers in there? How vile!

Trevor clicked the shutter several times before lowering the camera. "I think you need to drink that other drink, luv. Go on, sit up now and get it down you. You'll feel a lot better if you do."

I obeyed, draining the glass quickly. My head had begun to swim a little and panic had subsided. I still felt uncomfortable, awkward, embarrassed and terribly afraid though.

Over the following twenty minutes or so, I posed for Trevor, wearing all of the new clothes, the short skirts and dresses - without knickers. He urged me to spread my legs wide; draw up my knees and spread my legs; point to various parts of my genitalia, all manner of obscene poses.

Finally, Trevor put the camera down between the chair and the wall. I lolled on the settee, my chin resting on my chest and my legs stretched out before me. I felt very strange indeed. The room appeared to be moving, as did the settee I occupied. I had an insane urge to laugh, which I suppressed as I tried to focus on Trevor and the rest of the room. He was undoing his trousers. Somewhere in the back of my mind, something was telling me that an event infinitely more horrible than photographs was about to happen, but I found I really didn't care. I tried closing my eyes - that made the sensation of movement all the more powerful; I opened my eyes again and saw Trevor kneeling before me between my legs, his erect penis in his hand. He grinned.

"Reckon you're good and ready now, luv. Open wide, here I come!"

Being raped by Trevor was nothing like being raped by Terry. He did not set out to hurt me for a start, even though it did hurt being penetrated. I did not cry out. I concentrated all my efforts into trying to make the room remain still and over-ride the sensation of nausea which kept sweeping through me.

I couldn't say how long it took Trevor to complete the act; I lost all sense of time. When he finally finished and sat back on his heels, red in the face and panting, I found my voice.

"I think I might be sick in a minute."

Trevor got to his feet with a grunt. "Ah. That'll probably be the vodka, luv. Maybe I gave you a bit much for someone who ain't used to it." He fastened his trousers. "Come on into the kitchen with me." He reached out a hand and hauled me to my feet.

I was frightened because I could not stand unaided. My legs seemed to have taken on a personality of their own. They wouldn't do as I wanted. Trevor put an arm under one of my own and half dragged, half steered me out of the sitting room, along the hallway and into a large, bright kitchen. He flopped me over the stainless steel sink just as four glasses of vodka and coke mixed with semi-digested chips made their appearance.

Trevor held me up as I filled his wife's spotless sink with the vile contents of my roiling stomach. When I'd finished retching, he lowered me onto a kitchen chair.

"You just rest there a bit, luv. I'll get this all cleaned up. Uncle Trevor has been a bit silly, making you drink all that, hasn't he?"

Vomiting usually caused me to panic uncontrollably, but although panic was present, as ever, I found that I did not shake violently as I usually did. My arms and legs felt like lead and the sensation of movement continued, although now I found it less unpleasant.

"What you need now, my lovely," crooned Trevor as he unblocked the sink, "Is a nice little sleep. I'll just do this and bleach it all up nice and sparkly so the missus won't know, then you can come and have a nice lie down. I'll watch over you, don't you worry."

I wasn't worried. In fact, although I'd just been violently sick after having one of the most dreadful experiences of my life, I felt as if I hadn't a care in the world.

"Tell you what, luv. I'll make you some black coffee, how's that? It'll help sober you up a bit and after puking all that out you need a drink anyway."

Over the next hour or so, Trevor had me drinking black coffee with sugar in it. I didn't like it, but I did feel very thirsty. The first two cups came back almost immediately, all over the pristine red and white chequered floor, but Trevor didn't seem to mind. He kept up a constant monologue of reassurances and platitudes as he cleaned up the mess I'd made. I watched owlishly as he mopped the floor with a bleach solution which made my eyes water.

When two cups of coffee remained in my stomach and I no longer heaved and retched, Trevor gently washed my hands and face with a soft cloth and helped me back through to the sitting room. He explained that I should get dressed in my normal clothes and assisted with the tangle of clothing which I could not work out how to put on. Finally, he fastened the buttons on my blouse and pushed my hair back out of my eyes.

"There. You've been a good girl today. You lie down and have a nice sleep on the settee, luv. You'll feel better when you wake up. And this is for you."

Trevor held out a five pound note. I stared at it and made no move to take it.

"Go on, luv. You take it. You earned it. Put it in your pocket and keep it for something nice another day."

I accepted the note and stuffed it in the pocket of my skirt. Trevor plumped up a cushion for my head and gently pushed me onto it.

"There, there. A nice sleep; that's what you need."

I drifted off into a drunken sleep. Little did I know that what had just happened to me would become a regular part of my young life for a very long time to come.

9. Learning To Be Bad

Terry never mentioned anything about my time at Trevor's house. When he arrived to collect me, Trevor woke me up. I had a headache and my stomach muscles were sore from vomiting. I accepted a drink of water and sat on the edge of the settee whilst Terry and Trevor discussed the football match Terry and Russell had been to. Russell sat at the other end of the settee reading a comic book; occasionally he chipped in a comment about the football, but he didn't even look at me.

Dave came home just as we were preparing to leave. He stood in the hallway at the foot of the stairs covered in mud and grime; he grinned at me.

"Pity you can't stay. I'll see you at the club later on. Right now, I've got to have a bath. We won two nil and I scored a peach of a goal."

I ignored the result of the match. I had not been aware that Terry intended to take me to the Working Men's Club that evening. My stomach roiled inside me.

"I'm not sure if I'll be at the club. I've got a headache."

Terry patted my shoulder. "She will be at the club later, Dave. I'll give her an aspirin and she'll be fine by about eight this evening. See you later."

Russell exited the house first and Terry gave me a gentle shove to propel me out the door in front of him as he finished his conversation with Trevor. I caught the last few words:

"... yeah, got some great ones. She's a bit stiff and tense and but we'll soon fix that."

"She takes after the ice-maiden I married!"

Both men laughed uproariously. Trevor closed the door and Terry walked to the car carrying the shopping bags.

I fell asleep again as the car sped toward the village and home. When I woke, I felt sick again; I told Terry I felt unwell.

"Oh, you'll be all right in a bit. I'll get you something to eat and an aspirin."

Russell gave me a sharp look. "Why do you feel ill? Have you got a bug or something?"

"She had too much to drink round at Trevor's is all," Terry interrupted.

Russell grinned. "That's horrible. When I drank some of Dad's beer I was really sick and I thought my head would explode. Did you drink beer? Trevor let you? Dad was furious with me when I drank his and Mum went mental about it."

Terry laughed. "Yeah. I remember. You won't do that again in a hurry, will you, lad?"

Russell's question hung in the air, unanswered. That Terry knew I'd been drinking and didn't care, confirmed that he knew full well what Trevor had planned to do with me. Terry took the shopping bags filled with my clothes directly up to his bedroom. When he came down again, he told me where they were and instructed me to retrieve the short skirt and shoes just before going to school.

"But Mummy nearly always looks in my satchel!" I protested.

"Yeah, that's a point. She does. I've never understood that or worked out what she's looking for. Don't worry about it – I'll think of something later on."

Terry gave me some Disprin and two slices of toast to eat. He left me sitting at the kitchen table and went to the lounge room with Russell.

I struggled to eat the toast, but after a while I did begin to feel better. I drank the aspirin solution and also a glass of water. With nothing else to do, I went to my room and sprawled on my bed.

I dozed off to sleep again and only woke when Russell shook me and told me we were supposed to get ready to go out. I sat up and looked around the room, which was dark.

"Was I asleep very long?"

"About three hours, I think. Dad says you've got to wear one of those new dresses and the boots. You can go in his room to get them. Hurry up."

Russell went downstairs. I got up and made my way to Terry's bedroom door and opened it. The room was utterly black. I switched the light on and stared at the room I'd only ever seen with dim daylight seeping through closed curtains. It was just as messy as before, the bed unmade and clothes tossed around carelessly. A number of empty beer bottles stood on the dressing table. The pile of pornographic magazines was still beside the bed.

My stomach lurched with the knowledge that Trevor had taken pictures of me similar to those in the magazines. I turned away and rummaged through the shopping bags to find a dress and the boots Terry wanted me to wear. I also took a training bra, some tights and knickers before I hurried downstairs to the bathroom.

I felt very vulnerable and strange dressed in the new clothes. I could not get used to the short dress high around my thighs. When I sat in the back of the car, the dress rode up even higher and I had to keep tugging at the hem to keep my knickers covered! Terry noticed and grinned at me.

"Stop worrying about it," he advised. "All the other girls don't worry. It's all part of the fun. Just remember not to bend over too far at the pool table or we'll all see what you had for breakfast!" He and Russell laughed.

As it turned out, I had a great evening. I received many compliments, not just from men. Several women, wives of the men, told me I looked fantastic and how nice it was to see me 'coming out of my shell' a bit.

One girl, probably a year or two older than me and wearing 'hot-pants' along with a tight jumper and a great deal of make-up, looked me up and down before sighing theatrically.

"I wish I had legs as long and slim as yours!"

I glanced down at my own legs. "They're too skinny," I mumbled.

"I don't know who told you that!" the girl retorted. "You're so lucky. I'd give anything to have legs like yours."

"And I'd give anything to have a bust like yours," I replied.

The girl grabbed my arm and steered me toward the ladies toilets. "Shh! It's not all 'me'. Come on, I'll show you. Do you want me to put some make up on you?"

I spent more than half an hour in the toilets with Lynn. She painted my face with eye-shadow, blusher and lipstick and we giggled over the application of mascara - I kept blinking, making it difficult to apply.

She revealed that more than half of her bust, which I envied so much, was made up of carefully rolled tights! Lynn showed me how to fold the tights so they looked natural tucked inside the bra and under clothes. When I complained that my training bra probably wouldn't hold that much rolled up fabric, Lynn laughed.

"You just get a bigger bra, silly! I'm normally a 'B' cup, but I buy 'C' so I can stuff it full of tights and make my little knockers look like big ones. If I shove it all under what I've got naturally, I can even wear a low-cut top and have a big cleavage."

I absorbed all the tricks like a sponge. In Lynn's company, I felt like a young woman and privileged to be 'in' on the secrets of older girls. It was a novel feeling for me.

I thoroughly enjoyed myself for the rest of the evening. Dave was most attentive. Several times, he put his arm around me and hugged me.

"You're gorgeous!" he whispered, more than once.

I liked Dave, but I didn't like him touching me or hugging me. The relationship seemed to have changed suddenly. Whereas before, we had played darts and pool and talked about things as friends and equals, now Dave seemed to be acting in a totally different way toward me. When I shrugged out of another embrace, Dave looked hurt.

"What's wrong? I thought you liked me?"

"I do. You're funny and friendly ... and really good at pool. I just ..."

"What? Don't you fancy me? Is that it?"

I didn't know what to say. Dave was a tall, fine looking young man. Certainly, there was nothing wrong with him but, after what I'd experienced earlier with his father, being touched in any way by anybody made my skin crawl. It began to dawn on me that all men and older boys would want and expect the kind of thing Trevor and Terry wanted. The thought made my stomach turn. I knew if I told Dave I was not in the least interested in that, he'd not want to stay around me at all. I found my voice.

"It's not that, Dave. I was sick earlier today and I still don't feel quite right."

"Oh. Sorry, I hadn't thought of that. Dad was telling me and Mum how you were poorly at my house. What is it? Are you ill or something?"

"I don't really know," I lied.

"Well, I understand. It's just that you look so pretty tonight ... I don't want any of the other lads to start getting ideas, that's all. I want you for myself, got it?"

I nodded and glanced around the room. Only then did I notice the way the other older lads and young men were looking at me. They all had a similar expression on their faces every time they looked my way. Often, they winked or smiled.

Suddenly, I felt like a rabbit surrounded by foxes. Surely, clothes couldn't make that much difference? None of them had given me a second glance when I wore the old-fashioned, frumpy clothes Mother dressed me in. The rest of the evening, although I joined in with everything as usual, in the back of my mind, a feeling was growing. Clearly, all men were predators and wanted only one thing - one vile thing. What I could not fathom out at all was why any sane girl would undertake the degradation and humiliation of sex willingly!

Terry asked me if there were lockers at the school. I dimly recalled seeing some on my tour. They stood in rows in the cloakroom. Terry told me to find out and to get one as soon as I could. In the meantime, he suggested I put my shoes, tights and anything else I wanted to wear for school into a stout canvas bag which he placed just inside the garage doors. He told me to retrieve the things in the mornings, after Mother had searched my satchel. I pointed out that Mother often left the house very shortly after me and so would probably catch me. Terry shrugged and told me to get up a little earlier and leave the house earlier. Once I'd got a locker at school, I could leave my stuff locked inside it and change when I got there; I'd only have to out-wit Mother for as long as it took me to get a locker of my own.

On the Monday morning when I had to return to school, Mother seemed somewhat silent and distracted. I had the short, black skirt on beneath the long, grey pleated skirt and I dreaded Mother lifting the hem of the skirt and discovering my deception.

A full ten minutes before Mother usually told me to leave I picked up my satchel and headed for the door.

"It's too early to leave yet," Mother snapped.

I had an excuse prepared. "I want to be one of the first at the bus-stop so I can get a decent seat. If I get there last I might have to stand or sit right at the front near the driver where it smells horrible with all the fumes."

"You're so childish and petty! Go on, then. At least you're out of my sight. I might be able to eat something if I haven't got to look at your miserable, ugly face over the breakfast table."

Mother didn't bother to look inside my satchel. "I suppose you have got all your pens and books?"

"Yes, Mummy. I've always got everything I need."

"Right. Clear off, then. When you get home, you can wash up the breakfast things and peel the potatoes for dinner."

I left the house. Praying silently that Mother would not look out of the window and see me I darted behind the hedge and hurried to the garage. It only took seconds to grab my things from the canvas bag and stuff them in my satchel. Once I had them, I strolled innocently up the village street toward the bus-stop. I thought I might even have time to take off my long, white socks and ugly shoes and put the new shoes on before anyone else came to join the queue.

As it happened, there were already three lads waiting when I arrived, so I did not get the chance to change. This turned out to be fortuitous because, as five girls arrived at the bus-stop, Mother went past in her horrible three-wheeled car. She glared at me from the window as she turned into the Norwich road.

When I arrived at school, I hurried straight to the girl's toilets where I changed out of my loose, baggy blouse into a tighter, fitted blouse. I rolled up my horrible pleated skirt and tucked it into the bottom of my satchel with the folded up blouse. I undid my hair from the tight pony-tail Mother always made me wear and let it fall around my shoulders.

I had no idea how to make the large, loose tie-knot everyone seemed to wear. Inside the small cubicle, I tried again and again, but always ended up with the same tight, small knot. Outside, I could hear several girls laughing and chatting. I didn't want to appear foolish and felt anxious about stepping out of the cubicle.

When the noise subsided and I judged everyone had left, I cautiously opened the door. There was one girl, older than me, carefully applying mascara. I know she saw me in the mirror. I sidled out and approached her, shyly.

"Excuse me. I don't know how to make the large knot in my tie. Please, could you show me?"

"Hang on a minute, let me just finish doing this."

I waited, thankful that the girl had not sneered at me or made a spiteful remark. When she'd finished, she tucked the mascara tube into her bag and turned to me.

"I have to put my make-up on when I get here," she explained. "My father won't let me wear it to school."

I grinned. "I understand. My mother won't let me wear normal clothes or make-up at all. I have to change when I get here. Actually, this is the first time I've done it. I came here last week, but I got hit in the face with a football. It broke my nose and I had to stay at home for the week."

"Oh. That was you, was it? I heard about that."

The girl leaned forward and undid my tie. In a few deft moves, she'd turned it from the neat knot into the huge, loose knot that everyone else wore.

"There. You shouldn't need to re-do it for a week or so, you can just slip it on and off over your head."

"I will. I'll have to do it up small and tight every morning, or my mother will go mad. Can you show me how to do it myself?"

The girl patiently showed me how to make the loose knot and I thanked her profusely. She paused as she lifted her bag. "Haven't you got any make-up?"

I shook my head. "My mother won't let me get any. She thinks it's ... tarty."

"Hah! She sounds like my dad! Here, put some lipstick on, quick before the bell goes. Meet me here at break and I'll lend you my blusher, eye-shadow and mascara."

"What's your name?" I asked as I quickly applied the pale pink lipstick she offered me.

"Charlotte, but everyone calls me Charlie. Hurry up, I've got to go!"

"Thanks for your help. I'm Keri."

Charlie snatched at her lipstick and grinned. "See ya at break, Keri!"

She left. I stood and looked at myself in the mirror. I looked nothing like the person I'd always been. The girl in the mirror was a complete stranger to me. I smiled and turned to leave. It occurred to me that I had no idea where I was meant to be.

I trotted along the corridor to the Reception office and although the door stood slightly ajar, I knocked, before peering round the door.

"What do you want?" The secretary glared at me.

"Er ... I wasn't here last week because I got hit by a football. I don't know my timetable or where I'm supposed to be. Can you tell me, please?"

"Oh. It's you. I didn't recognise you. Weren't you given a timetable?"

I shook my head.

The secretary clicked her tongue and went to a filing cabinet. After a short time, she produced a piece of printed paper and thrust it toward me.

"Try not to get 'injured' today," her voice dripped sarcasm. "I'd rather not have your mother on the phone again with more complaints."

I took the sheet and fled.

Members of staff seemed both surprised and pleased that I had completed all the work set for me. I blushed as I was praised in each class. I overheard a few whispered comments from other students along the lines that I must be a swot and was sucking up to the teachers to curry favour.

The student's comments meant more to me than the praise from the staff. Clearly, to be 'accepted', I would need to do less work. With Mother constantly checking up on me, this would be very difficult to achieve.

Mr. Watson, the stern maths teacher, looked me up and down as he flicked through the pages of work I'd done.

"You look different today. I assume you've decided, for whatever reason, to mimic the rest of these ... young women. It clearly has not yet affected your work, which is of an excellent standard. Tell me, do you enjoy mathematics?"

I'd always hated and dreaded maths. I could hardly believe my ears. I flushed bright red, right to my ears and hung my head.

"Not really, sir. I've never been any good at it."

"I see. But this is your work, is it not?"

I nodded.

"Well, it's work of remarkable quality from someone 'not good' at mathematics. Good. Now, everyone, page sixty-seven of your text books. Who can explain to me how to find the area of a circle?"

I bit back the automatic answer. This was something I knew. I did not want to appear too clever in front of other students. I listened intently during class and realised that these students were being taught things I'd learned two or even three years previously. Sister Mathilda had been so frustrated with my low ability in mathematics, yet in this class, I was clearly one of the better students.

At break-time, I went to the girl's toilets and met up with Charlie. She carefully applied make up to my eyes and cheeks. She did not seem surprised that I had no idea how to do my own make-up nor that I possessed none of my own.

"We'll go into town at lunch-time," she said as she put her make-up away. "School meals are vile. Most everyone goes into town. Got any money?"

I shook my head. "My mother ..."

"Don't tell me. I bet she's paid for school dinners and won't let you have any money, right? Sounds like she'd get on really well with my dad. It doesn't matter. I've got some money. I nicked it out of my dad's wallet last night. We'll go into town and get some chips to eat and have a look at the make-up in Boots, all right?"

Charlie also had a locker. She suggested I leave my clothes and ugly shoes inside it so I didn't have to carry them about all day. I readily agreed. I couldn't wait until lunch-time. I felt awed by a girl who had the audacity to steal from a strict father. I asked about her mother.

"Mum? Oh, she died the year before last. It's just me and Dad now, the miserable bastard. I hate him."

"I wish my mother would die! My step-father too. All of them."

Charlie laughed. "Not all of them, surely?"

I nodded and grinned at her. "If they all dropped dead I could go and live with my Nana. She's lovely, but I haven't seen her for ages."

We spent almost the whole of that break-time in the girl's toilets, laughing and chatting. We compared Charlie's father to my mother and decided they should get together, having left us well alone, of course.

At lunch-time, I met up with Charlie and followed her out of the school gates along with many other students. We wandered into the town of North Walsham, stopping at the fish and chip shop. Charlie paid for our cones of chips with a ten pound note!

We sat together on the steps of the war memorial and watched the people going by. Not far away, a tall, extremely thin young man with an enormous blond afro hairstyle chatted animatedly to two young, black youths.

"That's Chris. He's the local stone-head."

"Stone-head? What's that?"

"You know! He does drugs; smokes cannabis all the time and talks a load of rubbish. He's nice enough though. He's always got fags anyway. Do you smoke?"

"No. My mum and step-father do though. It's horrible!"

"You should try it! It's well handy if your parents smoke. You can pinch their fags. Hey, Chris?"

The tall man turned. I could barely see his face under his huge mop of hair. I noticed immediately that he twitched his head repeatedly.

"Why does he jerk his head like that?" I whispered to Charlie.

She shrugged. "I dunno. He's always doing it. Sometimes, he stops talking and stares straight ahead, just twitching his head. At first, I thought it was him trying to toss the hair out of his eyes, but now I think maybe it's some kind of fit. Don't let it worry you, he's all right."

Charlie decided we'd meet with Chris after we'd looked for make-up. I followed her into Boots the Chemist where she quickly found the stands of make-up. Several times, as we were going through the different shades of eye shadows and blushers, mascara's and foundations, a lady came to stare at us. It made me uncomfortable.

"Why does that woman keep staring at us?" I whispered.

"Stupid cow. She thinks we're going to nick stuff, that's all. Take no notice; she's got nothing better to do. How about these? Shall I get them for you? You can pay me back another time."

I nodded. Charlie marched past the woman holding the make-up in one hand.

"Don't worry, missus. We're gonna pay for it," she snarled. "You ought to be watching those first years. They're more likely to rob the place than me. I've got money!"

The woman turned to look at a group of younger girls who were chattering by the nail polish. As soon as the woman's eyes were off us, Charlie slipped all but one piece of make-up in her pocket. We approached the tills and she paid just sixty-five pence for a tub of eye-shadow.

Once we got outside and away from the store, Charlie fished the mascara, foundation, lipstick and blusher from her pocket and dropped them into the bag with the eye-shadow. She held the bag out to me.

"There. You owe me sixty-five pence and something nicked. Fancy a cream cake before we go back to school?"

I accepted the bag and followed Charlie into the baker's shop where she bought two dairy cream éclairs. I had not eaten anything so nice since I last stayed with Nana. We made our way back to the war memorial, where Chris sat on the steps.

"Hi, Chris. This is Keri, she's my new friend. Be nice to her."

Chris extended a thin hand and took hold of one of mine. He brought it to his face and was about to kiss it. "All right, Keri?"

I snatched my hand away. "Yes, thanks."

"Don't worry about Chris. He's a softie, aren't you, luv?" Charlie sat down next to Chris and gave him a quick hug. "Give us a fag, baby," she crooned.

Chris fumbled in his pocket for a battered packet of cigarettes. He extracted two and offered them to me and Charlie. I declined. Charlie took both of them. She slipped one into the breast pocket of her blazer and produced a box of matches from another pocket. I watched as she lit the cigarette and inhaled deeply.

"So; are you going to Janice's party on Saturday?" Charlie asked Chris.

"Yeah, probably, even though I'm not invited of course. Hard to ignore with all that free booze flowing. Are you two going?"

Charlie roared with laughter. "Try to keep me away! I haven't been invited, but I'm damned well going. You should come too, Keri."

I nodded. I had been invited. It occurred to me that perhaps Charlie was not the sort of person I should really associate myself with. Even so, she was the only person who had been friendly toward me, other than Janice. I pushed my doubts aside and ate my cream éclair with renewed relish.

10. Party Plans and Mother Trouble

Even though I actually tried not to do well in lessons, I still achieved a high standard and often, praise from members of staff, particularly Mr. Watson, the maths teacher. This did not endear me to the other students at all. No-one was openly unpleasant to me at first, but I did overhear things said in a stage whisper about me being a swot and a snob and sucking up to the teachers. I tried to ignore it, but it was difficult, especially since more than anything, I wanted friends and to be accepted.

I spent every break-time with Charlie, either in the girl's toilet, where we sat on the edges of the wash hand-basins and chattered whilst others came and went, or outside, behind the science block, where Charlie smoked.

Sometimes, we were joined by a couple of boys and another girl called Lauren. All of them smoked and I came to realise, Lauren and the boys liked to 'drop Acid' and smoke cannabis regularly. They talked about their 'Acid Trips' and I listened in utter astonishment.

One day, one of the boys, I think his name was Eric, related how he had almost jumped off the top of the multi-storey car-park because, under the influence of this 'Acid', he thought he could fly! If it had not been for the presence of other lads, he would almost certainly be dead. Charlie, Lauren and the other boy laughed hysterically as he described the flying sensation. I found myself shaking inside.

"Don't you worry about how dangerous it is?" I asked.

"It's dangerous crossing the road," replied Eric, "But it's not nearly so much fun. Anyway, I'm not going to live my life being worried. Live for the moment because tomorrow you might die, that's what I say!"

Privately, I thought it highly likely that Eric would die, but I said no more because the small group had already made it clear that they thought me a coward because I would not join them in even cigarette smoking.

Every lunch-time during that week, I went with Charlie into the town of North Walsham. We trailed around the shops. Several stores sold make-up and perfumes, which Charlie often stole; she never got caught. Even though I actually knew she was intending to steal something, she managed to take and conceal things with ease so that I rarely saw her do it. I went with her into Department Stores and boutiques, where we looked at the clothing and accessories. Sometimes, Charlie took clothes into the fitting rooms to try them on. There were shop assistants waiting by the fitting room doors who monitored what people took in and brought out. I waited for Charlie to step out from behind the curtain to show me the outfit she'd selected. Nearly every shop we went into, Charlie showed me what she'd stolen when we were outside and a few yards away from the door. I had no idea how she managed it as all her activity seemed open and honest to onlookers, even though she was often rude to the assistants.

On Thursday, when I got home from school, I noticed a carrier bag tossed onto a chair in the sitting room. It had a note attached to it in Mother's rounded handwriting. I picked it up and read:

'These are for the party on Saturday. Try them on and if they don't fit, put them back in the bag and leave a note. I've got a late meeting tonight and will take things back tomorrow if necessary.'

I opened the bag and lifted out a dress. It was grey with three quarter sleeves, a button front, pleated skirt and belt. I don't believe I have ever seen anything so ugly. I stared at it in disgust. It was just the sort of dress one might see an old aged pensioner wearing to a Derby and Joan outing!

Further investigation of the bag revealed a pair of flat, grey shoes with bows on the front - again, the sort worn by old ladies. Beneath the shoes lay a lighter grey cardigan exactly the same as the ones Mother herself wore.

Tears of outrage filled my eyes and I threw the dress down on the chair. Why would Mother dress me like an old woman? I recalled all the lovely things I'd seen in the shops during my lunch breaks with Charlie.

The price tag on the dress lay face up and I noticed Mother had paid twenty pounds for it, from Debenhams. I searched the bag and found the till receipt. In all, Mother had paid over forty pounds for this horrible selection. I knew, from trawling the boutiques and shops, that I could have bought perhaps four fashionable dresses with matching shoes and accessories for that amount of money. No way was I going to try the offending garment on; I couldn't even bring myself to touch it any more than I had already.

I went to the kitchen and made a cup of tea. Russell came in and grinned at me.

"You seen that rag she wants you to wear on Saturday night?"

I nodded.

Russell dissolved into gales of helpless laughter. I watched him as he clutched at his sides and rocked on his feet.

"It's not funny!"

"Yes!" Russell gasped, "It is funny! Even Nana wouldn't be seen dead in that thing! You should go and give it to old Mrs. Meadowes, she might like it!"

I began to smile myself. It didn't have to be a problem, I thought. I knew Charlie would be going to Janice's party. We were a similar size; perhaps she was a little bigger than me, but surely, she could lend me something to wear which would be more appropriate.

"I can't wait till Dad sees it!"

Russell's remark snapped me out of my plans. Almost certainly, there would be a row between Terry and Mother because of the 'party' dress. Once again, I would be the cause of trouble between them. The smile vanished from my face.

"Maybe I'd better not show him?"

"Oh yes, you have to show him. She'll have you drawing an old aged pension if he doesn't stop her. She got me some new stuff too. Wait, I'll get it and show you."

Russell darted away and I stared into my cup of tea. Perhaps Mother really wasn't right in the head, as Terry so frequently suggested. I thought she must really hate me to want to humiliate me by dressing me in such obviously inappropriate clothing. When Russell reappeared carrying a Debenhams bag, I looked up.

"Look at this," he said, as he lifted a sweater. "It's for an old man! It clearly says 'Menswear' on the price tag! If we put this stuff on, we'd look like a couple of old fogies! I'm gonna get Dad to take me to Debenhams on Saturday and change this for something decent. You should come too."

"What else did she get you?"

"These horrible corduroy trousers. They're exactly like the ones my teacher wears. I'm gonna change them and get some flares instead. If Dad's in a good mood, I might even persuade him to get me a denim jacket as well."

I thought Russell was too young to be wearing flares and a denim jacket, but I held my tongue. The facts remained unchanged; Mother had purchased inappropriate clothing for both of us, not just me.

The next day, at school, I told Charlie about the dress and other things Mother had bought. She stared at me in horror.

"Bloody hell! I knew your old woman was strict, but that's just awful! She really expects you to wear it?"

"I haven't actually seen her. I'd already gone to bed when she came home last night. I heard her arguing with my step-father and the bag was still there this morning when I left for school. Mother wasn't there though. I don't know if she went out early or what."

"Right, well that doesn't matter. At lunch-time, we're going into town and we'll get something decent for you to wear tomorrow."

"I can't, Charlie! I haven't got any money! I had a five pound note last weekend, but I left it in the pocket of my skirt and it's gone. I didn't dare ask my mother about it."

"Hah! Having no money is no barrier! Haven't you learned anything at all with me? Nick something; whatever you want. I'll help - distract the assistant or something while you nick something really nice. Make sure it will fit though. I nicked a top last week and I didn't try it on; it's way too big for me."

"I ... I can't, Charlie! I'll get caught!"

"Yes you can. It'll be fine, you'll see. See you at lunch-time."

Charlie gave my shoulder a squeeze as she left. She meant well, I knew that, but even so, I'd had problems in the past with taking things which didn't belong to me and the thought of stealing from a shop terrified me. I wandered off to my lesson deep in thought.

By lunch-time, I'd made up my mind that the answer to the problem was, quite simply, not to go to the party at all. That way, I wouldn't have to wear the horrible clothes Mother bought me; neither would I need to steal anything and risk getting into trouble. I told Charlie this as we walked toward the shops.

"What? Are you completely mad? I never took you for an idiot before. That's just what your rotten mother wants you to do, you stupid cow!"

I opened my mouth to protest and shut it again without saying anything. Perhaps Charlie was right. Mother must have known that I'd refuse to go to the party wearing the dreadful clothes she'd bought me. Then she could scream and shout at me for being ungrateful, but take the things back for a refund nonetheless, secure in the knowledge that I was stuck at home, alone in my room instead of enjoying an evening with friends.

I followed Charlie into a boutique and listened as she advised me on appropriate party wear. Apparently, flared jeans and shiny, halter-neck tops were the 'in' thing. I tried to hide my embarrassment at not knowing what size jeans I should look for. The only jeans I'd ever worn were Benjamin's used work jeans, tied tightly at the waist so they would not fall down.

Charlie had me try on several pairs of jeans and trousers. With only a few exceptions, even the smallest sizes hung quite loosely on my skinny frame. Charlie fussed and chattered; she assured me that I needed the trousers to fit more snugly than those we'd tried, even though a glorious pair of copper coloured satin flares fitted me like a glove. I stood in the opening to the changing room red faced whilst Charlie explained to the assistant that I needed to find a pair of dark jeans in a smaller size.

One of the assistants volunteered to look in the stock-room. The other two busied themselves searching along the rails, both assuring Charlie that at least two styles came in the smallest size and they were certain they had sold nothing in that size recently.

I glanced at the copper trousers hanging on the peg in front of six pairs of jeans. I really wanted them, but they were seven pounds. Charlie caught my eye as she chatted to the assistants and lifted her eyebrows, jerking her head as she did so.

Quick as a flash, I unclipped the trousers from their hanger, rolled them as small as possible and stuffed them in the bottom of my satchel, piling books on top. I wondered what I could do with the empty hanger. My heart pounded wildly as I darted into the next cubicle and put the hanger on the floor beneath the chair in there.

By the time the assistants returned with Charlie chattering to them as if she'd known them all her life, I once again stood looking innocent and slightly helpless in the doorway of the cubicle in which I'd tried everything on.

I obediently tried on four more pairs of jeans and a long, floor-length skirt before Charlie announced that it was simply hopeless trying to find anything that fitted me properly and we should try somewhere else. She picked up the armful of clothes and gave them to one of the assistants.

"You could try Dorothy Perkins or Tammy Girl," the young woman suggested. "I think they've got some things in her size."

I knew they had because Terry had bought me a lot from both stores. However, I didn't want to wear any of the clothes Terry had bought for me because everything made me think of Trevor and the vile things he'd done to me and had me do. We left the store and as we walked along toward the memorial, Charlie grinned at me.

"You're so wet! You could have had at least three pairs of jeans from there. They weren't watching you at all! Loads of those jeans were just fine. Why didn't you nick a pair or two? I mean, I kept them busy for you, didn't I?"

"I took the copper coloured trousers," I admitted.

"You did? That's brilliant! I never even saw you and I'm an expert. We'll have to find something to go with them now. They really did fit you like a glove; they looked like you'd sprayed them on!"

I revelled in Charlie's praise of my shop-lifting talent; it meant a great deal more to me than the teacher's praise for my school-work. I felt confident and happy as we went from shop to shop, stealing whatever we wanted.

I stole an expensive mini skirt with a wide belt which I gave to Charlie. She stole a fancy halter-neck bra for me in a cup size 'B' so that I could pad it out with tights - which we also stole. Charlie stole a beautiful halter neck top for me which would match the copper coloured trousers perfectly. It was stretchy and shiny in many gold, red and copper diagonal stripes.

By the time we walked back to school for the afternoon lessons, eating chips from cones as we went, both our bags were bulging with stolen items. I felt absolutely no guilt whatever; in fact, as Charlie continued to praise me, I glowed with pride.

We carefully arranged to meet outside the hall where the party was due to be held. Charlie told me to wear the awful clothes Mother had provided for me and said she would bring the trousers, bra, tights and top and wait for me outside. We further arranged that I would go with Charlie to the nearby public conveniences to change and we would go in to the party together.

Mother was already at home when I got in from school. This I found most unusual, but I dared not comment. I changed out of my school uniform and sat down at the table in the sitting room to do my homework before Mother could nag me about it.

I jumped violently when Mother's harsh voice interrupted my concentration.

"Where did you get this? Stolen from my purse, I suppose?"

I looked up. Mother had a creased five pound note in her hand.

"Dad's friend, Trevor. He gave it to me last Saturday."

"Did he really? And why was he giving *you* five pounds?"

I bit back the retort which formed in my mind, which ran along the lines of 'I suppose that's what he always pays girls for vile photographs and sex'.

"Well?"

"Well, what? He told me to get myself something pretty. But when I went to get it from my skirt pocket, it had gone."

"You're a filthy little liar! You stole it, didn't you? Tell me the truth or I'll ..."

Help came from an unexpected source. I hadn't seen or heard Russell come in.

"Trevor gave it to her, Mum. He did. I saw him. Dad bought me some comic books and Trevor gave that money to Keri."

Mother gritted her teeth and turned toward Russell.

"Who asked you?"

Russell shrugged. "No-one, but you were going to bash her for lying and she's not lying, that's all."

Mother stared from Russell to me; she frowned.

"This is a conspiracy!" she yelled. "Now both of you are at it, lying to me!" She rounded on Russell and snarled, "Since when did you need to stick up for this slimy bitch?"

Russell stood his ground. "Why don't you just ask Dad?" I noticed the confident smirk on his face.

"Oh, I'm going out! You all make me sick!" Mother turned on her heel, snatched up her handbag from a nearby armchair and marched toward the hallway.

"Bye." Russell openly laughed as Mother slammed out of the house.

I bent down in my seat to retrieve the five pound note which Mother had screwed up and dropped to the floor.

"Russell, why is she like this? I wasn't doing anything wrong. She keeps searching all my stuff and accusing me of stealing. She takes down the posters I put in my room and puts pictures of bloody Donny Osmond and David Cassidy up instead. She's always nagging at me, no matter how hard I try."

"Dad says she's mental," Russell replied. "He thinks she needs locking up. He said she threatened to kill him. She's been reading too many of those murder stories. She said she's gonna poison him!"

I shook my head. Perhaps I was mental too; I'd considered poisoning all of them too. I felt relieved that Mother had gone out. At least I could be certain that the food would be safe later on. Also, if she wasn't at home, there was a good chance Russell and I would go to the club with Terry. I hated being at home now there were no animal friends; I still missed my dog terribly.

"Do you think she will poison him ... or even all of us?" I asked.

Russell flung himself into an armchair. "Nah. Dad says she lives in a dream world. She told me that she wants to take me and run away somewhere. When I said I didn't want to go anywhere with her because I want to stay with Dad, she started crying and raved on about everybody hating her. I do hate her; she's horrible. I wish Sylvia was my mum."

I had no idea Russell felt to strongly about Mother. Sylvia was a lovely woman and Russell's friend, Kevin was a lucky lad to have such a superb, loving mum.

"I hate her too. I've always hated her - but only because she hates me. I can't understand it, Russell. Nana isn't like it, she's patient and kind and ..."

"Not to me, she's not! Nana's always telling me what a spoilt brat I am!"

I couldn't imagine my mild-mannered Nana saying such a thing. I hadn't seen her in quite a while and missed her terribly. Briefly, I experienced a pang of guilt; if Nana knew I'd been stealing clothes and make-up ... this led on to my recollection of being drunk at Trevor's house and the vile things which had happened there. I shuddered.

"Did she actually call you that?"

Russell frowned. "No. She did say I was spoiled, but she didn't call me a brat. That's Mum's favourite word when she's talking about you."

I nodded and turned back to my books, although with Mother gone, there was no reason to continue with my homework. I nearly put it all away, but it occurred to me there was nothing else for me to do if I did. To my surprise, Russell got out a book and sat at the table beside me.

"Will you help me with my maths homework?" he asked. "I don't understand and I keep getting in trouble at school for not doing the work."

"Well, I'll try. I'm not too clever with maths myself, but I should be able to help a bit. Let me see."

When Terry came home, Russell had mastered the fraction problems which had confused him. He'd completed all his homework and a few extra sums that I invented to make sure he understood.

Terry glanced at us. "Where's the old bitch?"

"She got in a huff and went out because when she was accusing Keri of stealing that fiver, I told her Trevor gave it to her."

"Fuck! What did you do that for?"

Russell stared at Terry. "She was gonna bash Keri for stealing!"

Terry hesitated; then he shrugged. "Well I don't suppose it matters. It's nothing to do with her anyway. I suppose she didn't cook anything?"

"No. I wouldn't eat it if she did," Russell grinned at me. "Not after she said she wanted to poison you."

Terry sniggered. "The stuff she cooks is like poison anyway, I probably wouldn't notice! Right. Get changed, Russell and you go and put something nice on, Keri. We'll go to the club and have fish and chips on the way there."

I saw Lynn at the club and once again, she painted my make-up on for me. As she applied eye-shadow, I told her about the party I had been invited to the following evening and the truly horrible dress Mother had bought for me to wear.

"We've all heard about your mother, Keri. Poor woman, she can't help being crazy. It must be so hard, living with someone so ill. She probably means well."

I goggled at Lynn. "Have you actually *met* my mother?"

"No. But my parents have. Mum says your mum needs help. Everyone tries to be supportive of Terry, but he won't accept any help. I suppose he's too proud. My mum thinks you're a lovely girl and Russell is a nice lad too."

I decided to keep my thoughts to myself. It was quite frightening to realise that everyone at the club thought Mother was mentally ill and felt sorry for Terry, Russell and me. I couldn't get the thought out of my head that perhaps I was going to be just like Mother; this was far more terrifying. I quietly resolved *never* to have any children.

11. The Party And Other Bad Things

"Fucking hell! I cannot believe your bloody mother! You can't go out to a party looking like that! You look like an old aged pensioner!" Terry was furious.

"It's all right. Honestly. I'll be fine."

"It reflects on me, you know. Everyone sees you walking about looking ... well, just looking strange and they think it's something to do with me!"

"Yes, but the party is in North Walsham. No-one there knows you. Please, can we just go now? I don't want to be late."

Mother had tied my hair up in a tight bun on top of my head. The horrible grey dress hung like a sack to my mid calf and the belt did nothing to shape it as, even on the tightest eyelet, the natural waist of the garment hung to my hips. Mother merely complained once more that I was far too skinny. She'd forced me to wear white knee length socks with the vile, flat and ugly shoes.

Terry scowled. "I should go in there and give that old bitch such a damned hiding; then you could wear one of those dresses I got you and go out looking like a teenager instead of ..."

"Honestly," I interrupted, "It's fine. Can we just go before she decides to change her mind?"

Terry drove far too fast to North Walsham. His lips were pressed into a tight line of disapproval. I sat in the passenger seat and said nothing. I hoped Charlie would be as good as her word and be there, waiting for me, as she promised.

Terry pulled the car up close to the war memorial. He fumbled in his pocket and produced a five pound note.

"Here. You'll be all right walking from here. I don't want anyone to see you getting out of the car, you look so terrible. I know you haven't got any money, so this will be all right. You can get chips and maybe if you have to buy your own drinks, you'll get a few with that. I'll be back to pick you up at half past eleven. Make sure you're waiting right here."

I accepted the note and slipped out of the car. Terry hardly waited for the door to close before he sped off.

There were several people about in the town centre; most of them stared at me. I hung my head and crossed the road. Every time I saw any young people, I stopped and pretended to look at something in a shop window. Nobody spoke to me, although I did hear a few muffled bursts of laughter.

I approached the hall where the party was being held. There were coloured balloons each side of the door and a hand painted banner above it which read, 'Happy Birthday Janice'. I couldn't see Charlie anywhere.

After loitering close to the hall for about ten minutes, I walked on past and headed toward the far end of town. I felt utterly let down and deflated, not to mention cold. I hadn't brought a coat out with me and the November evening was becoming colder by the minute.

I sat down on a bench near the shops and tried my best not to cry. I couldn't believe Charlie would let me down, not after all she'd said and the plans we'd made. I wondered if she'd argued with her father and he'd stopped her from going out.

After several minutes of shivering, I heard voices across the street and raucous laughter which I recognised. I looked up and saw Charlie staggering along the road with Chris and several others. They were all laughing uproariously. Charlie carried a duffel bag over one shoulder and a bottle of something in her hand.

It took all the courage I could muster to stand up, cross the street and approach the group.

"Er ... Hello, Charlie. I've been waiting ages for you."

Charlie peered at me through her drunken stupor. "Oh. You've arrived. Your clothes are in here." She tossed the bag at my feet. "I thought you weren't coming," she slurred.

"I've been here for ages. I couldn't find you. Hello, Chris."

Charlie held out a bottle of something clear and staggered against Chris, who supported her, grinning as he openly groped at her breasts.

"Want some of this?"

"No, thanks. Where can I get changed?"

Chris pointed down the street at the public toilet building. "Why are you disguised as an old woman, man?" he queried. I thought he sounded a little drunk too.

"I'm not a man! And this horrible dress is what my foul mother bought for me to go to the party in. She likes me to look old and ugly."

"Hey, man. No need to get your knickers in a knot. Just a figure of speech, man. Your ole' lady sure made a good job of making you look ugly. I wouldn't fuck you if you were unconscious!"

Chris, Charlie and their mates screamed with laughter at the comment. Charlie tried to look serious.

"She's all right, Chris, just a bit dumb is all. Have a drink, Keri, you'll feel better!"

I recalled what happened last time I had a drink and shuddered. "No. You keep it. I'm going to get changed."

I picked up the duffel bag and headed toward the public toilets leaving Chris, Charlie and the others behind. As I walked away, I heard the sounds of someone being noisily sick; the others laughed.

The lighting was rather dim in the toilet building and the smell was horrendous. I peeped into a couple of filthy cubicles. One had urine and faeces all over the floor and seat, the other was filled to the top with screwed up toilet tissue. I retreated back to the outer door and peeped out; I could see no-one.

Barely inside the doorway, I took off the horrible shoes and peeled off my knee length socks so I stood barefoot on the concrete, which was incredibly cold – and damp. I opened the duffel bag and dragged out the copper satin trousers and the striped halter neck top. They were creased from being screwed up in the bag. I rummaged deeper, between two glass bottles, but there was no sign of either the bra or the tights Terry and I had stolen and she had promised to bring with her; there was an equal lack of 'platform shoes' she'd offered to lend me too. I couldn't wear the top without a lot of padding and I could not even use my socks as padding because there was no bra to hold them. I wasn't even wearing the training bra Terry bought me because Mother had stood over me whilst I dressed. Under the hated grey dress was a childish vest and huge, childish knickers.

I choked back a despairing sob. How could Charlie be so utterly thoughtless? I pulled on the trousers anyway because I was so cold; although they fitted well, they were too long without high heeled shoes and I trod on the hem, making them wet. My fingers were going numb with cold as I fumbled with the zipper and button. I slipped my bare feet back into the horrible flat shoes, which made the trousers bunch round my ankles and stood just outside the toilets with my back to the wall, shivering.

I looked up and down the street. There was no sign of Charlie, Chris or anyone else. I didn't know what to do. Certainly, I could not go to Janice's party looking the way I did but neither could I remain standing by the toilets all evening. I had no watch, but I knew it would be several hours before Terry came to collect me.

I remembered the five pound note Terry had given me and felt in the pocket of the dress for it. It was gone! Frantic, I turned back and sought around the floor, finding it eventually, crumpled up in a damp spot. It must have fallen from the shallow pocket when I pulled on the trousers. I snatched it up and smoothed it out as best I could.

I shrugged the ropes of the duffel bag over my shoulder and began to walk back to the memorial. I glanced at the jolly balloons outside the hall where the party was being held and heard dance music and the sound of people laughing and enjoying themselves.

Suddenly, I felt furious. Why was it that everybody else could have a normal life and enjoy themselves but I could not? Why did Mother go out of her way to dress me in a way which made me look stupid, old and ugly so that people would not accept me?

Why had Charlie let me down? It simply wasn't fair! I began to cry tears of helpless rage as I plodded along. An icy wind blew down the empty street and I shivered uncontrollably.

The lights of the fish and chip shop near the memorial drew me and I gripped the duffel bag ropes with one hand and the crumpled five pound note with the other as I drew closer. I hoped no-one was waiting in there. I really didn't want anyone to see me.

Mercifully, the shop was empty. I glanced up and down the street before stepping inside. A radio played behind the counter. The man sat with his back to me; he was doing a crossword in a newspaper. I cleared my throat to attract his attention and he looked round.

"Sorry, luv; can't have your sort in here. Can't serve you, I'm afraid. Off you go now." He turned back to his crossword puzzle.

I didn't understand. Why couldn't I go in there? What on earth could he mean by the phrase 'your sort'? I remained standing at the counter; the man ignored me. At length, I spoke.

"I'm sorry. I don't understand what you mean? Why can't you serve me, please?"

"Don't serve gyppos in 'ere, luv. Not even well spoken ones. Scares the other, proper customers away, see? You'd best go or I'll ring the police and have them remove you." The man did not turn to look at me.

"What? But I'm not a ... gypsy! I live in Swanton Abbot with my parents and my brother. And I go to school right over there!"

The man turned and looked me up and down. "Whereabouts in Swanton Abbot?" he asked, suspicion colouring his tone. "On the Common I suppose!"

I drew myself up and thrust out my chin. "No, of course not. Don't be stupid. I live at Holly Cottage."

"'Ent never 'eard o' that place," the man said mildly. You looks like a gyppo to me. What's yer name then?"

"Keri," I snarled. "My name is Keri. I'm fourteen; I go to that school just down the road. I'm cold and hungry and my friends have let me down ... and my step-father isn't coming to pick me up till after eleven o'clock. I just want some chips and soup or something else warm. I've got money."

I held out the crumpled, damp five pound note. The man stared at it and then at me.

"Why don't you just go to the phone box, call yer Dad and get him to come and pick you up now, if yer friends have let you down?"

I had no change for the public telephone box and didn't know how to use it anyway. I burst into tears and turned away. Now I had been mistaken for a gypsy! I thought of Mam and the beautiful, embroidered clothes she, Anna and Mia wore. None of them looked anything like I did; I must look like a tramp! I ran out of the fish and chip shop and across the road to the memorial, where I sat on the stone steps, buried my face in my hands and sobbed.

As the evening wore on, I saw several people enter the fish and chip shop. The scent of hot chips with vinegar and salt on them wafted across the road; at first, my mouth watered. No-one took any notice of me, huddled at the foot of the stone cross in my ugly grey dress which I'd wrapped around my legs trying to conserve some warmth. I'd stopped shivering; the cold of the stone cross seemed to have seeped into my bones and although I did still feel quite cold, I also felt sleepy.

Not long after I sat down there and the tears had stopped, I'd noticed a large street clock hanging outside the jewellery store; I spent more than two hours doing nothing more than watch the large second hand tick round and round its face. I vaguely wondered where Charlie and Chris had gone and why she had not come back for her bag.

At half past ten, I dug inside the duffel bag and retrieved my long white socks which I pulled on with numb hands before slipping my shoes back on. I'd have to take off the trousers before Terry arrived. I couldn't face walking back to those filthy toilets, I knew that. Anyway, my legs and back-side seemed to have gone numb and cramped; I wasn't at all sure I could even stand up.

Although several people were queuing up inside the fish and chip shop, a lot of them teenagers and young people laughing and joking, I groped beneath the skirt of the dress to undo the button and zip of the trousers. When I finally managed, I peeled the trousers down and slipped them off. Instantly, I began to shiver once more. I thought about putting the trousers back in the bag, but I realised I would have to either leave the bag where I was sitting or bring it home and explain it to Terry. That it contained alcohol might be a problem.

I snatched out the striped top and stuffed it and the trousers down the inside front of the horrible dress then I pulled the draw-string tight and put the bag behind me. Just as I did this, I heard an unmistakeable sound – the engine of Mother's horrible little three wheeled car; Terry told me he'd collect me at half past eleven. This was an hour early. I looked up just as the vehicle turned the corner and came into sight.

It was difficult standing up. Both my legs felt like lead weights and my back side was completely numb. As Mother pulled the car to a halt beside the memorial, I staggered down the steps toward her. She wound the driver's window down.

"You're drunk!"

My teeth began to chatter. "No, I'm not drunk, Mummy, I'm just really cold. I've been waiting for ages."

"I know when someone is drunk!" roared Mother through the open window. Several people on the other side of the street turned to look.

I shuffled around to the passenger door and opened it.

"Just wait till I get you home, young lady! I'm not putting up with that kind of behaviour! That girl assured me that there would be no alcohol available to minors! I shall go and see her father first thing tomorrow morning! Get in the car and don't you dare vomit!"

I struggled into the low seat and closed the door. As I did so, I heard shouts of laughter and a few loud comments along the lines of 'Oh, it's only that weird girl and her potty Mother'. I grimaced and hugged myself. I tried to wiggle my toes; pins and needles were beginning to hurt in both legs.

"I knew you couldn't be trusted!" Mother slammed the car into gear and pulled away.

My teeth began to chatter uncontrollably in the warmth of the little car. In trying to reply to Mother and defend myself, I bit my tongue. My whole body shuddered with violent shivers.

"What else have you done?" Mother screeched. "I suppose you've been taking drugs as well? Oh, my god, you're impossible. I shall thrash you within an inch of your life when I get you home! Just look at the state of that beautiful dress as well! Whatever have you been doing in it? I suppose you've been having sex with men again, haven't you ..."

I closed my eyes and let Mother's incessant nagging fade into the background. If Charlie was as unreliable as she'd turned out to be, I would need to steal my own bras, tights and clothes from now on. I wondered what the older girl would say on Monday morning when I asked her about the things she'd forgotten to bring with her. Then I mused on who would find the duffel bag and its contents that I'd left sitting on the steps of the memorial. All manner of thoughts drifted through my mind and I forgot where I was. I may have even drifted off to sleep.

I woke to a ringing slap around my ear.

"Get out of my car and get indoors, you filthy little slut. I'm going to teach you a lesson once and for all!"

I rubbed at my cheek and stumbled from the car toward the door. Mother came behind me and kicked my legs.

"Look at those socks as well! They're filthy dirty! Get inside, now!"

As I approached the door, Mother snatched at my hair, but it was still tied up in the tight bun so she shoved me roughly in the back. I fell into the back door and fumbled for the handle.

As I stepped inside the darkened kitchen, Mother's large hand caught me round the back of the head.

"Get off!" I yelled. "I haven't done anything wrong!"

Mother slammed the door and took hold of the shoulder of the grey dress to turn me to face her. I pulled away. I still had pins and needles in both feet; my back and legs ached and my fingers tingled and prickled as well. The sleeve of the dress tore with a loud ripping sound.

Mother pushed me with both hands. I stumbled forward and fell to my knees. "Now look what you've done!" she shrieked. "That dress was expensive and now you've ruined it!"

I crawled away and turned as I raised myself to my feet. Tears streaked my cheeks as I backed away.

"It's a vile dress! Even an old aged pensioner wouldn't be seen dead in it! I hate you! You make me look ugly and horrible so everyone makes fun of me!"

"How dare you speak to me like that?" Mother lunged toward me and I swept my arm up in a defensive manner. Unfortunately, my flailing hand caught Mother's chin. She went wild with fury and snatched up a frying pan, which she began to clout me with. All the time, she screamed abuse at me, reminding me how ashamed of me she felt, how I had utterly ruined her life and how she wished I were dead.

I warded off as many blows as I could, backing away further and further until I found my shoulders against the bathroom door. Quick as a flash, I stepped inside and slammed the door in Mother's furious face. I drew the bolt across and leaned against the wood, panting.

I had no idea why Terry had not come to collect me or where he and Russell might be. I could only assume that he'd argued with Mother again and taken Russell out to the club to get away from her.

As Mother began banging on the bathroom door with the frying pan, I stepped forward and removed the shiny, screwed up trousers and striped halter neck top from inside the dress. Ignoring the cacophonous noise, I pulled at the panel on the side of the bath until it came away slightly. I tucked the clothes inside the space behind the panel and leaned on the board hard so that it snapped back into place.

The door rattled under the rain of blows Mother hurled upon it, but the bolt held. I used the lavatory and ran hot water into the sink so I could hold my hands under the warm water until they went red. Eventually, I put the lid down on the lavatory and sat down on it. All I could do was wait, either until Mother exhausted herself and stopped her attack or until Terry returned with Russell.

At least the bathroom was warmer than the war memorial in North Walsham and there was no-one to stare or call me a gypsy or anything else. I ignored the tears seeping from the corners of my eyes and settled down to wait.

12. A Lot To Think About

Amazingly, once Terry had disarmed Mother and she'd fled to her room, shrieking death threats, Terry actually listened to what I told him. I didn't mention the stolen clothes, but I did explain that I had arranged to meet a friend who would lend me some clothes for the party – but that she'd let me down and I'd spent the whole evening cold and alone sitting on the war memorial.

"Well, I suppose that explains why you didn't make a fuss about wearing that ... that hideous rag and old woman shoes. You should have gone in the fish and chip shop; it would have been warm in there."

"I did, but they called me a gypsy and refused to serve me!"

"Really? Well. You'd best go make yourself a cup of tea and some toast or something. How did you tear that dress?"

"Mummy did it. She grabbed me and I was scared and pulled away. The sleeve just ripped; she's ever so cross about it."

"She's always cross about everything. Throw it in the bin when you take it off."

I ate several pieces of toast and had two cups of tea before I scuttled to my room in my vest and knickers, leaving the dress stuffed in the kitchen bin.

I quickly put on my nightdress and crawled into bed. However, I couldn't sleep. I could hear more raised voices from downstairs and I fretted, tossed and turned, all the time expecting my bedroom door to be flung open and some kind of attack to take place.

In the morning, Terry opened the door and called me. I sat up and stared at him in silence.

"The old bitch has gone off somewhere; probably gone whining to that Riley bloke. I'm off to football. You can come if you want or stay here."

"I'll stay here, thanks."

"All right, but if she comes back, she'll still go mental at you. Come to football. Trevor and Dave will be there and you can get hot soup and stuff from the club-house."

I considered what might happen if Mother returned and found me alone in the house. Terry's offer was by far a safer option. However, the November morning was very cold and I did not want to wear a short skirt.

"Can I wear my old clothes?"

"If you want to. It's a bit muddy at pitch-side anyway. Wear a coat and scarf too."

I enjoyed watching the football. Dave greeted me enthusiastically and stayed beside me throughout the match. I sneered at the pathetic goal-keeping efforts of the opposing team and remarked that I could do better with my eyes closed. Dave promised to test me out one day.

After the game finished and Terry had taken a shower, Trevor invited the three of us to his home for Sunday lunch. Terry accepted. I had reservations, but felt I could not protest.

It was only a short drive from the football ground to Trevor's home. Dave travelled with Terry, Russell and me and we sat in the back of the Consul, giggling and chattering. When we arrived, Dave tugged at my sleeve to get me to the front door more quickly.

"Come on! I want you to meet my mum. I keep telling her about you. She thinks you're an imaginary friend or something!"

Trevor's wife was enormously fat and not very tall. She had short, dark hair speckled with grey and rosy cheeks. She didn't look at all like the slender young woman in the wedding photograph I'd seen in the lounge on my last visit. She grinned and greeted me warmly; I liked her at once.

We sat together at the kitchen table and ate a well cooked roast dinner. I had to keep avoiding Trevor's eyes because every time he looked at me, I recalled the foul things he'd done when I'd been there alone with him. I found it difficult to swallow the food

Maisie gave me, even though it tasted equally as nice as anything Nana cooked.

"What's wrong, luv? You seem really nervous and upset." Maisie's look of concern made me want to cry. If only she knew. I shook my head.

"Aw, it's just her bloody mother again," Terry answered for me. He went on to explain about my disastrous evening out and the attack Mother launched upon me, assuming I was drunk or on drugs.

Maisie's hand flew to her mouth in shock. "Terry, that woman is dangerous! What if you hadn't got home in time? She might have killed poor Keri, and the dear child hadn't even done anything wrong!"

"I know; that's why I brought her with us today. It's just not safe to leave her at home any more. The woman's insane! She's constantly accusing me of seeing other women too – chance would be a fine thing, I haven't got time, what with work and everything!"

"Mum says she's gonna poison Dad," Russell said, with his mouth full. "We're all too scared to eat anything she cooks now!" He grinned; he didn't look at all scared to me.

"Well! You should go to the police or something," Maisie stated, righteously. "That can't be legal making death threats like that. And you've got enough proof. Everybody knows she's as nutty as a fruit cake. Can't you get her committed to an asylum or something?"

"I wish!" Terry shovelled more food into his mouth and chewed it enthusiastically. "This is so good, Maisie. You're a wonderful cook. Trevor's a lucky man!"

Maisie smiled indulgently at Trevor. "No. I'm a lucky woman," she said. "I've got the best hubby in the world!"

I nearly choked on the food I was trying to eat. I coughed and spluttered till my eyes watered. Maisie got me a glass of water and patted my back until the coughing fit subsided.

On Monday morning, I got myself ready for school and tried to avoid being in the same room as Mother for more than a few seconds at a time. Even so, she kept up a constant barrage of accusations and derogatory comments. I ignored them all. I knew, if I tried to defend myself in any way, she might attack me again.

When Mother went into her room to get something, I seized my opportunity. I grabbed my satchel and blazer and fled the house. I jogged up the village street in my over-long skirt and ugly shoes. How much easier life would be if I could just wear the nice clothes without having to wait until I got to school where I could find Charlie and get my things from her locker. I resolved to ask the secretary for a locker of my own as soon as possible.

I loitered around in the cloakroom for a good long time before Charlie finally appeared. She looked dreadful; she had big bags under her eyes and a red scrape-mark down one side of her face. I was horrified and forgot all about the things I'd planned to say to her about letting me down on Saturday evening.

"Oh, God, Charlie! What happened to you?"

Charlie grinned ruefully. "I fell down some steps on Saturday night," she admitted. "I was out of my head so I didn't feel it at the time, but it's well sore!"

"Really? I mean ... it wasn't your father or anything?"

"What? Oh no. He wouldn't hit me. He just nags and nags and nags. He didn't even notice; he's been drunk as a skunk all weekend. I'm sorry I didn't get to come in to the party with you. I had it off with Chris and then later, when he'd passed out, that mate of his. You know; the one with the really long hair."

I knew that expression well enough. I swallowed hard. "What? Chris raped you?"

"No, silly! He's a really good screw. He makes me all shivery inside! I only went with Ray because Chris was unconscious and I was randy as hell. He's not so good, but any port in a storm, eh?"

I didn't know what to say about this. I frowned in confusion. From what Charlie had said having sex was an enjoyable activity. I certainly couldn't imagine her doing anything she didn't like.

"Do you forgive me, then?"

"What?"

"For not coming in to the party with you?"

"I didn't go to the party."

Charlie stared at me as I fastened my shoes. "Yes, you did. I gave you the clothes and you went to change. You went to the party so I wasn't worried about going off with Chris, Ray and the others."

I couldn't change, Terry. You forgot to bring the bra and the tights. No way could I wear that top without those. You didn't bring the shoes either. I sat on the memorial all evening and nearly froze to death. Then it was my mother who came to collect me instead of my step-father. I was frozen stiff and she thought I was drunk. She thrashed me. I had to sit in the bathroom for over an hour before my step-father got home and stopped her trying to beat down the door."

"Oh. Sorry about that. I was a bit drunk. I had half a bottle of vodka before I even went out. Never mind. Next time I'll make sure I get it right. Come on, we'll be late. You've got Watson for maths haven't you?"

Privately, I thought there would never be a 'next time' but I said nothing. Charlie secured the door of her locker and grinned at me.

"See you at lunch-time."

I went to my class-room and made sure I was marked as present on the register the teacher called. When everyone moved from their chairs at the first bell and began to move toward the appropriate room for the next class, I darted into the toilets, where I waited until all had gone quiet. I had no intention of meeting Charlie at lunch-time.

I took two five pound notes out of my pocket and looked at them. One that Trevor had given me and the other, Terry had provided on Saturday night. I intended to go into the town and spend them before Mother or anyone else had the opportunity to take them from me. I didn't need to rely on Charlie or anyone else.

I peered out the door into the silent corridor. No-one was about. I slipped through the doorway without opening the door fully because it creaked. After another quick glance to check the coast was clear, I raced along the corridor, out the double doors and across the front playground to the double gates.

I didn't stop running until I was in the town centre. I stopped, close to the fish and chip shop which had refused to serve me on Saturday evening to catch my breath. I glanced across to the memorial and noticed the duffel bag I'd left behind was still there! I crossed the road and picked it up. Even the bottles of vodka were still inside! I hefted it onto my shoulder and walked along the road toward one of the shops Charlie and I had visited the previous week. I wanted a bra and some tights.

No-one commented on a schoolgirl out shopping during the morning. In fact, when I went into the shop that I'd stolen the copper trousers from, the sales assistants asked me if I'd found anything nice to wear and if I enjoyed the party on Saturday evening. I lied and said I'd found a lovely dress and had a wonderful evening. As they smiled and chatted to me, I began to feel guilty about stealing the trousers. Before long, I made my excuses, said goodbye and left.

I did very well with my ten pounds. I bought a pair of snug-fitting 'Brutus Gold' jeans, a padded bra and a pack of six pairs of tights. I still had just enough money with which to buy a cone of chips.

I crossed to the fish and chip shop, which had just opened. When I went inside and ordered a cone of chips, I waited until the man had served me and given me a few pence in change before speaking.

"Do you still think I'm a gypsy?" I asked.

"Eh? Don't know what you mean, luv."

"Saturday night. I was freezing cold, scared and my friends had let me down. You wouldn't serve me. You said I was a gypsy."

The man peered at me. "That was you, was it? Well, if you were in fancy dress, you should've just said so. You looked a right state; you look normal enough now, I suppose."

"I'd just like to tell you," I grated, "Just so that in future, you'll know. Gypsy women do not wear horrible, frowsy dresses. I've seen gypsies. They wear beautiful, embroidered blouses and bright skirts."

"Not *them*," the man replied. "I don't mean *them*. They're all right. I mean them scruffy buggers what steal anything that ain't nailed down. Them diddycoys what have never done a day's work in their lives. They're dirty, scruffy buggers, them are."

I'd never heard of 'diddycoys' but I didn't like the picture the man was painting, particularly since he'd mistaken me for one of these 'undesirable' types.

"Well, I'm not a gypsy nor a diddy ... diddy-thing like you said. I'm just a girl and I nearly froze to death on Saturday because of you."

The man grinned. "Well, you're very much alive now, ain't you? Sorry 'bout that, luv. It was an easy mistake to make. You should've seen yourself! I'll know another time, won't I?"

I glowered at the man and left the shop, savouring the salty chips. I had no intention of going back to school; I thought perhaps I should have saved a bit more money so that I could catch the bus home. I decided to walk. The November sunshine was bright enough, although too weak to be warm.

The only route back to Swanton Abbot that I knew was the one the bus took. I set off and quickly cleared the town. I screwed up my empty chip cone and put it in my pocket. There was no pavement along the road, so I kept to the edge, near the grass verge. I remembered that I was supposed to walk on the side of the oncoming vehicles, but I felt it didn't matter.

The road was not particularly busy and I was enjoying the walk. I looked up as I noticed a car which had passed me had pulled in at the side of the road. I kept walking, not altering my pace. As I drew level with the car, the driver, a man I judged to be in his thirties, leaned across the passenger seat and wound the window down.

"Where ya goin', luv? Wanna lift?"

"No, thank you. My mother will be along in a minute to pick me up." I lied.

"Only asking!" The window wound up and the driver sped off.

Nana had always drummed into my head that I should never accept lifts from strangers. I shook my head and continued onward. It was a long walk; longer by the bus route, which called at several small villages.

I paused in a tiny village and sat down on a bench beside the bus stop to rest. After a few moments, a lady wearing a mackintosh and coloured headscarf approached me.

"You've missed the bus, luv," she said. "There won't be another one 'till the school bus comes along at about half past three."

"It's all right," I replied. "I'm walking anyway. I just stopped for a rest."

"Where you walking to?"

"Swanton Abbot."

"Ah. Only three miles to go. Not too far. Not in school today?"

I hesitated. "I had a free period this afternoon," I lied. "I thought I'd walk home. I can't work in the school library, there are too many distractions."

"Want me to ask my hubby if he'll take you home?" the woman asked. "He works nights, but he's up and about now. I'm sure he won't mind."

No, I'm sure he won't mind either, I thought to myself. *He probably wouldn't believe his luck at having a schoolgirl to rape or molest.*

"No thanks. The walk will do me good." I stood up. "Goodbye," I added.

I saw the woman shake her head as I walked away.

I had plenty of time to think as I walked those three miles. Ordinarily, I would have been looking at the trees, fields and scenery, but on that day, I only plodded along, thinking about how disgusting men were and wondering at Terry's enjoyment of sex. It totally threw me how she could like such a thing. I began to think I should disassociate myself from her altogether. On the other hand, if I did that, I'd be back to square one with no friends at all.

I'd got almost to the door of Holly Cottage before I realised I'd walked all the way home, some nine miles, wearing the short black skirt, tight blouse and fashionable shoes. I stared down at myself in horror. I hadn't given a thought to how I was dressed!

Shaking with anxiety, I approached the cottage. Mother's car was not there; I hadn't expected it to be. I retrieved the back door key from beneath a flower pot. Since Terry had insisted we have no more to do with Sylvia, this is where the key was left every day.

I rushed indoors and darted straight to my room, undoing the school clothes as I went. It took only moments to change into one of my over-long, frowsy skirts and a baggy blouse. I stared at the clothes I'd taken off. The blouse had been worn every day for a couple of weeks and was badly in need of a wash, as was the short skirt. I knew I could not put them in the laundry basket. Mother would go insane if she found them.

I decided to wash both the items myself, by hand. I still didn't know how I'd dry them, but at least I could get them clean before anyone else came home.

I'd just finished wringing the skirt out when Russell came home. He stood in the kitchen doorway and watched me.

"Is that the skirt you've been wearing for school?"

"Yes. I forgot to change. I've left the long grey one at school in Charlie's locker. I've got another one upstairs, but I thought I'd better wash this stuff while I can. I don't know how on earth I'm going to get them dry without Mummy finding them though."

"Iron them dry," Russell suggested.

"I dare not use the iron. She'll know. Anyway, I might burn them."

"I'm going out with Kev in a while. How about if I get him to ask Sylvia if she could do them for you? Then she can give them to Kev and he'll give them to me."

"All right. But you will make sure Mummy doesn't find out, won't you?" I gave Russell the wet skirt and blouse.

"Yeah. Stop worrying. I'll get it sorted. But ..."

"What?"

"Will you do my maths homework for me? Fair's fair. I'm doing something for you."

I nodded. "Yes, but I'll do it on a piece of paper so you can copy it into your book."

Russell put the wet clothes on the draining board and went to get his school bag. He lifted out a maths book and a battered exercise book.

"There's two lots actually," he said. "I didn't do the class work either. I was writing notes to my mates and winding up the teacher."

I grinned. "All right. I'll do both, but you'll have to remember to copy them into your book."

Russell snatched up the wet clothes and left. I went into the sitting room and took out my school books. Since I'd missed class, I had no idea what I should be doing. I opened my own maths book.

Maybe, if I just did the work on the page after the homework I'd done on Friday, it would be all right.

I settled down to work, finding the problems easy. I worked my way through five pages before I remembered Russell's homework. I put my own maths book back into my satchel and opened Russell's text book. Once again, the problems and sums were all fractions. I understood fractions well so it took me very little time to work through several pages, using paper torn out of one of my own exercise books to work on.

I glanced at the clock. Nearly half past six. Mother should have been home an hour ago. In fact, Terry would be home very soon. I tidied away all the books and went to make myself a cup of tea.

Terry came in as I sat down to drink the tea I'd made.

"One left in the pot for me? Where's the old bitch? I notice her car isn't outside."

I shrugged. "I don't know."

I poured Terry a cup of tea and sat down again. "I ... er ... made a mistake today," I began.

"Yea?"

"Yes. I forgot to change before I came home from school."

"Won't matter. You've got another uniform haven't you?"

"Yes. I washed the things I've been wearing. I didn't know how to dry them so Russell took them round to Sylvia's to see if she could do it. You know, iron them and stuff." I waited for Terry to explode with rage.

"Good idea. Let me have them when they're done and I'll put them in the canvas bag in the garage again. You can collect them in the morning. Problem sorted. How come you forgot to change?"

"I was talking to my friends."

Terry said no more. He took his cup of tea and went into the lounge room. I wondered if he would suggest anything for tea. I went to the door of the lounge and knocked on it.

"What are you knocking at the door for? It's not locked, you know!"

I opened the door and peered into the room. "Shall I peel some potatoes or something? I don't know what we are going to have for tea."

"I've had a meal already. Do you know how to make scrambled eggs?"

"I think so."

"Right, well you do some scrambled eggs on toast for yourself and Russell. There's a program on that I want to see in minute. Make sure you wash up and tidy the kitchen so the old cow hasn't got anything to moan about." Terry turned back to the television.

I closed the door and went back to the kitchen. I knew Russell had to be home by half past seven. There would be little point in preparing food until just before then. I washed up the mug I'd used for tea and went to my room.

Once again, pictures of Donny Osmond and David Cassidy had been pinned to the board. I tore them down and screwed them up. So; Mother had been in this room, had she? I opened a few drawers and glanced inside. All my socks, knickers and vests had been sorted into neat piles. I mixed them up again out of sheer devilment. Why did Mother insist on having everything just so and why had she been in my room at all in the first place?

I opened the shopping bag and took out the jeans, bra and tights I'd bought that day. There was nowhere in this room that I could hide these things. I'd have to put them in Terry's room with all the other things he'd bought for me. It would only take a moment to open his bedroom door and tuck the jeans and things into the top of the bag which contained dresses and skirts.

I went from my room across the landing and opened Terry's bedroom door, switched the light on and stepped into the room.

The usual mess greeted me, along with the stale smell. I tucked the jeans into one bag and the bra and tights into another bag.

As I turned around to leave, I noticed a pile of large, glossy pictures on the floor near the bed. I walked over to them and bent to pick them up; I thought they must have fallen off the pile of Terry's pornographic magazines.

The pictures were close-up shots of a girl's genitals. My stomach knotted as I scooped them all together. I had a horrible suspicion that they must be of me, but then, I noticed a small hand in one picture. It had a bright ring on one finger. Not me, then. Morbid curiosity caused me to look through the pictures, which were mostly so close they really only showed genitalia and hands, one of which was large and obviously male. I gagged as I saw what the hand was doing and quickly turned to the next picture.

The little girl could not have been more than nine or ten years old. She had wavy blonde hair and enormous, blue eyes. Her face was fixed in a false, terrified grin. Between her legs protruded something huge and black.

I don't know how I didn't drop the pictures with the shock I felt. I bent and spread them out as close to how I'd found them as I could. Then I crept back to the doorway and switched the light off, closing the door quietly behind me.

Once back in my own room, I sat on my bed and shook with shock and anxiety. Who could that little girl be? Where had Terry got those pictures from? I felt physically sickened and allowed myself to dwell on the matter. I'd actually begun to like Terry a bit and see him as an ally against Mother. Those horrible pictures reminded me of the pain and humiliation he'd made me suffer on numerous occasions and renewed my disgust and hatred of him. It occurred to me that perhaps he'd not assaulted me for a long time because now I was too old for his tastes. The thought gave me a sense of relief, but the anxiety about the other little girl, whoever she might be, built until I felt I could scream.

I hurried back downstairs and sat in the kitchen so I was close enough to the bathroom if I was sick. My appetite had fled and the idea of food nauseated me. I'd just sat down when Russell came in. He handed me the beautifully dry and ironed clothes immediately.

"Here. You'd better hide them quick. Where's Mum?"

I accepted the clothes and stared at them. "Thanks. I don't know where she is. She hasn't come home."

"Good. She won't have a chance to try and poison me anyway. Is Dad home?"

"Yes. He's watching something on the telly. I've got to do you scrambled egg on toast for tea."

"Don't bother. I had some shepherd's pie and beans round at Sylvia's. She gave me some chocolate to give to you." He put his hand in his jacket pocket and pulled out a large bar of Cadbury's Dairy Milk. "She says to try and visit her soon as she's missed you and wants to know how you're getting on at school."

I accepted the chocolate and put it on the kitchen table. "I miss her too. I'll have to try and visit her soon. It's just hard for me because either Mummy or ... your ... er ... dad are here. I told him Sylvia was drying my clothes for me and he wasn't angry."

Russell grinned. "I expect he's forgotten already that he told us all to stop going round there. He never stays mad for long. What's on the telly?"

"I don't know. Do you think he'll let me go out?"

"Probably. I'm going in the lounge to watch telly with him anyway. Come and ask."

I did ask Terry if I could go out. He barely looked at me as he readily agreed that I could but that I should return by ten o'clock. He gave me two fifty pence pieces and settled back to watch the television.

Although I should have liked to wear my new jeans, there was always a chance Mother might return and catch me when I came in. I barely thanked Terry as I snatched the money from his hand. I grabbed my jacket and left the house, emerging into the darkened village street. I paused only long enough to fasten my jacket before making my way directly to Sylvia's house.

Martin opened the door. His face split into a delighted grin.

"She's 'ere, Mam!" Martin yelled. "Keri's come ta see ya!"

13. While The Cat's Away ...

Mother stayed away for the whole of that week. It made such a pleasant change to get up in the morning, dress in my preferred school clothes and walk up to the bus stop feeling normal and as if I fitted in with everyone else. A few of the girls even spoke to me a little bit.

Terry gave me money every day; enough for the bus to and from school, for lunch in the town rather than a school meal and with some left over – for sweets, Terry said. It may have been having money to which I was unaccustomed which caused me to undertake my next venture.

I met Charlie by her locker and told her how the previous week after speaking to her, I had been present in class for registration, but had then slipped out of school and spent most of the day shopping and how I had simply gone home afterward. She frowned.

"What about afternoon registration? You didn't think of that, did you?"

I shook my head.

"Well, it's a great idea, just so long as we make sure we come back for afternoon registration. I don't want the school contacting my Dad and saying I wasn't at school!"

I arranged to meet Charlie in the toilets after registration. Suddenly, the day seemed full of excitement and promise. I hurried off to the classroom.

After the class teacher had called the register, she took her spectacles off and looked around the room. She glared at me.

"Where were you last Thursday afternoon, young lady?"

I swallowed hard. "I was here, Miss."

"Well, you weren't here for registration! You girls really should take more care about getting back to class after lunch. I will mark you present this time, but in future, make sure you're actually here, do you understand? How will we know where you are if say, the fire alarm goes off?"

"Sorry, Miss."

The bell rang and I snatched up my satchel and fled. Several girls paused in the toilets before moving to the next class and I had to wait in a cubicle until all had gone quiet.

"Keri? Is that you?"

I heard Charlie's whisper and opened the door.

"I've got an idea. Let's not walk round the town. How about we go to Norwich? There're loads more shops and the market too. We could have a ball!"

I grinned. "That's a great idea! I've got some money for the bus as well. Come on, let's get going!"

We crept out of school silently and fled along the road toward the bus stop, laughing at our cleverness.

Buses ran regularly and we did not have long to wait. We sat at the back, on the long seat, chattering and giggling together. When adults on the bus glared at us, we glared back and went off into more gales of laughter at their affronted expressions.

I found being in the city to be exhilarating and exciting. Charlie knew her way about very well, so there was no chance at all of us becoming lost. We visited shop after shop and I took Charlie's lead, helping myself to all manner of beautiful clothes.

We changed out of our school uniforms into the fashionable clothing we'd stolen. Charlie even had the foresight to steal a couple of large, colourful holdalls, one of which she stuffed my satchel into.

"Without the uniforms and that giveaway satchel, no-one will know how old we are or suspect we should be at school," she told me.

We spent ages in Boots the Chemist, trying out perfumes and make-up. I noticed a lady with a red headscarf seemed to be watching us very carefully, so I made sure I stole nothing at all, even though I really wanted a perfume called 'Sea Jade'.

When we emerged into the winter sunlight, I followed Charlie across the road and in between the market stalls.

"I got two bottles of that perfume stuff you liked," Charlie said.

"You did? I never saw you take a thing and I'm certain that woman in the red headscarf was watching us!"

"She was. She's a store detective,"

I'd never heard of store detectives and I sat on the steps of the Guild Hall eating chips as Charlie explained all about them. I wondered what would happen if we were caught stealing and voiced my concern.

"That's easy," Charlie said, with her mouth full of chips. "If you get stopped, I snatch your bag and run. If I get stopped, you snatch mine and run. No use in us both getting nicked is there? Anyway, if we've snatched the bag the one who gets stopped won't be carrying anything stolen, will she?"

I didn't like the sound of this plan. I had a horrible idea that the police would be involved, whether there was a bag or not.

"Don't be so wet! I wonder about you sometimes. One minute you're great and fun to be with, the next minute you're acting the saint and being a wet blanket!"

"Sorry."

Charlie shoved me in a friendly manner. "Come on, let's go have a look in Debenhams and then we'll have to get the bus back to North Walsham or we'll miss afternoon registration."

The Department store was simply too easy to steal from. Both Charlie and I helped ourselves to beautiful coats, several tops and skirts and Charlie even managed a pair of shoes, which she took right under the nose of the assistant!

By the time we arrived at the bus stop, we were loaded down with bags full of stolen goods. It was quite difficult to carry everything without dropping things.

"I think I'll stay at school this afternoon, Charlie. For one thing, I'm really tired and for another, I have to try and make sure I do some work or the teachers will get suspicious."

"All right. But we'll do this again another day. I've had a great time and I've got some super stuff too. It was a great idea of yours."

When we got off the bus in North Walsham, we went into a cafe so that we could use their toilets to change back into our school uniforms. Charlie handed me the perfume and a great pile of make-up she'd stolen from Boots. We divided the clothing between us and packed it into the bags more carefully.

"I'll bung it all in my locker until after school." Charlie grinned at me. "What about your mother? Won't she find all this stuff and do something terrible?"

"Nah. It's all right. I'll just shove it all in my step-father's bedroom. She never goes in there. Anyway, she's cleared off. She might come home today, she might not. It's better when she's not there."

"Can't imagine not liking your mum," Charlie mused. "Sometimes, I really miss mine."

I had no idea what to say or do. It was the first time Charlie had mentioned her mother. Although she looked brash and over-confident most of the time, for that fleeting moment, she looked like a very small girl who was lost and utterly alone.

In the end, I shrugged. "You can have my mother for free! I wish someone would take her."

The melancholy moment passed and Charlie laughed. "Ever thought of putting laxatives in her tea?" she asked.

Giggling like loons, we made our way back to school. We arrived in plenty of time to stash everything in Charlie's locker and get to class for the register.

I sprayed myself with 'Sea Jade' before going back to class. It was a lovely smell; it made me feel very feminine all of a sudden. Several girls commented on it and asked the name of the perfume.

When Terry arrived home from work that evening, he also commented.

"You smell nice."

"My friend gave me some perfume," I replied. "She got it for herself but didn't like it. I've put it in the bag in your room. Is that all right?"

"Yeah. Not a problem. I mean, you can't leave it in your own room because that old hag will find it and there'll be hell to pay."

"Where is Mummy?"

Terry shrugged. "Dunno and don't care, so long as she stays away from here. She's probably with that Riley bloke or with her snooty mother."

At the mention of Nana, I felt a strange sensation – as if my heart had lurched in my chest. I swallowed and hung my head.

"What's wrong with you?"

"Nothing," I lied. "I just remembered my homework. Best go and do it."

I scuttled away and took out my books. I couldn't concentrate on the school work though. I kept thinking of Nana and how sad and disappointed in me she'd be if she knew what I'd been doing with Charlie. I hadn't seen her or heard from her for a very long time.

I tore a page out of one of my books and wrote Nana a letter. I told her I missed her dreadfully and that I loved her very much. I also asked when I could next go and stay with her and pressed her to pass on my love and best wishes to Great Uncle Bertie, Penelope, Great Aunty Ellen and Great Uncle John.

Writing the letter made me feel a lot better. I asked Terry for an envelope and he gave me a small brown one. He also found me a stamp. He didn't ask who I was writing to. Maybe he guessed; maybe he didn't care.

Every day for that week, Charlie and I escaped the school soon after registration. We did not go to Norwich again, but spent our time wandering around the shops in North Walsham. I don't believe I stole anything other than a pen and notepaper, but Charlie helped herself to just about anything that wasn't nailed down whether it was something she needed or not. Her locker became so packed with things, I had to take all the clothes I'd stolen in Norwich home. I stuffed them into the bags in Terry's room.

By Thursday, I'd become bold enough to wear the Brutus jeans and a stolen top to go out into the village. Terry made no comment, simply handing me fifty pence with which to get chips at the Wheatsheaf.

I trotted up the village street in my jeans and high heels. I had no friends to meet, but it was good to be out of the house and feeling confident. I approached the group of young people hanging out near the Jolly Farmers pub.

"Bloody 'ell! You scrub up well!"

The remark came from the youth, 'Nosh' who had spoken to me before. I grinned but said nothing.

One of the two girls I had seen in the village with the crowd spoke to me immediately.

"I like your jeans."

"Thanks."

I passed the time with group, laughing and chatting, messing about as teenagers do. I felt strangely elated, almost as if I were in a dream. Not only had I been accepted into this group, I was actually enjoying myself! Not that we did much. Mainly, it was jokes and chatter, banter from the lads and a lot of giggling and squealing from the girls.

At half past ten, we all moved down to the Wheatsheaf and waited by the back door of the building. I studied Janice's mother as she served chips at the door of the pub kitchen. She was a pretty, cheerful woman with sparkling eyes and an infectious smile. She laughed and joked with everyone. I didn't see Janice though.

Nosh walked me home. I thought he was just fine. His long hair intrigued me and although he occasionally made remarks about Mother and how strange my family members were, I thought I liked him well enough.

When we reached the driveway to Holly Cottage, Nosh stopped and caught my arm.

"Ain't ya gonna invite me indoors for a cup of coffee?"

I hesitated. "Um ... well, my step-father is at home and ..."

"Well, he won't mind me coming in for coffee, will he?"

"I ... er ... I don't know."

"Aw ... c'mon. I live right the other end of the village and I've walked all the way down 'ere with ya."

I decided to take the risk. "Come on then. You can't stop long though."

I led Nosh to the back door, which was unlocked. As we stepped through the doorway, Terry appeared from the direction of the sitting room. He grinned at me and nodded at Nosh.

"All right?"

"Um ... this is Nosh. He walked home with me and I ... er ... thought he could have a cup of coffee."

"Yea. Coffee. That's what all the lads want ain't it, son?"

Terry waved his hand. "Feel free. Just don't leave a mess in case the old bitch comes back. I can do without her griping and nagging. I'm off to bed. See ya."

I tried to look nonchalant, but I couldn't hide my surprise. For some reason, I'd assumed Terry would be less than welcoming.

I made two cups of coffee and led Nosh into the sitting room. He looked around and frowned.

"Ain't ya got a telly?"

"It's in there." I indicated the front lounge with a nod of my head.

"Well. Let's go in there and watch telly then."

I couldn't bear to tell Nosh that I wasn't permitted to go into the lounge except on special occasions or at Christmas. Frantically, I tried to think of an excuse, but whilst I hesitated, Nosh walked across the sitting room and opened the lounge door.

"Where's the light switch?"

I hurried after him, coffee slopping to the carpet from the cup I held in my shaking hand.

"Best we just stay in the sitting room and ... er ..."

Nosh found the light switch and stepped into the room. He nodded appreciatively.

"Nice."

Powerless to stop him, I watched as Nosh plonked his coffee on a small table and flung himself onto the white, leather settee.

"Nice, big telly. Put it on. There might be a film on or something."

I put my coffee down on the table next to where Nosh had placed his.

"Look. Um ... we don't use this room much and ..."

"I can see that. Go on. Put the telly on and come sit by me." He patted the seat next to him.

"Er ... no. I don't think so. I have to get up for school in the morning and I'd quite like to go to bed."

Nosh grinned. I noticed a wolfish glint in his eye.

"Is that an invitation, luv?"

"What? No, of course not!"

Nosh sprawled out on the settee. I noticed his big, greasy boots perilously near to the white leather.

"Oh, I think it is. You've been making sheep's eyes at me ever since the first time you saw me. I'll give ya a good seeing to. Drop yer jeans and lean over the arm of that chair and I'll get me tool out and give yer a good shaftin'."

"No!" I backed away.

"What, you don't want to now, eh?"

I leaned against the door frame and tried to still my shaking body.

"Thank you for walking me home," I managed. "But I'd like you to leave now, please."

"I only just got 'ere and I ain't drank me coffee yet! You're not telling me you don't even want a cuddle and a grope?"

I glanced toward the door to the stairs, which stood open. I wondered if Terry could hear what was being said.

"No! I don't want anything! I didn't ask you to walk home with me! You just came along!"

Nosh leaned forward and took a large mouthful of coffee, which he slurped, noisily.

"I only come down 'ere 'cos I thought I was gonna get me end away," he grumbled. "Now you want to kick me out without so much as a grope. There's a word for girls like you."

Anger came to my rescue. "And there's probably a word for boys like you who think girls are only for having sex with! Just get out and leave me alone!"

Nosh drained his cup and stood up. "I weren't really interested in you anyway, you posh tart. You've got no tits and you're as ugly as sin."

I stepped backward as Nosh approached me. "Well ... you're rude and unpleasant and ... and ..."

"Can it, luv. I've heard it all before. I'm going."

He pushed past me and went to the front door, which he opened. He glanced behind and grinned.

"Nice place you got here, I might visit again."

I said nothing but I scowled fiercely as Nosh slammed the door behind him. I rushed to the kitchen and caught up a damp cloth to wipe the table where Nosh has spilled a little coffee.

My heart pounded painfully. Why did all men and boys just want one thing? Was Terry actually a good example of maleness? Every man I'd met, including Dave, whom I actually quite liked, seemed to want only sex. I shuddered with revulsion as I took the cups back to the kitchen.

I tidied the kitchen, locked the back door and retreated to my room, deep in thought. Maybe Mother had done the right thing for me after all? None of the boys had even looked at me twice when I was dressed in frumpy clothes. It seemed, as soon as I wore fashionable or pretty clothes, every male in the vicinity instantly wanted to take the clothes off me and do unspeakable things.

I scrambled into bed and lay in the darkness, listening to the night sounds of the village. I wanted to be liked, perhaps even to be popular, but mostly, I wanted to be accepted. Yet I really didn't want to have boys and men crawling all over me with their vile demands. Perhaps I should just accept that I would be forever alone? I thought about Janice. She had not been in the group and her mother looked so cheerful and pleasant. Did she suffer in the same way?

There were so many questions rolling around in my mind, I found it hard to get to sleep. I had no idea how to deal with all these thoughts and feelings and I couldn't think of anyone I could talk to about them. Charlie would not be much good as she seemed to enjoy all the sex and attention. I couldn't go to Sylvia, I would be too ashamed. I wondered what Nana would have to say about it all. Then I wondered where Mother had gone. Perhaps I should try to talk to her when she came back?

I eventually drifted into a fitful sleep, waking frequently. It was a very long night indeed.

14. The World Turns Upside Down

Since I had not been attending classes for a week, I had missed a great deal. None of the teachers said anything about my absences although one or two remarked that it was good to see me back in lessons. I marvelled at the lack of communication between members of staff. I knew the school register had me as present every day, but due to my rapid escapes with Charlie after registration, every other staff member seemed to think I had been ill!

I quickly caught up with the work. In all honesty, in most subjects, I had already covered what the class were doing when I was at the convent. Fortunately, I was easily able to write a lot very quickly.

In maths, the fact that I had been working my way steadily through the textbook, without having been in the lessons meant that Mr. Watson made no comment at all about either catching up or my absences. He marked my work and left a comment at the end of each piece along the lines of 'good work' or 'well done'.

Mother had arrived home on Sunday afternoon. She gave no indication of where she had been and neither Russell nor I asked her. She had only been home a short while before an argument began between her and Terry. I went to my room in order to stay out of the way, but I could still hear the raised voices, although I had no idea about the subject of the row.

Charlie was as accommodating as ever with the use of her locker. As soon as she saw me, dressed in the over-long and frumpy clothes, she knew Mother had returned. It felt strange, having spent a week dressing as I wished, to be hurrying to change out of the dreadful clothes into my fashionable ones again.

Even though Charlie urged me to skip classes with her again, I resisted the temptation. I made several rather lame excuses and Charlie became frustrated and upset with me.

"Why have you suddenly become all goody-goody again? Is it because your Mum has come back and you're afraid she'll find out?"

Charlie stood with her hands on her hips and her eyes blazed with anger.

I shrugged.

"Kind of. I can't really explain, Charlie. Maybe next week? This week, I just want to try and catch up the work I missed. I can't have a bad report at the end of term. You've no idea what she'll be like if I've got a bad report."

Charlie subsided a little. "My Dad doesn't even read my report!"

"Really? Why not?"

"He says school is just a waste of time. He thinks I should get a job. He says I'll be happier working."

I considered this. The school leaving age was at that time, fifteen, but due to be raised to sixteen for the following year. I knew Charlie was fifteen. Technically, she could leave school if she wanted to, even before the end of the year.

"Do you think you will leave?"

Charlie shrugged and then frowned. "I dunno. I've thought about it. I suppose a job would be nice, but ..."

"I'd really miss you. You're the only real friend I've got!"

She grinned and hugged me. "Yea, you're a good mate to me and all. I guess I'll stay at the moment. Maybe I won't come back after Christmas. Maybe I will. I don't fancy sitting the exams because I'm useless and I'll fail them all."

"I'll help you." I saw her disbelieving expression. "No, I will. If you want to pass the exams, I'll help."

That might have been a pivotal point. One of those places in life where things can go either way with very different results. I had a sense of something important, although I couldn't articulate it. My offer of academic help hung in the air between us for a few precious seconds. Then Charlie laughed and shook her head.

"Nah. Who needs exams? I'm only gonna get a job in a bloody factory or a supermarket. I expect I'll get married or something and be a super boring housewife with hundreds of snot-nosed kids hanging off me day and night!"

"Well. You don't have to. Wouldn't you prefer to have some kind of career before you do all that?"

Charlie placed her hands on my shoulders and put a faked serious expression on her face.

"You're right. I shouldn't go getting married ... or having brats either. How about I swan off somewhere and become a film star? Or maybe a pop star? I could go to Hollywood and make my fortune!"

I shrugged her hands off me.

"Don't be daft. There're loads of other things you could do if you put your mind to it."

"Yep. And one of them is getting drunk, which is what I intend to do this morning. I'm meeting Chris and we're going to the park with a couple of bottles. You sure you don't want to come too?"

I shook my head.

"Here." Charlie gave me the key to her locker. "I won't be back in school today, so you may as well have this or you won't be able to change before you go home. You can give it me back tomorrow."

I accepted the key. I knew it would be pointless trying to dissuade Charlie from going to the park to get drunk, so I held my tongue.

I worked hard in all the lessons that day and actually quite enjoyed most of them, even maths. Mr. Watson surprised me in class by suddenly asking me what I wanted to do for a living when I had finished school.

"I want to be a vet."

Several of my class mates sniggered, mostly boys.

"An unusual choice for a young lady," Mr. Watson mused. "However, I am quite sure that you are more than capable. I understand there is a very long and difficult university course involved. You will need to study very hard and get good grades in your GCE examinations. Good. Now, how about you?" he turned to someone else in the class.

I thought about what I had just said. Did I really want to be a vet? I'd never seen or heard of a female vet; mostly, the only vets I knew of were men - and old as well. For several minutes, I drifted in thoughts of becoming a world-famous vet who saved animals in their thousands from abuse, disease and pain. Mr. Watson's stern tone brought me back to myself suddenly.

"For most of you it has to be said, you have no ambition and no prospects because you won't work and you won't try. With the exception of James, Kevin and Keri you all seem to believe that the whole world owes you something! I want some decent hard work from everyone in this class or there will be trouble. Understand?"

Most people murmured a gloomy acknowledgement.

After school, I rushed to Charlie's locker to change. I would have to take my clothes home as they needed a wash again. This meant that at least I could visit Sylvia - so long as Mother was not around. I put the key in my pocket and hurried to get to the bus stop.

To my absolute horror, I saw Mother's horrible little three wheeled car in the school car park as I walked past on my way out of the school. My heart began to thud painfully in my chest and I felt nauseous. Why on earth would Mother be at the school? Perhaps I should not take the bus and simply wait for her?

I stood stock still in the milling mass of students leaving the school. No-one spoke to me and no-one took any notice of my obvious distress. I was about to turn and head for the bus when Mother came out of the double doors. Her lips were pressed into a thin, angry line and she marched to her car without looking across the playground.

I swallowed hard, turned and pushed my way through the heaving throng of young people, heading toward the bus stop where the school buses waited. I didn't care who I barged out of my way or what angry remarks were made. I simply wanted to get to the relative safety of the bus.

The bus journey seemed to take less time than usual. It was probably due to my state of mind. It took the same route as always, around all the villages and hamlets. No-one spoke to me; I had such a lump in my throat anyway I would probably have been unable to answer if they had.

My feet dragged as I walked from the bus stop, down the village street toward Holly Cottage. I could see Mother's car in the driveway. She never usually arrived home this early and having seen her at the school, I had a very good sense that it was something to do with me. I wondered how long she had been home. Clearly, she would go via the direct route. How long would that give her? Ten minutes ... maybe fifteen.

I tried not to hesitate at the back door. To give any indication that I knew something was amiss would give Mother the edge. I walked boldly into the kitchen.

Mother sat at the kitchen table with a mug of tea and a cigarette. I tried to smile.

"Hello. You're home early today."

"And I wonder why that should be?" Mother's tone was acidic.

I shrugged. "Did you get an afternoon off work or something?"

I felt truly sick. I couldn't move from where I stood because Mother could catch hold of me if I tried to pass her. I glanced at the back door.

Mother stubbed out her cigarette. "I've got something to show you." She stood up.

I had to follow her through into the sitting room. Scattered over the settee and chairs were my fashionable clothes. All of them.

The ones Terry had bought and everything I had stolen. There were so many!

Stunned, I could not move or speak. So, she had been into Terry's bedroom and found everything. What had prompted that? It had to be something to do with the school. She must have found out everything.

"I've known for weeks that you were up to something," Mother's tone was light and conversational. "And I knew he had something to do with it as well. It was just a case of doing a little detective work. Of course, he has no idea I am onto him or his vile plans."

Mother swept a pile of clothing off an armchair, dumped it on the table and sat down. She lit another cigarette. I stood in the doorway not knowing what to do or say. I waited whilst Mother took a long draw on her cigarette.

"There'll be someone along in a few minutes to see you. I'm not putting up with any more of these conspiracies or your disgusting behaviour. You must think I am utterly stupid and without any intelligence at all."

Mother smiled a bright and brittle grimace. I saw her horrible, pale blue eyes glittering with triumph.

"You're going to be sorry, my girl. So very sorry. You see, you cannot win against me. I know exactly what you've been doing, where you've been and everything about you. No amount of skulduggery and plotting to outwit me will succeed. In short, I am cleverer than you and that pig put together."

I swallowed. Whatever was she talking about? Had she found out about my shop-lifting and missing school? What did she think Terry had to do with it all? My knees shook as I stood in the sitting room doorway. Perhaps I should simply flee through the kitchen, out the back door and keep running forever?

There was a knock at the front door. Mother smiled and stood up. She paused to stub out her cigarette in a nearby ash-tray; then went to answer the door.

I remained rooted to the spot. I could hear Mother speaking in a friendly tone and two female voices answering her but I couldn't see who it was. I watched as Mother took a step backwards.

"Do come in. I'm afraid there is rather a mess. The evidence rather overwhelmed me and I was very distressed. Having found it all, I meant to simply bring it downstairs and pile it up ready to be destroyed, but ..."

Two women entered. I recognised one of them immediately. This was the Social Worker who had visited the house before on the day when Mother had made me sick. I recalled how I had screamed and shouted, trying to convince the woman of my innocence.

Mother closed the front door and came into the room, stepping past the two women, who both stared at me and looked around.

"I really am so sorry." Mother scooped up my fashionable clothes from the settee in a huge double armload and flung them onto the table. She did the same with the things on the other armchair.

"Do sit down. I'll go and put the kettle on, shall I?"

Both women sat on the settee and Mother pushed past me to go to the kitchen.

"Hello, Keri." The Social Worker I had seen before gave me a tight smile. "This is Miss Armstrong, my colleague."

"Hello." The younger woman did not smile.

I neither spoke nor moved. In fact, I now felt as if I were in a dream world. I gazed out of the nearby window at a leafless tree I could see across the street. Behind it, heavy clouds threatened rain.

Mother came back from the kitchen with a tray. On it were three mugs of steaming tea, a bowl of sugar and a plate of small biscuits. She hesitated at the table, now covered in my jumbled clothing.

"You'd better put all that rubbish on the floor over there."

Still I did not move.

"Oh, for goodness sake, child. Can you not do anything I ask?"

Miss Armstrong stood up and moved some of the clothing. She did not put it on the floor, merely piled it further back on the table making enough space for the tray.

Suddenly, I found my voice.

"What am I supposed to have done wrong?"

"There." Mother looked triumphant. "She cannot even tell that her behaviour is in any way wrong or unacceptable! I certainly have tried everything to teach her right from wrong and to bring her up as a decent girl, but I am banging my head, metaphorically, against a brick wall. I'm sure she must either be mad or a very good actress. Although, to what ends I have no idea."

Mother sat down with her tea. "I went to the school today to explain the situation and let them know she won't be back and you'll never guess what they told me?"

The older Social Worker frowned. "So the problems are at school as well now?"

"Oh, yes. She's been absent from class more than she's been present! She's always there in the mornings and after lunch for registration, but never actually in class."

"Is that correct, Keri?" the older Social Worker addressed me, frowning.

"No, of course not! I go to school. I do my work as well."

I still had my satchel slung across my shoulder.

Mother stood up and snatched it from me. "Really? You do your work, do you? Well, let us just have a look at this 'work' you so diligently do, shall we?"

She put her cup of tea on the table and opened my satchel. Of course, the first thing she saw was the skirt, tights and blouse I had brought home hoping to persuade Sylvia to wash for me. Mother dragged them out and held them up.

"More clothes? This explains what the head told me. She keeps a supply of slutty clothes at school. I ensure she leaves here in the morning looking clean and decent, but once she gets to school, she changes into these ..." Mother dropped the blouse and held up the short skirt. "Just look at that! It's hardly more than a wide belt!"

"It's just the same as everyone else wears! You don't understand! I look old and frumpy in these clothes and everyone calls me names and laughs at me!"

Mother flung the skirt to the floor, snatched up her mug and sat down. "It is not the same as everyone else wears, Keri. It is very similar to the minority of dirty, sluttish girls who behave in a manner which is ..."

The older Social Worker interrupted. "I think you look very nice dressed as you are, Keri. Why do think you don't?"

"What? Don't you know *anything* about fashion? I look about forty dressed like this and it makes me a laughing stock!"

I noticed Miss Armstrong dropped her gaze to her mug of tea.

"Tell me, dear. Where did you get all these clothes from?"

"He bought them for her. I told you what he's like, always encouraging her. I've no idea what he's said or done to make her behave like this, but there is a lot of whispering and secrecy. I told you on the telephone that I'd found all these things hidden in his bedroom." Mother's expression was one of sneering triumph. "No decent father would behave like that. It's no wonder she's become the way she has."

I hesitated. Clearly, Mother didn't actually know anything very much at all. If Terry were here, he could tell her that he bought a few of the clothes but then I would be challenged as to where the rest of them came from. I tried to think.

"I thought you were going to look at my school work?"

Mother snatched up the satchel and pulled my books from it. "What work? If you haven't been in class, you cannot have done any work! Are you calling the head teacher a liar?"

I stuck out my chin in a defiant gesture. I knew I had caught up with all the work I'd missed and done very well in every subject. "Yes! Just check it and you'll see for yourself!"

Mother handed the books to the older Social Worker who opened the first one, which happened to be maths. She gazed at the pages for a few seconds before remarking in an uncertain tone of voice, "Well, there does seem to be an awful lot of very good work in here."

Mother took the maths book from the woman's unresisting hands and stared at it. "I knew it! All these years, she's driven me mad by pretending to be absolutely useless at mathematics! Why, I even employed an extra tutor for a while. Look at this!" Mother glared at me. "So, what was the pretence all about? Why would you try to make me think you were stupid? When I think of all the tears and tantrums and the disappointments ..."

"I can't win, can I? First, you accuse me of not being at school. Then, when I show you that I was and I have done all the work, you yell at me for doing well!" I tried not to shout, but my voice was certainly raised.

"I can't do this anymore. I really can't." Mother threw the maths book on the floor, put her hands over her face and began to sob.

Russell suddenly appeared in the sitting room from the kitchen. I hadn't heard him come in. He looked at Mother, weeping, glanced at the pile of clothes on the table and the two women sitting on the settee.

"What's going on?"

"Hello. You must be Russell? I'm Mrs. Waverley. I'm a Social Worker. I'm afraid your sister has been ... there have been some problems. This is Miss Armstrong. Have you had a good day at school, young man?"

Russell glanced at me and back to Mrs. Waverley. "Yes. Why are you here? Why are all Keri's things on the table? What has she been saying?" He indicated Mother.

"I think it is better that you don't worry yourself about it for the moment, Russell. Tell me, are you and Keri getting along any better?"

Mother took her hands from her face. Mascara tracks ran down her cheeks. "No. She still hits him and taunts and bullies him. All the time, every day!"

Russell looked nonplussed. "What? That's rubbish! We get along fine most of the time, don't we, Keri?"

I nodded.

"You don't need to be afraid any more, Russell. We know all about what you have to put up with." Mrs. Waverley put on a bright smile.

"What, like how she intends to poison us all? How she's gonna kill my Dad and all the stuff she says and does to Keri?"

"I beg your pardon?" Mrs. Waverley looked shocked. "Keri has threatened to poison you all?"

Russell stared at the woman as if she were completely mad. "Are you deaf? Not Keri, her!" He pointed at Mother, who sat with her mascara stained cheeks, her mouth open in astonishment.

"I think there must be some misunderstanding here," Mrs. Waverley began. "Your poor mother has told me and my colleagues about your suffering and how Keri has bullied and beaten you for years. I'm very concerned about the violence involved, Russell. Why would you defend your half-sister and say such dreadful things about your own mother?"

Russell snorted with laughter. "Keri's never bullied me and if she tried to beat me up I'd kick her back-side for her. It's all her. She's mad! She's always hitting Keri and dragging her around by her hair. And she's told my Dad she's gonna kill him. We're all too scared to eat anything she cooks now!"

Mother shook her head slowly from side to side. "I ... I don't know why he is saying such things. I can only think that his father has been telling him these things. We ... er ... we haven't been getting along at all well. He ... he ..." Mother paused and took a sobbing breath. "He sees other women a lot, if you know what I mean. He ... er ... he can be very violent. He's hit all of us more than once."

"He's never hit me!" Russell shouted. He turned to the two women. "You should take her away and lock her up in a loony bin! She's dangerous! Everyone knows about it except you!"

I reached out and put my hand on Russell's shoulder. "Be careful, Russell," I whispered. "I think ..."

"Keri! Step away from Russell, please!" Mrs. Waverley's voice was stern.

I dropped my hand. "Pardon? Why? I haven't done anything!"

Mother leaned toward the two Social Workers and muttered something. I didn't hear what she said. Miss Armstrong stood up and a meaningful look passed between the two women.

I stepped aside as the younger woman came and put her arm around Russell. "Can you show me your bedroom, Russell? I think Mummy needs to talk to my colleague for a moment."

"No! I don't know what you're doing here, but I'm pretty sure it's got something to do with her and all the lies she tells. I'm going round to Kev's. I want my Dad! Keri, come with me, we'll be all right round at Sylvia's place."

I moved toward the door, but Mrs. Waverley stood up and caught my arm. "I think, under the circumstances, Keri, it would be better if you stayed here, don't you? If Russell would prefer to visit his friend, that's fine, but we actually came here to see you."

I pulled away. "Well, I don't want to see you! I haven't done anything and I want to go with Russell."

Mother surged to her feet and grabbed hold of my other arm. "Hurry up, Russell, if you're going to see Kevin. And you jolly well stay here and do as you're told, my girl!"

I tried to wrench myself free of Mother's grip. Her fingers bit into the flesh of my upper arm like a vice.

"Get off me! Let go! Why are you doing this? It's only a few clothes! Da ... Terry bought them for me!"

Russell rushed toward the front door. His eyes were huge in his face and unshed tears glittered on his lower lashes.

"Thump her, Keri! Go on! Thump her and come on!" He opened the door.

Miss Armstrong moved uncertainly toward him. I struggled and twisted, managing to get my arm free of Mother. Mrs. Waverley took hold of my other arm.

"Now, now. Calm down, Keri! There's no need for any of this. Let us not have one of your outbursts. Sit down, please."

Russell hesitated in the open doorway. "Keri!" he wailed. "Come on! We have to get away from them!"

Mother snatched at my flailing arm and took hold of it with both of her hands. I twisted and shook off Mrs. Waverley, leaving my hand free. Mother's fingers were digging into me and it hurt. I swung my arm with all the force I could muster and felt my fist connect with Mother's head.

"Get off me!" I shrieked as loud as I could.

"Hit her again, Keri! Go on! Bash her evil head in!" Russell's voice held an edge of hysteria.

As my fist connected with Mother's head, she released her grip and I turned toward her.

"I hate you!" I yelled and swung my hand around hard.

The slap resounded like a gunshot and Mother suddenly stood stock still. Far from the shock I had expected, I saw triumph in her wicked, pale blue eyes. On her right cheek, my fingers had left four long, red welts.

"That's all I needed them to see. I'm finished with you now. I'll have a life again." The words were only just audible to me. In fact, I think I read her lips more than heard her speak. Before my eyes, Mother's eyes filled with tears once more and she cried out."

"Oh! You wicked girl! You struck me! *Again*!" She retreated to the armchair and flung herself into it, clumsily kicking over the mug of tea Mrs. Waverley had left on the floor beside the chair.

I glanced toward the front door and saw Russell's horrified expression. "Quick! Come with me," he pleaded.

I could not move. A tear trickled down Russell's cheek and he fled, leaving the door swinging open behind him.

Miss Armstrong glanced at Mrs. Waverley, who stooped to put a comforting arm around Mother's shoulders.

"We've seen quite enough, my dear. I'm afraid I agree with you absolutely. Keri is completely beyond control. We have a place arranged for her. I think it best if she comes with us now, don't you?"

Mother nodded and buried her face in her hands. She began to make sobbing, wailing sounds interspersed with the words, "I'm so sorry! I've tried everything! I don't know what else to do!"

"There, there, dear. Everything will be just fine." Mrs. Waverly nodded at Miss Armstrong, who crossed the room and began to bundle up all my clothes in her arms.

"What are you doing?" I demanded. "Those things are mine! You can't just take them!"

"They're very pretty things, Keri. Would you like to help me?" Miss Armstrong replied.

"Help you? What? You really expect me to help you take my things away from me? I haven't done anything wrong! Well ... now I have, I've clouted my mother, but apart from that, I haven't done anything."

"Why don't you help me put these things in the car, dear? We are going to take you somewhere safe. You do want to go somewhere safe, don't you?"

I paused. At last these people were listening! They had seen Mother's violence with their own eyes and had heard Russell defend me with their ears.

"Will I have to see her?" I nodded toward Mother, being comforted by Mrs. Waverly.

"Not if you don't want to, dear. I'm sure everyone will be much happier this way. It's a nice place we're taking you to. Come along, help me take your clothes out to the car, there's a good girl."

I rushed to the table and began to snatch up the jumbled clothing and shoes. "Can I get the rest of my things from my bedroom?" I asked.

"Yes, yes, of course you may, dear. Let Mrs. Waverley talk with your poor mother and you just help me to get all your things. I'm sure we've got some bags in the boot of the car to put them all in. Come along."

The Social Worker did indeed have a couple of very large, canvas holdalls in the boot of her car. We stuffed my belongings into one of them and returned to the house via the front door, which still stood open.

I led Miss Armstrong up to my bare room. She stood, looking about as I rummaged in a drawer for one skirt I wanted and under my pillow for Lambie. I stood there, in the middle of the room, clutching my tattered woolly lamb and a screwed up garment. I looked about.

Once again, Mother had pinned pictures of David Cassidy and Donny Osmond to my board. Beneath them, in the waste paper bin were my latest pictures, torn into little shreds.

"Don't you want to take the pictures down as well, dear?"

I laughed. "Nope. I *hate* those two slimy toads! Mother keeps taking my pictures down and putting them up instead. She thinks nice girls like them."

"Well, I understand a lot of teenage girls do."

"Not me."

"Oh? Who do you like?"

"Well, T-Rex is great and there's a band called Deep Purple who look just fine to me but I haven't heard anything by them yet."

Miss Armstrong smiled. "Come along, what about all your other things?"

"What other things? This is it. There's nothing else here I really want. Oh. Maybe my drawing books and notebooks. Wait a moment." I stooped to the bottom drawer and tugged it open. The books were in disarray. I deduced Mother must have rummaged through them for some reason. I gathered them up into a scruffy bundle.

"Nothing else. Can we go now? If we don't go in a minute, she'll probably pull all my hair out, punch and kick me half to death because I actually hit her."

Miss Armstrong shook her head. "But you've hit your mother plenty of times before, haven't you?"

I shook my head. "No. Only once, by accident. She was trying to kill me at the time. She went mental after that and attacked me with a cast iron frying pan. I had to lock myself in the bathroom for hours until my step-father came home and took the pan off her."

"Oh. Well. Perhaps you can tell me all about that as we travel?"

I followed the Social Worker down the stairs and out of the front door. She opened the rear door of the dark blue car and I clambered inside. Just as she closed the door, I noticed Russell coming along the street with both Sylvia and Malcom hurrying along beside him.

Mrs. Waverley came out of the front door and made her way to the driver's door of the car very quickly. Miss Armstrong slipped into the front passenger seat.

"Where are you taking my sister?" Russell began to run toward the car.

Mrs. Waverley started the engine just as Sylvia and Martin drew alongside the car. Sylvia knocked on the driver's window whilst Martin hung back a little.

Mrs. Waverley wound the window down a little. "Yes? Can I help you?" she addressed Sylvia.

"What you doin? You can't jus' come along 'o 'ere and tek that poor girl off like that! It's tha mother you should be haulin' away! You let 'er outta that car this instant or Oi'm callin' tha police roight now!"

"Please. Calm down, Mrs ...?"

"Oi 'ent tellin' you moi name now am Oi? Oi ent stupid! Oi wants that wicked woman arrested so Oi do! She'm a wicked cow and she bin bashin' and beatin' this lovely girl for years an' years. You jist let young Keri outta that car roight now. She kin come along an' live with us, can't she, Martin?"

Martin nodded. I saw tears streaking his cheeks. Russell clung to Sylvia's apron and wailed aloud, begging her to save me from the two women.

"I'm so sorry. Keri has agreed to come with us of her own free will. I think you must have misunderstood. Good day to you." Mrs. Waverly wound up the window and began to edge the car forward.

Sylvia placed both her hands on the window beside where I was sitting. I saw her tear-streaked face, but I couldn't hear what she said to me. Very slowly, so as not to hit Sylvia, Martin or Russell, the car pulled away. Within seconds, it was gliding along the village street.

I turned and looked out of the rear window. My last, lingering image of the place I called home retreated, leaving Sylvia, Martin, Russell and a flustered Mrs. Meadowes standing in the middle of the road, crying and wringing their hands in despair.

15. Garfield House

Neither of the social Workers said very much as the car sped along the roads. I didn't feel much like talking in any case. It had dawned on me as the vehicle left the village of Swanton Abbot that I might never see any of the people who cared about me again. I thought of Sylvia and Martin; also of Mr. and Mrs. Jones and Benjamin. Then my thoughts turned to Mam and the gypsies. I fought back tears.

Miss Armstrong turned in her seat and looked at me. "Are you all right now, Keri?"

I nodded and swallowed the lump in my throat.

"Where are we going?"

"Oh, it's not too far away. It's a very nice Reception Centre in East Dereham. There are a few children of about your age there already. You will have to be well behaved though."

I stared at my hands and said nothing.

When the car entered the town of East Dereham, I looked out the window at the shops. It looked similar to North Walsham, I thought. There were a few people hurrying along in the chilly November air; I saw a group of young people gathered outside a Wimpy bar. They were laughing.

I suddenly felt very lost and alone. The glee and relief to be finally free of Mother faded. I had no idea what to expect or of how I would be received in this place the Social Workers were taking me to. I wondered what a 'Reception Centre' actually was.

The car jolted over a level crossing and after just a few hundred yards more, drew up outside a very large, red-brick building with black, cast iron railings along the front. There was a driveway leading onto a paved area beside the building and I could see a mini-bus parked there next to a tall wooden fence.

The Social Workers got out of the car and Miss Armstrong went to the boot to collect the bags she'd put my clothes in. Mrs. Waverley came around to the rear passenger door and opened it.

"Come along, Keri. I think you'll be in time for tea. Make haste, dear."

I scrambled out of the car and followed the two women through the wide, open gate, along a short path between untidy shrubs and up three or four steps to an imposing door set between stone pillars.

Mrs. Waverley rang the doorbell. I could hear it echo inside. I heard the voice of a young child yell, "There's someone at the door!"

A middle aged lady opened the door. Her face had many wrinkles and looked quite stern, but she smiled when she saw the Social Workers.

"Oh. Hello, Mrs. Waverley. You made good time. I don't think they're quite ready. Do come in. I'll just show you into the sitting room for now. Perhaps you wouldn't mind waiting whilst I go and find Paul and Joss?"

Mrs. Waverley stepped inside; Miss Armstrong took my elbow and gently steered me ahead of her.

"This is Keri."

The woman looked me up and down and then smiled. "Hello, Keri. I'm Mrs. Webster. I help around the place. You'll get to know me soon enough. I expect you're hungry? Most young people seem to be hungry most of the time. It will be time for tea quite soon."

I didn't feel at all hungry. I had a knot in my stomach which seemed to twist at the mention of food. I shook my head.

"Oh. Well, never mind. Perhaps you'll want something later. I expect you're feeling quite nervous at the moment. Come this way, please."

I followed the women along a wide hallway which had beautiful red, cream and black ceramic tiles on the floor, laid out in geometric patterns. A slender, blonde haired girl about my own age stopped halfway down the wide stairway in front of us. She wore a very short skirt and had a pile of clothes in her arms. She stared at me. I turned away.

Mrs. Webster opened a door on the right and ushered us into a large, comfortable room with a thick, fitted carpet and at least twelve armchairs. I noticed a desk in the corner next to a filing cabinet. In the wide, bay window a table bore a large vase of flowers. The room was lit well and smelled of furniture polish and cigarette smoke.

"Do sit down and make yourselves comfortable," Mrs. Webster said. "I'll go and make a pot of tea and send someone to get Paul and Joss. Do you drink tea, Keri?"

I nodded. Somehow, I simply couldn't find my voice. I didn't feel exactly afraid, but everything seemed strange and alien. I sat in a green upholstered armchair and looked around the room. Mrs. Waverley began to speak to Miss Armstrong in hushed tones, but I ignored her.

An electric fire with fake coals sat in the wide hearth beneath an ornate, Victorian mantelpiece. I watched the lights flickering under the plastic 'coals' before lifting my eyes to a large print of Constable's 'The Haywain' hanging on the chimney breast.

Although there were various ornaments and furnishings, including full-length drapes, the contents of the room told me nothing at all about the people here. The only personal item I noticed was a small, blue teddy bear which sat on top of the filing cabinet next to a pile of text books. Even that told me nothing.

The door opened and Mrs. Webster entered bearing a tray with a teapot and several mugs. She set it down on a wide, low coffee table in the centre of the room.

"Paul will be along directly," she said as she poured the tea. "I'm afraid Joss is otherwise engaged at the moment, but I'm sure she'll be back in a little while. Do you all take sugar and milk?"

"No sugar for me." I surprised myself by speaking out.

"That's unusual," Mrs. Webster replied. "I think you'll be the only person in the house who doesn't take sugar!" She handed me a mug.

I accepted the tea and sat sipping at it whilst the Social Workers made small talk with Mrs. Webster. I thought the atmosphere felt a little awkward but I could not begin to understand why that should be.

The door opened again and an enormous man entered the room. He must have been over six feet tall and was extremely well built, even though he also had quite a large stomach. He had brown hair and a full beard and moustache darker than the hair on his head. He beamed at me and the three women.

"Hello! I got here at last! So sorry. Been busy setting up the dart board in the play-barn and then making the little darlings understand that throwing darts is a dangerous business if one isn't careful!"

In many ways, he reminded me of Great Uncle Bertie although he looked nothing like him. I think it was the joviality and the way everything he had said so far sounded like an exclamation rather than simple conversation.

"Hello, Paul," said Mrs. Waverley. "How nice to see you again. This is Keri. I think she's feeling a bit nervous and shy."

"I'm not shy," I snapped. "Hello, Paul."

Paul approached the table and poured himself a mug of tea. He retreated to the desk and flung himself into the large, leather chair in front of it.

"Good not to be shy. Get nowhere much in life if you're too busy being shy," he slurped at his tea.

I drained my own cup and stood to replace the mug on the tray.

"How old are you, Keri?"

"Nearly fifteen."

"All right. There are two or three kids your own age here at the moment. I'm sure you'll get to know each other quite quickly." He turned and rummaged through some paperwork on his desk. "We'll have er ... Valerie, yes. She can show Keri to her room and help her unpack and all that."

"I'll go and fetch her." Mrs. Webster stood up. "So nice to have seen you again, Mrs. Waverley; and your colleague." She left the room closing the door quietly behind her.

"Got any luggage, Keri?" Paul addressed me as if the two Social Workers were not there.

I nodded. "A bit."

"Good. Well, Valerie will show you to your room and then a little later, Joss will come and sort through your things with you to see what else you need. You'll definitely need a school uniform ... what you're wearing won't do at all! I can just imagine how you'll be teased and ripped to bits by the masses turning up looking like that!"

I noticed Mrs. Waverley smile and shake her head. She didn't say she thought I looked very nice in front of Paul like she had in front of Mother.

The door opened again and a girl peered into the room. I tried not to stare but she looked very strange. She had very short cropped dark hair, but no eyebrows or eyelashes! I dropped my gaze; I didn't want to offend anyone right at the start.

"Ah, Valerie! This is Keri. She's going to have the room right at the far end of the corridor. Would you take her up there, please? You can show her around the house a bit and help her unpack her stuff. Joss will come and see what she needs a bit later."

I made no move to leave my seat. I simply glanced between the Social Workers and Paul and then back toward the face at the door.

"Go on, Keri," Paul encouraged. "Off you go. You've got about twenty minutes before tea. Plenty of time to have a look around the place and meet at least some of the kids."

I stood up and walked slowly toward the door. Neither of the Social Workers said anything to me. Valerie opened the door wider to allow me to exit the room and closed it firmly as soon as I'd passed through.

"Bloody Social Workers! I see you've got the bitch, Waverley. I've never seen the other one. What's she like?"

"Um ... she seems all right."

"All right? None of them are all right. That's how they start, all nice and friendly, just to get you to trust them, then ... wham! They ruin your life for you!"

I was taken aback and did not know how to respond. I looked at Valerie in her fashionable jumper and a short, checked skirt which I liked very much. She wore platform shoes and had a number of chain necklaces dangling over the neck of her jumper. I wondered if I'd be allowed to wear nice things here at Garfield House.

Valerie lifted one of the canvas bags which had been left in the hallway.

"Social Worker bags," she commented. "Best go and empty them out 'cos they'll want them back before they go. Come on."

I lifted the second bag and followed Valerie along the hallway, past an open door wherein I could hear young children bickering and up the wide staircase.

Valerie paused on the landing and pointed to a passageway to the left.

"That's all the staff quarters down there. Paul and Joss's room, the duty worker's room and their private sitting room, kitchen and bathroom. We aren't allowed in there. I've never even seen it ... not that I want to!"

She led me straight ahead, pausing at each door to inform me of who occupied what room, pointing out bathrooms, lavatories, cupboards and so forth. The corridor seemed very long to me. Holly Cottage would have been swallowed a couple of times over just in the upper storey of this enormous house.

At length, we came to the end of the corridor where a white painted door stood open. Valerie entered the room with me on her heels. She tossed the bag she'd carried for me onto the bed and sat down next to it.

"Well. This is it. It was my room for a while, but now I share with Karen. Have you had your own bedroom before?"

I glanced around the room and nodded. This room was already brighter and more homely than my old bedroom at home. For a start, there was a lot more furniture. I noted a wardrobe and two chests of drawers, a bedside cabinet and a desk with a lamp on it. In the corner was a fire door only partially covered by a long, single drape. A small window above the desk had colourful curtains with tie-backs. I also noticed a small basin in one corner with a fluffy, blue towel on the hand-rail next to it. There was a large mirror above the basin.

I plonked my bag on the floor and sat down next to Valerie.

"Have you been here very long?"

She shook her head. "Not really. Maybe about ... three months. If I can stop plucking my eyebrows and eyelashes, they might let me go home soon."

I tried not to stare.

"It's all right. I know I look weird without any eyelashes and stuff but ... well, I can't help it. Just as soon as I notice a hair growing I just have to pluck it out. They took my tweezers away, but it's OK. I just go and buy some more!" She giggled.

Intrigued, I grinned. "But why do you do it?"

Valerie shrugged. "I dunno. I just do. That bloody Waverley woman reckons it's proof that my folks hurt me. What the hell does she know? I don't know who looks after my mum now I'm stuck here. My dad tried to visit me the other week, but they wouldn't let him be in the room with me on my own so I couldn't ask about my mum at all."

I felt confused. Did this mean that Valerie's parents had not hurt her but the Social Workers thought they had?

"What's wrong with your mum?"

"Oh, she's an alcoholic but she hasn't had a drink in nearly a year."

I didn't know what an alcoholic was and felt I did not want to show my ignorance. I nodded and was about to ask another question when a woman entered the room.

She was fairly stout and had long, straight, dark brown hair. Her skirt was a little too short, showing her fat, knock-knees. I looked at her face which was round and rather flushed. She carried a notebook and pen.

"Hello. You must be Keri? I'm Joss, Paul's wife and the house-mother here. I've come to make a list of the things you need. Oh! You haven't even started unpacking yet!"

"Joss, we only just got here and sat down." Valerie grinned at the woman. "I had to show her where the toilets and bathrooms are, didn't I?"

Joss put her notebook down on one of the chests of drawers. "Come on, let's get on with it. It will be tea-time soon. Are you going to help, Valerie?"

Between the three of us, we unpacked the clothes that Miss Armstrong and I had stuffed into the bags. Several things Joss set aside, claiming they needed either laundering or ironing.

"I wish Social Workers would learn to pack properly," she muttered.

Joss made a note of all my belongings on one page and then turned to the business of the things I would need.

"You'll need wash things for a start. And a toothbrush and shampoo. I didn't see any knickers, tights, bras or socks either, so we'll need all of those. I'll find you a new pair of knickers for the morning before we go shopping. And you'll need nightdresses and a dressing gown and slippers too. Or would you prefer pyjamas?"

"Nighties, please."

"Right. And there's only one pair of jeans. That won't do at all. And you'll need a coat and a jacket and ... let me see ... yes, a proper school uniform. I can't have you going out of here in that thing you're wearing! Don't you get teased about that skirt and blouse?"

I nodded.

"Well, we'll soon sort it all out for you. Now, I must go down and present the Social Workers with this list. It will be tea-time any minute. You can show Keri the rest of the house after tea, Valerie."

Joss looked around the room. "Have you got any posters to put up? Any photographs, ornaments, personal things? What about any jewellery?"

"My mother wouldn't let me have any of those things."

"Oh. Well, I expect you'll gradually accumulate them whilst you're here. I'd better hurry. See you in the dining room for tea, girls."

Joss hurried away. I sat down on the bed and looked up at Valerie standing nearby.

"What does she mean about 'going shopping'?

"Oh, that'll be tomorrow. First day they always take you into town shopping. To get all the stuff you need ... and if you whine enough, you'll get other stuff as well. Make sure you hold out for decent shoes. Joss has a blind spot when it comes to shoes. She's flat-footed so can't wear high heels. She tends to always look at flat, ugly shoes. Just tell her you don't like them. She won't mind."

I shook my head in wonder.

"At least you won't have to go to school tomorrow and maybe not all week, it depends on whether the Social Workers can arrange a place for you at the school quickly or not. I bet you'll be in my class. Karen is, and John as well, but he's weird."

"What's the school like?"

"Oh, you know. Crappy like every school. I hate it. Half the time I skyve off if I can. Sometimes, if we can get away, me and Karen go down the end of the field and get through the fence into the coach park. We can sit on the coaches and have a fag and eat crisps and stuff. Better than school."

I considered this as Valerie led me back along the corridor to the top of the stairs.

"Don't you get into trouble?"

"Nah. Not really. I mean, what can they do? They've already taken me away from my family. Sometimes, Paul gets really pissed off and says I can't go out that evening and once he stopped my pocket money for a week, but that's all."

I followed Valerie down the stairs.

"You get pocket money?"

"Yeah. Everyone does. It depends how old you are as to how much you get. How old are you?"

"Nearly fifteen."

"Fourteen then. You'll get the same as me, Two pounds twenty-five." Then, every three months or so, you get a grant for new clothes, shoes and stuff. Then they take you shopping again. Good, ain't it? Easy money."

As we reached the foot of the stairs, a gong sounded. I jumped violently and Valerie giggled.

"It's all right, don't panic. Just the gong for tea. Come on, I'll show you the dining room. You can sit with me and Karen."

We turned right at the foot of the stairs and went a short way along another passageway off the main hall. I glanced toward the room where I'd left the Social Workers with Paul. The door remained closed.

"They'll be in there for ages," Valerie told me. "They're probably telling Paul all about what they think of you and the stuff you've done or not done and everything they suspect about your parents too. They'll get it all wrong because they always do. They're useless."

We entered a spacious room filled with tables. Two or three children were already seated and Mrs. Webster bustled about, serving soup.

"But I don't like tomato soup!" wailed a small girl.

"Well then, you don't have to have it," Mrs Webster remarked. You can just have the sausage and chips but you'll have to wait until everyone has finished their soup first."

"But I want chicken soup!"

"I want doesn't get!" scolded Mrs. Webster. "What do you say?"

The child pouted. "Chicken soup!"

Mrs. Webster turned and saw me and Valerie. "Ah. Is Keri going to sit over there with you and Karen, Valerie? I don't know where Karen's got to, I'm sure. It's not like her to be late."

"I'm not late."

I turned and saw a pretty, dark-haired girl standing in the doorway. Her hair framed her face with natural waves and her dark, long-lashed eyes blinked as she stared at me.

"You're new."

"This is Keri," Valerie introduced me to Karen. "She just got here. The Social Workers are still here."

Karen looked thoughtful. "Which Social Workers?"

We moved together to a table in the window. Mrs. Webster came along behind with the large saucepan of soup. As we sat down, she ladled thick, creamy tomato soup into dishes set ready.

"There's more rolls in the kitchen if you haven't got enough here," Mrs. Webster said. "But remember you've got sausage and chips afterwards so you don't want too much bread."

"Never mind rolls, Mrs. Webster. Which Social Workers are here?" Karen lifted her spoon.

"Mrs. Waverly and Miss ..."

"Armstrong," I added as Mrs. Webster hesitated.

"Bugger. When is that stupid cow, Gainsworthy coming?" Karen flung her spoon down again in disgust.

"Don't swear, young lady! And Mrs. Gainsworthy will be here as soon as she can fit you in. Now eat up your soup."

Karen leaned back in her chair. "I don't want any bloody soup. A visit from my dad is what I want!"

"And I want chicken soup!" the little girl on the other side of the room piped up again.

"Mrs. Brown has gone home now, so you can have tomato soup or nothing. I haven't got time to start heating up a can of chicken soup just for one!" Mrs. Webster looked harassed.

A tall boy of about fifteen entered the room with another boy aged about ten.

"Chicken soup?" he asked. "Is there chicken soup?"

"No." said Mrs. Webster. "There's tomato soup, now sit down and let's get on. Paul and Joss will be here momentarily. Where are Sally and Michelle?"

I ignored the rest of the children and an increasingly more stressed Mrs. Webster and helped myself to a crispy bread roll from the dish in the centre of the table.

I surprised myself with an appetite I hadn't thought I had. I cleared the soup and roll and listened to Karen complaining about Social Workers to Valerie.

Several other people entered the room and sat down, but I was so interested in the things Karen was talking about, I barely noticed them. It seemed Social Workers could be very easily manipulated in order to get practically anything you wanted! The main complaint Karen had was that her Social Worker had not arrived as expected that day.

"So; does that mean that Mrs. Waverly is my Social Worker now?" I felt a little stupid, but Karen and Valerie didn't seem to notice.

"She might be, but she's a bitch, you don't want her. You might get the other one, what did you say her name was?"

"Miss Armstrong."

"She's quite young," Valerie remarked as she began to tuck into sausages, chips and beans that Mrs. Webster had placed in front of us. "I saw her when I went to the sitting room to get Keri and show her the bedroom."

"You'd best hope you get her, then," said Karen with her mouth full. "The young ones are the easiest to get round. Anything you decide you want, just lean on her and whine a bit. You'll get it eventually, especially if you can say you're being teased or bullied because you haven't got whatever it is."

"What? I can get anything?"

"Sure." Karen continued to eat. "It's great. They're so thick and they don't have a clue. It's not their own money they're spending, so why should they worry? I've had all the clothes, make-up, shoes and other stuff I've always wanted since I came here. My folks couldn't afford half of what I get now."

"I'll be going shopping with my grant in a couple of weeks. I'm gonna get some of those great, flared jeans with the embroidery on them." Valerie pushed her empty plate to one side and looked over her shoulder. "Mrs. Webster? What's for pudding?"

"Jam roly-poly and custard."

I was struggling to finish the mountain of sausage and chips. I felt pretty certain I would not be able to manage pudding as well.

"Do we have to have pudding?" I kept my voice low so that Mrs. Webster wouldn't hear me.

Karen grinned. "'Course not! You don't have to have anything you don't want. Don't be scared of saying you don't want or like something. And if ever anyone tries to push you, just pretend to cry or have a shouting match with them. Then you'll get your own way quickly enough."

I felt utterly bemused by what I heard. Life here would be as different by comparison to my home life as the convent had been, but in a totally alternative way. I found it hard to comprehend that material things were so easily come by and even harder to believe that getting into trouble seemed almost impossible.

After the meal, Valerie and Karen escorted me around the rest of the building. There was a large, comfortable sitting room with an enormous television and cupboards filled with toys and games of every sort. Karen introduced me to the three children in the room. The girl who had complained about the soup, was aged about six and named Mary. Two boys aged about seven and nine, brothers called Philip and Anthony. Both boys made rude faces at me and even ruder remarks.

"Ignore them. They're both crazy anyway," Karen shoved the younger boy away from her. "Let's go to the play barn for a while. I think Neil is in there. He's nice."

I followed the two girls out the back door and across a concrete area to a large building which stood slightly apart from the far end of the main house. The windows were brightly lit but glazed with safety glass - the kind with something resembling chicken-wire running through it. The building had a large door painted in all different colours. It looked to me as if a lot of people had painted graffiti on it. I could hear music coming from inside.

Karen tugged the door open and glanced over her shoulder at me. "Have you met Neil yet?"

I shook my head and followed Karen and Valerie inside.

The play barn was immense. It must have once been either an extremely large garage for about eight vehicles or some kind of other outbuilding. The walls were all painted in the same crazy designs as the outside door. Several tatty old settees and chairs were placed in groups with tables which had clearly seen better days.

On one table in front of the long bank of side windows a record player had been set up with the speakers either side. "Sherry" by the Four Seasons was playing - extremely loudly.

On the end wall a dart board had been erected and a man was busy playing darts with two teenage boys.

Neither of the boys took any notice of us but the man turned and grinned. "Hello, girls. Come for a game of darts?"

The man had shoulder length, light brown hair, a full beard and moustache, neatly trimmed and very straight, white teeth. He wore a faded, blue tee-shirt and fashionable, flared jeans.

"Hey, Neil. This is Keri. She's new." I noticed the way Karen held her head slightly on one side and the half-smile she gave. I'd seen older girls at the club behaving like that. I looked at the floor.

"Back in a moment, lads." Neil walked across the faded old carpet toward the three of us. He held out a hand to me.

"Pleased to meet you, Keri. Do you play darts, by any chance?"

"A bit, but I'm not very good."

"That's all right. Neither are any of us! Do you want to come and join in? I'm Neil. I'm one of the house-father's here. You've probably already met my mum, Mrs. Webster?"

I nodded.

Karen flung herself into one of the scruffy armchairs with her legs dangling over the arm. Her short skirt rode right up to the edge of her knickers but she didn't seem to care.

"Neil, will it be you taking Keri shopping tomorrow or Joss?"

Neil returned to the dartboard. "Uh. I dunno, Karen, why?" He threw his three darts inexpertly at the board. One landed in the wall below the board and the teenage boys laughed.

"I need some new tights; mine are all laddered and I haven't got enough pocket money to buy any more," Karen continued. "Will you get me some tights please, Neil? Please? Pretty please? I'll be ever so good!"

Neil turned and grinned at her. "Have you asked Joss? What did she say?"

Karen faked a pout. "I haven't asked her. She'll only tell me to make do. But, Neil! I'll look like a tramp going to school with laddered tights!"

The dark haired boy turned around and scowled at Karen. "Wear socks then, you stupid cow! Clear off! We were having a good game 'till you three turned up!"

"Shut up, John, you weirdo." Karen pulled a face at the boy.

"That's not very nice, John. I haven't done anything!" Valerie moved to the record player because the track had stopped.

"Put that song on again, I like it," said John.

Valerie ignored him and found something by the Beach Boys.

"I hate girls!" John yelled. He flung down the three darts he'd been holding, barged between the chairs and marched toward Valerie and the record player.

Neil sighed. He put his darts down on a small table. "Come on, John! Don't let's have an argument over a record. You're not the only one here, you know. You need to let the others use the record player as well."

I watched as John shoved Valerie away and lifted the arm from the spinning record. For her own part, Valerie did not seem in the least intimidated. She shoved John back and kicked out at him.

"Don't touch me, weird boy!"

"That's right, I'm the one that's pulled all my eyelashes out aren't I? Nothing weird at all about that!"

Neil crossed the large room very quickly and got between John and Valerie. "That's enough now. Come on, if you don't pack it in, I'll have to close up the place and lock it until tomorrow. It's only a record, John. Valerie, you shouldn't say such mean things. You know John likes only certain songs."

"He started it," Valerie mumbled.

Karen hoisted herself out of the chair. "Come on, Keri. I'm not staying in here to watch weird boy John have one of his tantrums. Let's go and watch telly. Come on, Valerie. Leave the whining baby here with Neil and Adam."

I didn't glance back as we left the play barn. I actually felt quite uncomfortable about the whole experience. I hadn't liked the way Karen appeared to flirt with Neil or the confrontation between John and Valerie.

As we made our way to the back door of the house, I asked Karen, "Are there often arguments and stuff here?"

Karen nodded. "All the time. Just make sure you learn how to hit harder than anyone else, kick better than anyone else and you'll be just fine. Everyone here can fight. Well, except Sally, but she'll cut you to bits just by speaking to you. Anyway, she's pregnant."

"Pregnant?"

"Yeah. She and George are keeping the baby as well. When she leaves here, she'll go and live with George at his mum's place."

I followed Karen and a still bristling Valerie into the sitting room. "But ... will that be allowed?"

Karen shoved little Mary out of her way. "Piss off, brat. Yeah, of course it'll be 'allowed'. Sally will be sixteen just before the baby's born so the social workers can't do a damned thing about it. Anyway, can you see Mrs. Webster letting them deprive her of her first grandchild? I can't!"

I sidestepped Mary, who was rubbing her eyes as if preparing to cry. "Sally is having Mrs. Webster's grandchild? I don't understand."

"You wouldn't 'cos you're new. George is going out with Sally. He does a bit of work here now and then. He's Neil's younger brother. And Mrs. Webster is their mum. See?"

"Um ... not really. If Sally is only fifteen, shouldn't George get into trouble? Why do Paul and the social workers let it go on?"

Karen shrugged. "Girls are always getting pregnant. It's just what happens. Half the time, they go to mother and baby homes and then the social workers get them somewhere to live. Some of them don't want to keep the brat anyway. They just leave. I dunno where they go."

Mary began to wail loudly. Karen glanced at the child. "Shut up, Mary! For God's sakes! You're always howling! I didn't hurt you."

From along the corridor, I heard Mrs. Webster's voice. "Why is Mary crying? Is she all right?"

"It's nothing, Mrs. Webster. Just a tantrum," Karen shouted back. She leaned down to the little girl. "Just shut up and I'll give you one of my sweets at sweetie time. All right?"

Mary stopped howling immediately and skipped off to the other end of the room where she picked up a teddy bear and hugged it. I watched the little girl talking to the teddy for a few moments.

"What happens now?" I asked.

"Well. When Mrs. Webster's done all the washing up and stuff, she brings the sweetie tin. We all get sweets. Then she and Joss take the little ones up for their baths. We're allowed out then. If we don't want to go out, we can stay here and watch telly or go in our rooms and do whatever we want. Do you fancy going out?"

"It's her first night, Karen. She might not be allowed." Valerie joined in the conversation. "I wasn't allowed out on my first night. They thought I'd run."

"Run? Where to?" I asked.

"Home, of course! I'll tell you something. If I do run, I won't go home. That's the first place they'll look!"

"Me neither," agreed Karen.

I couldn't imagine running away from this place, which seemed to be so easy-going and with very lax rules. So far, it had proved to be a much more pleasant place than home had ever been.

Briefly, I thought of Russell and then of Sylvia and Martin, Mrs. Meadowes and the Jones family. I might have become miserable, had I dwelt on those people and the fact I might never see any of them again. However, Mrs. Webster entered the room bearing a large tin and I was quickly distracted by its contents.

We were allowed two 'sweets' each. They weren't single sweets, but large confectionary bars. I chose a Mars Bar and a Crunchie and sat down in front of the television with Karen and Valerie whilst Mrs. Webster herded little Mary from the room and began yelling for Philip and Anthony.

16. Shopping With Joss

I slept remarkably well in view of the fact that I was in a strange place. The bed was both comfortable and warm, although the laundry smelled different to what I was used to.

I had taken a book from the sitting room downstairs and read until my eyes were so tired the words swam on the page, believing I would never be able to sleep. I actually fell asleep with the bedside lamp on. I have a vague memory of a shadowy form leaning over to switch the light off, but I didn't wake properly.

Neil shook my shoulder gently to wake me in the morning.

"Hello. Time to get up. I hope you slept well?"

Bleary eyed, I sat up and looked around. Neil grinned at me.

"You won't be going to school today, Keri. You can wear whatever you like. Joss is taking you shopping. You've got about half an hour before breakfast. I left a flannel, toothbrush and toothpaste over there on the basin for you. See you at breakfast."

Neil left the room and pulled the door closed behind him. I lay back on the pillows and stared at the ceiling.

I suddenly occurred to me that I had left my home and former school - and I still had the key to Charlie's locker in my pocket! Poor Charlie! She would not be able to get to any of her belongings. I wondered if she would miss me; I couldn't even write to her because I didn't know her home address.

I worried over this little problem as I washed and dressed. I found a new pair of pretty knickers in my size on the chest of drawers. Joss must have put them there for me. I inspected them before I put them on. Mother would never have bought me such pretty underwear! There was a panel of lace in the front of these and they weren't huge and thick either! I wore my Brutus jeans and one of the tops Charlie had stolen for me.

Perhaps Neil or Paul might have an idea of how to get Charlie's key back to her. I rummaged in the pocket of my ugly school skirt, found the key and left it on the bedside table. Then I wondered what to do with the dirty laundry. No-one had told me where to put it. I folded the clothes and left them in a pile on the chest of drawers. I could find out soon enough what to do with them.

When I went in search of the lavatory, I heard the unmistakeable sounds of someone being noisily sick coming from the first toilet room I came to. My stomach roiled.

Valerie opened her bedroom door, saw me and grinned.

"Don't worry. It's only Sally with her morning sickness. She's in there for ages every morning. There's another loo just over there."

Valerie pointed. I hurried along the passageway to where she indicated. When I came out, little Mary was leaning against the opposite wall, clutching a teddy bear.

"Will you hold my teddy?"

"Pardon?"

"I don't want him to get germs, see."

I accepted the tatty old bear the child held out to me. "Don't forget to wash your hands."

Mary frowned. Her little face was serious as she informed me, "I never forget. I hate germs!"

I stood outside the lavatory, feeling rather foolish holding the teddy bear. Karen paused on her way along the corridor.

"I see Mary has collared you already?"

I nodded.

"She's obsessed with germs at the moment. They've been teaching them about it at school and Mary takes everything so seriously. It's really funny. If you tell her something has germs on it, she won't touch it!"

Mary emerged from the toilet and glared at Karen as she snatched her bear from me.

"You were talking about me!"

Karen scowled. "I've got better things to do than to talk about you! Coming down to breakfast, Keri?"

I followed Karen down the stairs and into the dining room. Mrs. Webster and another lady I hadn't met before were busy setting out the tables.

"Morning, girls," Mrs. Webster smiled. "Nearly ready for breakfast. Keri, this is Mrs. Brown, she does most of our cooking for us. Will you want a cooked breakfast today, dear?"

"Cooked breakfast?"

"Yes, dear. You know; bacon, eggs, tomatoes and mushrooms. The usual stuff."

I was used to snatching a slice of toast in the mornings, although Mother sometimes cooked breakfast for Russell and Terry. I hesitated.

"How about I do you one anyway, luv?" Mrs. Brown, a very stout lady with curly, brown hair and twinkling eyes, paused and looked at me. "You can see what you can manage. Most of you young people are always hungry, but I expect you're still a bit nervous, being in a new place and all."

I nodded. "Thank you. I'll do my best. I don't usually eat much for breakfast."

"You'd be surprised, dear. Some of these kids had never even heard of breakfast before they came here!"

Karen and I sat down at the table we'd occupied at tea the previous day. "Philip and Anthony were half-starved when they first came here," Karen informed me. "You should've seen the little buggers eat! Keep an eye on them though, they'll pinch your sweets if they can and they think nothing of going in your room and nicking stuff. Have you got a bag?"

I shook my head.

"Well, when you go shopping today, tell Joss you haven't got a bag and she'll get you one. Then, anything you value, you can keep in your bag. We're not allowed to take the bags to school, but that's all right because everyone is at school in the day so stuff in your room is safe – nothing can get stolen. If you're stuck here, someone will 'keep you occupied' all day so you don't get bored."

Actually, I consumed the most enormous breakfast, starting with cereal. I gazed along the sideboard in the dining room. Cereal of every variety left me spoiled for choice. The milk was ice cold and creamy, totally different from that which Mother used to buy.

Mrs. Brown certainly was a good cook. The bacon was just crispy enough, without being burned and fried eggs were cooked to perfection, with the yolk still soft so that I could dip my toast into it. These tastes and textures made me think of Nana. I wondered if she knew that I had been taken away from Mother and if she did, what she thought of it all. I did not mention Nana or my family to Karen or Valerie. Neither girl seemed to notice anything amiss, even though I barely spoke during the meal.

When everyone had left for school, I wandered into the kitchen, where Mrs. Webster and Mrs. Brown were washing up the breakfast things.

"Can I help?"

"If you want to, Keri. I have to say, we don't very often get offers of help!" Mrs. Webster handed me a tea-towel. "Joss will be taking you shopping when she gets back from taking the little ones to school. Are you looking forward to that?"

I shrugged. "Not really."

Mrs. Brown turned to stare at me. "Will you just listen to the girl! Don't you tell any of the other kids that! They'll all think you're quite mad. Shopping trips are real treats around here."

I dried a couple of plates. "Oh. Well, when my mother took me shopping, she always bought stuff I didn't like, that's all."

"Never mind," Mrs. Brown continued. "It will be different for you this time, dear. You'll see. Now, let's finish this job and we can all have a nice drink together before you go out with Joss."

I met George whilst we worked. He poked his head around the kitchen door to say hello to his mother.

I stared at the young man. He was tall and slender with a mop of light brown, curly hair. He wore faded, flared jeans and a tie-dyed tee shirt. He winked at me.

"Paul wants you to take the minibus to the garage for a service, George," said Mrs. Webster. "He says the brakes need something doing to them. Can you fit that in today?"

"Yep. No problem, Mum. Who's this?" he indicated me with a nod of his head.

"This is Keri. She arrived yesterday. Now, off you go. I'm sure you've got work to do. No need for lallygagging about!"

George grinned, leaned in the door and filched an apple from the fruit bowl on the counter and left.

Mrs. Brown made me a cup of sweet coffee with frothy milk and sent me to the sitting room with it.

"You just wait in the sitting room, dear, whilst we have our coffee here in the kitchen. Joss will come and get you when she's ready to go. You can put the telly on if you like. I think there are some schools programmes on about now."

I scuttled away with the hot coffee. I didn't put the television on, but sat on a comfortable settee and sipped at the drink whilst looking around the room. I saw every imaginable board game; a stack of jigsaw puzzles and a huge box of Lego.

Setting my drink down, I explored the contents of the tall cupboards and many drawers. I found art and craft supplies in plenty, including a full set of oil paints and stacked canvasses. One cupboard was filled with dolls and equipment for girls.

Another held an assortment of toy cars, trucks and Meccano - clearly for boys.

I had just closed that cupboard when Joss arrived. She held out a parka-style jacket with fake fur around the hood.

"Having a look round?"

I nodded.

"Well, if there isn't anything for you in any of these cupboards, you just let me or Paul know what it is that you want and we'll see about getting it for you. Have you got any hobbies?"

I hesitated, unsure of what Joss meant.

"What do you like to do in your spare time?" Joss held out the jacket. "Put this on. It'll probably fit you and do until we can get you a coat of your own. It's Valerie's, but she told me you could borrow it to go shopping."

I accepted the jacket and tugged it on. "Um ... well. I don't do very much. I like to draw. Sometimes I write poetry ..." my voice tailed off.

"Oh. Do you like music? What about dancing? I know all you young girls are keen on the latest dances."

I shrugged. "I've never tried."

Joss gave me a quick hug. "Never mind. You'll soon settle in and I bet you'll be surprised at the things you like, once you have an opportunity to try. Come along. We've got a lot to get. If you're good, we'll have lunch in the Wimpy. How do you fancy that?"

It was a short walk into town; just a few hundred yards to the level crossing, then there we were at the shops. Our first stop was at a large shoe shop. I trailed after Joss through the door.

Almost immediately, a slender, well-dressed woman approached. "Hello, Mrs. Holdsworth. How nice to see you again so soon! Is this another of your residents?"

Joss smiled and urged me forward. "Yes. This is Keri. She arrived yesterday. We'll need all the usual things and ... I think, yes, a pretty, fashionable pair of shoes to wear out as well. Poor girl. Her mother dressed her like an old woman!"

The lady reached out and took my hand. "Well. We'll find you lots of pretty things to wear on your feet today! Come and sit down, dear. Do you know what size shoe you take?"

I felt extremely awkward. Particularly when I told the lady my shoe size. She frowned.

"Hmmm. Well, there's a challenge for me to meet." She patted my hand. "But don't you worry about a thing. "We're very cosmopolitan here and I'm sure I can help."

To my amazement, there were quite a variety of pretty shoes in a size nine. Mother used to take me to the Clarks shoe store, where my school shoes for the convent had to be ordered in because the shop only held stocks up to size eight in women's shoes. It was a novelty to be shown so many attractive pairs of footwear.

I found Joss to be very liberal minded; not at all like I'd been told. She didn't even give the flat, ugly shoes a second glance. A pile grew beside the chair I sat upon. We must have been in that shop for the best part of an hour. I felt as if I were dreaming when Joss insisted I have a pair of fashionable, patent boots with laces criss-crossed up the front.

"I'll get someone to drop them round at Garfield House for you, Mrs. Holdsworth. You don't want to struggle around the shops with all these boxes, do you?" The lady handed Joss a hand written receipt. I didn't hear how much my shoes had cost, but it must have been an awful lot because there were no less than nine boxes stacked beside the counter.

Joss had insisted I needed Wellington boots for muddy walks, the patent boots, two pairs of fashion shoes, stout hiking boots, a pair of shoes for school, slippers, sport shoes and hockey boots.

We left the shoe store and walked further into the town. Several people spoke to Joss as we encountered them. I felt as if everyone knew her and liked her.

We went into the Littlewoods department store and Joss urged me to select underwear, nighties and a dressing gown. I had never seen so many pretty things which were available to me. Joss's enthusiasm soon infected me and I began to enjoy myself.

When it came to buying bras, I barely hesitated before telling Joss my problem of having not, so far, developed any breasts. I even told her how Mother frequently complained about it.

"Oh, not to worry, Keri. It's not such an unusual problem. Everyone develops at their own pace. There are ways around it, I can assure you. There are plenty of padded bras to be found; some of them have 'extra' pads to add to them. Let's have a look, shall we? I'm so sorry your mother was angry with you for not developing quickly. It's such a shame when mothers and daughters let silly things like that get in the way of their relationship."

Joss bought three nighties - all of them pretty and modern; in fact, one was a 'baby doll' set! She urged me to select a long, black, silky dressing gown which had embroidery on the back and would match the black, fluffy mule-style slippers I'd chosen in the shoe store. A dozen pairs of knickers, four bras, six pairs of ankle socks - to wear under jeans and four packs of six tights were added to the basket.

Joss suggested I look at the jackets and coats in the store, but pointed out that there were plenty of other stores to visit before I made any final choice.

In actual fact, it was in a small boutique in a side street that I found the coat of my dreams. I believe they are still called 'Afghan' coats even today. This one was a pale beige coloured suede with multi-coloured embroidery all over the outside. The whole of the inside was some kind of hair or fur. I tried it on and it came to my mid-calf. I thought it was quite the most beautiful coat I had ever seen! When Joss told the assistant she'd take it, I nearly fainted because it was incredibly expensive.

"You know what you need now, Keri?" said Joss, conversationally as we left the boutique.

"No. Surely, we've got everything? All these things must have cost a fortune!"

"Nonsense! Every child gets a grant for clothing and other necessary things when they come to us. You should get some of those super jeans with wide flares and embroidery up the sides. I know a lovely little shop that has them. Would you like some of those? They'll match your coat perfectly."

"Yes, please!" I recalled the conversation with Karen and Valerie the previous evening. I hoped they wouldn't be jealous.

I remembered as well, the advice I'd been given, to ask Joss for a bag whilst we were in the store which sold the jeans.

"Oh, I'm so glad you asked! I'd quite forgotten that," Joss exclaimed.

I chose a purple and green shoulder bag which had embroidery and tiny beads all over it. Joss insisted we buy another bag as well, for school. This was plainer, but nothing like the old-fashioned satchel Mother had made me use.

Joss helped me to choose practical but still fashionable school clothes, even getting me to try several skirts and blouses on before she bought them, just to make sure they fitted me properly.

By the time we struggled to the Wimpy bar with our many bags, I had really warmed to Joss. She chattered about all sorts of things and I completely failed to notice that she learned a very great deal about me.

During the meal of burger and chips, I talked to Joss about all aspects of my life, as if I'd known her for years. I told her how I'd been expelled from All Hallows and how the argument had come about. I related the dire circumstances which led to the death of my beloved dog, Tammy.

When Joss ordered more coffee, I relaxed even more. I explained how Benjamin and I spent time with our dogs, the things we had in common, how our friendship had grown and my frequent visits to the farm without Mother's knowledge. I even told her about Mam and the gypsies!

Joss listened to my animated description of the old, gypsy woman and her caravan with shining eyes.

"How simply wonderful, Keri! Not many people get to spend any time with real Romany's. I think you've been very lucky indeed. Tell me, please. Did you not do anything with your mother at all?"

"Like what?"

"Girly things ... you know, going shopping together and the cinema or to visit museums, things like that."

I shook my head. "No. The only time Mother ever took me shopping was for school stuff; she always chose the ugliest things she could find ... expensive things, but then she scolded me for the money I was costing her! I couldn't win. She'd never have bought me anything like the lovely things here." I indicated the shopping bags.

"I thought as much," murmured Joss.

"Mother says I ruined her life," I added. "She was always telling me she hated me and wished I'd die and she was always cross with me, even when I'd done nothing wrong."

"Poor child. That must have been very difficult to cope with?"

I nodded and drained my third cup of coffee. "It was. I tried so hard, Joss, but she was never pleased with me. If she knew even half of the dreadful things I'd done ... she'd ... well, she'd probably kill me!"

"What 'dreadful' things, Keri?"

That simple question was enough for me to pour out all my wicked doings with Terry. From skipping school to our day in Norwich and the shop-lifting spree to the regular escapes from school, hiding fashionable clothes in Terry's locker. I even told Joss how

Terry got drunk and had sex with Chris on the night of the party that I didn't get to go to.

"Is that all? Goodness, I thought you were going to tell me you'd killed someone or something!" Joss smiled. "If that is the whole extent of your wickedness, Keri, I don't think we will have the problems we thought we might have in looking after you. I hope you don't mind, but I have to ask you something?"

"I don't mind. You've been kind to me and you haven't told me you hate me or that I'm horrible or a waste of space."

"The information we have is that you ... er ... how can I put this? We've been told that you're very promiscuous. Do you know what that means?"

I shook my head.

"It means that you have sex with lots of boys. I won't judge you; of course not. It's just that, well, we might need to have a medical examination done. Can you tell me the truth?"

I looked Joss in the eye. "The only people I've ever had sex with are my step-father and his friend, Trevor. Ever since my step-father married my mother, he's done things to me. Horrible, disgusting, painful things. I'm sure my mother knows. She's always calling me a slut and she's always telling people that I have sex with every boy or man I can get my hands on. It's not true. No way would I willingly let anyone touch me. I hate sex. I think it's filthy and disgusting!"

Joss stood up and hugged me. "Thank you for telling me, Keri. Now. Let's get all these bags home. You'll be wanting to sort through all your new things and put them all away."

Joss and I gathered the bags together and left the Wimpy bar. A light drizzle had begun, but I felt better than I had since I'd told Mam about my family. I felt almost as if I were walking on air as we headed back to Garfield House.

17. Yet Another New School

Although I spent the whole of my first week at Garfield House without having to attend school, I had an inkling of what I might face when Karen came home on Thursday with a black eye and a split lip.

Mrs. Webster fussed around her with cotton balls, antiseptic and ice. Joss fumed at Karen's tale of being attacked by a gang of girls as she left school and stomped straight to the office to inform Paul.

Once Mrs. Webster had dismissed Karen with a bag of ice to hold on her eye, I had an opportunity to speak with her.

"What happened?"

"Oh, the usual stuff. I just wasn't quick enough today. I moved right into a fist or two instead of moving away. I landed a couple of really good kicks and punches myself though."

"Usual stuff?" My stomach knotted with anxiety. "You mean this kind of thing happens a lot?"

Karen nodded. "Most of the kids are all right. It's just a few. They go on at us about being in care. You know; remarks about our families and how we're not as good as everyone else. I generally give as good as I get, but these particular girls have been after me for a while."

"Why didn't you tell anyone they were threatening you?"

Karen snorted and gave me a look which suggested she thought me mentally ill.

"Are you kidding? Don't you know what happens to snitches? If I grass them up it'll just get worse. I'm not gonna take it lying down though. I'll get those bitches tomorrow, you see if I don't!"

I turned away and stared at my hands for a few minutes. I didn't want to get into any fights or trouble. To learn that I could be picked upon simply because I lived at Garfield House was a shock. I'd thought everything would be just fine once I was dressed like other girls my age.

"Isn't there another school you could go to, Karen?"

Karen flung the bag of ice on the table. "Nope. Even if there was, d'you think it would be any different? It's all right, Keri. I can take care of myself. There're any number of things I can do to get my own back."

"Maybe it might be best to just keep your head down and do nothing. I mean ..."

Karen stood up and scowled. "I'm not a coward! If you honestly think I'd just take this kind of shit from girls who're no better than me, you're wrong! I can't help the way my family is or anything that happened! I didn't ask to come to this shit-hole! I could've managed if they'd just left me alone to get on with it. It was only a six month sentence anyway!"

I shrank back from Karen's anger. "I'm sorry. I was only trying to help."

"Well ... don't! It's my problem and I'll deal with it!"

As Karen flounced from the room, Valerie entered. Her eyes were red and her cheeks tear-stained.

"Are you all right?" I asked, even though I almost expected Valerie to shout at me as well.

"I hate that school!" Valerie burst into tears and sat down on the edge of the chair Karen had vacated.

I didn't know what to do or say. I stood close by, feeling utterly helpless as Valerie sobbed. I felt intense relief when Joss entered the room and hurried to put her arms around Valerie. Even so, I still felt like an intruder and I crept out of the room and headed toward the kitchen. I could hear Mrs. Webster telling Mrs. Brown about Karen's injuries.

I entered the kitchen and asked for a piece of fruit as a way to interrupt. Mrs. Webster waved me toward the fruit bowl and continued speaking to Mrs. Brown.

" ... and I heard her tell him she'll contact the Authorities if he doesn't put a stop to it. That's five times so far this term! I'd just like to give their parents a piece of my mind!"

Mrs. Brown shook her head. "Mind you, we've only heard the one side of things. You've got to admit, both Karen and Valerie can be very difficult at times. We don't actually know why these girls keep attacking them, do we?"

I swallowed the piece of apple I was chewing. "Will I get beaten up as well?"

Both women turned to me. Mrs. Webster grimaced. "Not if I have anything to do with it, you won't, dear. Don't worry. Joss and Paul will get to the bottom of it. I'm sure it will all be sorted out by the time you start at school on Monday. Don't let it worry you. Off you go now. Why don't you go over to the play barn and see if there's anyone there?"

I walked across the yard to the play barn clutching the apple and trying, with limited success, not to allow myself to panic about having to go to a school where I might get bullied and beaten up.

As I approached the building, I heard 'The Witchdoctor Song' playing loudly. I guessed John must be inside. I'd not had a great deal to do with John. He didn't seem to like anybody very much. I hesitated at the door, which opened suddenly.

"Are you spying on me?" John glared at me.

"What? Of course not! I just came over here to ... well ... I dunno really. Karen's angry and Valerie's upset. They got beaten up at school today."

"Yeah. I know. I heard all about it. Shouldn't hit girls, it's not right."

I recalled how John had shoved at Valerie a few days before. "You do."

John shook his head. "No. I might shove them and shout but I don't hit girls. My Nan would never forgive me if I hit a girl."

"Oh. Can I come in?"

"I'm not stopping you. Just don't stare at me or watch me or anything."

I wandered inside and slumped into an armchair which had a torn seat. For several minutes, neither of us said anything at all. The song played over a second time. I turned toward John.

"Are people nasty to you at the school as well?"

"People are always nasty to me. I'm used to it because I'm weird."

"People are usually nasty to me too. I think I must be weird as well."

Strangely, John grinned and turned back to the record player.

Later, when we were all in the children's sitting room watching 'Top of the Pops' on the television, I saw Karen huddled on the end of the settee furiously writing something. I wanted to speak to her, but I had no idea of how to open the conversation.

Neither Karen nor Valerie went to school the following day. After breakfast, Paul called Karen into the office, leaving me with Valerie in the children's sitting room.

"Is she in trouble, do you think?"

Valerie shook her head. "Nope; not yet. He'll just want to hear her version of what happened. He's probably making a fuss with the school. She will be in trouble if she doesn't give him some names though. Last time, Paul got really angry with her because she wouldn't give him names."

I considered this. "Why won't she say who did it?"

Valerie turned away. "I won't either. I'm not stupid. I know how much worse it will get if I grass them up."

I felt extremely uncomfortable and not a little afraid. Anxiety about what might happen to me the following week when I started at the school caused my hands to shake. I dared not speak, for fear that my voice would quaver; I didn't want Valerie to know I was scared.

A little later, when Paul was speaking to Valerie and Karen together, Neil peered round the door into the sitting room.

"All on your own?"

"Paul's talking to Karen and Valerie."

"Yeah, I know. Neither of them will say who the trouble-makers are. The school says it's them. Have they said anything to you?"

I shook my head. "Only that they can't say, because if they do, it'll all get much worse. I don't think it's everyone, just a few girls."

Neil nodded. "I thought it would be something like that. Trouble is, bullies tend to rely on the fact that their victims will stay silent. Then there's the 'I'm not a grass' mentality to contend with as well." He sighed. "Come and find me when Paul has finished with those two. I'll unlock the play barn for you all."

During the course of that day, as I passed the time with Karen and Valerie, I learned that Karen's dad was in prison. She claimed he'd got into a fight which was not his fault, but that police had blamed him. He also would not give any names as to the real perpetrators.

Karen talked animatedly about 'Teddy Boys'. Clearly, she greatly admired this particular group of people. I learned about the clothes they wore and the kind of music they listened to. I was shocked to learn that Karen had spent long periods with her father and a group of these 'Teddy Boys' as they got drunk, fought and got into various other unsavoury situations.

"What? Your own father let you get drunk and go with them?"

"Course. It was great. We were going to run to Ireland but ... well, that was when the fuzz turned up and all hell was let loose."

"Fuzz?"

"Police."

I'd never heard the expression before and I giggled.

"We used to call the police 'pigs' when I was at home," Valerie volunteered.

We all laughed at that.

The weekend passed too quickly for me. I could not stop worrying about attending the new school, even though there were plenty of new experiences for me. I went to the cinema on Saturday morning with Karen, Valerie, Adam and John. Later, we walked around the town, window-shopping.

On Sunday, nearly all the children at Garfield House piled into the mini-bus and Neil drove to some heath land. We raced about playing what Neil called a 'Wide Game'. Essentially, we were split into two teams. The object of the game was to sneak up to a central point and 'capture' a flag. In truth, I did not do well. I quickly became exhausted because I'd had very little exercise since leaving All Hallows School.

I slept poorly Sunday night, not least because my muscles ached from the activity during the day. Also, my fear and anxiety grew to immense proportions. I tossed and turned all night long.

By Monday morning, I was so frightened about the school I felt sick and could barely eat any breakfast. I wanted to beg to be allowed to stay at Garfield House but I didn't dare.

Neil took the little ones to school because Joss came with me, Valerie, Karen, Adam and John. The boys walked a little ahead of us; I thought they were embarrassed. My own steps dragged. It wasn't very far to the school, but more than once, Joss encouraged me to keep up.

The school was reasonably modern - at least, compared with the one I attended in North Walsham. Joss led us along a wide corridor and stopped at a cloakroom.

"Right. You two girls just go about your business as usual. Remember; try to keep away from the people you don't get along with. Staff will be watching from now on. Anything that happens will come back to me and Paul. Off you go; and I hope you have a better day than last Thursday. I'm taking Keri to meet the Head. I expect she'll be in your class. See you later."

"Good luck. See you later," Karen whispered to me.

I followed Joss to the Headmaster's office and waited whilst Joss spoke at some length to the School Secretary.

The Headmaster was a slight, short man with a completely bald head and round, horn-rimmed spectacles. I cannot recall his name. He spoke to me pleasantly and asked a few questions about the level of work I'd completed in various subjects. He further asked me if I generally enjoyed school.

The Secretary escorted me to a classroom and introduced me to the teacher, a slender, blonde woman with a ready smile. I cannot recall her name either!

I sat at a desk in the middle of the room with a bespectacled girl on one side and a very fat boy on the other. The boy grinned and greeted me, but the girl looked at me as if I were something disgusting and turned her face away.

I saw Karen and Valerie seated two rows in front of me, but neither acknowledged me in any way. I wondered why not.

I do recall that the first lesson of my first day was History. Although I'd already covered what this class was doing, I set to enthusiastically and produced some good work. The teacher was pleased with me.

When the bell rang to indicate the end of the lesson, I was very surprised that none of the students moved from their chairs. Instead, the teacher gathered her books and bags and left the room.

As soon as she'd gone, everyone began to chatter and laugh.

The fat boy turned to me and grinned. "What was your name again?"

"Keri. What's yours?"

"Gordon. It's French next. You any good at French?"

I shrugged. "I suppose I'm all right, but I don't like it much. How about you?"

"Not bad; better than History! Have you just moved here?"

My stomach knotted. I wondered if I should try to lie about where I lived. How would Gordon react to the news that I lived at Garfield House?

"It's all right. I know you're in the children's home. Just be careful with those girls over there." Gordon jerked his head toward the back of the room.

"Why?"

"They're a bunch of spiteful bitches, that's why. They'll find something to moan about and then they'll start on you. Best avoid them, if you can. Most of us do!"

The French lesson passed quickly and I found I'd already covered most of what the class had been doing. Both Valerie and Karen got into trouble for not having done the expected homework and were given after school detentions. The sniggers from the back of the class told me that the girls Gordon had mentioned thought it was funny.

When the bell rang for morning break, the French teacher left the class quickly and there was pandemonium as students rushed to either get out of the room or move into groups. I sat at my desk and waited to see what Karen and Valerie would do. Neither turned to speak to me. I wondered if I'd upset them in some way. I'd just decided I would go and speak to them when a girl appeared at my shoulder. I looked up at her. She had a thin face and heavy eye make-up. Her dark hair was drawn into two bunches high on the sides of her head.

"So; you're sat next to Fat Gordy. How do you stand the smell?"

Gordon had just stood up. He ignored the girl and moved away across the classroom. I should have liked to ignore her as well, but I already had an idea that this might be seen as a way to pick on me. I smiled.

"I can't say I noticed, to be honest. But I probably smell pretty bad myself."

The girl looked puzzled for a split second then scowled. "Right. So you're a smart-arse are you?"

I made an exaggerated gesture of trying to look at my own back side.

"So what're you in the children's home for? Lying? Stealing? Prostitution?"

"All of the above, plus I beat the hell out of my mother and tried to kill my family," I lied.

"What? Really?"

"Yep." I stood up. "Did you want something?"

The girl backed away a step or two. I was at least four inches taller than her. "So they sent you to the children's home? How come you didn't go to prison, if you did all that?"

I stared at her intently. "I'm only fourteen. They don't send children to prison. I expect they'll lock me up somewhere next time I try to kill someone though."

I noticed a small group of girls standing in the back corner of the room. They were watching me and the thin girl intently. I took a step toward her.

"I get terrible ... er ... episodes of temper. I never know when I'm going to get mad and go crazy. Neither does anyone else."

The girl took another step back. "Well ... you shouldn't be allowed to come to an ordinary school if you're like that! They should send you to a special school!"

I moved quickly to snatch up my bag. "I expect they will as soon as I've done some real damage here. What's your name?"

"Tracey. Stay away from me! I don't want any trouble from you." She turned and hurried to the back of the room. I paused and waited until all the girls were looking my way, smiled a cold grimace at them all, before turning and trotting out into the corridor.

In truth, my heart was pounding and I felt quite nauseous. I wondered if my lies would be believed. As I leaned against the wall, Karen and Valerie approached me.

"What did that cow, Tracey say to you?" Karen demanded. "Did they guess you're at Garfield House? We thought maybe if we didn't speak to you, they might not know."

"Yeah. She knew already," I replied. "I told her I got put in there for beating up my mother and trying to kill my family ... amongst other things."

Valerie gasped. "Did you?"

"No. Don't be stupid. I thought if I could make them think I'm violent and trouble, they might leave me alone."

"I never thought of that," Karen muttered. "They're always saying stuff about my family and I get so mad I just scream and shout stuff back at them."

We walked along the corridor to a double door which led onto a wide playground.

"I don't care what they say about my bloody family. I hate my parents anyway. If they say nasty things it can never be as bad as the truth."

We sat together on a low bench. "I just hope you never have to prove that you're as hard as you claim to be," Valerie said. "Can you actually fight at all?"

"I've never really tried. What would happen at Garfield House if I hurt someone at school?"

Karen and Valerie looked at one another and then at me. "I dunno. Maybe they'd send you to a lock-up place."

"What's a lock-up?"

Karen looked serious. "It's like a prison. They keep you locked in, twenty four hours a day."

I shrugged. "Doesn't sound so bad to me. Do you have to go to school?"

Valerie grinned. "Probably not. Don't go and get yourself locked up. We're only just getting to know you. I'd miss you."

"Yeah. Me too." Karen added. "I kind of like you, Keri."

For the rest of the day, the group of girls avoided me. Valerie and Karen kept me company at lunch and during the afternoon break. When the bell rang for the end of school, Karen approached me.

"We've got half an hour detention. Can you tell Joss? You can find your way back home all right, can't you?"

"Yeah. I remember the way. See you later."

As I made my way to the school gate, Gordon approached me. He was red in the face and puffing with the effort of hurrying to catch up with me.

"Aren't you worried, Keri?"

"About what?"

"Tracey and all her friends are waiting for you outside the school gates."

I stopped and stared at Gordon. "What for?"

"Well ... usually when they wait like that it's to start a fight. They like to taunt your friend, Karen. And that Valerie as well. The one with no eyelashes?"

I considered this information. "Do they pick an actual fight?"

Gordon shrugged. "Sometimes. Usually, they just say nasty stuff and wait for Karen or Valerie to get upset and start shouting. Then they start a fight. Will you be all right? Shall I walk with you?"

"Thanks, Gordon. No. You go on ahead. Maybe I'll see you tomorrow. Thanks for the warning. I'll be fine."

I didn't really feel at all like I'd be fine. I wondered if perhaps I should go back inside and wait for Karen and Valerie. I heard screams of laughter and looked across to the gate. Gordon had walked out into the road to avoid the girls. He put his red face down and plodded past. A car hooted at him.

How much worse could it be than when Terry thrashed me or Mother set about me? Several of the girls were shorter than me. Surely, if I had to, I could defend myself? I walked on, my heart thudding painfully in my chest and my stomach knotted with anxiety.

"Hey, Keri!" A girl's voice shouted over the general hubbub of young people talking and laughing.

I looked up. A dark haired girl, standing beside Tracey was smirking at me.

"How's your mother's whoring going?" the girl yelled.

"She's probably making a fortune," I replied. "Why?"

"Your dad in prison is he?" another girl called.

"Nope. They haven't caught him yet."

"When you gonna start whoring, like your mother?" That was the dark haired girl again.

"Already have," I snapped. "And I make a lot of money too. Shall I try and get you some customers?"

"I should slap your face for that!"

"Go on then. But can you hurry up because I've got money to be making."

The girl hesitated. I walked up to her and realised I was a lot taller than her. "Why do you want to pick a fight with me? I haven't done anything to you ... yet."

The girl blanched. "I'm not picking a fight. I just think you're scum and you shouldn't be at this school, that's all."

I put my head on one side. "Yes. I am scum. Always have been. Do you think I'd be here if I had a choice? I used to go to a private boarding school ... until I got expelled for trying to kill a girl I didn't like. This place is a crummy shit-hole. Anyway, I don't intend to be here long."

"Why?" the girl asked. I noticed she looked kind of nervous.

"Because next time, I won't try to kill anyone. I'll just do it. I'm clever. I know all about poisons, you know."

The girl took a step back and bumped into a slightly taller girl with blonde hair, who shoved her.

"Don't get me involved with her! I don't want trouble like that!"

All the girls moved out of my way. I strode confidently forward and continued walking without looking back.

18. Teen Life At Garfield House

Karen listened with great interest later as I related events at the school gate. She laughed at the idea of my being a mad, violent psychopath.

"What would you actually do if one of them took a swing at you, Keri?"

I shrugged. "Dunno. Hopefully, it won't come to that. I know I can fling my arms about. It wasn't all lies. The day the social workers took me from my house, my mother was hurting me, as usual. I did thump her ... but I don't know if I hurt her or not."

"I can't imagine fighting with my mum. Mind you, I can't remember her all that well. She ran off with some bloke about five years ago. If my dad ever finds them, he'll kill them both, for sure."

Valerie joined us and we went to the play barn. For once, John was not in there and we could choose which records to play.

On that day and several others like it, I learned that the girl with dark hair, Emma, had been taunting Karen ever since she'd been at the school. She'd pretended to befriend her first in order to learn all she could about Karen and her background. I thought this a particularly mean tactic and made a mental note to somehow find out all I could about Emma. Maybe I'd get the chance to hit back on Karen's behalf.

I learned to dance a little, although I was clumsy and found it difficult to remember all the 'moves' in the popular dances of the time. I laughed with Karen and Valerie when I made a fool of myself or got it dreadfully wrong.

We spoke a fair bit about our families and how life had been before coming to Garfield House. It came as some surprise to me to find out that mine wasn't the only mother who claimed her life had been ruined. Valerie related tales of her mother being in a drunken state and doing or saying the most awful things. In fact, Valerie suggested that perhaps my mother had been drunk when she said such things to me.

I couldn't recall ever having seen Mother drink alcohol at all. I knew Terry liked a few pints and sometimes, a shot of whisky, but Mother always had a very negative attitude to alcohol.

"No. It wasn't drink, Valerie. I never knew her to drink anything but tea or coffee. I think she's mad to be honest. All I know is that she was always angry and it was somehow my fault."

"My mum never got angry at all," Karen interrupted. "Mainly, she never did very much. She hugged me and all that and sometimes, she played cards with me in the evenings. She used to cry a lot."

We were allowed to go out in the evenings after tea. I quickly got used to the town of East Dereham with its coffee bars, shops and other places where young people gathered. Karen and Valerie seemed to know all the best places to go.

I attended my fist 'disco' one Friday evening in early December. I was so excited as we got ready. Karen and Valerie helped me with makeup and my hair. We spent simply ages on making ourselves look splendid.

I was surprised at how dark it was inside the hall where the disco was held. There were coloured spotlights on the walls which flashed on and off creating strange shadows in the crowds of moving young people. The music hurt my ears it was so loud. When a strobe light came on at the beginning of a music track which had a heavy, bass beat, I felt almost frightened and looked around for Karen and Valerie.

Both were dancing enthusiastically and grinning widely. I pushed my way between people to reach them.

"It's really hot in here!" I bawled. I knew neither of them had understood what I said. I tried again, this time with gestures. "I'm hot! I'm going outside for a while!"

Karen nodded. I pushed and shoved my way through the crowd until I came to a fire door which had been propped open with a fire extinguisher. I stepped out into the cold evening air and leaned against the wall. I think I knew then that the disco scene was not for me. The crowds made me nervous, the music was too loud to be able to hear it properly and the scent of all the mixed perfumes and after-shaves made my head swim a little.

A tall young man wearing the latest in flared jeans and a tight fitting tie-dyed shirt in a tunic style stepped out of the door and stood beside me.

"'Ello, darlin'. Wanna buy some drugs?"

I stared at him. "Pardon?"

"I got some acid and some blow. 'S good stuff."

"Is it?" I replied, weakly.

"Yeah. Five for a quarter of blow and three for a tab."

"Er ... no, thanks. I haven't got any money."

The young man edged closer to me. "You can give me the money tomorrow, if you like. You look like a girl who knows how to have a good time."

I stepped away. Suddenly, I very much wanted to return to the safety of Garfield House. I wished fervently that I hadn't gone outside on my own. If Karen were here, she'd know what to do.

The young man followed me. "C'mon, darlin'. You know you want some really."

Fortunately, anger came to my rescue. I glared up him. "Well. You're very much mistaken! Why would I want to take drugs? I'm not stupid, as you quite clearly are!"

The young man looked puzzled. "Hey! I was only offerin'!"

"Don't bother! Now, get out of my way. I have to find my friends."

I shoved him roughly with both hands and darted past, back inside the darkened hall, where the music and heat hit me like a sockful of wet sand.

Ignoring protests from irritated people, I shoved and pushed until I finally found Karen and Valerie. They were with two young men. Both were grinning like fools. I tugged Karen's sleeve.

"I'm going home!" I yelled.

"What? Why?" Karen shouted back.

"Some bloke just tried to sell me drugs!"

Karen sniggered. The young man standing next to her frowned.

"And I've got a headache," I added, hoping this would be a reasonable excuse.

Karen grabbed my arm and dragged me toward the cloakroom where the volume of music was a little lower.

"What's up? We only just got here! You'll never get a boyfriend if you go home now."

"I don't want a boyfriend! Karen, I can't hear myself think in here. It's too hot, the lights hurt my eyes and that bloke trying to sell me drugs has made me feel sick."

Karen shrugged. "Please yourself. I'm staying until half past ten. Neil is meeting us outside and walking home with us. It's only a quarter to nine now!"

"I'll see you later."

With no further ado, I collected my coat from the cloakroom and hurried to the main doors. There were several young people on the steps of the hall. All were laughing and chattering gaily. I mumbled 'excuse me' several times as I pushed between them and headed off, along the dark street toward the town centre.

The familiar smell coming from a fish and chip shop drew me and I wandered toward it, checking to see if I had enough money for a cone of chips. I paid little or no attention to several large motor-cycles parked against the kerb as I counted my small change.

I looked up and saw a large number of leather jacketed bikers crowded on the pavement outside the chip shop. They stepped aside as I approached.

"Nice coat, love," one of them said.

I glanced toward the man who had spoken. He looked about twenty five, although it was difficult to tell because he had a full beard and very long hair.

"Thanks."

Another biker spoke up. "Hope you're not all on your own, love. Not safe, walking the streets on your own, you know."

"I'll be all right, thanks. I only live a little way away." I stepped inside the chip shop and waited behind a couple of women.

"It's disgustin', is what it is," one of the women muttered.

"Shouldn't be allowed," the other agreed. "If I'd known they'd all be hangin' about 'ere, I'd have sent me ole' man fer the damned chips."

I quickly realised they were referring to the motor-cyclists outside. I glanced over my shoulder. The men weren't doing anything, just standing talking. One or two were smoking cigarettes and one was squatting down beside an enormous black motor-bike, fiddling with something.

The women gave their orders, collected their suppers and left. I turned and watched the bikers move aside to let them out of the shop.

When I'd bought my chips and added copious quantities of both salt and vinegar, I went to the door of the shop and stood there, looking at the man fiddling with his bike.

"Like bikes, do ya?" one man asked.

I stuffed a couple of chips in my mouth and nodded. When I'd chewed and swallowed them, I looked up at the man and said, "I've never been on one though. I bet it's an ace feeling."

The man's face cracked into a wide grin. I noticed he had a scar on the side of his face.

"Sure is, love. Best feeling in the world."

"Yeah. Until you fall off!" another man shouted.

Everyone laughed, including me.

"What's wrong with that bike?" I asked, nodding toward the man squatting on the kerb.

"I think it's a blocked fuel line. He'll soon have it sorted. We only stopped here because of that. You say you live locally? Are there any biker-friendly pubs around here?"

I shook my head. "Sorry. I've got no idea. I'm in a children's home up the road. I don't go into pubs ... I'm not old enough."

The bearded biker stepped forward, frowning. "What? You're under sixteen? What the devil is that home you're in thinking of to let you wander around the streets on your own at night?"

I glanced across the road at a large clock outside Littlewoods store. "It's not late. Only nine o'clock. I was supposed to be at the disco ... only ..."

"Ah. I see. Well, listen to me, love. You should go straight home. Don't hang about in the street like this. You never know when there could be trouble. I wouldn't let a kid of your age wander about the streets. Didn't you like the disco?"

I shrugged. "Not much. The music was too loud, the lights hurt my eyes and some bloke tried to sell me drugs!"

The bearded man scowled fiercely. "What? He needs his head kicking in for that! I hope you said no?"

I stuffed more chips into my mouth and nodded.

"Right. Where do you live, exactly, love?"

I swallowed the chips and pointed along the high street. "About two hundred yards past the level crossing down there. It's not far. I'm going home as soon as I've eaten these chips, I promise."

The man nudged another biker standing close by. "Give us your brain bucket for a moment, man."

I finished the chips and put the empty cone into the waste bin outside the chip shop. The bearded biker handed me a black, open-faced crash helmet.

"Here. Put this on. I'm taking you home. Right now."

I looped my shoulder bag over my head and accepted the crash helmet. It never occurred to me to be anxious or to refuse. I couldn't manage to fasten the strap under my chin. One of the bikers helped.

"You'll be all right with Jez, love. Best you go home. Hope you enjoy your ride!"

Jez went to a gleaming, black and chrome machine and stepped astride it. I watched as he kick-started it. The engine roared into life, the sound echoing up and down the street.

"Come on, kiddo. Hop on. Put your feet on those foot-rests there, hang on around my waist. If I lean to one side, you lean with me, all right? The bike won't fall over."

I scrambled astride the machine and wrapped my arms tightly around Jez's middle. He used his feet to edge the bike forward, away from the kerb.

"Tap me on the shoulder when we get to your home, all right?" he yelled, over the throbbing of the engine.

The bike pulled away smoothly and headed off along the high street. It was the most wonderful feeling! The wind whipped at my hair sticking out from beneath the crash helmet. As Jez leaned into the corner which led onto the Norwich Road, I remembered what he'd said and leaned with him.

All too quickly, the bike crossed the level crossing and I had to tap Jez on the shoulder to tell him we had arrived. He pulled up, right outside Garfield House. I scrambled off the bike and fumbled to undo the helmet.

Jez reached up and undid the catch for me. I lifted the helmet off and handed it to him.

"Thank you! Thank you so much! That was wonderful!"

"No problem, love. Glad to have been of service. Just you remember though. Don't go wandering about at night on your own. It might have been anybody outside the chip-shop tonight. And that's another thing ..." he grinned at me. "Don't accept lifts off strangers in future neither! You need to get more street-wise, girl. Carry on like you are and you'll get yourself raped or killed, understand?"

I nodded. "I knew you were all right, though."

"I might not have been. A lot of blokes would've taken advantage of you and your trusting nature."

Out of the corner of my eyes, I noticed a curtain move in the large, bay window at the front of Garfield House.

"But bikers and Hell's Angels have always been nice to me."

"Well ... I'd like to hope that they would. But just you remember, even some bikers and Hell's Angels aren't trustworthy. You be careful now. What's your name, love?"

"I'm Keri. And you're Jez. Thanks for looking after me, Jez. Bye!"

I turned and walked through the gateway.

"See ya, Keri!" Jez called.

I paused to watch as the motor-cycle roared away. When I moved to walk to the back door, I saw Neil hurrying toward me.

"Who was that? Have you been on a motor-bike? Why aren't you at the disco?"

"It's all right, Neil. I didn't like the disco. The music was too loud. I just bumped into a friend on the way home, that's all. He gave me a lift."

"Well. I suppose that's all right then. Who was the friend?"

"Just someone I met a year or so ago in Norwich," I lied. "He was on his way to ... well, anyway, his friend's bike broke down."

Neil escorted me into the house. "I'll make you a cup of cocoa in a while," he said. "I'm not sure what Paul and Joss will think about you going on a motor-bike. You can expect at the very least, a telling off. Next time, if you don't like something, go to a public call box and ring us. One of us will come and collect you, understand?"

I nodded.

"Right, go and hang your coat up. Then you can go in the play room and watch telly, if you want."

John and Adam were watching a film on the television. I flung myself into an armchair and tried to pay attention enough to understand what had happened so far.

"Why aren't you still at the disco?" Adam asked.

"I didn't like it. So I thought I'd come home, that's all."

John snorted with laughter. "You're right. You are weird, Keri. I thought all girls were mad for discos. I hate them. The music's too loud, they play all kinds of rubbish and there are too many people. And everyone stares at me."

John had more or less summed up how I felt about the disco experience.

"Some crazy bloke tried to sell me drugs as well."

Adam looked across at me and scratched his blond head. "What kind of drugs?"

I hesitated. What had that man said? "Er ... something called 'acid' and another thing called 'blow'."

Adam nodded. "That's LSD and cannabis. What did you say? Did you buy any?"

"Don't be stupid! Of course not!"

"Well. Make sure, Paul, Joss and Neil don't find out or no-one will ever be allowed to go out to the disco again."

I wondered why Adam had not gone to the disco, but I didn't ask. I settled down to watch the film, but I didn't really concentrate on it. I was far too busy remembering the sensation of being astride the big motor-cycle and the sense of freedom it gave me.

19. Neil: A Wolf In Sheep's Clothing

I think it was around the second or third week at Garfield House that Neil offered to dry my hair for me one evening. I had no plans to go out or do anything much other than slouch about in front of the television. I still found it a novelty to have the TV available to me every day until bed-time.

I'd had a bath and washed my hair and I arrived in the playroom - or children's sitting room - wearing my night clothes, dressing gown and a towel twisted round my head into a turban. Neil was watching a show with the teenagers; he looked up.

"Want me to dry your hair for you, Keri?"

"Pardon?"

"With the hair dryer. Hang on, I'll go and fetch it." Neil lifted himself from the armchair and trotted out of the room.

Sally was curled in the corner with a book. I hadn't had a lot to do with the girl as she kept herself apart from the rest of us. I did notice her glower at me and shake her head though. Before I could think of anything to say, Neil returned with a hand-held hair-dryer which he plugged in close to one of the side tables.

"Come on. Come and sit down here and we'll soon have your hair dry. It's not good for you to sit about with wet hair all evening."

I sat down in the upright chair and looked at the hair-dryer with curiosity. I'd never seen one before.

Sally looked up and scowled. "That's total rubbish and you know it! Leave her be!"

Neil smiled benignly at Sally. "Cheer up, Grouchy! Why don't you ask George to rub your back for you? I'm sure he's in the office with Paul and Joss." He untwisted the towel from my hair. "Good grief! What a mess of tangles you have here, Keri! Did you bring your comb downstairs?"

I shook my head.

"Never mind," said Neil, "I'll just get another one from the cupboard." He disappeared out of the room again.

"You should get to bed now, Keri, while you've got the chance," Sally's tone held a warning.

"Why?"

Before Sally could reply, Neil returned to the room. She shook her head and pretended to read once more. From the corner of my eye, I noticed Valerie whispering to Karen and my new friend shaking her head.

John stood up quite suddenly. "I'm going to bed."

"Good night, John, sleep well." Neil's voice sounded as if he were suppressing laughter as he began the unenviable task of combing out my thin, wet hair.

I found it a very strange sensation to have someone combing and drying my hair. The only people who had ever touched my hair were Mother or Nana. Whilst Nana did her best to get the snarls out gently, Mother had cruelly ripped the comb through the tangled strands, tugging and pulling with no regard to my comfort or protests of pain. This experience with Neil was altogether different from both.

Neil patiently teased the tangles out, working from the bottom of the hair up toward the roots. Not once did he tug or pull. Although Nana had always tried hard not to hurt me, it felt so strange to me. As Neil's hands brushed the nape of my neck once or twice, I shivered.

"Are you all right, Keri?" Neil sounded genuinely concerned.

I nodded but did not reply.

As Neil took up the dryer and began to blow warm air onto my hair, which he lifted and held out at an angle, I shivered again. It felt very pleasant indeed. I was only fourteen and extremely naive. I had no idea that this was a ritual which would lead to other things and so I enjoyed the experience.

When my hair was dry, Neil patted me on the shoulder and told me to go and take a look in the mirror which hung in the wide hallway. I gathered my dressing gown around me and re-fastened the tie-belt which had become loose as I sat - and trotted out of the room.

I could barely recognise the girl in the mirror. Her hair was beautiful! I'd never seen my hair anything but straight and lank, even immediately after washing it. The dryer and Neil's hands had lifted it at the roots and it looked fluffy and tumbled past my shoulders in a fine haze. Somehow, it looked as if my volume of hair had increased by about tenfold! I grinned with delight.

"You could do with the ends trimming a bit really," Neil patted my behind. "Even so, it looks really nice. It's a lovely colour."

"Thank you so much, Neil!" I exclaimed. "It does look really good. How did you manage it?"

Neil tapped the side of his nose in a conspiratorial manner. "That's my special secret," he grinned. "I think it deserves a hug, don't you?"

I flung my arms about him and hugged him before dashing back into the playroom to see what Karen thought.

She looked up at me from her position on a settee and frowned. "Yeah, I suppose it looks all right, but it makes you look a lot older. You'll pay for it though, you see if you don't."

"Whatever do you mean?" I squeezed between Valerie and Karen on the settee.

"You'll find out," muttered Karen, darkly. "I suppose I should have warned you, but it slipped my mind. It's been a while now."

"What has? What are you talking about?"

Neil came back into the room. "Anybody like a cup of cocoa?"

Everybody asked for a cup, including me.

"Ah. I'll need a hand, then. Come on, Karen. You can come and help. I'll give you an extra biscuit as well, how does that sound?"

"No, thanks. I'm watching this. Valerie will help you."

I sat between the girls as they both tried to avoid helping Neil. I thought their behaviour very odd. I opened my mouth to offer my help, but Karen kicked my shin hard. I glared at her.

"All right. I'm sure I'll manage on my own." Neil left the room.

I turned to Karen. "What did you do that for? It hurt!"

Karen nodded. "Good. But it got your attention. I want to talk to you, that's all. Anyway, if you go out to the kitchen with him, he'll try to ... you know ..."

Puzzled, I shook my head. "What? I don't know! He's so nice, yet you talk as if he's some kind of ... bully or something."

Valerie snorted and Adam leaned over from the other settee as if to better hear what Karen said.

"Oh no, not a bully. Bullying is the last thing he'll do to you!" Karen looked furious.

I sighed. "Just tell me!"

"He'll get in your knickers."

This remark came from Adam. I noted the smirk on his face as he spoke.

"What? Don't be crude! That's horrible! He's always so nice ... to all of us!"

Karen scowled. "You haven't learned a damned thing, have you? No-one is ever nice to kids like us without a reason! Adam's right. He'll get in your knickers and worse! How do you think Sally got pregnant?" This last remark came in a lowered tone and hissed between Karen's teeth.

"What? But ... you said she's going out with George and ..."

"Stop talking about me!" Sally raised her voice. "It's none of your business who I'm going out with! Just shut up about it. You're only jealous, Karen!"

Karen stood up and glared at Sally. "No! I'm not jealous actually. I'm just not a slapper and a stupid tart like you!"

Before anyone else could say anything, Sally launched herself from her chair and rushed across the room. With one hand she grabbed Karen's short, curly hair, dragging her head to the side. The other hand came round in a fist and hit Karen square on the nose.

For her own part, even though she was off balance, Karen threw a punch or two of her own, connecting to Sally's ear, which made the enraged girl scream in fury.

Valerie and I managed to wriggle out of the way and move across the room whilst the two girls slapped, punched and kicked at one another. My heart pounded in my chest but I could not bring myself to get involved. Apart from anything else, I didn't want to get hurt. Blood streamed from Karen's nose as she writhed away from Sally's grip.

Neil rushed into the room and immediately began to try and separate the girls. A heartbeat later, Paul and Joss appeared at the doorway. Paul darted forward and grabbed hold of Karen, hauling her bodily away from Sally, who strained in Neil's grip.

"She called me a slut! I'm not putting up with that!" Sally screeched into Neil's face.

Karen remained quite still as Paul held her. "No. I didn't call you a slut. I said you're a slapper and a stupid tart!"

"Enough!" Paul shouted.

I cringed. I felt Valerie's hand groping to snatch mine. I clung to that hand as if my life depended upon it.

"My office. Now!" Paul roared.

Neil manhandled Sally past me and Valerie; Paul let go of Karen and gave her a small shove between the shoulder blades. "Go on! Move!"

Karen stood still and turned a defiant face to Paul.

"So make me! There's nothing you can say that I want to hear! She is stupid and she's clearly a slapper - or she wouldn't be pregnant by one of your workers!"

Paul's face darkened. I noticed a vein throbbing in his temple. "Just you shut that filthy mouth of yours, young lady, and get yourself into my office or you'll be very sorry indeed!"

Karen folded her arms. "No. And you can't make me sorry!"

I held my breath. I felt certain Karen would be hit, but Paul simply sighed and gently shoved at Karen's back again. "Very well. Up to your room. No television or sweets for one week; you won't be going out for a week either. Off you go. I've got to go and calm Sally down."

"That's not fair!" Karen yelled. "*She* hit *me!*"

"Yes, but you made nasty, provocative remarks. I'm not surprised she hit you, to be honest. That was an awful thing to say to her. Now, go to your room before I add to your punishments. Joss will come and see to your face, although I think your nose has already stopped bleeding."

Karen opened her mouth as if to reply, but either thought better of it or decided to humour Paul. She dragged the back of her hand under her nose, stared at the smear of blood and marched out of the room.

"You two can finish making the cocoa," Paul indicated me and Valerie. "Karen won't be having one. You can have a couple of biscuits each, then when you've washed the cups, you can all go to bed."

He left the room.

Adam turned back to the television screen, saying nothing. Valerie tugged at my hand.

"Come on, let's finish the cocoa."

I allowed Valerie to tow me toward the kitchen. I felt shocked and confused. I'd never seen such defiance before - except my own attempts to defy Mother, which always ended in violence.

I didn't help at all but stood owlish as Valerie poured hot water onto the cocoa set out in mugs on the table. She filled them all.

"But Paul said ..."

"I don't care," Valerie sniffed. "I'll take hers up to her in her room. He won't know. They'll all be in the office for hours mollycoddling Sally. It's all her fault!"

I opened the biscuit tin and peered inside. "I still don't understand what it was all about. And I thought Paul was gonna hit Karen. I was scared, Valerie – and I don't mind admitting it."

Valerie put three cups on a tray and took the lid of the biscuit tin from my unresisting fingers. "He might have hit her. You never really know with Paul. Although, usually, if he's gonna hit someone, he makes sure either Joss or Mrs. Webster are there as witnesses. He must be in a good mood or something." Valerie replaced the lid of the biscuit tin and placed it on the tray with the cups.

"Carry that through to the playroom. I'm taking this up to Karen. I'll be back in a minute."

She took up the fourth cup and hurried from the kitchen. I stared at the tray for a moment or two before lifting and carrying it, very carefully, because my hands were shaking, into the playroom.

Adam looked up. "Oh, good. I wondered if you'd bring the biscuit tin. Karen always puts a few on a plate."

I set the tray down on a low table and helped myself to a cup of cocoa.

Adam took a handful of biscuits and leaned back on the settee. "I guess you learned a bit about Sally tonight, eh?"

I nodded. "I thought she was quite nice until she attacked Karen. She's very quiet though."

"Quiet ones are always the worst," Adam replied, dipping a chocolate biscuit into his cocoa. "I suppose Valerie's taken Karen a drink?"

I nodded. Adam grinned. "Paul knows full well she would do that, you know. He also knows that we'll all share our sweets with Karen this week. They can't stop us. We have to stick together sometimes, even if we don't like each other all that much. I saw Karen give Sally a really good thump alongside the ear. I hope it knocks some sense into the silly, snooty little cow."

I sipped at my cocoa. "You don't like Sally?"

"No-one does. She is a slapper, just like Karen said. And that other thing Karen was trying to tell you is true as well. If it's not Neil, then it'll be George, maybe even Paul."

I hung my head. "Is it really true, Adam? They've all been so nice to me ever since I came here. I'm sure none of them would hurt me."

Adam shook his head. "You're not too bright, are you, Keri? They won't thrash you or beat you or anything like that, but they all do stuff we don't like. I tried telling my social worker about it but all I got was punishment; no-one believed me. So now, I just keep my head down, do as I'm told and keep my mouth shut. I won't be here much longer anyway. I'll be fostered out somewhere I expect."

I swallowed. "So; you're telling me that stuff happens here but no-one will do anything about it?"

Adam nodded. "Yep. They won't believe you. You've gotta remember. We're 'troubled' kids, us lot. Liars, thieves and worse. Who's gonna listen to a liar?"

I thought for a while. Suddenly, Garfield House didn't seem like such a wonderful place to be after all. I no longer wanted the cocoa.

"I think I'll go to bed now."

"Wash your cup before you go. Or you'll have Mrs. Webster after you in the morning. Night, Keri."

I washed, dried and put away my cup before making my way up the stairs. As I crept past Valerie and Karen's room, I could hear low voices. I didn't knock on the door or even pause to listen.

I took off my dressing gown and crawled into bed. Although I had a book to read, I just lay and stared at the ceiling for quite a long period of time. I don't know what I was thinking, if anything.

I jumped when I heard a gentle tapping on the outside of my door. Before I could answer, the door opened and Neil peered into the room.

"Are you all right, Keri?"

"Yes."

"That must have been quite upsetting for you to witness. Luckily, it doesn't happen too often."

Neil entered the room and sat on the end of my bed.

"It's all right."

Neil studied me for a few seconds. "Well. It's not all right at all. We don't encourage fighting or violence here at Garfield House. Joss tells me that you had a rough time at home and that your Mother and step-father hit you often. Is that right?"

I nodded.

"Well, I just want to reassure you that it won't happen here. Not even if there are fights between the kids. Understand?"

I nodded again.

Neil stood up and came to stand beside the bed. He straightened my covers for me and brushed my hair back off my forehead.

"Try to get some sleep. It will all be fine by the morning."

I tensed, waiting for ... I didn't know what I was waiting for.

Neil smiled and turned away.

"Good night, Keri. Sleep well."

He left the room, closing the door quietly behind him.

20. The First House Meeting

I'd been at Garfield House for about a month when Mrs. Webster announced there would be a 'house meeting' that evening. She further informed us that any plans we had made for the evening would need to be put back.

I noticed the expression of disgust on Karen's face, although she said nothing whilst Mrs. Webster was in the room. Valerie shook her head and began to eat, also saying nothing.

When Mrs. Webster went to fetch something from the kitchen, I nudged Karen.

"What's the matter? What is this meeting thing and why do you look so cross about it? Were you planning on going out?"

Karen scowled. "You'll find out for yourself later on. All I'm gonna say is keep your trap shut. If they pick on you, only say the least you can get away with."

This didn't give me any answers. I opened my mouth to ask further questions, but Mrs. Webster re-entered the room and Karen frowned at me. I subsided and tucked in to the hearty breakfast in front of me. I couldn't imagine what the problem could be.

On the way to school, I asked Karen and Valerie for more detail. Valerie blushed and hung her head; Karen growled a reply.

"It's all about sex. They want us all to talk about sex. It happens every month or so."

"Really? I don't know anything about sex!"

"Ha! You will do!"

Valerie stared at her feet as we plodded toward the school gates. "I hate it," she muttered. "One day, I'm gonna run away from here!"

"Me too," Karen mumbled.

"Where would we go?" I asked.

251

Karen shrugged. "Doesn't really matter where we go so long as we go. We could go together, all three of us."

Valerie looked hopeful. "When? Today?"

Karen shook her head. "Not today. We haven't got any money and anyway, they'll be more or less expecting it today won't they? You ran last month, just before Keri came."

As we hung our coats up in the school cloakroom, I looked at Valerie with new eyes.

"You ran away last month? You didn't say!"

Valerie shrugged. "Nothing to say really. I didn't get far. Paul picked me up and took me back to the house, that's all. I cried a bit and said some stupid stuff about my family and they left it at that."

I felt intrigued and wondered why neither girl had mentioned this escapade before, but I had no time to ask because the bell rang for lessons.

In just a couple of weeks I had learned that it didn't sit well with the other students in the class if I did well in my school work. Apart from anything else, if I worked hard and produced quality homework, it rather negated my claim to be a trouble-maker and dangerous. This was a shame because I really enjoyed a lot of the lessons and I put much more effort into not doing well than I would have if I'd simply worked!

Several staff members spoke to me. They usually made comments along the lines of knowing that I could do much better and wondering why I did not apply myself to the set work. If the comment was made in front of the class, I simply shrugged or stared rudely away in the opposite direction. If the interview was personal I usually muttered 'sorry' or some other platitude. In all truth, I regretted what I'd said to the other girls in order to remain unmolested; I should have liked to throw myself into the school work instead.

After school, I accompanied Valerie and Karen on the short walk back to Garfield House. Both girls were subdued and seemed irritable and anxious. Their mood infected me to some degree.

All too soon, the afternoon wore away, we'd had the evening meal, cleared up and the little ones had been bathed and put to bed. An atmosphere of gloom and impending doom hung over the playroom as we sat waiting to be summoned to Paul's office. The television was on, but I didn't pay any attention to it; I'm not sure anyone did.

When Joss came to tell us that the meeting was about to start, she looked flushed and had a strange expression on her face which I couldn't identify. She stood in the doorway of the playroom as we all filed past her and entered the large room which doubled as sitting room and office.

I noticed the way the room was lit as we entered. The main overhead light was not on but several side lamps glowed softly. The room had a faint orange tint, accentuated by the fake flames of the fire.

I sat down in an armchair and looked around at the others. Karen had a fierce scowl on her face; Valerie looked close to tears. I glanced across at Adam, who looked resigned. John sat in a chair as far away from everyone else that he could find and I noticed his head nodding and his lips moving silently. After a few seconds, I realised he was repeating the words of the Witchdoctor Song over and over to himself.

Sally looked the most relaxed. She sprawled on a sofa with her legs outstretched. George sat next to her. She leaned her head on his shoulder and I watched as he slipped his arm around her. Sally looked content, but she could not see George's face. I could; he looked very fed up, bored almost.

I became aware of soft music playing and I concentrated on hearing the words. I had no idea what to expect at all, but judging from the body language and the expressions on the faces of my peers, it would not be enjoyable. I began to feel very anxious myself.

Paul sat at his desk, studying some paperwork. He did not turn to look at or speak to any of us. Joss sat down close to him; I noticed she twisted her fingers together and I wondered if she felt anxious as well.

The door opened and Neil came into the room with a large tray full of steaming cups which he set down on the coffee table in the centre of the room.

"Coffee all round. Help yourselves to milk and sugar. I'll just pop and get the biscuit tin," Neil exited the room again.

Joss immediately stood up and added milk and sugar to two cups. She carried one to Paul and sat down again, cupping the mug in her hands.

I waited until all the others had helped themselves and Neil had returned before I stood up to get one of the cups for myself. I didn't like coffee much, but I did not want to look childish or feel left out.

Paul looked up, once Neil had sat down with his own cup.

"Right. Here we are again. We've had a fairly quiet month; only one fight and only one call to the school to sort out Karen's problems."

I saw Karen's face darken with suppressed anger, but she said nothing.

"So," continued Paul, "How are things at school now, Karen? Everything sorted out?"

"S'All right, I suppose," Karen sounded sulky.

Joss leaned forward a little. "Only 'all right'? You haven't been attacked again, have you, Karen?"

Karen shook her head.

Paul turned his attention to me. "How about you, Keri? How are you getting along at the school?"

I sought for something to say. "It's better than my last school."

Paul smiled. "Well. That's good. Have you made any new friends yet?"

I shook my head.

"Never mind, I'm sure you will do. Have you made any other friends, in the town perhaps? You've been going out with Karen and Valerie a fair amount, haven't you?"

Again, I shook my head.

"That's strange," Neil interrupted. "That you've not made any other friends, Keri. You're not shy, are you?"

"Not really. It's just ... well ... most people are a bit ... I don't know ..." my voice tailed off. I noticed Karen flashing me a furious glance.

"I understand." Paul smiled. "I know it isn't easy for kids living in a place like this. Other people don't understand and get suspicious. It can be difficult to deal with. Just remember, Keri. If you have any problems, come and talk to one of us about them. We'll do what we can to help and advise you."

I nodded and sipped at my coffee. It tasted bitter; I wished I'd put some sugar in it but I didn't feel able to draw attention to myself by getting up and doing so at that time.

"Right." Paul turned and shuffled through some papers on his desk. "Adam. It looks like we might have found a possible foster home for you. As soon as we hear any news we'll let you know. Are you looking forward to leaving and going to live with some new parents?"

"I can't wait," Adam muttered.

"Good, good," Paul beamed. He ignored the sarcasm in Adam's tone. "I understand the family already have one foster son but he'll be leaving them soon. There are other children in the home as well. I'm sure it will all be perfect for you. The family live just outside Norwich."

I think if it had been me about to move into a foster-home, I would have been brimming with questions, but Adam seemed disinterested, which I thought was surely strange.

Paul turned his attention to Sally. "And how are you, Sally? Everything going along all right? Has your morning sickness eased up a little?"

"Not really," Sally replied. "I feel sick almost all day. I'm either throwing up or stuffing my face. I'm still getting big, though. Can I have some maternity dresses soon?"

"I can ask the doctor if there is anything they can give you for the sickness, Sally," Joss said. "It has gone on for rather a long time. As for the maternity clothes, the grant came through just yesterday, so we can go shopping at the weekend, if you like."

Sally smiled. "Thanks, Joss. Can George come too?" She turned her head on George's shoulder to look up at him. "You want to help me choose some maternity clothes, don't you, George?"

"Uh ... if I'm not working, I'll come, honey-bun." George forced a smile.

Sally snuggled closer to him, but he looked uncomfortable to me.

Paul spoke to each of us in turn. I lost interest and listened to the music, letting Paul's voice drone on in the background. I dimly recall hearing something about a holiday in the summer, but I really paid little attention.

" ... my old friend ... I've come to talk to you again ..." the music was soothing and pleasant. I'd never heard any of these songs before. " ... because a vision softly creeping, left its seeds while I was sleeping ... and the vision that was planted in my brain ..."

"So ... who can tell me about masturbation?" Paul's voice had increased in volume. I jumped and looked around me guiltily.

No-one spoke.

"Come on! One of you must be able to talk to us about it. How about you, John?"

I glanced at John. His lips still moved and his head nodded ever more vigorously.

"John!" Paul bellowed.

John stopped moving and muttering to himself and stared at Paul. "What?"

"Masturbation, John. What is it, how is it done and why?"

"Dunno."

Paul sighed theatrically. "For goodness sake, John! Are you even in the same room with us? This is serious. Every young person needs to know how to masturbate properly!"

A slow grin began to form on John's face. "Cut it off and put it in a pie," he said.

Sally giggled, but Paul frowned. "You're not taking this meeting seriously, John! I've just told you about a holiday we are all going to have next year and then you are facetious when I ask you a perfectly civilised question. A sensible answer, lad. Right now, please!"

I saw panic spread across John's face; then he simply seemed to shut down. He resumed his nodding and mouthing of the Witchdoctor Song. For a few seconds, everyone stared at him saying nothing. Then Paul shook his head and turned to me.

"Right, Keri. You tell us about masturbation instead, please."

I swallowed. I had never heard the word before and I had no idea what it meant. I swallowed and glanced over at Karen, who resolutely refused to look at me. Not wishing to appear stupid, I shrugged and said, clearly, "Why me?"

"Because you are of the age when you should know, Keri. So tell us, what do you do to pleasure yourself?"

"Well I like reading and I draw quite a lot. Sometimes I write poetry, although it's not very good."

Joss shook her head and Paul glared at me. "So, you're being smart as well are you? How does not going out at all for a week and no sweets sound?"

Confused, I stared back at Paul. "Why? What have I done? I don't understand!"

"She doesn't know what you mean, Paul," Joss spoke quietly.

"That's because she's stupid!" Sally interrupted. "You don't know what masturbation means, do you?"

I turned toward the older girl and noted her smug, self-satisfied expression. Since I already looked more than stupid, I had nothing to lose.

"All right! So I don't know what it means! But I still haven't done anything wrong!"

"All right! All right! There's no need for that attitude," Paul intervened. "Why didn't you simply say you didn't know, Keri?"

I shrugged. "Didn't want to look stupid, I suppose."

"Right. Well, let's ask Valerie instead. Come on, Valerie. I know you know the answer to the question. You can tell us all about it."

I sat for the next hour, squirming in my seat and feeling more anxious and uncomfortable than I ever had in my life before as Valerie haltingly described things I had never imagined. It sounded dirty, filthy and sickening to me. The songs I'd heard earlier played over again. I tried to shut out the room and the tremulous voice, but I failed. I began to feel sick to my stomach.

Eventually, Valerie faltered to silence.

"Anyone got anything to add to all that?" Paul smiled at all of us. No-one spoke.

"Right then. That will do for this month. Off you go. You can all have cocoa and biscuits before bed. Neil, would you see to that please?"

I couldn't wait to get out of the room. Without looking at Valerie or Karen - or anyone else, I fled to my room, taking the stairs three at a time.

"Look at that!" Paul called. "She knows now and can't wait to try it all out!"

I heard laughter as I raced along the landing. My head was swimming and I wanted to find somewhere safe. In the absence of a hole to crawl into, my bedroom seemed the safest bet.

I flung myself onto my bed and pulled a pillow over my head. Although Valerie's words had been halting and often she stammered, she had described things I'd had no idea about at all. At least it now made sense to me why men wanted to do things to girls, although I could not begin to imagine the things Valerie had described.

Apparently, sex was supposed to be pleasurable. From all I had heard, it seemed I should be thinking of sex all the time and finding ways in which to make myself feel 'good'. I couldn't bear the idea of having to touch myself, especially not in the ways Valerie had described. As for the way she had described how boys masturbated, I had very unpleasant memories of Terry and the things he made me do. My stomach churned. If he could have done those things for himself, I wondered, why then did he force me to do it for him?

I struggled to understand everything I'd heard and wondered if I would ever stop hearing the echoes of all Valerie had been forced to say.

I jumped when I heard someone knocking on my door and sat up. The knocking continued without pause. Eventually, I stood up and crossed the room.

"Who is it?"

The knocking continued. I opened the door.

John stood there, his hand raised to knock some more. He frowned at me when I said nothing at first.

"What do you want?" I asked.

John lowered his hand. "Your cocoa is ready. Neil said I must come and get you."

"Oh. Well, I don't want any cocoa. I'm going to bed."

John regarded me stolidly. "You have to come down anyway. I know how you feel. It's horrible but it's over now for another month or so. Don't get like me about it or you'll have to pretend you're mental like I do."

"So, you're not really 'weird' or 'mental' then?"

"Don't tell anyone."

I warmed to John and actually felt a little admiration for him. It made me realise for the first time that I was not the only resident of Garfield House pretending to be something I wasn't.

"You do it very well. I won't say anything, I promise."

John grinned. "You do a pretty good job of being hard as nails yourself. You can look truly evil when you glare. Those girls at school are scared stiff of you."

I followed John along the landing and down the stairs to the dining room.

"Hello, Keri. I thought you wouldn't want to miss out. We've got cakes!" Neil offered me a steaming cup of cocoa as I entered the room.

I took the cup and watched John weave round all the tables one by one before coming back to the table by the door. I hid a smile as I sipped at the cocoa. He really was very clever at pretending to be mad.

21. Trouble Is My Middle Name

Although life at Garfield House continued as 'normal', I was deeply disturbed by everything Valerie had been forced to say about masturbation during the meeting. Everyone I encountered I regarded with disgusted suspicion. I resolutely decided that I would never, ever do any of the things I had heard described.

These feelings certainly got in the way of any normal interaction I may have had with most people I met. Completely unaware of how I came across to people, I privately sneered at everyone, thinking they had no idea at all of my thoughts and feelings. I actually thought everyone was utterly disgusting and depraved. Unknown to me, this showed clearly on my face.

At school, everyone, except Karen, Valerie and fat Gordon avoided me as completely as possible. The girls - the ones John had told me were terrified of me - kept away, but if they had to speak to me, they were incredibly polite. As for boys, they left me well alone. I experienced none of the teasing banter or laughter which other girls often seemed to enjoy.

This had a beneficial effect on my work. I found that I could produce excellent quality class work and homework with no remarks made at all. I began to enjoy school - except for the cookery lessons, which I hated with a passion.

One Tuesday, I moaned to Karen as we walked to school.

"I wish I could think of a way to get out of cookery. I hate it. I might pretend I'm ill and get the staff to send me home. What do you think?"

Karen grinned. "That won't work. They'll make you sit in the office all day with a bucket. I've got a better idea. Meet me at break by the water fountain. I'll see if Valerie wants to come too."

As it turned out, Valerie did not wish to join us because she really enjoyed cookery. I gave her the food ingredients I'd been supplied with that morning by Mrs. Webster and hurried to meet Karen.

We lingered by the water fountain for most of the break period. When the bell rang and students began to rush back toward the classrooms, Karen grabbed my hand.

"Come on! This way!"

Together, we darted down between the school buildings and the high hedge. Dragging me along behind her, Karen sprinted a short distance along the edge of the playing field until we came to a gap in the hedge. She shoved me in front of her.

"Quick! Get through there before anyone sees us from the windows!"

I scrambled through the hedge, snagging my school jumper on twigs and thorns. I found myself in a wide, concrete area filled with coaches.

Karen stumbled through the hedge behind me, glanced about and ran toward a large red and orange coach. I followed her and watched as she pressed something on the side of the bus. The door hissed open.

"Come on! We can sit in here until lunch time, or all day if you want. I brought some crisps and sweets. I was gonna try and pinch a couple of sausage rolls, but there were too many dinner ladies in the canteen when I went there."

We made our way right to the back of the coach and sat down on the plush seats.

"I've got 'Jackie' magazine in here somewhere," Karen rummaged in her bag. "It's last week's but it will keep us busy for a while."

I peered out of the back window of the coach. "What if the driver comes back?"

"He won't. These coaches are here all day, every day. We'll be fine. I've done this before ... loads of times."

We curled up on the seats and ate the crisps Karen had brought with her as we chatted about nothing very much at all. The time flew by and I felt surprised when Karen suddenly glanced at her watch and announced it was lunch-time back at school.

"So we have to go back through the hedge?"

"Nah. We'll walk out of the coach park and around past the shop. There'll be loads of kids hanging about by the shop and the chip-shop further down the road. Everyone will assume we've just been out to get sweets or something."

We brushed the crisp crumbs onto the floor, collected our rubbish and left the coach. Karen pressed the button to close the door behind us.

"There. No-one will know we were ever here."

Nobody said anything at all about our absence from the cookery class. At home, when Valerie produced a very large apple pie, Karen told Mrs. Webster we'd eaten ours and this was accepted without question.

The coach park became a regular haunt for me and Karen, sometimes Valerie as well. We planned our days according to what lessons we wished to avoid. For me, cookery was the only thing I really detested. I knew Valerie and Karen avoided other lessons, but knowing that meant I never asked Gordon or anyone else where they were.

In the evenings, I went frequently to a coffee bar with Karen and Valerie. We drank frothy milk shakes, giggled and laughed together over nothing and generally behaved much the same way as all the other teenagers we saw.

One evening, a very tall, slim young man with a close resemblance to Elvis Presley approached the table where we were sitting.

"Hi. I've seen you girls in here a lot recently. Do you live locally?"

Karen stopped laughing and looked the young man up and down. "Who wants to know?"

"I do." He turned an empty chair and sat astride it, resting his arms on the chair back. "I'm Anthony. What are your names?"

Karen hesitated. Then she nudged Valerie and said, "This is Valerie."

"Hello," Valerie mumbled.

I scowled at Anthony.

"Ah. And this is Keri," Karen continued.

"What about you? What's your name?"

"Karen. Now, did you actually want anything? We've got to go home in a minute and you're taking up our time."

I grinned at this open snub, even though I thought the youth was quite attractive.

Anthony seemed unperturbed. "Just thought I'd like to get to know such pretty girls; that's all."

"Well. Now you know our names. We're busy. Where's your girlfriend? She dumped you or something? You're spoken for, aren't you?"

Anthony shrugged. "What if I am? It doesn't mean I can't talk to other people. I like your coat, Keri. It suits you."

Karen stood up. "Come on, you two. We'd better get back."

Without another word, both Valerie and I left our seats and followed Karen to the door.

"See you again, girls!" Anthony grinned widely. I noticed he had beautiful, even, white teeth.

"Don't say anything!" Karen hissed as she opened the door.

We walked back to Garfield House in the chilly December air.

"Who is he, Karen?" I asked.

"The local pretty boy. He is to be avoided. He has an enormously fat, aggressive and possessive girlfriend. She has a reputation for clouting people she thinks he fancies."

I thought about this for a few moments. "What school does she go to? Ours?"

Karen grinned. "She doesn't go to school, idiot! He's nineteen. I think she's about eighteen. Anyway, she works in the supermarket. She's usually in the coffee bar with him. You must have seen her? Fat, with long, orange hair. She always wears clothes that are about two sizes too small for her and her fat rolls hang over the top of her jeans."

I recalled the girl Karen had described. She was nearly always in the coffee bar, talking too loudly, laughing raucously or making rude remarks to other people at the top of her voice.

"Why on earth would a bloke like him be going with her?"

"From what I heard, she's a bit of a bike," Valerie interrupted. "I think she's slept with just about every bloke in town. She'll get fed up with him after a few months and sink her fat paws into some other poor victim."

I shuddered. It was bad enough imagining normal people indulging in sex and masturbation, but the thought of the fat girl having sex with Anthony truly disgusted me.

In the weeks leading up to Christmas, Anthony spoke to us at every opportunity. Whenever his fat girlfriend was absent from the coffee bar, he made his way over to us and struck up a conversation. I learned he lived at home with his mother; his father had died some four years previously. He worked at a local garage as a trainee mechanic ... and he loved motorbikes.

My own interest in motorbikes soon became apparent. Several times, Anthony brought magazines and brochures over to where we sat in the corner and enthusiastically chatted about them. I read avidly and gazed at pictures of gleaming machines, often asking questions, which Anthony readily answered.

He told us that he very nearly had enough money saved to pay the deposit on a Norton 750 Commando. He showed us a well thumbed and rather greasy copy of the sales brochure for the bike.

Two days before Christmas, as Karen, Valerie and I were leaving the coffee shop, we heard the deep throb of a large motorcycle approaching from behind us. We stopped and turned to stare.

The enormous, black machine pulled up outside the coffee shop and the tall, lean figure turned out to be Anthony when his head emerged from under a black crash helmet.

"Got it!" he called to us. "Come and see!"

Without hesitation, I raced back to admire Anthony's latest acquisition. Karen and Valerie followed more slowly.

"Oooh! Anthony! It's beautiful! Is it heavy?"

"Heavier than I'm used to at the moment. I only had a one two five before this. But I'll soon get used to it. Sit on it, if you want."

He hauled the machine onto its main centre stand and twisted the throttle so the engine revved loudly. It made even more noise than the bike I'd ridden on with Jez. I grinned and scrambled astride it, flicking my long coat behind me so it partially covered the rear wheel.

"You're a biker born," remarked Anthony approvingly as I twisted the throttle and felt the power of the engine between my knees. "You'll need to get yourself a decent leather jacket though. I can't take you for a ride in that coat, it would catch and we'd be off in a trice!"

I beamed up at Anthony. "You'll take me for a ride? That'd be wonderful!"

Anthony leaned around me and hugged me with both arms until I gasped for breath. "I sure will! You're so pretty and I like you a lot. Apart from anything else, you like my bike! I'd like to think perhaps you like me as well ... just a little bit?"

I twisted in Anthony's hug. "Yeah. I like you. You're all right. And I don't just like your bike, I love it!"

Anthony released me and stepped back. "Get hold of a leather as soon as you can and we'll go for a spin, all right?"

I nodded as I clambered off the machine. "I'll do my best. I can't wait! See you, Anthony. I've got to go home now."

"See you, Keri. Have a good Christmas."

I bounced along, beside Karen and Valerie. "That's just the most beautiful bike I've ever seen!"

"And it's probably the most beautiful mistake you'll ever make," Karen retorted. "If that fat cow finds out you've been anywhere near Anthony, there'll be trouble, count on it."

I stopped walking and glared at Karen. "Why? I haven't done anything. It's the bike I like. I suppose Anthony is all right, but I'm not interested in him."

Karen shrugged and we continued walking.

As we approached the level crossing gates, Karen nudged me urgently. "Look out! You might try telling her you're not interested in her boyfriend!"

The fat girl attacked me so fast, I hardly knew what had happened. I saw a brief flurry of orange hair, blue coat and heavy make-up before the punch landed square on my nose. I stumbled backwards and fell over, landing on the railway tracks. My head was spinning and blood poured from my nose and a split lip, cascading all down my beautiful Afghan coat.

"You stupid little tart!" the fat girl roared, rushing toward me as I lay prone. "I'll kick your bleedin' head in!"

I shook my head, spraying droplets of blood in all directions and tried to gain my feet, but before I'd even got halfway upright, the girl kicked me viciously in the ribs and I stumbled again, gasping for air.

"Bloody hell!" I heard Karen shout as the world spun dizzyingly about me. "You can't do that! Valerie! Grab her! Help me stop her!"

There was a scuffle and some loud cursing, during which time I found my feet. I struggled upright, shaking my head again, trying to dispel the sick, dizzy feeling. Blood ran warm into my mouth and down my chin. I stared at Karen trying to restrain the fat girl. There was no sign of Valerie.

As I hesitated, the girl got away from Karen and came at me again. I saw the ham-sized fist this time and ducked, but I was dizzy and the movement sent me reeling and retching. I spat out a mouthful of blood.

"I'll kill you! I'm gonna kill you!" the fat girl screeched.

Something seemed to go 'snap' inside my head. I stood up straight, retched hard and balled my hands into fists. "Not if I kill you first, you fat cow! You're insane!"

I swung a punch and barely noticed it connect. In fact, I thought I'd missed, so I swung again, with the other fist. This time, I felt a sharp, stabbing pain as the girl's teeth cut my knuckles open. She stumbled backward a few steps.

"How dare you!" she bellowed. "You'll not get away with hitting me, you little care-home tramp!" She surged forward and lunged at me again.

The punch glanced the side of my head. I ignored it, making a swipe with my right hand, which distracted the girl. She ducked right into my left hand, which I used reflexively to grab hold of her long, orange hair at the front, right above her forehead. I drew my right fist back and pounded it into her face, once, twice, I don't know how many times.

The girl kicked and writhed and screamed, but I had learned the grip on the hair from Mother and I couldn't have let go, even had I been inclined to. I felt the impact of the girl's foot on my knee. Rather than release her, I shoved her backward and took a swing with my own right leg - which had plenty of experience of kicking hard, having learned drop-kicks from footballers.

My foot caught the girl full in the crotch and she screamed in agony. I took the opportunity to haul her face around to my own.

I cannot explain exactly how I felt. At the time, I put the fact that everything seemed to be tinged red to having blood in my eyes. Now I know it was pure, unadulterated rage which gripped me. I'd been thrashed and beaten all my life and never been able to retaliate effectively. Something inside me had broken and my fury knew no bounds. I wanted to kill her. I saw her cut and bleeding face, her tangled hair, a few long hanks of which were clinging to her coat and the look of terror and horror in her pale eyes. I spat a mouthful of blood into her face and drew my fist back for the punch which would finally slay my attacker.

Suddenly, I struggled against strong arms that gripped me. I made animal noises as my left hand was torn from the girl's hair and I growled like an enraged dog when I found my arms pinned to my sides and I was lifted bodily off my feet.

The fat girl sank to her knees, gasping and spitting both blood and teeth. A pool of blood appeared between her legs and began to spread. I laughed like a maniac and struggled in the vice-like grip which held me. Dimly, I heard Neil's voice, as if it were coming from a very long way away.

Gradually, the red mist cleared and even though I still felt dizzy and disorientated, I was able to see a large crowd of people gathered. I allowed my body to go limp; only then did I become aware of the pain I felt and the fact that my breath was unsteady and my side hurt unbearably with every indrawn gulp of air.

"It was her what started it, I saw it!" A woman called out. "Them three girls was just walkin' along and that fat girl just flew at them and attacked. I thought she'd knocked that girl out! Who'd have thought anyone so slight could cause that much damage, eh?" She chuckled.

Another woman standing beside her added. "She had it coming. She's a trouble-maker, her. She met her match at last. Where's that boyfriend of hers?"

Anthony pushed through the crowd and stood, looking stunned at the scene. He glanced at his fat, bleeding girlfriend and then approached me, still being held by Neil.

"Oh, Keri! I'm so sorry! I know what she's like; I should never have even spoken to you." He turned to Neil. "Will she be all right?"

"Don't worry, we'll look after her," Neil assured him.

I heard the sound of sirens and looked up. A police car, closely followed by an ambulance bumped across the level crossing and came to a halt.

I watched as the ambulance men attended to Anthony's girlfriend. They loaded her onto a stretcher before approaching me and Neil.

I don't recall what was said, but after several people had spoken to the police and the ambulance driver had ensured that Neil would take me to the hospital himself to be checked out, I was allowed to be led the few hundred yards back to Garfield House.

I had two broken ribs, several loose teeth, a split lip and my nose had to be cauterised again to stop the bleeding. Other than that, just a few bruises and scrapes; I think I got off quite lightly. I never faced any charges because Anthony's fat girlfriend had been witnessed to be the attacker and was also extremely unpopular in the town. Not only that; she was eighteen and so an adult and I was only fourteen. I know she had to go to Court, but whatever happened to her, I never knew.

I actually learned a great deal from the event. That I *was* dangerous, just as I'd claimed to be. Also, that people attacking, rarely seemed to consider that their victim just might be able to defend themselves. I already knew that pain was a transient thing and it would pass. I'd had enough beatings in my life before.

In fact, when the hospital did X-Rays on my ribs, nearly all of them showed evidence of having been broken in the past. My surprise at learning this caused a lot of confusion amongst the hospital staff. Records were checked and re-checked; they thought it passing strange that I had never been brought to Casualty before with the obvious injuries I'd suffered in the past. For my own part,

I merely wondered how many other bones had been broken which no-one knew about.

22. Christmas and A Foolhardy Venture

Christmas at Garfield House was like nothing I had ever dreamt of. At home, Christmas had always been a miserable affair, despite the gifts and food. Mother always seemed to be waspish and the presence of extended family always made me nervous.

Finding a woolly stocking on the end of my bed was my first surprise. I'd never had a stocking before, despite traditions. At home, 'Santa' always left a pile of unwrapped gifts inside a pillowcase in the adult's lounge. A stocking full of wrapped gifts was far more exciting. I set to opening the presents at once.

I found a small, fluffy 'cat' teddy, some items of makeup, several sweets, a superb set of graded drawing pencils, clip-on ear-rings and some pretty hair ornaments. I set the little fluffy cat on my pillow and tried the ear-rings on.

I found having to look in the mirror rather unpleasant. I had two beautiful black eyes and my top lip was still swollen where it had split when Anthony's girlfriend first punched me. I forgot about the ear-rings as I leaned forward to peer more closely at my damaged face.

My bedroom door burst open; Valerie and Karen bounded into the room.

"Happy Christmas, Keri!" Karen bawled. "Get dressed, quick! Hurry up, there're loads more presents downstairs!"

"Look at the state of my face," I moaned.

"Does it still hurt?" Valerie asked.

"My nose feels like it's stuffed with a ton of cotton wool and my lip is really sore. I can't smile or it splits again and bleeds."

"That's all right. You never smile anyway," Karen joked. "Can you still frown and glare?"

I winced as my instant grin stretched my sore lip. "I'll give you glare! You made me snigger and now there'll be a taste of blood on my eggs and bacon!"

"Extra protein," Karen remarked. "Will you please get dressed now? We've been up for over an hour already."

I left both girls in my room whilst I dashed to the toilet. When I returned I dragged some clothes on as quickly as I could whilst Valerie and Karen inspected the things I'd been given in my stocking.

We rushed downstairs to find we were the last to arrive in the dining room. Overnight, someone had decorated the room with garlands and tinsel. A small Christmas tree bearing lights and baubles sat on the windowsill. Christmas songs were playing on a tape recorder which rested on the floor just inside the doorway.

Everyone else was already seated as we entered the room to a chorus of "Merry Christmas!" The three of us hurried to our table, the closest to the little Christmas tree. A small gift lay at each place setting.

"Can we open these now?" Karen asked, of no-one in particular.

"Happy Christmas, Karen. Of course you can, dear. I'll bring you a cooked breakfast in a moment. Would you like cereal or porridge this morning?" Mrs. Webster bustled about the room, her wrinkled face beaming.

"Have we got cream to have with the porridge?" I asked.

"Yes, dear. I'll fetch it in to you when I bring the porridge."

I tore open the small package. Inside, I found a pair of tights with a five pound note wrapped around them, tied with a fine, red ribbon. Both Valerie and Karen had the same. We discussed what we'd likely do with the extra five pounds.

After breakfast, everyone trooped into the office where Paul and Joss waited beside an enormous Christmas tree. I saw heaps of brightly coloured packages piled up under the tree and my lip split again when I grinned with anticipation.

Paul handed out the gifts, one by one. Joss, Mrs. Webster, Neil and George all helped the little ones open theirs. Karen, Valerie,

John, Adam and I all opened ours together. Sally sat on a chair in the corner with gifts piled on her lap. She looked ill and made no attempt to open anything.

Mainly, the gifts were clothing, every bit of it as fashionable and pretty as I could have wished for. Clearly, Joss had been very busy shopping for all of us. In addition to this, I'd been given a large sketch book of quality cartridge paper, a book of poetry and a set of acrylic paints with a selection of brushes. The last gift I opened contained three boards which would ordinarily have been used for oil painting.

It seemed in the few short weeks I'd been resident at Garfield House, Joss knew me far better than my own mother ever had. Delighted, I chattered happily to Valerie and Karen as we compared gifts. Everyone looked pleased and happy.

When all the paper had been cleared away, Paul solemnly handed out envelopes with our names on them. Inside mine, I found nearly fifty pounds! I couldn't believe it; I'd never dreamed of having that much money all at once.

Each of us gave the money to Paul and watched as he recorded the sum in his ledger. I held on to the five pound note I'd received with the tights at breakfast. Paul didn't say anything.

The day passed all too quickly for me. I'd never had such fun. We played 'Twister' and ended up in a heap on the floor, our legs and arms all tangled together. There were many other games, including 'charades', which I thoroughly enjoyed.

At lunch time, Mrs. Webster produced the perfect Christmas meal. Crackers and streamers were on every table along with real glasses which contained fruit juice mixed with lemonade. I noticed Sally ate virtually nothing. Her face appeared tear-stained and she spoke not a word.

"What's wrong with Sally?" I whispered to Karen as we tucked into our meal.

Karen shrugged. "Dunno. And I don't care. She's a bitch. Maybe George dumped her or something."

"It can't be that," Valerie volunteered. "He's been right by her all day so far, but she hasn't spoken to him at all.

I didn't dwell upon Sally's misery or apparent sulking. We all helped Mrs. Webster clear up after the meal. The kitchen was so packed with people all working at crossed purposes that it took far longer than it should have done to get the washing up done.

"Right, we're all off to the play barn now for some more games," Paul boomed. "Let's work off this big dinner so we've all got room for the splendid tea we'll have later on. Chop, chop, come on, everybody!"

I hardly recognised the play barn. All the furniture had been moved to the sides of the huge space and so many decorations festooned the walls and ceiling that the brickwork could hardly be seen at all.

By five o'clock, I felt exhausted, but happy. The games had involved a lot of dashing about and other exercise. Even John joined in willingly, but Sally sat in an armchair on her own. I noticed Joss speaking quietly to her several times, but Sally shook her head and wiped at her eyes and nose with a grubby handkerchief.

Tea turned out to be as special as lunch had been. So many treats, all in one day. I ate far too much and felt quite uncomfortably full by the evening. I felt relieved to be able to slump onto a sofa with Karen and Valerie to watch television.

Boxing Day saw us all pile into the minibus about an hour after breakfast. Neil drove us to some heath land, where we played a long 'Wide Game'. I had become much fitter during my time at Garfield House and despite my broken ribs I managed to run about a little, although I quickly became breathless.

The rest of the Christmas holiday passed too quickly. We went shopping with Joss in pairs. Karen came with me on our trip. I learned that money was set aside to 'do' Christmas for each child in care. Any money that Joss had left over after buying gifts had been given in the envelope Paul handed out. I didn't spend a great deal whilst out shopping as Joss had thoughtfully provided just about everything I could possibly want.

Joss said it would be good to try to save the money for spending on the holiday, which would be in June. Since I'd never had a proper holiday, I found the whole prospect more exciting than I could put into words. We would be going to Jersey, in the Channel Isles, for a whole two weeks. The holiday became a regular topic of conversation between Karen and me. She'd been on holidays before with her parents and knew all about camping.

The first time we attended the coffee shop after Christmas, I was overwhelmed by the greetings we received. Although my black eyes had healed so there was barely a yellow shadow across my nose and cheeks, I still felt rather self-conscious. I found it awkward to have people peering intently at the remains of the bruising whilst they made comments about Anthony's 'ex' girlfriend.

Anthony himself seemed withdrawn and extremely subdued about the whole affair. He insisted on buying me several milk-shakes and on more than one occasion, he apologised for the fight.

About the fifth time Anthony said 'I'm so sorry about everything, Keri,' I turned to him and remarked, in an acid tone, "If you knew it was likely to happen, why didn't you simply dump her - or leave me alone?"

"I tried to dump her. Several times. She just would not have it."

"What a complete wuss!" Karen interrupted. "What, did she beat you up as well?"

Anthony blushed, although he said nothing. I wondered just what had gone on between him and the fat girl, but I decided not to ask. The fact that she no longer came to the coffee shop, nor even seemed to work at the supermarket any more was quite enough for me. The less I knew about her the better!

When I returned to school, I found that almost everyone treated me with the utmost respect and deference. Except Gordon, who grinned at me and said, "So you really are as hard as nails! I'm glad you're all right."

"Just between you and me, Gordon, my ribs still hurt and it was bloody awful. I scared myself by fighting like I did. I wouldn't want that to happen again. What if I'd killed her?"

"From what I heard, it would have been self-defence if you had," Gordon replied. "She's been a force to be feared in this town for so long. Everyone was scared of her, even her own family. You're not the first person she's attacked and beaten up, although you're the only one who got the better of her. Just make sure we stay friends, Keri. I never want to be on the receiving end of your temper!"

I enjoyed Gordon's company. He was straightforward and uncomplicated. Karen thought I was mad, spending time with the fat boy and sneered when I pointed out he had a great sense of humour and was actually interesting to talk to.

"Everyone will be saying you're going out with him, if you're not careful," Karen grumbled.

"Well. Maybe that's not such a bad thing? Just because he's fat doesn't mean he's not a nice person. I'm too skinny and he doesn't seem to mind that!"

"You're daft," Karen laughed. "It's well fashionable to be skinny, like you. I suppose he's harmless enough. I just wouldn't like anyone saying I was going with him. I'd be embarrassed."

"Let them say what they want, Karen. Just so long as they leave us all alone, I'm happy."

One weekend, I didn't spend any of my pocket money. There was nothing I needed. I shoved it into my purse and spent the day painting. Neither Valerie nor Karen went out that weekend either.

On the following Monday as we walked to school, Valerie spoke in a low voice.

"I'm running today. It's my mum's birthday and I'm gonna see her if I can."

I stopped and stared at her. Karen walked right into me.

"What?" Valerie demanded.

"Don't be so daft," Karen said. "Your mum will be the first person they contact. They'll just bring you back!"

Valerie took on a defensive stance. "She'll lie and say she hasn't seen me," she protested.

Karen snorted derisively. "What? Do you think they won't search the house?"

"They might not. At least not for a day or two. I'm going anyway."

I have no idea at all what prompted me, but I heard my own voice say, "I'll come with you. I'm fed up with this place."

"Oh, God. I suppose I'll have to come as well," Karen muttered.

"So, what do we do? Shall we go now?" I asked.

"Nope. Need to get registered as present at school for one thing," Karen replied. "Got any money?"

"Well," I replied. "I've got my pocket money and a couple of quid I held onto. How about you two?"

"I've got nearly ten pounds," Valerie admitted. I've been saving and hoarding as much money as I can. I hid the five quid from Christmas and I've been keeping the odd pound or fifty pence here and there."

"Right. That's good. I've got just over a fiver myself. We'll meet by the water fountain at break time, all right?"

I couldn't concentrate on the first lesson of the day, which was History. I spent the lesson struggling with myself. Why had I offered to run away with Valerie? I wasn't exactly unhappy. It would be a week or more till the next house meeting. There was no discernable reason why I should leave the security and easy life I'd discovered here. I wondered if I could somehow back out of the venture without losing face.

"What's wrong?" Gordon whispered to me when the teacher's back was turned.

"Nothing," I replied. "Just thinking, that's all."

By the time the bell rang for break, I'd found no excuse to remain and resigned myself to an adventure with Valerie and Karen. We gathered by the water fountain as planned.

"Right. When the bell goes for the end of break, we'll run down by the hedge and get through into the coach park as usual," Karen began.

"I don't want to waste the whole day sitting on a coach!" exclaimed Valerie. "I just want to see my mum."

Karen rolled her eyes. "We're not going to sit on a coach, dummy! If we go through the coach park and turn left out of the exit, we can be on the main road in no time. How far is it to your mum's place?"

"It's the other side of Norwich," Valerie replied. "I was gonna take the bus."

"We could do that. To get as far as Norwich anyway. The thing that bothers me is these damned school uniforms. If you'd said last night, we could have brought a change of clothes with us this morning."

"I have brought a change of clothes," Valerie replied. "I've got false eyelashes and make up as well. Will you put them on for me, Karen?"

"Course. But we'll have to go sit on a coach to do that."

When the bell rang, I dashed along by the hedge and squeezed through the gap. Karen headed for the usual red and orange bus, but when she opened the door, we heard whispering voices. We looked at one another in confusion.

Karen climbed the steps and made her way to the back of the coach whilst Valerie and I crouched at the front. I heard an indrawn gasp of breath, then Karen's angry voice.

"What are you three doing here?"

The unmistakeable tone of Tracey's voice answered her. "The same as you, by the look of things. I hate maths."

Karen stomped back to where Valerie and I waited. "It's Tracey and her stupid friends," she muttered. We'll have to get on one of the other buses. Come on."

We followed Karen between three or four large buses until she stopped at one right in the middle of the park, surrounded on all sides by other vehicles.

Once we'd opened the door and made our way to the back, Karen angrily stamped her foot. "Of all the cheek! That's our hideaway. How in the hell did they know about it? And that's not the only thing. With six people missing from a lesson, staff are bound to start looking for us all. We'd better get a move on. Come on, Valerie, get changed and then I'll fix those eyelashes and make up for you."

Valerie looked totally different with eyelashes and drawn in eyebrows. I would never have recognised her. In her jeans and smart top, she looked a lot older as well. Once again, I worried about the venture.

"You know, she'd easily pass for someone who should be out and about on the bus," I began. "We'll be spotted really quickly though in our uniforms. Maybe we should just let her go on her own?"

I saw the expression on Karen's face. "I'm only saying," I added, lamely.

"Karen applied some make up to her own face and turned to me. "Shall I put some slap on you as well? We might get away with being fifth formers on a study break if anyone asks."

"Go on, then," I agreed.

With our faces made up, we left the coach park, carefully avoiding the orange and red bus.

"If they see us, they'll open their stupid mouths and blab," Karen growled.

In no time at all, we were on the main road and waiting in a bus shelter for the bus to Norwich. My misgivings grew by the minute. I profoundly wished I'd kept my mouth shut and not agreed to this stupid idea.

23. On The Run

We encountered no problems with catching the bus. The driver took our fares - we even paid 'half-fare' and it didn't cause him to even raise an eyebrow. No-one on the bus gave us a second glance. We sat at the back and chattered, mainly about Valerie's mum and the need to buy her a gift and birthday card.

When we got to Norwich, Karen suggested we spend some time going round the shops, not least so that we could get something different to wear. I knew this meant we would have to steal clothes, something I hadn't done since before I went to Garfield House. I found I didn't want to, but I couldn't think of a way to say so and dissuade Karen from her planned course of action.

I followed Karen and Valerie into Dorothy Perkins store and tried to pretend I was interested in the things they were looking at. I saw Karen take a pair of jeans and stuff them in the waistband of her skirt. I glanced around, guiltily. Surely, if I'd seen her, other people must have done as well?

We left the store shortly afterward and wandered into the market, where Karen ran to the public toilets to change from her school skirt into the jeans. While she was gone, I asked Valerie if she had any ideas about a gift for her mother.

"Well. Ideally, I should try to get her a bottle of vodka or something like that."

"That's alcohol, isn't it? I thought you said your mum didn't drink anymore?"

"I forgot about that. I don't know what to get her. What do you think?"

I thought for a while. I had no idea what to get as a birthday gift for someone's mum. I considered suggesting perfume, but rejected it before I'd even spoken as I knew Valerie had only a little money.

I looked toward the public lavatories, where Karen had gone to change. A large stall stood nearby selling flowers of all types.

"What about just a pretty card and some flowers?"

"Flowers? What good are they? She can't eat them or do anything with them!"

"Well. No, I suppose not, but they'll look pretty. She'll think of you when she looks at them. I remember my Nana saying it's always nice to receive flowers."

Karen appeared wearing the jeans and a top I hadn't even noticed her steal.

"Flowers? How old are you, Keri? How many girls would give their mum flowers for her birthday?"

I shrugged, feeling small. "Dunno. Just seemed like a good idea. What else could she get her? By the way, the label is still on that top."

Karen tugged the price tag from the shoulder of the top, making a small tear in the fabric, and threw it down on the ground at our feet.

"Are you gonna get yourself something to wear, or what?"

"I'm no good at nicking stuff. I'll get caught," I lied.

Karen changed her tone. "C'mon, Keri! I thought we'd have a great day today, but so far, you've been a bit wet. What's wrong?"

"What'll happen when they catch us?"

Karen grinned and Valerie chuckled. "They have to catch us first!" They both spoke together.

"Well, how come you got caught last time, Valerie?"

"Oh, I walked out of the school gates and Paul was about. He saw me. He waited to make sure I wasn't going back to the house, then he came after me. No-one saw us go this time; we've got a head start. They won't know where to look first, since it's all three of us."

I thought about my bedroom at Garfield House and all my lovely things that I'd left behind. I sincerely wished I hadn't offered to go with Valerie. In fact, if I'd kept my mouth shut, Karen wouldn't have taken it into her head to do the same. It was all my fault. I sighed.

"You didn't really want to come, did you? Why did you say you'd come with me?" Valerie's tone was accusing.

"I dunno. I just said it on the spur of the moment. I've never had as much as I've got now. I quite like it at the house. Anyway, I like you two. You're good friends."

Karen shook her head. "Well it'll all be there when we get back, dummy! Get a sense of adventure, why don't you? Come on. Let's get some chips from the chip-van and then I'll go and get you something to wear, since you're too chicken to get it for yourself!"

I followed them to the chip van and waited in line to be served. Once we'd got cones of chips, we sat on the steps of the Guild Hall to eat them.

"Where are we gonna stay?" I asked, with my mouth full.

"Oh, my mum will let us stay at hers. It's all right. She's really nice ... most of the time," Valerie assured me.

"Is it far? To your house I mean?"

"We'll have to get another bus," Valerie said, her brow wrinkling as she thought. "It's too far to walk."

We finished our chips and Valerie stopped at a stall selling cards to buy a pretty card for her mother. Karen and I waited whilst she wrote inside it.

"I won't be able to get her a present as well," Valerie said. "By the time I've paid the bus fare, I won't really have enough left to get anything decent. My mum won't mind, though. I bet she'll be really pleased to see me."

Karen went in to Tammy Girl on her own and returned to the market a few minutes later with a brightly coloured dress tucked into her jeans. She pulled it out and tossed it to me.

"I reckon that'll fit you. It's all I could get. They were watching me like a hawk from the minute I went in there."

I snatched the dress up and went to the public lavatories to change. The dress did fit, but it only had short sleeves. Since it was still cold, I pulled my school cardigan on over the top of it before returning to the steps of the Guild Hall.

"Still got your school gear?" Karen asked.

I patted my bag and nodded.

"Come on. Let's get a move on. Which bus do we need, Valerie?"

The bus stop was crowded with shoppers, several of whom stared at us. I began to feel uncomfortable and intensely worried. I hoped it didn't show on my face. I tried to look nonchalant and as if I were exactly where I should be.

We couldn't all sit together on the bus because it was too crowded. I sat next to a woman with a huge wickerwork shopping basket piled high with produce. She was quite large and her elbows kept digging me in the ribs when the bus went round corners. I kept my eyes to the rail in front of me, glancing now and again at Valerie, who sat next to a young woman with a screaming baby. Karen had found a seat at the back of the bus.

The journey seemed very long to me. Every time I looked at Valerie, she was smiling happily. Clearly, she knew where we were. I felt lost and not a little afraid. When I saw Valerie stand up, along with several other passengers, I hurriedly left my seat, looking behind me to make sure Karen was coming too.

The other passengers dispersed quickly and the bus moved away.

"Where to now?" Karen asked.

"We'll go down the alleyways," Valerie replied. "Just in case anyone is around here looking for us."

I looked around. The houses resembled the council houses in Swanton Abbott somewhat, except these were obviously older and not so well looked after. None of the gardens I could see were tended; most had very long grass and weeds in front of the shabby doors and windows. Some had piles of rubbish and junk, old toys and broken vehicles.

I trailed after Valerie and Karen. Neither seemed to think there was anything remotely odd or unpleasant about the area. We passed a house where two small children, aged about three, were playing in the mud. Neither had shoes on and one little girl looked particularly unkempt. Her dirty hair was tangled at the back of her head and her clothes were ill fitting and covered in mud and other debris. I wanted to stop, but Valerie walked past without a second glance. Karen turned to look at me and raised her eyebrows in a silent question.

"Those kids," I began. "They ... er ... well. They look a bit cold."

Karen shook her head and put her finger across her lips to indicate I should keep quiet. I nodded. We followed Valerie into a narrow alleyway, where overflowing dustbins and other rubbish were heaped outside every gate. The smell was appalling. I clenched my teeth and tried to breathe shallowly so as not to inhale the scent.

We came to a road. Valerie peered out of the alley and looked both ways.

"All clear," she said. "No-one about. Come on. It's not far now. Just over there, along another alleyway and then I'll be home."

We crossed the road and entered another narrow passageway, even more fetid and unpleasant than the first. The rotting remains of some creature lay against the wall on one side. I turned my face away. It looked like it might once have been a cat. Valerie didn't seem to notice.

She stopped at a battered gate and tried the handle. The gate creaked open. Valerie turned to Karen and me and grinned widely.

"I guessed the back gate would be unlocked. She never remembers to lock it. Come on!"

A huge quantity of empty bottles, stacked up in torn bags, was the first obstacle we had to negotiate our way around. A rusted old pram sat in the middle of what had once been a lawn but was now choked with weeds at waist height. The back windows of the house were smeared with grime and the door clearly hadn't been painted or cleaned for several years. Valerie turned the door handle and shoved at the buckled wood.

I almost hoped the door would be locked. More than anything, I wanted to get away, not just from this house, but the whole area. Once again, I bitterly regretted my rash actions in going with Valerie. On the other hand, I didn't like to think of her being here alone.

Eventually, the door opened and Valerie stepped inside. I noticed the expression on Karen's face as she hesitated to follow. Clearly, she felt much the same way I did.

"How do you know your mum is home?" Karen asked.

"Oh, she'll be here. She hardly ever goes out. Come on. Come in. I'll fix us all a cup of tea or something after I've said hello to Mum and given her the card."

I crept over the threshold into a room which looked and smelled like a war-zone. *It must be a kitchen*, I thought frantically to myself, *there's a cooker in the corner*!

Pots and dishes half-filled with rotting food lay on every available surface. The floor was thick with ground in grime and several bags and boxes, filled with empty bottles and other rubbish lay scattered about so we had to step over them. I noticed torn net curtains hanging at the window. These were covered in dust, spider webs and grease. My stomach churned.

"Wait here a minute. I'll go through and see where Mum is," Valerie whispered.

She stepped carefully over a pool of something which looked remarkably like half-dried vomit and disappeared through a doorway into a dingy room beyond.

As soon as Valerie had gone, Karen turned to me. Her face was screwed up with disgust. "This is horrible! Do you think she had to live like this before she came to Garfield House?"

I shrugged. "She did say her mum was ill and that her dad couldn't really cope."

We both jumped at a loud, shrill voice, which came from the room Valerie had entered.

"Fuck off! Leave me be! I haven't had any!"

I stood, rooted to the spot with panic. Karen's eyes were wide with anxiety.

I held my breath and tried to discern what Valerie was saying. I could hear her voice, soft and reassuring. The shrill voice came again.

"Is it really you? Where have you been? I've been so scared. Get me a drink, there's a good girl."

I had no idea what to do or say. Clearly, Karen felt as at a loss as me. We looked at each other in mute concern. Valerie came back to the kitchen and grinned at us.

"It's all right," she said. "She was asleep. She thought I was someone else. You can come in and meet her now ... if you want. I'll make us all a cup of tea, shall I?"

Karen glanced around the filthy room. "No, it's all right, Valerie. We'll be going now that you're safely at home. Um ... we thought we might go and visit my dad, since we're out and able to go where we want. Will you be all right?"

Valerie looked crestfallen. "I thought you two might stay and help me clean up a bit," she mumbled.

The very thought of touching anything in this stinking hovel of a house made my skin crawl. I could tell Karen had even stronger misgivings than me. Even so, it seemed particularly nasty to simply abandon Valerie here.

"You shouldn't be the one to clean up, Valerie," Karen began.

Valerie planted her hands on her hips and glared at the two of us. "Well, who else is gonna do it?" she demanded. "I never used to let it get this bad when I was here. Mum can't do it."

"Why not?" Karen asked.

"She's ... she can't. She's not well."

"Valerie! Who have you got out there? You'd better not be talking about me!" The shrill and querulous voice from the other room made me jump.

"It's all right, Mum. It's just a couple of my friends. They're gonna help me clean the place up a bit," Valerie replied.

"Valerie! Don't say that! I can't help you. It's ... well ... your dad should do it, not us." The words were out of my mouth before I could stop them.

"Huh! I thought you two were my friends! Some friends you are, when you won't even help me to help my mum! I wish I'd come on my own now!"

A movement out of the corner of my eye made me turn around toward the back door, which still stood open. Two policemen were clambering their way up the path, stumbling over the bags and boxes of rubbish. I opened my mouth to shout a warning, but heavy knocking sounded through the house. Clearly, the police were out at the front as well.

I nudged Karen hard in the side and looked about me wildly, looking for somewhere to run to. Valerie's eyes widened as the police officers arrived at the door behind me. She turned and fled into the dingy room beyond.

Neither Karen nor I moved. One officer took hold of my arm whilst the other stepped past both of us to pursue Valerie.

"Which one are you, love? Karen?"

I tried to shake his hand off. "No. I'm Keri. She's Karen. We haven't done anything! Are you taking us to prison?"

The officer laughed. "No. Nothing so dramatic as that, love. We've just got to take you back to the home in East Dereham. There're folks worried about you all. What did you run away for?"

I opened my mouth to reply, caught Karen's expression and shut it again. From the dingy room Valerie had fled to, I heard the unmistakeable sounds of her crying and her mother's shrill voice swearing and shouting at the policemen. The officer who went in there had opened the front door to admit more officers.

Karen and I walked quietly when we were led through the filthy, darkened room toward the front of the house. I caught a glimpse of somebody thin and frail looking, wrapped in blankets on a grubby settee. She swore and protested, claiming the police were intruders and should be arrested. Valerie struggled like a mad thing, planting a kick squarely on the knee of one of the officers who grappled with her.

Outside, there were three police cars drawn up at the side of the road. I was led to one of them and helped into the back seat by the officer who had spoken to me in the kitchen. I turned and saw out the back window of the vehicle that Karen had been placed in one of the other cars. Valerie still screamed and struggled at the roadside. Two officers were doing their best to restrain her, with limited success.

During the journey back to Garfield House, the police officer spoke pleasantly to me. He asked me more than once why I had felt the need to run away. Eventually, even though I knew I should keep quiet, I said, "I didn't want Valerie to go home all on her own. It's her mum's birthday. That's all."

I only half listened to the lecture the officer gave me. Something about asking Social Workers or getting the staff from Garfield

House to arrange visits and not cause the police to have to waste their time dealing with irresponsible runaways.

When the car drew into the area next to Garfield House, I felt intense relief when I saw Joss hurry out of the kitchen door to greet us.

"Into the office straight away, please, Keri. Paul is waiting to speak with you."

I scuttled past Joss, through the kitchen and on toward the office with a sinking heart. I wondered what punishment Paul would mete out to me. More, I worried that the other two cars had not arrived at the house with the one I travelled in. What if Karen and Valerie had been taken somewhere else?

I began to cry before I reached the office door. I bitterly regretted my actions that day and greatly feared the consequences.

24. The Aftermath

I felt very small, standing in the middle of that huge office room with Paul standing by the fireplace. He seemed even larger than ever before and he was a big man anyway.

"So," Paul began. "Here you are. Did you enjoy your little escapade today, Keri?"

I shook my head and whispered, "No."

"I am surprised that you did something so stupid, to be honest. I thought you had settled down well. Are you unhappy here, Keri?"

"No." I sniffed and wiped my eyes with the sleeve of my cardigan, smudging eye shadow and mascara across my cheeks.

Paul paused. I looked up at him through a film of tears. He frowned.

"Then why did you do it, girl? Was it the other two, pressuring you into it? I can well believe that of Karen but not Valerie."

I thought of the filthy hovel Valerie had taken us to. Then I thought about the fact that Valerie had been quite prepared to clean it all up and look after her mother, who was clearly deranged, if not actually ill. My own home life had involved nothing by way of responsibility and even if Mother was foul, my home had always been clean. I couldn't imagine the kind of life Valerie had led. Perhaps she'd not even gone to school before coming to Garfield House.

"It's Valerie's mum's birthday today," I blurted. "She said she was gonna run away so she could see her mum. I offered to go with her. It wasn't Karen's fault at all."

"I see." Paul pursed his lips and drummed his fingertips on the mantelpiece. "And were you welcomed with open arms? I mean, Valerie was making a birthday visit after all."

I shook my head. "No."

Paul stepped toward me and I cringed, expecting to be hit. He stopped and stared at me in surprise.

"What's this? Why are you afraid of me, girl?"

"I ... I ... don't know," I stammered. "I'm sorry."

"Yes, I can see that." Paul placed a huge hand on my shoulder. "I think perhaps you've learned something from this day. Young people don't always know what is best for them, but perhaps you're beginning to realise. You made no attempt to go to your own home, Keri. Was that simply because you wanted to help Valerie?"

"My mum would've killed me if I'd gone home," I muttered.

"Quite so. Very clear thinking there." Paul steered me toward a chair. "Sit down, Keri."

I sat; my hands twisted round one another and I didn't know where to look.

"Everyone is here for a reason. You seem quite clear in your own mind, why you are here. Have you perhaps had a chance to think about why Valerie might be here and why visits between her and her mother are not arranged?"

"Her mum is ... ill," I began. "She's strange and scary as well."

"Right. Now you're an intelligent girl. I cannot talk to you about other kids or the reasons they are here, but I think today, you probably saw enough to be able to make up your own mind. Hopefully, that will be enough to make you realise that behaviour like this is unacceptable. Have you thought about the worry and concern you've caused?"

I shook my head. Tears trickled down my cheeks unchecked.

"Well, let me tell you about that. The school staff were frantic. It is their responsibility to make sure children are safe whilst at school. If you just walk out, they don't know where you are or what trouble you may have got into. It is not possible to look after someone who isn't there."

I said nothing.

"Of course," Paul continued, "They are obliged to let us know that they've 'lost' you and the other two. We knew you weren't here, so we had to call the police for help with finding you. I have no idea how many policemen were sent out to search for you all, but it would have been a great many."

"Does my mother know what I did?" I whispered.

"Yes. Of course, we had to inform her that you were missing. She would have had police visit her to see if you had gone home."

I shuddered. Mother would not have been at home; she'd have been at work. I could imagine her outrage if police turned up at her work, looking for me.

"I bet she's really angry," I ventured.

Paul grimaced. "Your mother is less than delighted; let's just say that, shall we? Anyway, to get back to what I was saying, you've caused a great deal of worry, trouble and upset today."

"I really am sorry, Paul."

"Right. Well, you'll have to be punished, you must realise that. So you will not go out, either on your own or with the others - or even on any trips we have planned - for two weeks. And there will be no sweets for two weeks either. Understand?"

I nodded. I couldn't believe I'd got off so lightly with barely any punishment at all.

"Right. That's all. I expect you're hungry, so if you go to the kitchen, either Joss or Mrs. Webster will fix you something to eat. I want no more of this. You're far too bright to allow yourself to get dragged down by those who have a lot less to lose than you. Off you go."

I hesitated because I still found it almost impossible to believe that Paul had not hit me for what I'd done. I didn't really go out a great deal anyway and the loss of sweets would be easy. Before I came to Garfield House, I'd rarely had sweets.

"Go on, girl. Go and get something to eat, before I change my mind and think of a worse punishment!"

I leaped from the chair and scuttled out of the room. I paused in the hallway, but no-one was about. I made my way to the kitchen, where Mrs. Webster and Joss were drinking tea together.

Joss stood up and approached me. I cringed a little as she reached out to me and swept me into a hug.

"I was really worried about you, Keri! I can't believe that you, of all people, would do something so utterly foolhardy. At least you're back safe now. Are you hungry?"

"A bit," I admitted. My mind reeled with the shock of how Joss had greeted me. I knew what would have happened if I'd run off like this when at home. Mother would have been icy and pleasant only so long as the police were present. She would never have hugged me or offered me food.

"Have the police gone now?"

"Yes, dear," Mrs. Webster answered. "But there'll be another policeman or two along in a minute, bringing Valerie and Karen back."

I sagged with relief. I had really worried that Valerie and Karen might be taken somewhere else. Valerie had run away before, even though she didn't get very far.

"In fact, there they are now," Joss said, glancing toward the wide kitchen window. "I'll just pop out to meet them. Mrs. Webster will get you something to eat, Keri." She left the kitchen and I heard the back door open as Joss went to greet the policemen bringing Karen and Valerie back.

I had thick, hot, vegetable soup with crusty rolls. I tried hard to ignore the noise coming from the hallway, but I could hear Valerie screaming and shouting abuse. Karen never made a sound.

"I should go up and have a nice, hot bath, if I were you, Keri," Mrs. Webster advised, when I'd finished the soup. "Bring your laundry down as usual. That's a very pretty dress. I haven't seen it before. Is it new?"

"Yes. I don't like it much though."

Mrs. Webster tried to hide a strange smile. "I expect it was all you could get at the time," she murmured.

I knew she thought I'd stolen the dress. I wanted so much to tell her I hadn't done so, but I couldn't. Not without letting on that Karen had stolen it for me. In fact, I began to think that I may just as well have stolen the garment myself. Surely, accepting things I knew to be stolen was as wrong as actually stealing it for myself?

I thanked Mrs. Webster for the soup and hurried out into the wide hallway, heading for the stairs. I saw Karen standing by the wall with a burly policeman standing next to her. The office door was closed, but I could hear Valerie shouting and screaming and deeper voices too. It sounded as if a policeman and Paul were trying to calm her. Karen grinned widely at me and winked. The policeman simply frowned at me.

I darted up the stairs and along the landing to my room. Everything was exactly as I'd left it that morning. I sagged with relief. I curled up on the bed and hugged Lambie and the little cat teddy I'd had for Christmas.

None of us went to school on Tuesday. A lady came from the Education Authority and spoke to us each in turn. She was very severe, but I quickly realised she had no actual power to 'do' anything to any of us.

Later, the young social worker, Miss Armstrong, visited. My interview with her was brief. She already knew all she wanted to know from Paul and Joss - probably from the police too. She tried to be stern but I could see her heart wasn't in it. She asked me several times if I was happier at Garfield House than I'd been at home.

"I do like it here," I replied. "I only went with Valerie because ... well ... she's my friend. She wanted to see her mum so badly."

The social worker left, assuring me that she would come and visit me again very soon and take me out for coffee.

I wandered into the playroom, where Karen sat on a settee with her feet on the coffee table.

"So you've seen your social worker?"

"Yep. She's really nice. She didn't tell me off at all."

"That's because it's the first time you've run. They're always nice the first time. My social worker will be along in a bit, I expect. Silly old bag will lecture me and moan and groan at me. Still, it was an adventure, wasn't it?"

"Is Valerie all right?"

Karen shrugged. "She's never really all right, is she? She's still moaning at me because I didn't want to clean up that shit-hole of a house with her. I reckon she must've done all the cleaning when she was at home."

I sat down next to Karen. "What about her dad? I wonder why he doesn't do it?"

"Dunno. It's weird. My dad would never let a place get like that. Even when he's drunk, he still tidies up."

"My mother kept our house so clean it made me nervous. She's a fanatic. She even used to go through my drawers and cupboards. If it wasn't all tidy and neat, she threw the stuff out and made me sort it all out into piles."

Karen snorted. "You should've thrown the stuff at her and told her to get stuffed!"

"Yeah," I agreed. "I could've done that. If I wanted to be beaten half to death!"

We laughed together. My home, Mother and everything I'd suffered seemed such a long way away. The laughter increased. Between gulps of air, I explained how Mother would have reacted when the police went to her work. I could just imagine the expression of outrage and shame on her face. I laughed until my sides ached.

Valerie took a very long time to recover and become the smiling girl I'd known before we ran away to visit her mother. She cried a lot and began to pull out the hair on her head as well as her eyelashes and eyebrows.

Karen and I tried to cheer her up but she could not forgive that we'd been unwilling to clean her mother's house with her, even though we'd all been taken away by the police before any of us had a chance to do anything.

After a week, Joss decided that Valerie and I would exchange bedrooms. I would move in to the room Valerie presently shared with Karen. I felt pleased at the prospect, but Valerie seemed withdrawn and sulky. I tried to ask her if she found the move agreeable, but she refused to answer me.

"Don't worry, Keri. You can always change back when Valerie feels a bit better. It's just temporary, I think. She needs some space for herself and time to recover. She's very upset and she worries about her mum." Joss reassured me as she helped me move all my belongings.

Apart from when I was at boarding school and shared a large dormitory with eleven other girls, I'd never had a shared bedroom. Karen and I enjoyed ourselves immensely, organising all my stuff. I thought it would be just grand to have someone to talk to at night. Karen agreed.

"Valerie always goes straight to sleep," Karen complained. "If I try to talk to her, she just grunts. And she snores!"

I giggled. "I don't think I snore, but I talk in my sleep, so you'll have some company at least!"

I found out why Sally had been so unhappy at Christmas time purely by accident. Karen and I had been drinking cocoa and I took the cups back to the kitchen. As I approached, I heard voices. Mrs. Webster and Mrs. Brown were talking together. I waited in the corridor, unsure as to whether I should just barge into the room.

"Well, of course, she's all alone in the world now," Mrs. Webster said. "Except for the baby, of course. I can't understand why she would say she no longer wants it."

"Grief can get you like that," Mrs. Brown replied. "Losing a parent is always hard, but for someone as emotionally disturbed as Sally, it must be unbearable. Don't worry. She'll come round. You'll still have your grandchild. I mean, even if she refuses to keep the baby, you and George can keep it, can't you?"

"I'm not sure about that. I just hope she comes to her senses before it's born. George will be heartbroken if he loses this little one. And so will I."

I made a noise in the corridor to alert the women to my presence. Both stopped talking abruptly when I walked through the door with the cups.

"Shall I wash these up, Mrs. Webster?"

"No, dear. It's all right. We'll deal with it. Off you go."

I hurried away to tell Karen what I'd overheard. None of us knew much about Sally or her circumstances, so it was a juicy piece of gossip to be shared and mulled over.

25. The Ugly Truth About Rage

My punishment for running away had been easy. I barely missed the sweets and when other kids offered me some of theirs, I refused. As for not going out, it gave me a chance to catch up on some reading.

Both Karen and Valerie moaned constantly about being grounded. I thought they really only did it to try and wind up the staff. Neil, in particular, became agitated fairly quickly when they pleaded and wheedled. I found it all quite amusing.

At last the punishment had been completed and we could once again go into town and visit the coffee shop. Anthony listened as Karen and I told him why we hadn't been there for two weeks. Valerie sat silent, her face screwed up in a fierce scowl.

Spring arrived and the days began to lengthen. I felt invigorated and full of life. Valerie began to come out of her shell again. It was good to see her smile and hear her laugh now and then.

The days passed quickly. I worked hard at school and actually obtained a couple of commendations. Gordon was an ever present figure in my school life. He had a terrific sense of humour and knew some really funny jokes. Karen began to join Gordon and me at break times. After a week or two, Valerie and two other girls came along too and we sat together, chatting and laughing.

We were sitting on a long bench one day, howling with laughter at one of Gordon's jokes, when a couple of older boys came along. They stood in front of us and stared. When the laughter subsided, one of the boys spoke.

"Oi, Gordie. How come such a fat git gets a crowd of girls round him every day? Good in the sack are you? I s'pose you've shafted every one of these tarts."

Sandra, a small, quiet girl, who had a wonderful sense of humour, glared at the boys.

"You've got a mucky mind, Vince. We sit with Gordon because he's good company. Unlike some others who only have one thing on their mind!"

Vince stepped forward and grabbed Sandra's arm. "How do you know I wouldn't be good company as well?" he growled.

The other boy looked uncomfortable. "Leave her alone, Vince. This isn't a joke anymore."

Vince turned and scowled. "Shut up, you wuss. I'm just seeing if this tart wants to spend some time with me."

Sandra struggled in Vince's grip. "Let me go, you pig! You're hurting me! If you were the last boy on earth, I'd jump off a cliff. You're horrible! Now, leave me alone or I'll scream."

Vince hauled Sandra to her feet. "I like it when they scream," he leered.

I had no idea the rage was coming, but quite suddenly, I felt a feeling similar to that when Anthony's girlfriend attacked me at the level crossing. I stood up. My fists were clenched tightly.

"Leave her alone," I grated.

"Er ... Vince ..." the other boy took a step backward.

"Sod off, Paul. This is my business! I want to know why this snooty little tart won't spend time with me and would rather sit here with all the misfits."

Red began to tinge the edge of my vision. I could feel myself beginning to shake. I took a step forward.

Vince reached over to me and pushed me in the chest dismissively. "Sit down, you weirdo. I'm not talking to you."

Something snapped. I took a step back and swung a punch. It connected with the side of Vince's head and he staggered, letting go of Sandra's arm. He turned to me and made a grab at my school blouse.

It was as if he were moving in slow motion. I found it easy to dodge away from his grasping hand and swing another punch, this time, aimed at his nose. There was a satisfying spray of blood, also in slow-motion. Distantly, I could hear voices and panicked screams. Someone yelled 'fight' but it sounded like it was coming from the bottom of a metal dustbin.

I saw the punch coming toward my face and stepped quickly to the side, aiming a kick at Vince's leg. I didn't feel my foot connect, but I saw his face twist and he stumbled, landing heavily on one knee. I took my chance and grabbed at his throat.

"I told you to leave Sandra alone," I roared, squeezing his neck as hard as I could with one hand.

Vince flailed his arms, but I kicked them away. "Apologise!" I said.

Vince's eyes were bulging and his face turned a deep shade of red. I shook him by the throat. "Apologise to Sandra!"

"Aaargh! I'm ... I'm ... s ... sorry!"

I shoved at the creep as I released him and he tumbled backward, spluttering and coughing. I was about to kick him in the stomach when someone laid a hand on my arm.

"You've done enough. You can leave it now." I recognised Gordon's voice and turned toward him.

"Come on. Come with me. Let's go to the water fountain and get a drink," Gordon said, gently.

I let him lead me away. The crowd of students parted to let us through and closed again behind us. Everyone seemed intent on watching Vince grovel on the floor, choking.

I noticed several staff members rushing toward the crowd, but I followed Gordon to the fountain, where I took a long, cool drink of water as he patted my back. I stood up, let my hands hang in the flow of dwindling water and then wiped them over my face. Gordon smiled at me.

"Better now?"

My body began to shake. I felt nauseous. I couldn't speak because there was a huge lump in my throat. Gordon took me by the arm and led me over to a bench near the wall. We sat down.

Gordon took one of my hands and held it in both of his. "Weather's getting warmer," he observed. "It'll soon be summer again. I like the summer, even though I sweat such a lot. I go swimming quite a lot with my dad and my uncle. I bet you're a good swimmer, Keri."

I nodded.

"I like gardening as well. My dad's got a lovely flower garden at home. Sometimes, I go and help him on the allotment. Last year, I grew a massive pumpkin. It was so big I couldn't lift it and we had to wheel it home, all through the town in a barrow. It made a super Hallow'een lantern. The spuds Dad grows are great, we have them fresh. He digs them up; we wash them and cook them ..."

I sat and let Gordon speak to me of all manner of little things. His voice was soothing and after only a few minutes, I forgot my anger and became interested in what he was telling me.

"My step-father's dad used to grow vegetables in his garden. When he dug up the potatoes, I'd pick them up and put them in a basket to take in to Nanny."

Gordon let go my hand and grinned at me.

An irate teacher approached. "What are you two doing?" she demanded.

"Nothing, Miss. We were just talking about gardening. Potatoes actually." Gordon looked up at the teacher innocently.

"What do you know about that kerfuffle just now?"

"Kerfuffle?"

"You know what I mean. That fight."

"What fight?"

The teacher glared at us and stormed away, shaking her head.

Gordon gave me a quick hug. "It'll be all right, Keri," he murmured. "No way will Vince tell the staff he was beaten up by a girl. Maybe he'll think twice before he starts on a girl again. You were great. You do understand why I stopped you, though?"

I felt sick.

"I wanted to kill him, Gordon! If he hadn't apologised, I think I might have strangled him!"

"No. You wouldn't have done that. I wouldn't have let you."

I sincerely wished I could believe Gordon. I knew, deep down, that if the event had occurred when there was no-one else about, I may well have continued and either strangled Vince or kicked him to death. The feeling of nausea came back and I began to shake.

"Here," Gordon offered me a Polo mint. "Suck on that. It'll make you feel better. I bet you feel all sick and shaky."

I accepted the sweet and sucked furiously at it. Gordon was right. It did make me feel a little better.

By the time the bell rang to indicate the end of break, I felt almost normal and trailed into class behind Gordon. Several of the students clapped as I entered the room.

I blushed and sat down at my desk. I didn't know what to do or say.

Gordon sat next to me and turned to class. He waved a little. "Thank you, thank you," he called. "The show is now over. Autographs after school, please!"

Several people laughed and I grinned as well. By the time the teacher entered the room to begin the lesson, everything had returned to normal, although I felt somewhat distracted. This was the second outburst of uncontrollable rage I'd experienced in just a few months. I hoped it wasn't an indication that I would turn into a fiend like Mother, but I greatly feared it meant just that.

26. Some Events and The Holiday Begins

Several things happened over the next few weeks and months, including my fifteenth birthday. I had some really lovely gifts, mostly clothes and art equipment. What pleased me more was the amount of birthday cards I received. I'd never had so many! Mrs. Webster let me choose the meal for that day and she also made a wonderful cake, all covered with pretty icing and candles. I received a card from Mother which contained a ten pound note. I had hoped to hear from Nana, but the postman brought nothing.

Probably the most important event at that time was my decision to begin smoking. It happened a few weeks after my fifteenth birthday. I look back now and wonder just why I wanted to do something so stupid, considering I'd always found the smoke from other people's cigarettes to be foul.

Karen and Valerie started before me. I grew used to them budgeting their pocket money so they could buy cigarettes. Frequently, I had to lend one or other of them a few pence - not that I ever got it back!

All the staff at Garfield House smoked, as had both Mother and Terry. Even Nana had smoked! I don't recall anyone ever saying smoking was bad for the health; even doctors smoked in those days - in their office whilst seeing patients!

I remember the day quite vividly. Karen, Valerie and I were sitting on top of the large bunker situated halfway between the house and the play barn. The sun shone brightly and we watched the younger kids playing in the yard. Karen produced a packet of twenty cigarettes - something no-one could usually afford. She offered one to Valerie, who took it, commenting on the size of the pack.

"Neil bought them for me," Karen replied, smugly.

My eyebrows shot up. "Really? Whatever for?"

Karen blushed a little and shrugged. "I dunno. I guess he was just feeling generous. Want one?"

I hesitated. What harm would it do? It might even make me look a bit more grown up. I thought about Neil and all the stolen cuddles and caresses we had together whenever he found me alone. For the first time, I began to wonder if he did the same with Karen. I shook myself; of course not. I was special. Neil told me so. He loved me, he said and thought that one day, we could be together somewhere nice.

"Come on, stupid! You want one or not?" Karen sounded impatient.

I drew a cigarette from the packet and stared at it. Valerie giggled. She was already blowing smoke rings with hers. Karen lit a match; the flame hardly wavered, the air was so still.

"Come on, Keri! You have to put the end of the fag in the flame and suck on it!"

I did so. The cigarette lit and a cloud of acrid smoke went into my eyes, which watered. Karen laughed.

"You're funny," she remarked, taking a long draw on her cigarette.

I sucked another mouthful of smoke and let it flow out of my mouth. Again, it went straight into my eyes.

"Don't waste it," warned Valerie. "You have to inhale the smoke. Like this." She sucked on her dwindling cigarette and then held her breath for a few seconds. I watched as she blew a stream of smoke from both nostrils and her mouth all at once.

"How do you do that?" I asked.

"You kind of swallow it," Karen interrupted.

I sucked at the cigarette again until my cheeks bulged ... and then I swallowed. Instantly, I began to cough, retch and splutter.

Karen thumped me between the shoulder blades and laughed loudly.

"Keri, you're so daft! You can't eat it; it's smoke! You breathe it in!"

The coughing fit continued, interspersed with hard retching. My eyes streamed and my ears rang. I felt incredibly foolish.

Valerie handed me a bottle of cola she'd been holding. "Here, have a swig of this, that'll help."

I grabbed the bottle and gratefully took a small mouthful. As the coughing subsided, I noticed some of the little ones staring at me. Mary frowned, her little face appearing severe.

Somehow, I managed a weak smile and waved at the child, who turned away. Whilst coughing, I'd dropped the offending cigarette. Karen picked it up and handed it to me. There was still at least half of it left.

"You have to persevere," she said. "I coughed my heart out the first few times I inhaled. You'll get the hang of it eventually."

Even though my first attempt at smoking had nearly made me sick, I so wanted to 'fit in' that I did persevere. Within a week or so, I was smoking just as if I'd been doing it all my life! None of the staff said anything to any of us. They must have known, not least because every one of us asked for a cigarette every now and then.

About a week later, when I was in the play barn alone, playing records, Neil entered. He looked out the door and closed it quietly before rushing over to embrace me.

I didn't much like Neil's kisses. His beard and moustache rubbed against my chin and cheeks, but I responded as I should. He groped at my bottom and lifted my skirt up to my hips. I clung to him and let him put his hands inside my knickers. After a little while, Neil pressed himself against me.

"Can you feel that?" he asked. "You turn me on so much!"

As far as I was concerned, I hadn't actually done anything except respond to his kisses, but I nodded anyway.

Neil eased my knickers down to my knees and began to fumble with the zip on his jeans. I did nothing to assist him, but he didn't seem to mind. I pointedly did not look at his penis; I didn't want to see the foul thing.

Using the table as a support behind me, Neil fumbled and shoved at me with his penis and his hand. He didn't hurt me at all, but I really would have preferred him not to do it. I didn't want to let him down or disappoint him though, so I stayed quiet.

When he'd finished, Neil made a show of helping me with my underwear and tidying himself up. He put his hand in the back pocket of his jeans and brought out a pack of twenty Player's number six - the same brand of cigarettes Mother smoked.

"We'll have a smoke now," Neil told me. "You can have this packet. I've got some more."

I put another disc on the record player and smoked the cigarette Neil gave me. I looked at the packet, which he placed on table beside me; I thought about when Karen had a full packet of twenty cigarettes. I wanted to ask if he'd given them to her as a reward for sex, but I didn't dare.

Neil stubbed his cigarette out, bent forward to kiss my forehead and left with a cheery wave. I sat down and picked up the cigarettes. It seemed I was doing a lot of things I didn't really want to do. I wondered if Neil really cared about me as he claimed he did. Was I really the special girl he'd waited for - or was this just another man getting what he wanted from me, but this time with trickery and gifts? I couldn't allow myself to believe that Neil was like that. He really did seem to care for me; he nearly always managed to give me extra sweets, biscuits and money, whether I'd had sex with him or not. I tucked the cigarettes into my skirt pocket and turned the volume up on the record player.

I did very well at school during the summer term, both in sport and the academic subjects. With the bullying and snide remarks having stopped, I felt quite comfortable at the school and able to work to the best of my ability. I won a couple of awards in high jump and long distance track running, along with coming in the top three in my class in every subject, including maths.

At the end of term, I promised Gordon I'd try to call him during the holidays and took his telephone number. He even said he might come into the town to the coffee shop one Saturday.

Joss took each of us shopping for holiday clothes in the last week of July. I enjoyed my trips with Joss; she had such good taste and never seemed to be critical or discouraging about the things I chose for myself. In fact, she often complimented me and found accessories which would match my choices.

I bought a one piece swimsuit and also a very small, turquoise coloured bikini. I worried about how foolish I might look wearing a bikini due to my lack of breasts, but Joss told me not to concern myself with such things. The holiday would be fun, she said. I began to look forward to it; everyone did.

We travelled down to Weymouth on a Friday at the beginning of August, leaving in the small hours of the morning when it was still dark. Paul drove his huge Saab saloon car with a low trailer affixed to the back into which were packed all the tents and luggage. Joss travelled with Paul in the car along with Mary and two other small children. Neil drove the minibus with all of us older children as passengers.

The minibus was stuffy and smelled of diesel fumes, in spite of all the windows being open. Valerie was sick ... several times. Neil had brought along bags for this eventuality. My stomach churned at both the noises Valerie made and the knotted bags piled beside her seat.

In the darkness there was nothing to be seen, but as dawn approached, I concentrated on looking out the window at the passing landscape. I think everyone dozed off to sleep at one point, except me and of course, Neil, who was driving.

Despite Valerie's unfortunate condition, Neil encouraged us to sing silly songs for part of the journey. Valerie joined in, but she often stopped singing to be sick again. I marvelled at her resilience.

By the time we arrived at Weymouth I felt more than slightly sick myself. I refused food when Paul and Joss offered. No-one seemed to mind. Joss patted my shoulder.

"Never mind, Keri. Perhaps you're a little sick from the long journey? We'll get you something once we're on the ferry. There are plenty of cafes and shops on board. Are you looking forward to the ferry trip?"

I nodded, even though the trip on the ferry hadn't even crossed my mind. In fact, I'd given no thought at all as to how we'd get to Jersey. I don't think I even knew where it was!

The ferry was like a floating town and I walked around the decks with Karen and Valerie, astonished at all I saw. There were indeed shops and cafeteria's; also bars. I'd never seen anything like it. People crowded everywhere, laughing and joking. Children ran about, dodging between adults and other children, tables and chairs.

Joss managed to shepherd us all into one large cafeteria and found a couple of tables where we could all sit together. She brought soft drinks for all of us and hot drinks for herself, Neil, George and Paul.

I agreed to have a sandwich after Joss persuaded me I would feel better if I ate something. I think I got halfway through that sandwich before I began to feel very sick indeed. I put it down and looked around wildly, panic building inside me. *I couldn't be sick*!

"What's wrong?" Karen nudged me.

Clenching my teeth, I replied, "Karen, I feel sick!"

Joss looked up. Mary had fallen asleep on her lap. "Karen, could you go with Keri and find the toilets, please? Poor Mary is so tired. She's been quite grizzly. I'm afraid if I put her down, she'll wake up again."

Karen stood up and tugged at my sleeve. "Come on. I saw a sign for toilets over there. You'll be all right."

My stomach roiled and churned as I followed Karen. The boat hadn't even left the harbour yet! My heart hammered against my ribs and I fought back the urge to run and find the way off the boat before it set out over the deep, grey sea.

Karen found the toilets and thrust at the door. I bumped into her as she stopped and turned back to me, shoving. "That's gross! Come on, let's find some other toilets. There must be more than this. I'm not going in there!"

I caught a glimpse of the floor as the door swung closed. It was covered with vomit. I managed to control the urge to retch and quickened my step, following Karen as she ducked between crowds in search of another toilet.

We actually found several more ladies toilets, but every one of them reeked of vomit and most had pools of vomit either on the floor or in the basins. I couldn't bring myself to enter. My stomach muscles were clenched tight against the urge to vomit myself and I shook with a mixture of the effort to control myself and fear.

Whilst we'd been looking for some decent toilets, the ferry had left dock. The constant movement made me feel even worse.

"Karen, I feel like I'm gonna die! I have to get out of here!" I spoke from between tightly clenched teeth.

Karen put her arm around my shoulders. "Come on; let's go up onto the deck. You'll feel better in the fresh air. Also, if you need to throw up, you can lean over the side!"

We found our way along several corridors and up more than one flight of metal stairs. Eventually, we came onto one of the main decks. There were so many people; mostly, they were sitting in deckchairs with drinks. I glanced at the railings on the edge of the deck. Karen shepherded me toward them.

I looked down at the grey waters and the white-tipped waves and felt panic overwhelm me completely. I needed to go to the toilet - but I knew I could not. Nothing would drag me into those befouled closets. I clung to Karen, my eyes wide with terror.

"I've got to get off!"

Karen smiled uncertainly. "No. You'll be all right, Keri. I'm here. Don't worry about being sick. Loads of people get sea-sick. I'll stay with you if you're scared. I've been on ferries loads of times before. If you look at the horizon it's easier. Wait there. I'll go and find us a chair each and we'll sit here together."

Before I could muster a reply, Karen darted off between groups of people, leaving me clinging to the railing. I felt dizzy; the nausea intensified as did the pressing urge to go to the toilet. Yet I couldn't move.

When Karen came back, dragging a couple of plastic chairs, I sank to my knees on the deck, my hands still clinging to the railing above me.

"Come and sit down, Keri. We'll be fine. Come on. You can't stay like that!"

I managed to shake my head, but the movement made me feel even worse. I saw Karen frown. She looked very worried. I tried to speak, but all that came out was a kind of strangled groan.

Neil found us about half an hour later. Karen was beside herself with worry for me. She hadn't dared to leave me to fetch help. She'd somehow managed to convince herself that I'd jump off the boat if she turned her back. She may have been right!

I spent the whole ferry crossing on my knees clinging to that railing with Neil and Karen on either side of me. I couldn't speak; I couldn't move. I actually wanted to die. I cannot explain how I did not vomit because the nausea was constant. I retched a few times and then went rigid with fear. Neither can I explain how I did not lose control of either bladder or bowels. The journey took around four and half to five hours. It felt like forever!

In fact, it might seem bizarre, considering I have such very vivid memories of the rest of the journey, but I cannot recall disembarking from that ferry at all. It must have been traumatic. Maybe it is a mercy I have no memory.

I do recall travelling in the minibus again. Neil drove very slowly, following Paul's car and trailer. I remember looking out the windows at the glorious scenery and as we climbed a hill, I glanced at the sea, which looked blue, sparkling under the midday sun.

I'd never been camping in my life before and so I was worse than useless when it came to erecting tents. I followed instructions and did everything asked of me, yet I still felt surprised when all the tents were up.

Karen, Valerie and I were sharing. We crawled inside, dragging our sleeping bags and luggage behind us. Although the space was cramped, we all giggled and chattered as we unpacked what we'd need.

I cannot now recall the exact location of our camp site. However, it must have been on the western coast of Jersey because, once the tents were all pitched and everyone had eaten - even me - we trekked along some roads and pathways to St. Ouen's Bay, where we played on the sand for a few hours.

Later, the adults took us all into the town of St. Helier, where we had a meal in a very crowded restaurant before exploring the town streets. Everything was so entirely different from Sheringham, which is the only seaside town I can remember going to as a child.

I overheard Neil speaking to Paul and Joss about 'duty free' items. Karen nudged me and drew me aside.

"Fags and booze are super cheap here because they're tax free. Make sure you buy plenty of fags as soon as you get the chance. Perfume and jewellery are dead cheap as well."

"How come?" I asked. "What's tax?"

Karen grinned. "It's what the government charge for us to have the stuff we want back home. Over here it's all different. My dad used to go over to France all the time to get cheap fags and booze. He bought my mum loads of expensive perfume and jewellery as well. All duty free."

Karen seemed a lot wiser to the ways of the world than I was. I just accepted that things were cheap over here in Jersey and put the reason for it to the back of my mind.

A little later I noticed Karen talking earnestly to Neil. I watched from under my eyelashes. Neil glanced around, then gave Karen a packet of cigarettes. He hadn't touched her or made any move to cuddle her or anything. For some reason, I felt intense relief.

Back at the camp site, Neil and Paul built a fire in the centre of our circle of tents. Joss fried sausages over the flames to make hot-dogs for everyone whilst Neil strummed on his guitar. Before long, everyone was singing along, even the little ones.

The sun sank beneath the waves amid faint wisps of orange, pink and purple clouds. I'd never seen anything more beautiful. A faint breeze blew across the dying embers of the fire. Joss had put the little ones to bed and Neil had gone off somewhere with George. Paul stood up and stretched.

"Right. You older kids can stop by the fire for a little longer if you want. Keep the volume of your chatter low because the little ones are sleeping. Joss and I are turning in now. We'll all be up quite early in the morning, so don't stop up too late. Night, everyone."

We all chorused 'Good night, Paul'. John and Adam began a conversation about ghosts and hauntings. For a while, Karen, Valerie and I listened to their tales until Karen snorted derisively.

"That's all utter rubbish! At least tell a scary story that's believable!"

Offended, the boys retired to their tent; we could hear them grumbling about what spoil-sports we were. I lay back on the sweet grass and looked up at the sky. It looked like a swathe of dark blue velvet studded with glittering spangles.

"How come the sky never looks like this at home," I asked, of no-one in particular.

Valerie giggled. "S' a different sky at home."

"Karen shoved her. "Don't be daft! The sky's the sky, everywhere!"

I let them bicker and stared upward. I'd studied a little astronomy in the Physics lessons at All Hallows. I knew each star was actually a distant sun, far out in space. It simply amazed me that there were so many! I found myself imagining someone else, far away, looking up into the night sky and seeing our sun as a tiny pinpoint of light.

"You reckon there're other people out there, Karen?"

"What? In space, you mean?"

"Yeah."

"Dunno. I asked that in science once and got sent out of the room for being childish. My dad used to tell me stories about UFO's though. There probably are other creatures out there. What do you think, Valerie?"

Thus began our conversation about aliens and UFO's. We crawled into our tent and talked long into the night. Karen knew lots of stories about Government cover-ups, alien spacecraft spotted and photographed and other, unexplained sightings. Long after Valerie and Karen had fallen asleep, I lay in my sleeping bag, wondering about distant worlds and civilisations and listening to the small noises of the night

27. Vague Recall of Hell Holiday

Considering how very vivid my memories are of that first night at the camp site, I am confused as to how it can be that, for the rest of the holiday, I have only disjointed remembrances. There was horror - in abundance, but my mind seems to have blocked out an awful lot. Trying to remember what happened, in what order is almost like trying to recall what one did when leglessly drunk.

Being drunk is something I'd only experienced once before, whilst at Trevor's house, when my stepfather accepted money for Trevor to have sex with me. It was not an experience I ever had any intention of repeating. However, during that holiday with the children and staff of Garfield House, I was hopelessly drunk several times.

I cannot recall how it is that a young teenager, only just fifteen years of age, could even be allowed into bars and clubs. I have vague memories of flashing disco lights, very loud music and - whisky ... lots of it.

Common sense tells me that the staff must have known or been aware. After all, we were in their care. Why were we in the town of St. Helier during the evening anyway? How is it that Karen and I fell about, laughing like fools, drunk as we were, and no-one reprimanded us? I have a vivid recollection of Karen tripping over a table leg and sprawling at my feet, yet managing to keep her glass of whisky and ice upright and intact!

A tall, slender French youth, with dark, shiny hair down past his collar, laughed with us and helped Karen into a seat. I recall his eyes and his pretty smile but not his name. Unfortunately, I also recall the long, long night of sordid sex with him - although I can't remember anything other than that the hotel room was luxurious and plush. I do not know which hotel it was or how I came to be drunk and apparently willing to indulge in all kinds of sexual activity with gay abandon!

That I had a headache in the morning - along with twenty pounds in crisp, five pound notes is another vivid recollection. I remember Karen showing me her fifty pounds and telling me I was a fool to have accepted less than her.

We sat on the sands of St. Brelade's bay in bikinis that day. Karen and I openly flirted with virtually anything male in the vicinity and received a great deal of attention. I ate far too many ice creams, none of which I bought for myself. I can recall Joss building sandcastles with little Mary and Neil playing Frisbee further down the beach with the young lads.

I have recollections of seeing Valerie emerge from our tent looking rumpled and distressed, followed shortly thereafter by a muscular, tanned young man who spoke to Paul and wandered off.

On another day, at St. Ouen's Bay, Karen and I were in the surf with surf-boards! I cannot recall how we acquired the boards; nor why we were in the water, apparently unattended. I managed to get astride my board and ride a few low waves. The undertow felt very strong and I was afraid. A large proportion of that holiday involved me feeling frightened, but I cannot remember why.

On that day, Karen and I paddled out past the surf and sat astride the boards on the blue water. We chatted, but I can't remember the conversation. I have a vivid recall of looking behind me and seeing an enormous wave curled right above us and the immediate conviction that I was about to die. Before I could react, the wave swept us up and we were both engulfed in swirling water. I didn't know which way was up and only came to the surface because I clung to the surf-board with a death-grip.

I floated, forlorn on the water, coughing, spluttering and weeping because I thought I had survived and Karen must have drowned. A huge, burly man on his own surf-board paddled over to me and spoke kindly. I sobbed out that we'd been caught in the freak wave and I thought my friend had drowned. He escorted me back to the shore and walked up and down the beach with me, trying to locate Karen.

Neil encountered us as I became ever more hysterical. He explained to the man that Karen had come ashore several minutes beforehand and was quite safe with the group from Garfield House. I ran to find Karen, leaving Neil talking to the man. I didn't thank either of them.

When I found Karen, I clung to her and sobbed that I feared I'd lost her; that she'd drowned. She echoed my feelings. Apparently, she'd searched for me for a long time before going back to fetch Neil. We spent the rest of the day together, but we were neither happy nor carefree. I can't remember why that should be. After all, we were firm friends; we were on holiday and had escaped a watery death!

I recall the group trip to Jersey Zoo - now the Durrell Wildlife Conservation Trust. It was the first time I had ever visited any kind of zoo at all, I can tell readers that no zoo I have ever visited since could even begin to match up to it. I spent a great deal of time with little Mary during the zoo visit. She held my hand and her eyes were huge in her petite face as she stared at the animals. I do not recall Karen being present at all on that trip. This in itself is an enigma to me as we were inseparable by then. I have horrible worries about what may have been happening to her.

The whole holiday lasted for two weeks, yet in my mind, it lasted very much longer than that. The mind is a strange thing sometimes. So much of my past is vivid, the happiness as well as the horrors, yet those two weeks are singularly different. Looking back now, as an adult, I have deep suspicions that I (and the other teenagers) may well have been drugged for part of the time, although that is just pure speculation on my part.

I'm pretty certain that we toured the German hospital and the underground tunnels which had been in use during World War Two. I'm certain that I would have been very interested in this, had I been myself. However, I can remember little or nothing about any of it!

I recall an encounter with a Jersey cow. It must have been during a visit to a working farm, but I cannot recall that much. I only remember the gentle cow, with her large, liquid eyes, leaning against my hand as I scratched her neck. Karen felt fearful of the large animal, but I'd grown used to cows during my time on the farm with Benjamin; I thought the Jersey cows were so beautiful and all had very gentle natures. Clearly, they were quite used to people and enjoyed the petting and fuss made of them.

The one day which remains most vivid in my mind began with another trip to St. Brelade's Bay. I had taken to walking everywhere barefoot - day and night. In fact, I believe I was insistent that I would never wear shoes again. As we descended to the sands, Karen and I noticed what appeared to an abundance of pebbles strewn across the expanse as far as the eye could see.

I trod on one of these 'pebbles' and felt instant pain. I hopped about and lifted my foot to see what could possibly have damaged my leathery skin, hardened from several days walking barefoot on all surfaces. Squashed against my foot was the most enormous 'wasp' I'd ever seen. It wasn't quite dead and I yelled for help.

Karen supported me whilst Neil removed the offending creature. It was whilst we were busy with this that the Bay lifeguards began to evacuate the beach. The 'pebbles' were a massive swarm of hornets! I was not the only person to have been stung. The lifeguards treated me, along with many others, before I was able to limp back to the group from Garfield House. We went to a different beach that day.

Later, I recall being in one of the night-clubs, dancing with Karen to one of the most current popular songs. We were approached by the big, burly man who had helped me to search for Karen after the big wave swept us apart.

I have extremely vague recollections of both Neil and Paul being present and of large quantities of whisky being consumed. Again, I must have been very drunk for these memories to be so vague.

Later, for some reason, I was on a beach with the big man. An electric storm made a wonderful light show overhead, accompanied by rumblings of thunder - yet I can still remember being able to see the stars above me.

The man was rough and groped at me, tearing off my underwear. I began to struggle and cry out. Several times, he shook me and told me to be silent. I did not obey him. I was afraid and felt desperately sick, causing even more fear. When he flung me to the sand and forced my legs apart, I began to scream in earnest.

I found myself scooped up into the man's arms. He walked down the sloping beach and into the water. I struggled and fought, but he held me easily. When he was just above his knees in the waves, the man spoke to me, forcing me to listen to what he was saying.

"If you don't shut the fuck up screaming, girl, I'll drop you in this water and stand on your head. Understand? They'll find your body tomorrow when the tide goes out, but I'll be long gone."

I listened to the swish and drag of the waves and fell silent. I stopped struggling. He carried me back higher up the beach and flung me to the sand.

"Open your legs, slut."

I did not exactly obey; I just allowed my body to go limp. That man must have weighed seventeen or eighteen stones and it was mainly muscle. As he thrust and thrust inside me again and again, I recalled a snatch of conversation from earlier on when he'd bragged about the boxing matches he'd won.

He tried to kiss me once or twice but I turned my head away in disgust. When he grabbed my hair to force my face to his, I bit the end of his nose - hard. He roared in pain and struck me a back-handed blow across my face.

I have no further recollection of that rape. Sometime later, I became aware of myself again. It had begun to rain and I shivered uncontrollably. I still felt sick, had no idea where I was or how to get back to my camp-site and my knickers were missing entirely.

I struggled across the sand and somehow got my bearings. A policeman found me wandering the streets of St. Helier. I babbled on about the rape and my missing underwear. He was kind and extremely disturbed by my story; I now think he may well have been concerned at my youth and the condition I was in - drunk.

I was taken back to the Garfield House camp site in a police car. Paul, Joss, Neil and George all gave very creditable performances of having been worried out of their minds, not knowing where I was. I remember feeling so confused and upset. Of course they knew where I was - they'd been there - until the man took me down to the beach.

I insisted I'd been raped. The police spoke with Joss and Paul for a long time before talking to me again. They implied that I was known to be promiscuous and had obviously fallen out with the man I'd gone off with. I angrily insisted I had not. I told the policeman who'd picked me up that I bit the man's nose because I was too afraid to struggle further as he'd threatened to drown me.

Unfortunately, I could not give them a name, only a vague description. I was not taken to hospital, nor examined by a doctor. I find this all incredibly strange now that I think back on it. The fact is, those staff members must have known what was going on, yet they behaved as if they didn't. I was labelled a 'difficult' and 'trouble-making' teenager and the police went away.

I told Valerie and Karen what had happened to me when we were in our tent together. I cannot recall the conversation save that Karen shook her head and hugged me.

"Always best not to struggle, Keri."

A few days later, we had to take the ferry back to Weymouth. I hadn't forgotten how I felt on the trip over. On a flat, calm sea, I'd been so sea-sick I wanted to die. I begged Joss to let me stay behind or find another way to get me home.

"Keri, this is an island. You have to cross the sea to get home. Don't worry, you'll be fine. The only other way to get home would be by plane and we can't afford the air-fare. I bet you'll be absolutely well on the trip back. Don't make any more fuss now, dear. You'll scare the little ones."

I sobbed and wept. I could not face travelling by sea again. I really thought I wanted to die. In fact, all the alcohol and sex seemed like nothing in comparison to the journey home.

A heavy storm swept in as we travelled to the port. Rain lashed the minibus and thunder drowned out what people said to one another. I heard Neil mention to John that the ferry might be cancelled if the sea were too rough. I sat, huddled in my seat, praying that all ferries would be cancelled for ever.

We waited a very long time before finally boarding the ferry. The storm still raged and there was a lot of discussion about ferries being cancelled. I shivered and shook with trepidation, but finally, found myself herded up the metal gangway onto the boat, which rocked alarmingly, despite its size.

Still barefoot, somehow, I managed to stub the big toe on my right foot against the metal grating. Blood poured from the wound and a flap of skin dangled from the toe tip. Joss fussed and tutted, insisting the wound would need stitching.

Hence, I had to visit the medical officer as soon as we were on board. He did stitch my toe, after having given me a long lecture about the foolhardiness of going barefoot everywhere. I barely heard him. Already, my stomach roiled and I wanted to die.

The doctor actually took pity on me and gave Joss some travel sickness tablets to give me. He said he thought he would be dispensing a great many before the journey ended. Unable to swallow even the smallest of pills, I chewed the tablets up and managed a gulp of water. I limped after Joss until we found the rest of the group. Joss handed me over to Neil.

Before the ferry even left the harbour, I began to weep and shake. I convinced Neil that I would die if I couldn't at least go out onto the deck. At last, he steered me along passageways and up stairs until we came out onto the rain lashed deck.

Surprisingly, a lot of people were gathered on deck. Mostly at the rails, where they were vomiting. My stomach churned ever faster. Neil steered me toward the prow. Like me, he'd noticed somebody vomit and the wind snatching it, flinging it into the face of a person a few feet away - who also vomited.

I remained crouched by the railing, my back firmly to the other sea-sick travellers. Neil spoke to me, but I cannot recall anything of what he may have said. I lived in a tiny little world all on my own. One filled with thunder, lighting, rain and the ever present, heaving sea.

One of the ferry officers came along and spoke to Neil. He said something about it being inadvisable to remain on deck throughout the journey as the sea was particularly rough. I refused to move. I don't think I could have moved anyway, even had I been willing. The officer went away when it became apparent that I flatly refused to move.

He returned a little later with life preservers for both me and Neil and some stout, stretchy ropes, which he wound around the railings and us. He made some comments about the possibility of losing his job before he left us.

I remember nothing but fear during that journey, which took over seven hours, rather than the four hours it was scheduled to take. Mountainous waves reared up and then crashed to either side of the boat, which pitched and rolled as if made of balsa wood.

I should have vomited. Neil did - several times. Somehow, it never actually happened; I just felt so ill I wanted to die. Those seven hours seemed longer than the whole of my life put together to that point!

Mercifully, I do not recall the journey back to Garfield House. It is possible that I slept in the minibus. Everyone had been sea-sick, even a lot of the crew. I think I might have been one of only a handful of people who did not actually vomit!

I do vividly recall the pleasant sensation of being in familiar surroundings, in my own bed again. I'd left Lambie behind for fear of losing him. I snuggled up to the soft, battered old woolly lamb and, despite my extremely sore toe, fell asleep.

28. The 'Label' Begins To Fit

The holiday in Jersey that I can only vaguely recall changed me in several fundamental ways. The foremost of these changes was my sudden determination to use my body to get whatever I wanted at the time.

I'd only ever had unpleasant experiences of sex and actively disliked everything about it. I had never had any pleasure from the activity and could not understand what the great 'kick' was all about. By the time I returned from the holiday, my attitude had changed. I still detested the activity - or even any reference to it - but I had learned that if I wanted something, I could promise sex as a reward.

During the first week back at Garfield House, I believe I had sex a good half dozen times, always willingly enough - and always to get something I wanted. It never crossed my mind that what I was doing could be wrong or in any way unacceptable. Karen seemed to have a similar philosophy.

The older teenage boys in East Dereham had no idea what had hit them. Sometimes, for something as insignificant as half a packet of cigarettes, their every whim was met by one or other of us!

The frightening aspect of all this is that never once did either Karen or I take any precaution to avoid pregnancy or disease. When I think back, I regard myself as having been extremely lucky not to have caught some vile sexually transmitted disease or found myself pregnant.

Sex and my willingness to use it as a tool was not the only thing to have changed. Joss seemed cool toward me and Paul openly scowled at me several times. Neil ceased his groping and fumbling whenever we were alone as well. I had no inkling of why this should be until I overheard Mrs. Webster talking to Mrs. Brown one morning before breakfast.

"Yes, there was such a to-do about it all. It's shocking, is what it is. That one girl could cause so much trouble!"

"Yes, but do you think she might have actually told the truth? I mean, she'd lost her underwear and everything and was certainly upset and frightened, from what I've heard."

Mrs. Webster snorted derisively. "I suppose there might have been a grain of truth in it, but there is no doubt in my mind that the little witch led the man on in the first place. Joss tells me those girls all ran wild over there, drinking and everything."

"Well ..." Mrs. Brown began, uncertainty tingeing her tone. "She's always seemed so polite and so quiet. I'd never have thought her a wild trouble-maker like Paul says she is."

At this point, I realised the women were talking about me. I hesitated in the passageway, listening.

"She's just like all the rest of them. Thieves, liars and sluts all of them. I mean, they wouldn't be here if they were decent girls in the first place, would they?"

I'd always liked Mrs. Webster. It made me feel sick to learn that she thought of me as nothing more than scum. Part of me wanted to barge into the kitchen and shout at the women; tell them it was true and I had been raped; let them know that Paul and Joss were not the wonderful carers they appeared to be. The other part of me cringed in shame and led to me remaining outside the door to hear still more.

"They need locking up, if you ask me," Mrs. Webster continued. "It's the only way anyone will ever be able to control them."

"That's a bit extreme," Mrs. Brown replied. "Anyone would think they were criminals, the way you talk!"

"Not yet, perhaps, but they will be; every last one of them'll end up in prison, whether or not she gets knocked up with some brat."

I slunk away. Mother had always told me I would end up in prison. If she only knew the wicked things I'd done without being caught! I wandered into the playroom and flung myself into an armchair. Adam came into the room just behind me.

"What's up with you?"

"Nothing. I'm just fed up."

"I'm going to my new place the day after tomorrow. Joss is taking me shopping for clothes later. Shall I ask if you can come too?"

I shook my head. "I'm not in Joss's good books just now. Best you don't."

Adam grinned. "They found that bloke who attacked you. Did you know?"

Interested, I sat up straight in the chair. "No-one told me."

"Well, they wouldn't. You made them look bad because you got yourself into such a situation. It just proved you weren't being looked after. You shouldn't have been drunk anyway - not if Paul and Joss had kept an eye on you. There's going to be an investigation. That bloke got thrown off the island for what he did to you."

"How did they find him?"

"Well, there obviously weren't that many boxers wandering about with teeth marks in their noses. I'm only telling you what I heard Joss and Paul talking about with Neil. I'm not supposed to know any more than you do."

I hung my head. "Will I get in trouble, do you think?"

Adam grinned. "Doubt it. They'll all be falling over themselves to make sure the place runs like clockwork if the social workers are sticking their noses in. You'll probably have to talk to a social worker though and tell her what happened. I bet Paul or Joss will tell you what you've got to say too. I know they're worried you might let the cat out of the bag."

Adam left the room and I settled back in the chair to think. What, exactly, could I tell the social worker? I couldn't remember most of the holiday. I knew I'd been very drunk several times. I'd felt sick a lot and afraid, although I couldn't remember what I was frightened of. I didn't want to talk to anyone about it at all, save perhaps Karen.

At breakfast, Mrs. Webster behaved in her normal, cheery manner and smiled at me just as much as everyone else. I thought it strange she could have said all those things and yet show no sign of her true feelings toward me and the others. I couldn't eat much; Mrs. Webster noticed.

"Oh, Keri, you've left most of your breakfast! Are you all right, dear? You don't feel unwell, do you?"

"No. I'm fine, thanks. Just not hungry."

Mrs. Webster patted my hand. "That's good. Off you go. I think Neil is taking some of you out later on."

I nudged Karen as we left the dining room. "Come upstairs, I want to talk to you."

Once we were safe in our shared room, I told Karen what I'd overheard Mrs. Webster saying.

Karen shrugged. "No surprise there. She's always been an old bitch, if you ask me. You're too trusting. Someone calls you 'dear' or 'love' and you immediately assume that they're nice and more than that, that you can trust them. All this lot are just like most social workers. You can't trust any of them."

"But ... she's always been so kind to me!"

"Ha! If you think someone being kind to you is a reason to trust them, you're mad. I'm always super suspicious when anyone is nice to me. The first thing I ask myself is what they want."

"What? Me as well?"

Karen shoved my shoulder. "No, not you, idiot! It's gonna take something serious for me not to trust you anymore."

I grinned. "Actually, there's something else I wanted to tell you."

I explained what Adam had said to me about an investigation being held into what happened in Jersey.

Karen frowned. "Wow. That could go very badly for all of us. If Paul and Joss get kicked out, who knows who we might get instead."

"What do you mean, if they get kicked out? They could get sacked from here?"

"Sure. They only have to be found to have done something really badly wrong; then they'll be in all kinds of trouble. I should think, if the social workers find out even half of what went on over in Jersey, we'd all be sent away and this place would be closed."

I hung my head. "I can't remember half of what went on over there. The biggest and most horrible memory I've got is that bloody boat!"

"There's a lot I can't remember either. Probably because we were so drunk most of the time. But ... we're not allowed to be drunk, don't you see? If it comes out that we were all out every night, getting rat-arsed and all the rest of it ..."

"Adam said a social worker will want to talk to me about it."

Karen nodded. "Yeah. At the very least ... talk about it. I wouldn't want to be in your shoes!"

I considered this for a few moments. "Actually, I think if they talk to me, pretty soon they'll want to talk to everyone else as well. What if I refuse to speak?"

"Knowing social services, if you refuse to tell them anything, they'll say you're being difficult for a start. Then there'll be an even deeper investigation."

I felt so afraid. The holiday had been pretty dreadful, but in general, I'd had a better life at Garfield House than I'd ever had at home with my family.

"Will they send me away somewhere else, Karen?"

"I dunno what they'll do."

I sat in silence, twisting my hands into my bedspread. I didn't want to be sent anywhere else. More, I didn't want to be separated from Karen. She was the first true friend I'd ever really had.

"I'm going to run away," I muttered.

Karen snorted. "Yeah. And we'll just be caught straight away like we were before and be in even worse trouble!"

"We don't have to be caught."

Karen paused and tilted her head to one side. "What? I don't know what you're getting at."

I leaned forward and took hold of Karen's hands. "Last time, it was on the spur of the moment, wasn't it? Valerie had planned to go, but we hadn't. We just went along with her. What if we plan it properly? I mean, if we'd got proper clothes and some money, make-up and stuff ..."

"Well. Where would we go?"

I shrugged. "Dunno. Not back to your home or mine, that's for sure." Briefly, I had an image of Mam, the gypsy woman in my mind. "Actually, I think I know somewhere we can go first. Somewhere they'll never think of looking. Safe and with good people."

Karen stood up and went to the window. "How will we get there?"

"Well. I suppose we can get there by bus, but we'll still have a bit of a walk afterwards. Don't worry, it's all country lanes. Most likely we won't be noticed."

"Right. So we need money. Got anything left from your holiday money?"

I shook my head. "Nope, and I haven't got any fags either. What about you?"

"I've got four hundred fags I nicked from Neil and Paul. They thought they forgot to put them in Mary's bag. I took them and split the packs up. I put forty fags in each pocket I own!"

I grinned at Karen's cunning. "That was smart. What about money?"

"Nope. Not a penny. We'll have to sort that out somehow. Any ideas?"

We spent a large proportion of the morning laying our plans, both for getting hold of money and finding which bus would take us anywhere close to Swanton Abbot and the Common, where I knew the gypsies should be. We swore to each other that we would tell no-one else of our plans.

I had a very good idea how I could lay my hands on some cash. That afternoon, Karen and I declined to go off with Neil and the others on a trip. We both claimed we'd already made plans to meet friends at the coffee shop.

Joss admonished us to be back for tea at six o'clock, gave us a pound each to buy coffee with and let us go. We waved at Valerie as she sat in the mini-bus, scowling.

"She feels left out," Karen told me as we made our way down the street. "Maybe we should be a bit more careful, or she'll want to come with us."

"I suppose we could take her as well," I mused.

"No." Karen interrupted. "We can't. She'll want to run straight home to her mum, you know that."

I had sex three times that afternoon. Karen went off with a couple of local lads, so I'm not entirely sure what she got up to. I had seventeen pounds in my pocket when we met up again. Karen had done better - she had over thirty pounds.

"You should ask for more," Karen advised me as we walked home.

I explained that one of the boys I had been with had bought some condoms. We laughed and giggled about it all the way home. It never once occurred to me that there might have been a reason for the boy's purchase.

We planned and schemed for three days. I couldn't say how many times I disappeared into the park with boys for some kind of sexual activity. I had made the decision to raise money for our run-away adventure and so I did not allow myself to worry as to how I got it. Sex still disgusted me. I could not allow myself to dwell upon the sweating, grunting, usually spotty youths who clambered over me, mauling and groping. Probably, my disdain of them protected me somewhat. It made the activity more bearable to dissociate myself and think of how wonderful life would be for me and Karen with the gypsies.

Valerie became suspicious and accused Karen and me of deliberately leaving her out of our activities. We both apologised and claimed we had boyfriends in town that we'd been spending time with. Unconvinced, Valerie challenged us as to their names and addresses.

Karen managed to divert the question by suggesting we go to the cinema together the following evening. Valerie readily agreed and we all went together to ask if we could go.

Just as Joss agreed that a trip to the cinema for the three of us would be a very good idea, Karen asked if we could go swimming in the afternoon as well.

"Well ... Neil and George are both busy tomorrow, girls. I've got to be here and Paul has got to go to a meeting, so there'd be no-one to go with you."

"Oh come on, Joss! We're fifteen! We can walk to the swimming pool and back! We can all swim anyway. It's not as if there are no lifeguards or anything!"

Joss smiled. "Yes, you're right. Of course you can go. I keep forgetting how grown up you all are now. I'll make sure I remember to ask Mrs. Webster for some swimming towels in a while, ready for the morning."

"Joss, I'm supposed to be going shopping with Neil tomorrow. I can't go swimming," Valerie grumbled.

"Oh. I'd forgotten that. Perhaps you want to delay your shopping instead, Valerie? Neil could go with you to the pool then."

"No. It's my turn to go shopping and I'm going," Valerie insisted. "Why can't you two go swimming next week instead?"

Karen grinned. "How about we all go swimming next week as well?"

Valerie nodded and Joss smiled. "That's all settled then. Off you go, girls. You've got a few minutes before tea."

I used my 'few minutes' to take a very quick bath. I felt that I smelled of sex. At least, I imagined I could smell it on myself and it disgusted me. I wanted to be clean.

When I came out of the bathroom, Karen was waiting. She grabbed my arm and tugged me toward our bedroom. "Listen! It's perfect. Now we have an excuse to have bags with our stuff in it - and no-one to supervise. We'll be long gone before they work out that we didn't go swimming!"

It dawned on me how Karen had successfully manipulated Joss into letting us go swimming alone. She knew full well that Valerie would not pass up her shopping trip. I admired her deviousness. Impulsively, I hugged her.

"Karen, I'm so excited. I shan't sleep tonight, I'm sure!"

"Shh! Keep your voice down," Karen warned. "We have to act normal this evening. If any of them even get a sniff of what we're planning, it'll all be ruined."

It was so hard, trying to 'act normal' since I had no real idea of what normal was for me. I watched television as I often did. I had another bath and washed my hair too - another normal activity. Neil did not offer to dry my hair for me though. I had to ask him and he seemed less than thrilled when he agreed.

In fact, the evening seemed to last forever. I kept looking at the big clock on the wall and the hands were dragging by so slowly I felt sure the clock must be broken! I guzzled my evening cocoa really quickly, burning my mouth in the process. Joss came into the playroom carrying swimming towels, swim-bags and our one piece costumes.

"Here you are, girls. The bikinis are a bit small for the local pool. You'll be fine in the one piece suits. Make sure you take your hairbrushes with you. You can't come out of the pool looking like scarecrows!"

Karen argued about the swimsuit, insisting she wanted to wear her bikini. I didn't dare argue. I felt too nervous about being caught out. I admired the way Karen seemed no different to the way she always was.

Sure enough, Joss ended the argument by saying Karen could wear the one-piece swimwear or not go swimming, so Karen agreed, apparently reluctantly. Satisfied, Joss bade us goodnight and left the room.

Once in our room, Karen advised me to everything we usually did, including reading, talking about silly stuff until someone came to tell us off and being rude to them when they did!

In fact, it was Neil who poked his head around the door and ordered us to stop messing about and go to sleep. Karen smirked at him.

"I will if you'll get me some new tights while you're shopping with Valerie tomorrow, Neil."

Neil grimaced. "Just shut up and go to sleep, Karen!"

"Will you get me some tights, Neil? Please?"

I watched as Karen smiled coyly and fluttered her eyelashes at him.

"Yes, yes, all right. And I'll get you some as well, Keri, but only so long as I don't hear another sound from this room!"

Karen giggled. "Night, Neil!" She dived under her covers and made loud snoring noises.

Neil shook his head and closed the door.

We waited about an hour before getting quietly out of bed to huddle beside Karen's bed with a torch. We sorted through our make-up and perfumes, cramming everything into a small make-up bag each. We counted our money. We had nearly seventy pounds between us, plus whatever we would be given for swimming. Karen split the money equally and concealed it in small amounts inside tights and briefs which she stuffed into the swim bags.

Next, we each selected a change of clothing which we rolled up as small as possible and crammed into the bags beside our underwear. Karen managed to wrap the swimsuits so tightly into the towels that they fit with no problem, leaving space for our hairbrushes, which we would put in just before we left.

"Are we ever gonna come back here, Karen?" I whispered.

"Not if I can help it," she replied. "Only if we get caught. Do you reckon we could live with these gypsy friends of yours?"

"I don't know. If we can't, I'm sure they'll help us find somewhere we can go safely. I ... er ... I don't know whether to take Lambie or not."

Karen shook her head. The shadows danced against the bedspread. "Best leave him. Anyway, if they see he's gone, they'll know we're gone too. Also, you're a bit old to take a teddy with you!"

"I've had him since I was a baby, Karen. My Nana made him for me."

"They don't throw our stuff away, you know. Not ever. I've seen people go missing before. After a few weeks, they just pack up all their stuff and keep it in storage ... ready for when they find them I suppose."

As I snuggled into bed that night, I cuddled Lambie really tightly, sniffing at his woolly body which still had a very faint scent of lavender about it. I felt excited, afraid, elated and terrified, all at once. The part of me which had any common sense told me I was being a fool and had no need to run away. I thought of Mother and how annoyed she'd be with me. Then I smiled to myself. The prospect of Mother being enraged with me but having no way to vent her fury was highly amusing. In fact, it may even have been the deciding factor. I fell asleep in the wee, small hours, still clutching Lambie close to my heart.

29. The Adventure Begins

Much to my own surprise, I awoke feeling rested the next morning. In many ways, I felt grateful that everything remained as it had always been at Garfield House. I ate a good breakfast and did my chores willingly. I even offered to help with extra chores. Mrs. Webster sent me to see Mrs. Brown in the kitchen. Apparently, there were a great many potatoes to peel.

Mrs. Brown chattered in her friendly manner, although I noticed she didn't once mention the holiday. She asked me if I was looking forward to going swimming in the afternoon.

"Yes. I'll feel safer in the pool than I did in the sea!"

"I used to go in the sea when I was a young girl. Sometimes, the waves were so big they knocked me off my feet. Of course, I was a strong swimmer in those days. Are you wearing your bikini, dear?"

I paused. "No. Joss thinks we should wear the one piece suits in the local pool as the bikinis are very small."

Mrs. Brown nodded. "Quite right too. We can't have any of the boys there getting silly ideas into their heads. You've had enough man trouble already in your short life ..." Mrs. Brown clapped her hand to her mouth and turned to me. Her cheeks were scarlet. "Keri! I'm so sorry! I didn't mean ..."

I shook my head. "It's all right, Mrs. Brown. I know that you've been told about what happened on holiday. It was horrible, but even so, it wasn't as bad as what my step-father used to do to me."

Mrs. Brown fussed with her apron. "Huh! And he needs shooting, if you ask me. Still, least said, soonest mended. If you've finished those, dear, you can go."

I put the peelings in the bin and washed my hands. Once again, I began to have second thoughts about running away. Everything seemed to be so ... secure and ordinary. A lump formed in my throat and I thought of Lambie, being left all alone whilst I ran off to goodness alone knew where.

"Are you all right, dear?" Mrs. Brown laid a hand on my arm.

"Yes, yes, I'm fine, thanks. See you later." I hurried from the room to find Karen.

We had no opportunity to be alone and unobserved during the morning, so I couldn't discuss my feelings with Karen. At lunch time, Valerie sat with us as usual, so I couldn't even give any hint then either.

About an hour after lunch, Neil came to the playroom to collect Valerie for her shopping trip. "What time are you two going swimming?"

Karen glanced at the clock, which read nearly two thirty. "Around now, why?"

"I'm just asking. If you want to wait a bit longer, Valerie and I will be back in a couple of hours and we could all go together."

"Oh, Neil! We can't! We're supposed to be meeting friends in the coffee shop after! We can't change our plans now! Karen sounded quite put out.

Neil shrugged. "Fair enough. Just make sure you're back in time for tea. I don't want to have to trudge all the way down to the coffee shop to fetch you both. Ta-ta; see you later. Come along, Valerie."

Once we were alone, Karen whispered, "Right. At least we know we've got three and a half hours clear before they even start wondering where we are. By the time they've sent Neil to look for us at the coffee shop and he gets back to tell them we're not there, it'll be closer to seven o'clock, making four and a half hours. Are you ready? I'm dead excited. I can't wait to meet your gypsy friends!"

How could I possibly tell Karen I was having second thoughts? After all our planning and getting money together, the scheming and plotting. Everything was set up. All we had to do was walk out the door.

"You're not too scared now, are you?"

I looked into Karen's brown eyes. "Kind of. Things can get pretty shitty here, but I've been happier here than I ever was at home."

"Yes, so have I, if I'm honest. But even so, I don't want to face any bloody social workers asking awkward questions. Just imagine, if they find out what we got up to, Joss and Paul would be sacked and we could have other, far more horrible people here. Best we just go."

The reminder of what might happen once social workers arrived to interview me was just the spur I needed. "Come on. Let's go before I change my mind."

We called a cheery farewell to Mrs. Webster and Mrs. Brown as we left, via the back door, our swim-bags swinging on our shoulders. Both women waved and smiled and told us to enjoy our swim.

Karen had acquired a bus timetable the previous day. She fished it out of her pocket and studied it once we were away from the house.

"Right. If we head down to the pool, but instead of turning off, we stay on that road, there's a bus stop just a few hundred yards further on. There'll be a bus in about ten minutes. We should make it all right. Got your money ready?"

I nodded and hurried along beside Karen. Neither of us spoke. Maybe we were too excited. I wondered if Karen felt as anxious as me. I greatly feared being caught. We found the bus stop without trouble and had only been waiting a couple of minutes when the bus arrived.

We paid our fares and scuttled right to the back. There were few passengers and nobody took any notice of us.

"I hope you know where to get off," Karen whispered.

"I'll recognise it, don't worry."

Although only around twenty five to thirty miles, the journey was prolonged, mainly because the bus went through just about every village on its way toward North Walsham. Karen and I spoke little, each deep in thought.

As the bus rumbled along the road and I saw the Jolly Farmer pub, my heart began to pound in my chest. Nothing had changed at all! I have no idea why I thought anything would be different. A couple of lads stood beside the pub with their bikes, but none of them looked at the bus.

"We'll have to get off in a little while," I whispered to Karen. "Then we've got a long walk. I'm scared now, in case the gypsies aren't there."

Karen shrugged. "Won't really matter if they're not. We've got money. We can go where we like. I'm hungry though; I could do with something to drink too."

We got off the bus at the crossroads at the other end of the village and watched the vehicle trundle away in a cloud of diesel fumes. Karen looked at the high hedges and the grass verges filled with cow parsley, nettles and dock.

"Wow. You're a country bumpkin at heart aren't you?" She grinned to let me know she was joking.

I turned into the lane which would lead round the back of the village and ultimately the track leading up to the Common, beckoning Karen to follow me. "If not for my horrible parents, I'd have loved it here. There're loads of really good people in this village, apart from the gypsies."

As we walked, I told Karen about Benjamin and the farm; how Mr. and Mrs. Jones had helped when Tammy was hurt. I spoke of Sylvia and her son, Martin; Mrs. Meadowes and her fierce geese. Karen listened, asking a question now and then. We were exposed as we strode up the track toward the Common. I worried we might be seen and someone would tell Mother.

"From what you've told me about the people here, if anyone did see us - and recognise us, no-one would go running to your mother."

I knew there was truth in that statement. Mother seemed to have made no friends in the village. Of those who had befriended her, they quickly fell out with her once it became known how she behaved toward me.

We reached the stile and clambered over it. Karen surveyed the wide, rolling expanse of short grass and heather with its few clumps of gorse and stunted trees. "I hope you know where you're going, Keri. If I don't get a drink soon, I'll likely die of thirst. Why didn't we bring a bottle of cola with us?"

"Would've looked suspicious. It's all right; I know where I'm going. It's not too far now."

I felt intense relief and pleasure as we came to the top of the rise and looked down into the familiar hollow. There were the coloured wagons, grouped together. The horses stood beneath a few trees slightly to the rear of the camp.

"Wow! Those are real Romany wagons! And you know these people? I was always told they didn't like outsiders. We won't be in any ... you know ... danger or anything, will we?" Karen's eyes were wide.

I shook my head and linked my arm with Karen's. "Come on. I expect Deefer is underneath one of the wagons watching us. He'll come out in a minute, barking his head off."

As I spoke, the yellow dog appeared. Strangely, he didn't bark; he stood, sniffing the air and wagging his tail.

"Deefer?" echoed Karen.

"Yep. Dee fer Dog! He belongs to Mia. There he is."

"I don't like dogs much. Our next door neighbour had dogs and they went for me and Dad one time."

"Don't worry. Deefer won't do anything. He's very obedient." A lump rose in my throat as I noticed the dog casting about with his nose in the air. He knew it was me approaching. I thought he was looking for Tammy. My poor dog! A pang of loss stabbed at me and I fought back tears.

Before we actually got into the camp, Mia appeared and then raced to a wagon. As we stepped forward, past the fire-pit, Mam opened her door and came down the steps with her hands outstretched.

I pulled away from Karen and ran to the old gypsy woman, tears spilling down my cheeks. Mam enfolded me in her arms, her tiny hands patting my back. She didn't speak. For several minutes I remained in the old woman's embrace. I could smell the herbs she used to wash her hair and the spices she'd been using in whatever she'd been making before we arrived. I felt a deep sense of peace and I knew the old woman truly loved me.

When Mam finally released me and looked into my eyes, I grinned widely. I could hear Mia chattering to Karen and I glanced to the side. Deefer sat at Karen's feet, the absolute picture of obedient dog.

"Now, Keri. You can sit down and tell me how it is that you are here. That there's been more trouble in your life, there is no doubt. And I see you have another friend." Mam held her hands out to Karen, who sidestepped Deefer and accepted the old woman's greeting.

"Ah. Another troubled soul. Come, child, come and be welcome here. Mia! Tell Anna there'll be two more for supper."

Mam led the way into her wagon. I stepped inside; nothing had changed. The familiar brightly coloured cushions and drapes made me feel safe and welcome.

We sat on the long seat which doubled as Mam's bed whilst she prepared drinks for us. Neither of us spoke. I think Karen felt unsure and didn't know what to expect. I simply waited for the old gypsy to open the conversation.

We sipped elderflower cordial from brightly coloured glasses. Mam sat between us. When she spoke, she sounded ... distant.

"So you've travelled, Keri. You don't like the sea?"

Karen spluttered into her drink and stared at the old woman in amazement. I stifled a snigger. Mam's statement hadn't really surprised me. The old woman always seemed to know things without any rational explanation.

"Mam, it was dreadful! I felt like I wanted to die. I'm never going on another boat as long as I live, I swear it!"

Mam chuckled to herself. "Oh, you will go on another boat, child. Just not for a long time. Strange that you focus on sea-sickness when other, far more terrible things have happened to you since we last met. Will you tell me about them?"

We sat in the cool wagon, a small breeze riffling through the open doorway making the drapes flutter. I described to Mam how the social workers had come to the house and taken me in spite of Sylvia's protests. I went on to describe Garfield House and life there.

"So you're happier at the home than you were with your mother." Mam patted Karen's hand. "And you've found a true friend as well. What of your Nana? You haven't mentioned her to me."

I shook my head. "I haven't heard from her at all, Mam. I think she's probably forgotten me."

"Nonsense! What is far more likely is that your mother has manipulated the poor woman into believing she is not permitted to contact you! Later this evening, you shall write a letter to your Nana. I shall see that it is posted." Mam hesitated before continuing. "I sense a darkness; something you haven't told me. Why can I not believe that you are secure and happy at the home? Is it simply because you have obviously run away, the two of you? I think there is something else. Something far more sinister. Do you not trust me, child?"

I glanced at Karen, who looked distinctly uncomfortable. "It's not that I don't trust you, Mam. It's ... well ... I ..."

Karen began to speak. At first, her words were halting and hesitant, but after just a few moments, with the old gypsy woman's hands resting on her arm, she spoke more freely. Even I gasped in shock as Karen told Mam about abuse on a massive scale. Neil's groping and fumbling with me whenever we were alone seemed as nothing compared to the things Karen spoke of. She'd been at Garfield House much longer than me.

Mam did not interrupt. Her face looked serene and calm as she listened, but somehow, I could sense the outrage and fury roiling beneath that calm exterior. When Karen began to describe events on Jersey, my body began to shake, even though it sounded as if she were relating a dream. Several things seemed almost real, but as I grasped at them, Karen added more and the memories slipped away again.

I now understood why Karen detested Sally. Karen had been George's girlfriend first. She too had fallen pregnant, but she'd had a miscarriage. George switched his attentions to Sally and never bothered with Karen again, leaving her to grieve for her lost child and an indifferent man all alone. I also understood much better how Karen's attitude to the sex abuse made her so apparently strong. She accepted it, even relished it to a certain degree. She'd learned, far more quickly than me, how to use her body to get what she wanted.

Mam stood up and refilled our glasses. She stood in the middle of the wagon, a diminutive figure, but somehow so much larger than life. More real than anyone else I'd ever known. Although her face remained calm as she handed us the refilled glasses, I knew she was furious.

"And you, Keri? Have you suffered the same as Karen?"

I shook my head. "No. So far, it's only been Neil who has done anything to me, but he hasn't hurt me at all. I ... I thought he cared about me!"

Karen snorted into her drink, but she didn't say anything.

"What happened to you on Jersey, Keri? Can you remember?"

"Not really. There was a French man. I spent all night in his hotel room. There was lots of sex, but he didn't hurt me. I think I liked him but I can't really remember. Mam, I was drunk most of the time. The rest of the time I felt dizzy and sick and nothing seemed real. I got raped one night. He was a huge fellow. He told me he was a boxer. He did hurt me. He scared me as well. He was going to drop me in the sea and stand on my head until I drowned." I paused to sip at my drink. "He hit me, I think. Anyway, when I woke up I was alone on the beach. There was a big thunderstorm and I couldn't find my knickers. It was ever so cold. I got up and wandered into the town. I found a policeman. He was kind to me."

Mam frowned. "That must have been very inconvenient for the so-called carers from the home. Were you examined, Keri?"

"No. He took me back to the camp. Paul and Joss told the policeman I was ... what's the word ... it means that I sleep around."

"Promiscuous."

"Yes, that's it. I got told off, in front of the policeman. I yelled that I had been raped and I'd bitten the man's nose. I didn't think anyone believed me but the other day, Adam told me that they found him. The man who raped me. Adam says he was kicked off the island and that there was going to be an investigation. That's why we ran away."

Mam pursed her lips. "And you came to me. You knew I'd welcome you. You knew I'd listen."

I nodded and opened my mouth to speak but Karen interrupted me. "Yet you're probably the only person who can't do anything about it. No-one would listen to a gypsy, right?"

Mam smiled at Karen. "You're old for your years, Karen. Yes, that's about the sum of it. If I went to the police or to County Hall and related all you've told me, they'd tell me I'm a mad old woman and ignore everything I said."

"Yes. I've met gypsies before, although no-one like you. We can't live here with you either, can we?"

Mam pulled her shawl tighter around her shoulders. "Probably not. But even so, you're staying tonight ... perhaps a few nights ... whilst I think about what can be done. You'll have a couple of days of peace at any rate."

Karen grinned at me. I hugged myself, delighted that I could stay at the gypsy camp, even if only for a day or two. Mam beamed, her dark eyes twinkled in her lined cheeks.

"Go and find Mia, you two. Spend an hour or two being children in the fresh air. I want to talk with Anna; when the men come back, I'll need to speak with them as well. Don't wander too far. We'll call you when supper is ready, although I expect Deefer will know anyway."

We drained our glasses and left Mam's wagon. We found Mia with the horses. The girl asked us no questions, simply accepting we were there and treating us as if she'd known us all her life. Before long, we were running about, throwing a stick for Deefer, talking together of simple things. Garfield House, Jersey and all my other troubles melted away into the warm summer air. I felt unburdened and safe. I could see Karen felt the same.

30. Mam's Plan

Karen and I stayed for two days and two nights with the gypsies. We shared the bed in Anna's wagon. At first, I was appalled at the prospect of Anna and her husband sleeping on the ground beneath the wagon, but after much laughter and reassurance, I ceased my protests. Anna explained that, since it was summer and nights were warm, she and her husband would suffer no discomfort. Only when she told me they sometimes slept under the wagon anyway, if the night was very hot, did I accept that Karen and I had not caused them any undue trouble.

Despite Karen's taunts of my being a country bumpkin, she settled into gypsy camp life just as easily as me. We lugged wood and water; we helped to prepare food and even to groom the horses, although we both felt unnerved by the gentle giants.

We only saw the men folk at the end of each day because, even though we got up just after dawn, they had already left the camp to work on the farms. The men treated us with respect - very much in the same way they treated all the women of the camp.

Mam helped me to compose a letter to Nana. I did not speak of any of the horrors; only of my love for her and my belief that she'd been duped into believing she was not permitted to contact me. I had to say I'd run away from the home, but I assured Nana of my safety and that I was with good, trustworthy people who would care for me. Somehow, it didn't seem to be enough. I hesitated before signing my name at the end. Mam noticed, of course.

"I am certain your Nana loves you, Keri. She will be worried; that is only natural. But soon, she'll realise that, of all people, you contacted her, to let her know you are safe and well. That will mean a lot. Perhaps, one day, you'll be able to visit with her again; for now, this will be sufficient."

No-one from outside the camp visited during those two days, which Karen and I considered fortunate. I enquired of Mam as to whether she'd seen Benjamin and Shep at all since last year. The old lady smiled.

"He's been to see us a couple of times. He is growing into a fine young man. He misses you, Keri. When you've left and I judge you to be safe, I shall send word that I've seen you. I have a plan. Later on, during supper, I'll explain everything. For now, you can go find me some dry heather and small sticks for kindling the fire. Off you go!"

Much later, after we'd eaten, we sat quietly as Mam explained what she had in mind. Firstly, my undated letter would be passed between various groups of gypsies until it reached a town far away, when it would be posted. This avoided the police being able to track where I'd been when I wrote it. This news pleased me because I'd worried about the letter. I didn't want Mam or any of the others to get into trouble for looking after us.

Next, Mam explained that she had a great many extended family members throughout the county of Norfolk and some even much further afield. She intended to give us a letter we could show to the people she directed us to. We would be taken in and cared for. Most of these people had given up the wandering life and settled down into ordinary houses and businesses. The only thing Mam needed to know was whether Karen and I had any preference as to where we went.

"I've always wanted to live near the seaside," Karen blurted out.

"And you, Keri?" Mam's eyes glittered in the light of the small flames of the camp fire.

I shrugged. "I'd like to stay here with you, Mam."

The old lady shook her head. "I'd like nothing better than to have you, child, but you would quickly be found and taken back to that ... place. With the best will in the world, such secrets as two 'new' girls in the camp are hard to keep quiet. If it were just family, there'd be no problem. As it is, people in small villages talk far too freely."

"I know, Mam. I don't really mind where we go. If it is half as nice as here, I'll be happy."

"Right then. I've a mind to send you to a distant cousin of mine. He lives in Great Yarmouth with his wife and family. He runs a business as well. It is the height of the summer season; I'm sure he'll find work for you both, accommodation too. I trust him and I know he'll look out for you. How does that sound?"

Karen and I looked at one another before nodding in agreement.

"How will we get there, Mam?"

"I've thought about that as well. The safest way of course, would be for one of us to take you. But that's out of the question. We never usually leave this site until the end of the season. Things like that are noticed, even though people have such a low opinion of gypsies. It will have to be on the bus or perhaps by bus and train. I have a little money I can give you."

"There's no need," I blurted out. "We've both got money. Plenty enough for bus fares, no matter how far away it is."

"Very well. Tomorrow you'll set out. Try to get word to me, Keri. At least let me know you are safe. Alberto will always pass on messages for you. He's a good soul, even if he is a little brusque and rough around the edges."

That night, both Karen and I fell asleep almost as soon as we went to bed. All too soon, we woke to Anna's cheery call. Karen chattered excitedly about the new life we were about to start but I found little enthusiasm. I couldn't conquer the longing I felt to remain with Mam. Deep down inside, I knew I would never see the old lady again and it upset me.

A steady rain fell; it had rained nearly all night. Parts of the camp were muddy, but no-one seemed to mind. I asked Anna if she and her husband had got wet and felt relieved when she assured me they had been snug and dry all night. The dismal skies reflected my mood but I kept my tears in check somehow.

After breakfast, which we ate in Mam's wagon, the tiny gypsy woman handed us each a piece of fabric.

"I haven't much that I can give you to remember me by, but these I stitched with my own hand. Ordinarily, I'd sell them, but I want you each to have them."

I unfolded the square to find it was a handkerchief. In one corner, the letter K was surrounded by tiny, violet flowers. Tears sprang to my eyes and I choked back a sob.

"Now, now, Keri. Don't get upset. Life is for living and I've lived most of mine. If I helped you to avoid any more pain and abuse, then I have done well enough. You have the whole of your life ahead of you - both of you. There will always be events over which you have no control, but for the most part, your lives will be whatever you make them."

"You make it sound as if we'll never see you again, Mam," Karen said.

"Not in this life, child. But know this: all those we have known and loved in our journey through life, we shall meet, know and love again. It's not so bad."

I rushed to Mam and hugged her, my tears dripping off the end of my nose and onto her shawl. "Mam!" I sobbed. "I don't want to go!"

Mam returned my embrace in silence. She held me as I wept and gradually, my tears slowed and I felt peace descend upon me. I don't know how she did it; perhaps she simply let her love flow into me. When I'd stopped weeping, she hugged Karen, who, despite her hard exterior, had tears in her eyes as well.

We left mam's wagon and found Mia and Deefer waiting outside with the other women. The whole atmosphere felt muted and quiet as if the camp were a little world all on its own in a sea of rain and heather. The fresh scents of the Common prickled my nostrils.

Anna and Mia hugged us both. Mia solemnly gave us each a tiny bunch of white heather – for good luck, she said. Anna gave us each a miniature bottle of perfume she'd made herself. The other women of the camp hugged us and wished us well.

Mam looked up at the sky. The rain had slowed to a light drizzle. She seemed to think for a few seconds, before reaching up to lay a hand on each of our heads.

"May the blessing of Light be upon you - Light without and Light within. May the blessed sunlight shine upon you; May Light shine out from your eyes like a lamp set in the window of a wagon to welcome the wanderer out in the storm. May the blessing of the rain be yours; may it beat upon your spirit and wash it clean, leaving a shining pool where the Truth of the Mother herself glows. May the blessing of the Earth be on you; soft under your feet as you pass along the roads, soft under you as you lie out on it, tired at the end of day; and may it rest easy over you when, at last, you lie out under it. May it rest so lightly over you that your spirit flies free from under it quickly – up and off; on its way home. Always remember, especially when the night is dark and the storm rages, the Mother of All is with you and always will be."

As if on cue, the clouds parted a little and a ray of sunshine glowed through the tiny raindrops. I felt awed and full of wonder. I'd never heard such a prayer, not in all my time at the Convent nor anywhere else.

"Mam," I croaked, "Who is the Mother of All?"

The old lady folded her hands in front of her. "She'll find you, Keri. You're young yet to learn of such things. But I have seen something of what life holds for you and I know She'll find you."

"And me?" Karen asked.

"Yours is a different path, Karen, but you will be happy eventually."

We stood there, in the drizzle, knowing we had to leave but unwilling to depart. I stared around at the brightly coloured wagons, the horses, their coats steaming slightly as the drizzle ceased and the small group of women. I wanted to fix it in my mind so I would never forget it.

Karen broke the silence. "Come on, Keri. We have to get back down to that crossroads and catch the bus to North Walsham. If we miss it, we'll have to wait an hour and we might be seen."

I tucked the handkerchief Mam had given me into my pocket and hefted my swim-bag on my shoulder. "Thank you, Mam. Thank you all for everything you've done for us. I wish I could say something to you as wonderful as you've just said to us."

Mam grinned widely. "Be off with you! Your thanks are enough. Have a safe journey and give my love to Alberto when you see him. Farewell."

With that, the old woman turned and walked slowly up the steps of her wagon. She closed the door. I knew, in that closing, a light had just winked out of my life. One I would never forget.

31. Off To Great Yarmouth

If Karen hadn't urged me onward, we would have missed the bus. My legs seemed unwilling to walk away from Mam and her family. Tears ran unchecked down my face and I sniffled miserably. Karen made no comment on my emotional state. Although she'd only spent a couple of days at the camp, she too recognised the unique qualities Mam had in abundance and had become emotionally attached herself.

We waited at the crossroads in the steady drizzle. There was no proper bus stop. On the country lanes, between villages, passengers simply waited for the bus to come along and waved their hands at the driver for him to stop.

I felt sure we'd missed the bus and was about to suggest we retreat into a field to hide for an hour or so when the bus rumbled round the corner. Karen darted out and waved her hands and the bus came to a stop right next to us.

The driver opened the automatic door and grinned. "Mornin' girls! Hope you dint get too wet waitin'."

I followed Karen up the steps and waited whilst she paid the fare for both of us. Once I'd stepped onto the bus and the door had closed, my heart somersaulted in my chest. Just a few seats along, there sat Mrs. Meadowes with her wicker shopping basket on her knees!

The old lady's eyes widened slightly as she recognised me. She glanced about and back to me. To my utter astonishment, she shook her head slightly and raised her fingers to her lips in a gesture of silence.

I caught Karen's arm and pulled her into the seat behind Mrs. Meadowes, who did not turn around or acknowledge us in any way.

"Why are we sitting here? Don't you want to ..." Karen began.

I nudged her to silence and put my hand close to her ear to whisper, "The old lady in front of us. She's my Mother's neighbour. She recognised me, but she's not going to say anything! It just seems right to sit here. Keep quiet. Please."

"Are you sure she won't tell?" Karen mouthed.

I shook my head. I sincerely hoped I had not misinterpreted the signal. I took the handkerchief Mam gave me out of my pocket and unfolded it, inspecting the tiny embroidery stitches. Karen took hers out too and we compared them. The flowers I had glanced at earlier, when Mam gave it to me, turned out to be Violets, with sprigs of Rosemary between them. I recalled the Shakespeare play, 'Hamlet' and muttered under my breath, "Rosemary for remembrance."

"What's this flower and leaf?" Karen asked, showing me her handkerchief.

I studied the pale, yellow flowers and the sprigs of deeper green with them. "I think they're primroses - and that stuff I'm pretty sure is Thyme - that's an herb."

"How did she know I like yellow?" Karen asked.

I grinned. "Best not to ask how she knows anything! She just does."

The bus stopped and a slender elderly lady climbed the steps. When she'd paid her fare, she sat next to Mrs. Meadowes, who greeted her warmly. Instinctively, Karen and I stopped talking.

"Oi 'eard there's bin police down your way last night," the elderly lady said.

Mrs. Meadowes nodded. "Tha's roight. Them bin ta see that woman lives opposite moine. Oi watched be'ind the curtain!"

"Phaw! What you reckon it was this time then? Reckon she started thrashin' the little lad an' all?"

Mrs. Meadowes shook her head so the cherries on her hat wobbled. "Naw. The father wouldn't let that happen! Oi wondered iffen she'd had a go at someone loike she done with our Sylvia. Oooh, Oi would've laughed to see 'er dragged away, so Oi would!"

"So them dint drag 'er off or anything?"

"Naw. Oi watched out the window fer over an hour, Oi did. Them coppers just come out the house, got in their car and drove off. Moind you, Oi kept watchin' loike. The man come out an' went off in 'is car. 'E looked a bit ... you know ... miffed."

"From what Oi 'eard, 'e always looks miffed," the other woman replied. "Oi 'opes summat 'orrible 'as 'appened to 'er, the wicked witch that she is. Did you ever foind out where they took the young girl from there?"

"Naw. Sylvia tried roight hard, so she did. She wanted to adopt the girl. Said she was a roight nice little lass. She went into Norwich to see them social worker people more 'n once. They wouldn't even let her write or 'phone the girl." Mrs. Meadowes paused and the other lady nudged her.

"What? Not at all?"

"Naw. O' course, once that woman found out, she created merry hell and then there was the big fallin' out. Oi tole you all about that before. Still, Sylvia weren't gonna stop there. She even went and seen the local MP. She tole him all about the beatin's and how that poor dog suffered an' all. She tole me none of them believed 'er and said she'd been taken in by the girl's lies! Imagine that! Sylvia seen the child and cared for 'er but they reckoned she couldn't prove nothing!"

Tears sprang to my eyes once again as I listened to the women. Clearly, Mrs. Meadowes was doing her best to let me have as much information as she could. To learn that Sylvia had fought to have me for her own choked me. I wanted to ask questions, pass on a message to Sylvia perhaps, but I knew I could not. To my surprise, I felt Karen's hand clutching at mine. I turned to look at her and knew she understood.

The bus stopped many times on the way to North Walsham; nearly all the passengers were elderly and they all seemed to know one another. Pretty soon, the conversation between them all meant we could hear little of what Mrs. Meadowes said. Even so, I learned that Farmer Jones had done very well with his pigs and Benjamin had won a scholarship to an even more exclusive school.

When the bus arrived at North Walsham railway station, the elderly passengers had already disembarked and we were the only people left. As we passed the driver on our way out he asked us, "Off somewhere nice, girls?"

"Yeah. We're going to see my auntie," Karen replied, before I could open my mouth.

"Where's that, then?" the driver asked as he stood to adjust the destination of the bus with a handle in the roof above him.

"Wouldn't you like to know!" Karen retorted.

The driver laughed. We hurried into the station building and watched out the window until the bus pulled away again.

"Right," Karen began. "We got this far all right. Do you think that old woman will keep her mouth shut about seeing us?"

"I think she will. She really dislikes Mother. I expect she's worked out now that the police were at my mum's place because I've run away."

"Well, we'd better not hang about now," Karen cautioned. "Let's get the tickets and get ourselves to Great Yarmouth."

The train journey lasted about an hour and a half and was uneventful for us. We watched families clearly going to the seaside for the day despite the drizzle; groups of young people on an outing together and couples enjoying each other's exclusive company. Absolutely nobody even glanced our way.

By the time the train pulled in at Great Yarmouth station, the rain had ceased and strong sunlight made the puddles gleam and sparkle. I thought of Mam's blessing immediately. Karen strode confidently out of the station concourse and onto the street beyond. She rummaged in her swim-bag for the letter Mam had given us the previous evening.

"All we have to do now is find this place," she said, pointing at the address.

"Well. We can't exactly go and ask a policeman, can we?"

Karen giggled. For no reason I could think of, I began to laugh as well. We moved along the street, laughing, having no idea where we were going. Pretty soon, we came to a main shopping street thronged with people.

Karen nudged me toward the Woolworth's store. I don't recall what we bought; something small and insignificant, no doubt. However, the reason for Karen taking me into the store soon became apparent. When we approached the till, the lady smiled and made small talk, which Karen responded to in a very friendly manner. Just as the lady handed her the change, Karen said, "Oh. I wonder if you could help me. I'm looking for this address." She showed the lady the envelope containing Mam's letter.

The lady looked at the address and smiled. "Oh, Alberto! I can tell you how to get there, dear, but he won't be at home at the moment. Can I ask why you want him?"

With rattlesnake speed, Karen explained that Alberto was our uncle. She wove a complex tale about our mother being unwell and sending us to stay with him and his wife for the summer. I stared at the ground so the woman would not register the astonishment on my face! Karen sounded incredibly convincing.

The lady directed us to go along the sea-front until we found a particular ice-cream parlour. She felt sure Alberto would be at work there and told us that if he were not, anyone there could telephone him and get him to come there quite quickly.

Karen thanked the lady, grabbed my hand and towed me out of the store.

"Enjoy your stay, dear! Tell Alberto Margie said 'hello'." I glanced back to see the friendly cashier waving. I waved back, feeling foolish and as if attention had been drawn to us.

We found the sea-front and ambled along it, peering into shop windows and stopping to inspect hats, postcards and other seaside paraphernalia. It felt as if we were just on a day out! We passed several places selling ice-creams and even more restaurants, all of which had enticing smells coming from them.

Eventually, Karen stopped in front of a large establishment which appeared to be both cafe and shop combined. "This is it, I think," she muttered.

We walked hesitantly through the double doors, which stood open. Karen wandered toward the cafe side and approached the counter where a harassed-looking man served a lady with at least six children.

When the woman and her wailing children had moved away from the counter toward a large table, the young man looked up. "Can I help you?"

"Um ... we're looking for Alberto. Is he here?" Karen took the lead.

"Nope. But he'll be back in about half an hour. You wanna wait?"

Karen treated the young man to one of her special smiles. "That'd be great. We'll have a drink while we're waiting. Two colas, please."

As the young man filled the glasses, Karen studied him. She nudged me and whispered, "He looks a bit like Anna; reckon he's Alberto's son?"

"Maybe," I whispered back.

I paid for our drinks and we sat at a small table in the corner where we could see the street and people coming into the cafe. At one point, I froze in horror as I saw two policemen walking along slowly, looking about as if searching for something. They stopped by the door. I shrank back into my seat and kicked Karen's foot to draw her attention to them.

"Don't worry about it," Karen muttered. "If you cringe every time you see a copper, they'll figure you've got something to hide. Just stare them down if they look at you."

The policemen moved away and I let out the breath I hadn't realised I was holding. Karen seemed unruffled and nothing like as nervous as me. She chatted about loads of insignificant things. Mainly, I simply agreed with her. I felt very anxious and exposed. I longed for Alberto to appear.

After little more than an hour and a second glass of cola, a man wearing smart black trousers, white shirt and a bright red bow tie approached us. He was not particularly tall but he carried himself in a very upright posture. His hair was thick and black threaded with silvered grey; he had a small moustache.

"Good afternoon," he began. "I understand you two ladies are waiting to speak with me?"

I looked up at the man and he smiled, showing very white teeth.

"Are you Alberto?" I asked.

"I certainly am, my dear, but my friends call me Al. How can I help you?"

Karen produced the letter from her pocket and handed it to him. "We've been told to give you this," she said. "I'm Karen and this is Keri."

Alberto accepted the letter and opened it. We watched as he read through it, frowning. He folded the letter in half and placed it in his trouser pocket before pulling a chair from another table and sitting down beside us.

"How old are you two?" he asked in a low voice.

"Fifteen," we replied.

Al ran his hand through his hair in a distracted manner. "This is very difficult, you understand. I really don't want any trouble. I've worked very hard to build up these businesses of mine and I've stayed within the letter of the law."

"Does that mean you can't help us?" Karen asked.

Al hesitated. "No. I can help you, but you'll have to understand certain things before I do."

"Like what?" I asked.

"I'll give you work. Both of you. And I've got a bed-sit empty in one of my buildings. You can have that. It's supposed to be for one person, but it won't hurt for you to share. You can't use your real names, though. Eventually, some nosy copper will come asking after you. How long have you been gone?"

"This is the fourth day," Karen replied, promptly.

"Right. Well, they never report runaways on the news - not unless they think they've come to some harm. So that helps a bit. It doesn't mean they're not looking for you, though. You'll have to change how you look and think of some new names."

"OK." Karen agreed.

I said nothing.

"I can't employ you both in the same place, so you'll be split up during the daytime. Is that all right?"

"What sort of 'employment' are we talking about here?" Karen asked.

"Poor girl. You really are suspicious, aren't you?" Al replied. "One of you can work in here and the other can work at my fish bar just round the corner. I need some extra workers as I've got a couple of staff on holiday. No-one will think anything much of it. I often take on seasonal staff."

Karen and I looked at one another. I felt excited at the prospect of working and earning money. Karen still looked suspicious.

"Can you think of names?" Al asked. "Only, if you're going to work for me, I'll need to show you around and introduce you to everyone."

"I'll be Fiona," Karen said. "What about you, Keri? Any name you like?"

"Amy?" I suggested.

"No. That's awful! What about something more ..."

"Anna," I stated. "I'll be Anna."

"Good," said Al. "Now, I'll take you and introduce you to the other workers, show you your bed-sit and then we'll fix you a meal. I expect you're hungry?"

Al stood up and we followed him to the counter. The young man was busy, making some sort of ice-cream dessert.

"Don, this is Fiona and Anna. They'll be working with us for a while. You look like you could use another pair of hands in here." Al turned toward us and added, "This is my grand-son, Don."

"Hello," Karen and I chorused.

Al stopped to collect his jacket and then led us out into the busy street. We trailed after him, moving along the sea-front, dodging tourists and holiday-makers, children and groups of youths.

Al led us into a crowded fish and chip shop, which also doubled as a restaurant. The two women working at the counter looked up as he entered and smiled.

"Ho, there, my dear daughters! Busy?"

"Very," one of the women replied as she served fish and chips onto plates.

"Good. Good. That's what we like to see. These two here are Fiona and Anna. They've foolishly agreed to help me out for a while, since we're so short-handed."

"Oh, that's great, Dad. When can they start?" the other woman said as she poured more chipped potatoes into the deep-fat fryer.

"Tomorrow morning, light of my life. And you're not having both of them. One of them will be working with Don." Al turned to us and pointed at each of the women. "My two daughters, Carole and Louisa. Carole is Don's mum."

The women gave us a brief greeting as they continued with their work. Al turned toward the door.

"Come on, girls. Let me show you where you're staying next. It's not far. Have you got everything you need?"

"Like what?" Karen asked.

"You know; toothbrushes, soap, towels and all that stuff. The place is furnished but I'll have to bring you some bedding. Most people bring their own, but I suppose, as you're 'travelling light' I can help out."

We followed Al along a street not quite as busy as the sea-front. Several people smiled and greeted him. It seemed he was well known. I recalled what the woman in Woolworth's had said.

"We asked directions to your house in Woolworth's. A woman called Margie sent us to your cafe and said to tell you 'hello'," I told Al.

"Did you say who you were?" Al enquired.

"No. We said you were our uncle and our mother is ill so has sent us down to stay with you until she recovers," Karen replied. "Does it matter?"

"Hmmm. Maybe not. I'll just make sure that Carole, Don and Louisa know that you're supposed to be their cousins."

Al stopped outside a door between two shops. He pulled a large bunch of keys from his jacket pocket and unlocked the door, revealing a flight of stairs. He switched a light on.

"Go on up. I'll follow. Second door on the left."

We preceded Al up the stairs, which were carpeted with a clean, if rather old, stair runner. A second flight of stairs led up to the next floor. In front of us were five doors, all painted gleaming white. Al puffed a little as he reached the top of the stairs.

"Too many fine cigars I think," he said, ruefully. "Right. That's the bathroom. You share that with the other tenants. This will be your room." He moved past us and opened a door on the left with one of his keys. "There. Will that do you?"

We followed Al into a very large and spacious room. Two large, bay windows faced us. They had faded curtains hanging at them. Between the windows stood a chest with a television on it. On one side of the room a double bed took up one corner. In the other corner, a large wardrobe stood. Between them, two chests of drawers, one with a large mirror.

On the other side of the room were several cupboards, a small, two ring electric cooker, a sink with a tiny draining board and a small refrigerator. Next to the door where we stood, a small settee faced the television and windows.

Neither Karen nor I spoke. We stood, looking around the huge room, grinning like a pair of fools.

"It's clean," Al began to explain. "My wife does the cleaning, so I know it's done properly. There're plates and cutlery and stuff in the cupboards. All you'll need is bedding and towels. I can fetch those down to you later on. Will you be able to manage crammed in here together?"

"It's lovely. Thank you so much," I breathed.

"Yep. It'll do just fine," Karen agreed, moving further into the room.

"Right," said Al. "I won't charge you anything for this week. Wouldn't be fair, especially not since it was Mam that sent you to me. How is she?"

I turned to look at the man. "She's fine, Al. She speaks very highly of you. She said you could get a message to her if we wanted you to."

"Yes. I can do that. I probably won't see her before Yule, but I can certainly relay anything you want to tell her. Or letters. I can make sure she gets those too. I'm glad she's well again. Did you know she was really sick last winter?"

I hadn't known. I hadn't even thought to ask the old woman how she was! I hung my head, tears threatening. How could I have been so selfish?

"Clearly, she didn't tell you that. Just like her. Never mind. You say she was well and that's good. Right. I'll give you a key. Please, try not to lose it. I spend a fortune having new keys cut all the time. You can leave your things here. I'll show you where you can get personal stuff you might need. Will you need an advance on your wages?"

"Wages?" I echoed.

"Of course, wages! What? Did you think you would work for nothing?"

Karen laughed. "No, thanks. We've got some money to be going on with. Can I use the toilet before we leave?"

We both used the toilet. The small bathroom was spotlessly clean and smelled fresh. I felt as if I were in a daze. Suddenly, we had jobs; we had somewhere to live - together. Surely, life had suddenly been kind to us both!

Karen looked after the key. Al showed us a small supermarket close to the building, which we noted was number seventeen and located between a shoe shop and a bookmaker. He took us back to the fish and chip shop and presented us with enormous plates piled high with crispy chips and battered fish.

As we ate, we discussed where we would each work. Karen seemed very keen to be in the fish and chip shop. I had no preference. I'd never had a job before. In all honesty, I was a bit anxious, hoping I wouldn't make a fool of myself by being incompetent. We agreed that I would work at the ice-cream parlour.

Al had already left the premises by the time we finished our meal. Carole winked at us as we returned the plates. "So you two are our long lost cousins, are you?"

I blushed and Karen opened her mouth to speak but Carole simply laughed. "It's all right. You don't have to explain. Probably best we don't know, eh? You'll fit in just fine. Which of you is going to help us tomorrow?"

"That would be me," said Karen.

"Right. And you're Fiona, aren't you?"

Karen nodded.

"Can you get here for half past nine, Fiona? I'll find you an overall and a hat ready for the morning."

"OK," Karen agreed. "See you tomorrow."

"I wonder what time I have to be at work?" I asked Karen as we made our way back along the sea-front.

"Best call in and ask," Karen replied. "And we'll need to get an alarm clock as well. I don't want to oversleep on my first day!"

We stopped at the ice-cream parlour and waited until Don had time to speak to us. He really did seem to be rushed off his feet. I asked what time I should arrive for work.

"We open at ten," Don replied. "If you get here for around half past nine, I can show you everything you need to know. You worked in a place like this before?"

I shook my head.

"Oh. Well, you'll soon pick it up. You won't be on your own. I'll be here. We'll soon get you used to it. It's a very long day though. Ten until eight. You'll get breaks, of course, but you need to wear comfortable shoes because you'll be standing for a lot of the time."

We stopped off at the supermarket and bought several things including something for breakfast the next day. Karen became worried when the shop clearly did not sell alarm clocks. We asked at the till, where we might find somewhere that did and the lady directed us along the street to a very small shop which appeared to sell everything.

When we arrived back at the bed-sit, we found Al had been there. The bed had been made up and there were four towels on the dresser. On top of the refrigerator stood a kettle, packs of tea and sugar and a pint of milk.

Karen put our bag of shopping down beside the cupboard and flung herself down on the settee. "Mam was right. He's a dead decent bloke, isn't he?"

"Yep. I can't believe that anyone related to Mam could be anything but decent," I replied as I fiddled with the alarm clock we'd just bought. "I don't know how to work this thing!"

Karen took the clock and peered at it. "What time shall we get up?"

"I dunno. About eight?"

Karen fiddled with it for a few minutes and set it down on the floor. "If I've done it right, it should go off in a minute."

Sure enough, within a minute or so, the little clock rang an extremely loud alarm. Karen pounced on it to switch it off. "That's all right then. I'll set it for eight, although I bet we'll already be awake well before then."

We hung our few clothes in the wardrobe and placed our makeup and hairbrushes on the chest with the mirror. I left Karen watching the television, although the picture was a little fuzzy, whilst I went to have a bath. When I returned to our room, swathed in towels, Karen went for a bath.

Later, curled up on the settee with a hot cup of tea each, Karen looked at me and said, "Do you think we'll be all right, Keri? I mean, this place is fine for us, isn't it? So long as we don't get caught, we could stop here and make a new life for ourselves."

"I dunno, Karen. It's weird. We're gonna have to do everything for ourselves."

"So? I'm damned sure I can look after myself!"

"We've got to think about food and ... well ... washing our clothes and stuff like that. I don't think I can cook much."

"Shut up, you ninny! We'll learn! How hard can it be? As for washing, I'm sure there's a launderette round here somewhere. Anyway, we'll have wages by this time next week. We'll be able to buy our own clothes and everything!"

I tried to feel reassured, I really did, but deep down, I was frightened. It was one thing to think about being independent but quite another finding that all of a sudden, I really was responsible for myself.

As we settled down in the unfamiliar bed, I thought about Mam and wondered how ill she'd been. I should have asked about her health but I'd been so consumed with my own troubles I hadn't given a thought to anyone else. I found it difficult to get to sleep, not just because of my gloomy and regretful thoughts. Karen moved about quite a lot and several times, she struck me with knees and elbows. I moved to the outside edge of the bed and stared at the reflection of a street light on the ceiling until I dozed off into an uneasy sleep.

32. Full Time Work and An Encounter

Karen and I actually did not need the alarm clock after all. Both of us woke naturally shortly after seven. We breakfasted on cereal and toast, although Karen complained we'd forgotten to buy marmalade!

We counted our money, finding we had just a little over fifty pounds left between us. This was a great deal of money for two teenage girls, but we both agreed that we'd 'worked' for it and so we could do with it as we wished.

"I'm going to dye my hair black," I announced. "I might cut it shorter as well. Why don't you dye your hair blonde?"

Karen snorted. "Not a chance! Everyone thinks blondes are stupid! Anyway, I'd look daft with blonde hair, brown eyes and black eyebrows. I might have my hair cut short though."

"Al said we'll need to change the way we look. I can only think of changing my hair style and colour. What else could we do?"

Karen shrugged. "Probably get some different clothes. They'll know what we took with us by now, won't they?"

"Let's go shopping then," I suggested. "Before work. How long does it take to dye hair?"

Karen screwed up her face in thought. "My mother used to do all kinds of stuff with her hair. She was always white blonde. I seem to remember her with horrible, smelly stuff on her head about once a month. I think it takes about half an hour. Tell you what, let's get a dye and I'll do yours for you."

Although only shortly after eight in the morning, we left the bed-sit and hurried down the stairs into the town. By the time we found a chemist it was nearly half past eight. Karen picked out a pack of hair dye which had a picture on the front of a woman with glossy, jet black hair.

"This'll do. Come on; we'll have to get a move on or it won't be done before work!"

We ran all the way back to the bed-sit. Karen skimmed through the instructions, put on the plastic gloves and told me to use one of our swim towels because we shouldn't get dye on any of Al's.

The stuff smelled dreadful! My eyes watered and Karen had to open one of the big windows to let some fresh air into the room. I perched on the edge of the settee with the vile liquid on my head. I could feel it dripping down my neck. Karen giggled as she wiped it away with tissues.

"You won't be able to cut your hair too short for a while. It's stained your neck. I can't get it off!"

I jumped up and peered into the large mirror. A small drip had formed beside my ear. I snatched up a tissue and wiped it away; it left a dark stain.

"Quick! Get the soap!" I yelled. "I'll have to scrub this off. Surely, it must come off skin!"

By the time we'd rinsed the stuff out, scrubbed at the stains on my skin and done our utmost to clean the stains off the basin and tiles in the bathroom; it was nearly twenty past nine. I rubbed vigorously at my hair with the enormous swim towel and felt dismayed when I saw the black streaks across the multi-coloured fabric.

I brushed my hair and stared at myself in the mirror. I looked totally different. Gone, at last, was the pale, mousy brown I'd always hated. The girl in the mirror looked older and quite severe.

Despite the fact that my hair remained damp, I quickly applied my make-up.

"Wow. That's a real change! I think you look fabulous!" Karen breathed. "I might dye mine as well. I don't think you need to cut your hair. It looks kind of 'right' at that length.

"We'll do yours tonight after work shall we?" I replied. "Come on; we'll have to run or we'll be late on our first day!"

"I like your hair. I nearly didn't recognise you when you arrived," Don commented as I presented myself for work at the ice-cream parlour.

"Thanks. I'm having it cut later as well," I replied.

"It looks nice long," Don replied.

Although I felt flattered by his compliment, the only thing I could focus on was the word 'nearly' in his first remark. I felt I would definitely have to cut my hair. I wanted to look completely different.

I had no time to dwell on such matters though. Don showed me how the automatic coffee machine worked and instructed me on the need to wash my hands frequently. There were a multitude of different ice-cream desserts I'd need to learn about, although Don told me to ask him the first few times so he could make them, showing me what they involved.

I mastered the till easily enough, although I had to tot up totals mentally before entering them. I explained to Don that mental arithmetic had never been my strongest talent. He grinned and taught me, very quickly, a method of manipulating numbers to arrive at a total quickly.

"Actually, it probably doesn't matter that much if you're a penny or two out either way. Few customers will argue and if they do, just apologise and tell them you made a mistake. I'll fix any problems anyway. Don't let yourself get worried or het up. Best way to deal with this job is to be friendly toward the customers. Chat to them; pay them compliments; ask about how their holiday is going. A friendly, smiling face means that a lot of small mistakes are overlooked. If you make a big mistake, just smile sweetly and explain that you're new and you'll do better next time."

Don made it sound so simple. The reality, once the doors opened at ten, nearly overwhelmed me in the first half hour! I couldn't believe how many people flooded in. Families with small children and groups of young adults, all laughing and chattering together. Most of them hardly seemed to give me a second glance, so intent were they on getting ice-creams and drinks and finding a table to sit at.

One of the jobs involved collecting dirty plates, dishes and cups and wiping the tables clean. Of course, virtually as soon as this had been done, someone else sat down with more!

Crockery and cutlery also had to be washed, dried and stacked. I wondered, as I dried my hands for the umpteenth time, just how Don had managed to do all the work on his own. In a short breather, I asked him.

"Well, I did my best, but it was impossible, to be honest. I've only been in here alone for two days and I was about ready to tell my grandfather he could take a running jump! Then you came along. Usually, there are three of us in here. Sometimes four. They've gone away on holiday though. Al advertised for replacement staff, but nobody applied. I think it's because the wages are so low."

"Oh. Good job I came along then, isn't it? I didn't ask about the wages. I've no idea what they are!"

"Well. You're a casual worker, aren't you? I'm not supposed to tell you, but I get a pound an hour, which is pretty good. You'll probably get about seventy-five pence an hour. Of course, it's all money. It soon adds up."

The way Don spoke of wages made me wonder if I should be disappointed at the rate of pay, but since I had little idea of the going rate, I couldn't comment.

"You won't pay any tax. I do. But even that isn't so bad, once you get used to it. I do pretty well through the summer season. It's not even that bad in September and October because people still seem to want ice-cream and coffee, even if it's pouring with rain. Winter is not a good time to have this kind of job though."

I learned to make wonderful ice-cream desserts with exotic names like 'Banana Longboat', 'Knickerbocker Glory' and 'Strawberry Sundae'. Mostly, they involved fruit, ice-cream - of various flavours - cream and a sticky sauce. All were incredibly popular.

Don made me take a break at about one. I sat on a deck-chair, outside in the bright sunshine at the back of the premises and enjoyed a cup of frothy coffee and several cigarettes. I looked up and noted the gulls strutting about on the rooftops. Their cries were ever present. I wondered how I'd never noticed them before.

At around three thirty, just after Don returned from his own break and I'd managed on my own, a crowd of long-haired men wearing leather jackets, grubby jeans and heavy boots entered.

"Ooops. Here comes trouble," Don muttered.

"Trouble? Why?" I asked.

"Bloody Hell's Angels. If they're in here, no-one else will want to come in. Anyway, they might start a fight and smash the place up."

The group approached the counter. I stepped in front of Don and gave my best smile.

"What can I get you fellows?"

"'Ello darlin'" a very tall man with lank, greasy hair almost to his waist, leered.

"Hello," I replied brightly. "What'll you have?"

"What you got?" the man replied.

"Leave her alone, Tool! Fer Chrissakes, shut up!" The man who had spoken shoved the man out of his way and stepped to the front. Although he could only be described as 'rather grubby', he was handsome, in a rough kind of way. Blue eyes twinkled under sandy brows and his thick, sandy-brown hair was pulled back to the nape of his neck and tied loosely with a leather thong.

"Do you do that 'frothy' coffee in here?" the man asked.

"We do," I replied.

The man beamed. He had beautiful, even, white teeth. "Great! Right. I'll have one of those - please. This lot will have ..." he turned and looked at the group behind him.

Don leaned forward and muttered in my ear, "Aren't you scared of them?"

I turned and looked at him in astonishment. "No. Why should I be? I bet they're a really good bunch - once you get to know them."

Don shook his head. "I'll leave you to it, then. I may as well get the washing up done. There'll be no other customers in whilst they're here." As he spoke, a family hastily vacated their table, the mother shooing her two young children ahead of her toward the door.

"Right." The handsome man turned back to me. "That's five of your frothiest coffees, three teas and one cold milk. You do serve cold milk?"

"Yep. Is that cups or mugs?"

"Oh, mugs. Definitely mugs." He grinned again.

"Right. Well, you go and find yourselves somewhere to sit and I'll bring them over to you."

The men moved toward the back of the room where a long table with ten chairs around it would accommodate them. I busied myself with making up their order.

As I walked across the room with the tray, one of the men exclaimed loudly, "Fuck's sake! You dirty bastard!"

I marched to the table and set the tray down. I put my hands on my hips and glared at the men. "You can stop that right now! This is a family place. If you want to start shouting and swearing, you can take yourselves somewhere else, understand? My boss didn't want to serve you at all, but I said you'd behave yourselves. Don't make me a liar!"

I unloaded the tray, distributing the mugs where the men indicated their choice. As I went to move away, I noticed the very tall man had his feet up on one of the chairs. I stopped and glared at him. He winked at me!

In one, swift movement, I shoved his feet off the chair and pushed hard at his shoulder. "Get your boots of my chairs!" I growled. "And I mean it. If you don't behave ... out you go. Got it?"

"Sorry, miss," the man replied. The others laughed at him.

I turned and went back to the counter.

After about ten minutes, a family came in. The leather-jacketed men were speaking together at the back of the room, but I'd not heard any swearing and there was no raucous behaviour at all. Don served the family.

Within a few moments, the trickle of customers once again became a flood and we were overwhelmed with requests for everything from ice cream sundaes to mugs of strong tea. I made sure I shot a stern glance across the room now and then, but it wasn't necessary. The men behaved perfectly.

As we worked, Don asked me, "How come you managed to keep them so quiet and well behaved? Every other time I've had that sort in here, they've been dreadful."

I shrugged. "You were the one who told me to be friendly. I've never had any problem with bikers. They're just people."

"Yes, I know, but you shoved that man's boots off the chair like you were his mum and he didn't say anything!"

I grinned. "I wouldn't recommend you try it, Don. I probably only got away with it because I'm a girl. Just be friendly to them and they'll be friendly to you."

When the men got up to leave, the room was filled to capacity and there were several people waiting to be served. They filed out quietly, the handsome man bringing up the rear.

"I stacked the cups up, love, so you can clear them quickly. Looks like you're well busy today," he said.

I looked up from the sundae I was constructing. "Thanks very much. And thanks for being quiet, too."

He flashed me a brilliant smile before leaving. My heart fluttered in my chest and I spilled strawberry sauce on the counter!

Later, when we'd both finished our first day of real work, Karen and I exchanged stories as we ate the fish and chips she'd bought home with her. Karen shuddered when I spoke about the Hell's Angels.

"I'm glad they didn't come into the chip shop," she remarked, with her mouth full.

"They're all right," I replied. "I like bikers. They've always been good to me."

"We should go out this evening," Karen said, ignoring me and changing the subject. "These long hours are gonna be a right pain. We won't get to see anything of the town or meet any new friends or anything if we don't go out in the evenings."

My feet hurt from the hours of standing, but I said nothing. I'd really enjoyed my first day of work and apart from my sore feet, I hadn't noticed the long hours at all.

"I tell you what," Karen added. "I'm gonna get sick of bloody fish and chips soon enough. We'll have to get some shopping in tomorrow morning and see what we can cook for ourselves."

We wandered along the sea-front, occasionally stopping to peer into shop windows. Many shops were still open, which I found to be strange at nine o'clock at night.

"It's the seaside, Keri. They have to stay open late. I found out today that in the winter, this place can be like a ghost town. They have to make as much money as they can in the summer. Anyway, Carole was talking about people not having as much money as usual this year. Apparently, a lot of people are only working three days a week. Something to do with the government and oil prices. I didn't understand half of it, to be honest. Anyway, we're lucky to have jobs at all, even if it does mean working till eight every night."

"Well, at least we don't have to get up early like the gypsy men. They were up and gone before dawn," I replied. "They were working every day, weren't they?"

"Oh, I dunno what it's all about. Nothing to do with us anyway. Come on; let's go home, I'm fed up with dodging tourists and drunks."

Once we'd bathed and had a hot cup of tea, I told Karen I intended to buy some sharp scissors the next morning and asked her if she'd cut my hair for me.

"Well ... I'll try," she agreed. "Although I've never cut anyone's hair before. I might mess it up."

I laughed at her serious expression. "It won't matter, Karen. If you do make a real mess, I can go to a hairdresser and get it fixed - maybe in my lunch break. Are you gonna dye your hair?"

"Nope. I thought about it, but I've always rather liked my hair. It goes with my eyes and anyway, it's taken ages to grow."

"Aren't you worried about being recognised?"

"Nah. I mean, they're hardly gonna be looking in a fish and chip shop for me, are they?"

I wondered just where 'they' were looking. Since I knew they'd already visited Mother, the police would probably try to visit Nana as well. Other than that, they would have no idea where to search for me.

"You reckon they've been to see your dad?"

"Oh yeah. Even if he knew where I was, he wouldn't tell them. He hates the police. He knows I can look after myself. I expect they'll be visiting my aunts and friends as well. They won't find anything. This is the first time I've been to Yarmouth. No contacts or family here. We'll be all right, don't worry so much."

"I'm not worried," I lied.

We watched television for a little while, but neither of us enjoyed the programme. We turned it off and clambered into bed. I fell asleep quickly that night. I must have been more tired than I realised.

33. Disaster Strikes

Three days later, Karen did cut my hair, although not quite as short as I'd wanted. I thought she'd made a very good job of it. Where it had been almost to my elbows, it now came to just below my shoulders. I'd always worn it with a centre parting and Karen changed this to a side parting.

"There. Even your own mother wouldn't recognise you now," she crowed.

I grimaced. The thought of Mother discovering and recognising me was not at all pleasant. As far as I knew, she didn't visit Great Yarmouth. She preferred the quiet, small town of Sheringham – if she went to the beach at all.

"Karen, I wish you'd do something to change how you look," I complained. "What will I do if you're recognised and caught?"

"Nothing," Karen replied, shaking her long, curly hair so it tumbled down her back. "If either of us is caught, we say nothing about the other, all right?"

I frowned. "But surely, they'll know we're together."

"Not necessarily. If I'm caught, I'll lie in my teeth and say we split up in Norwich and I don't know where you went. You say the same about me. All right?"

I nodded. "Even so. If you changed how you look we could ..."

"Well, I'm not going to, so you can just stop moaning about it. Anyway, there's a boy I like. I think he likes me too. If I suddenly go blonde or something, I might miss my chance with him."

I sighed. Karen had mentioned this lad several times. I hoped she'd remember to use her assumed name of Fiona if she got talking to him. My own assumed name, Anna, had fallen flat on its face on the first day. Don had decided I looked like a cat because of the way I'd done my make-up. He called me 'Kitty-Kat' all the time. I didn't mind; I liked cats and actually felt flattered.

The Hell's Angels had come into the shop every day after my first day of work. Don no longer worried about them; only a few people turned away when they saw the men. Mostly, people got on with their ice-creams and drinks and either didn't notice them or ignored them.

The men were in the shop when the refrigerated unit used to hold all the tubs of ice cream suddenly made a groaning noise and stopped working. Don flung his hands in the air in frustration.

"That's just great! Now I'll have to ring the engineer and wait who knows how long for him to get here. How am I going to keep these ices frozen?"

Don and I were peering at the grille on the bottom of the unit. A few sparks came out. We both stood up and our heads bumped together when the handsome man spoke.

"Want me to take a look for you? I'm pretty good with electrical engineering. It might be something as simple as a fuse or perhaps a wire has burned out. These things can get pretty hot in the summer weather."

Don hesitated.

"Seriously, man. Tramp's a wiz with anything electrical. Let him have a look. Might save you a few quid - and the ice-cream won't melt either," one of the other men called.

"Well, all right," grumbled Don. "But if you can't fix it, I'll still have to call the engineer and he'll likely complain that someone else looked at it first."

"Yeah. And likely be my father or one of his cronies," Tramp joked. "Come on, move over. Let's have a look-see."

I'm not entirely sure what the fault had been. Needless to say, the man named 'Tramp' - a particularly unpleasant name - got the unit running again in just a few minutes. Don grinned gratefully.

"Thanks very much. How much do I owe you?"

"Nothing, man. It was simple enough. You've been good to us, just returned the favour, that's all. I think we'll have another coffee, if we're not putting other customers off."

"Sure," replied Don. "Kitty-Kat, get these guys some more coffee - and don't charge them either."

When I took the tray of drinks over to the table, the man called Tramp spoke to me.

"Kitty-Kat, that's an unusual name. Mind you, you do look a bit like a cat."

I blushed. "Thanks."

"I've always been rather fond of pussies," commented the tall man.

The others laughed.

"Shut up, Tool. These folks have been good to us and we'll keep it civil, all right?"

The man Tramp called 'Tool' grinned up at me. "No offence meant, darlin'. I usually open me gob before I've engaged me brain."

I had no idea what the offensive remark had been, so I smiled at the man before I walked away.

Much later, I blushed horribly when Karen explained to me what 'pussy' meant! Only then was I offended. Thank goodness I hadn't understood at the time. That man would have been highly amused by my embarrassment.

The days passed quickly for me and Karen. We grew accustomed to getting up and going to work, shopping for the simple ingredients required to make small meals, although we often ate out as well.

We kept our bed-sit surprisingly tidy for a couple of teenagers. When Al's wife had been in to clean, we only knew because the carpet had been hoovered and the bed linens changed.

We acquired several more clothes and swapped them between each other regularly. Karen found a launderette fairly close to the bed-sit and we soon mastered the coin-operated machines.

Three weeks or so passed and we still found ourselves very busy at work. One evening, Karen said, as we walked home, "I think the kids all go back to school this week. It'll be good not to have to go to school, won't it?"

I actually quite enjoyed school and I felt an inexplicable pang of regret before I nodded, agreeing with her.

"I suppose, once the kids are back at school, we won't be so busy."

"Probably not. I'm not complaining, though. So long as we've still got jobs. Your people are back from their holiday, aren't they?"

I nodded. "Yeah. It makes life a lot easier not having to clear tables, wash up and serve customers all at once. I don't think that woman, Clara, likes me much though. She told me off yesterday for talking to the Hells' Angels. She said they shouldn't be in the shop at all. Mind you, Don stuck up for me and told her how one of them fixed the fridge unit for him and she shut up. Have you seen much of Al?"

"He drops in now and then, usually for wages. Have you seen him much?"

I had seen Al. He'd explained to me that, come October, he would have no choice but to let me go from the ice-cream parlour. He suggested I try looking for another job for the winter months. He also told me that Karen and I could stay in the bed-sit for as long as we liked, just as long as we could pay the five pounds a week rent. I hadn't liked the implication of that. If I couldn't find alternative employment - and the prospects were bleak - I'd have no money with which to pay the rent.

I explained this to Karen and she shrugged as if it didn't matter. "Oh, we'll be all right. Bound to be some other work we can get and there's loads of places for rent. Half the people in them at the moment will be gone by the end of September. You worry too much!"

The next day, after work, I headed back to the bed-sit. Usually, Karen arrived a few minutes before me, but today, the outside door was locked and there was no sign of her. I leaned against the doorway and waited.

After about half an hour, I became very worried and retraced my steps. The ice-cream parlour was closed and locked up, so I made my way further along the road to the fish and chip shop. I eased my way past the few people waiting to be served and managed to attract Carole's attention.

"Do you know where K ... I mean, Fiona is?" I asked, in a low voice.

Carole frowned at me. "Come in here and wait out the back. I want to talk to you, young lady." She lifted the flap which separated the serving area from the main shop and ushered me through.

I waited in the back room, staring at bins of chipped potatoes, trying to still the sudden pounding of my heart. I hoped Karen hadn't been rude to someone or been sacked.

Carole came through and closed the dividing door behind her. I noted her stern expression. "Just what have you two done?"

"Pardon? Nothing!"

"Well. I don't take kindly to policemen barging into my fish restaurant and arresting my staff! You must have done something! They were looking for you as well. I know your name isn't really Anna. Is it Keri?"

I nodded miserably.

"So what did you two do?" Carole's tone softened. "It must have been pretty bad for there to have been six policemen coming after your friend. Don't worry. I didn't tell on you. I was furious and they seemed convinced enough that I didn't know you."

I breathed a sigh of relief. "We ran away from a children's home," I confessed. "We haven't done anything bad at all. Please. Don't send me back there!"

"Really? Is that all? How old are you?"

"Fifteen."

"Good grief! Only fifteen? I thought you were both at least eighteen! Whatever did you do to get sent to a children's home in the first place?"

I looked Carole in the eye. "My step-father raped me and my mother thrashed me. All the time. They killed my dog too."

Carole's hand flew to her mouth in shock. She reached forward and embraced me in a bear-hug. "Don't worry," she soothed. "You'll be safe, I'll see to it. We won't let the police take you." She patted my back and stroked my hair. "Your friend 'Fiona' fought like a mad thing. It took four of them to cart her out of here.

I could well imagine how much of a fight Karen would have put up. However, my own immediate problem sprang to the front of my mind.

"Carole. Karen had the key to our bed-sit. Without that, I can't get in! What shall I do?"

"Fortunately, that's a problem I can do something about. Al's always got spare keys. You wait in here and I'll ring him. He'll come and let you in. You might have to wait a while though. Shall I bring you something to eat? You can go sit in the rest room to eat it."

I nodded. "Yes, please. I'm starving."

Carole took me through the back preparation room and showed me a small lounge which had a kettle and several mugs on a tray next to a pack of tea-bags and milk.

"Make yourself at home. You can make yourself a drink. I'll bring you some dinner. There's a toilet and hand-basin through there." She pointed along the corridor.

Left alone, I allowed myself to cry. I didn't know how I would cope entirely on my own. Already, I felt bereft and lonely. I imagined all kinds of horrors Karen could be enduring.

When I'd snivelled for a while, I got up and made myself a cup of tea. I had just sat down with it when Carole came back bearing a plate of cod and chips.

"Get that down you, girl. And when you've eaten it, you might want to go and wash your face! Your eye make-up is all smudged. I expect you've been crying a bit, eh?" She sat down on a nearby chair.

"I'm scared, Carole. What if they catch me as well?"

Carole studied me in silence for several minutes. I picked at the food; my appetite had fled.

"Well. There's no reason why they would catch you, as long as you stay well hidden - in plain sight. I would never have known you were only fifteen. Did you dye your hair after you left the home?"

"Yes. I cut it shorter as well. I've stopped wearing my high heel shoes, so I don't look so tall but I can't think of any other way to disguise myself!"

"I can. I'll get you some glasses. If you wear glasses it can change your face completely. Don't go in to work tomorrow. When Al comes and lets you in, go indoors and stay there until I come, all right?

I nodded. "All right. You're not just saying that, are you? You won't tell the police where I am?"

"Not likely! Al would not be best pleased about the ice-cream parlour being raided by the police as well. I expect they've been to question him anyway. We'll find out when he gets here. Now. Eat up your supper, wash your face and wait for Al. He'll go back to the bed-sit with you and make sure you're all right. I've got to get back to work."

Carole gave me a brief hug and hurried out of the room. I did my best to eat the meal she'd brought me, despite a lump in my throat and a sick, twisting feeling in my stomach.

I actually waited nearly two hours for Al to arrive. He came into the sitting room where I waited. He looked very worried; his brow creased with anxiety and he wrung his hands constantly.

"Listen, Anna ... I mean, Keri. I don't want any trouble, understand? I've had the police cross questioning me for hours. I think I managed to convince them that your friend was alone when I met her. I told them she came in here looking for work and I hired her as a casual. I hope I haven't caused her any problems. I told them she said she was sixteen and her family were staying here for the summer. I gave them an address on a caravan site and told them that's where she told me she was staying. It won't throw them off for long, but maybe just long enough."

I gulped. "Will you get in trouble if they find me and realise you lied to them?"

Al waved his hand. "Well, it won't make me exactly popular, but I won't go to prison for it if that's what's worrying you. Come on. Let's take you home. Carole will come in the morning. She'll have a key so you won't have to open the door for anyone knocking."

I followed Al through the shop, which was being cleaned. Carole nodded at me and mouthed "See you in the morning."

Although it was getting late, there were still a lot of people about. No-one took any notice of me as I walked the short distance to the bed-sit with Al. He opened the outside door and then solemnly gave me the key, along with a replacement key for the room.

"Try not to lose these ones, eh? As I said before, I spend a fortune on replacement keys. Now, you get yourself in bed and wait for Carole to come in the morning. It'll be quite early. Everything'll be all right, don't worry. Night."

"Goodnight, Al. I'm sorry we caused you so much trouble. I'll do my best to make sure you don't get any more."

"Never you mind about it, love. Mam told me to look after you and I will, to the very best of my abilities. In fact, I think I'll keep you on through the winter. Maybe you can help my wife with the cleaning of the bed-sits or something. Go on, get to bed!"

Al patted my hand and turned away. I slipped inside and closed the door. I switched the light on and looked at the stairway. I really didn't want to go up to the room I'd shared with Karen; it wouldn't be the same on my own. With a sigh, I plodded up the stairs.

When I reached the landing, I jumped as a young woman came out of the bathroom with a towel wrapped around her head.

"Hello," she said. "I think you live next door to me. You're in there, right?" She pointed at my door.

I nodded.

"I thought there were two of you in there?" The girl looked around me, onto the staircase.

"No," I said. "Just me. You probably saw my friend. She stopped here the other night."

"Oh. Right. See you." She turned and I watched her walk along the landing and enter the next door on the left. I waited until the girl had closed her door before opening my own.

Everything was exactly as Karen and I had left it that morning. Of course, it would be. I picked up the towel Karen had left on the end of the bed. The room seemed unnaturally quiet and very much bigger than before. I switched on the television and sat down on the settee, oblivious to the programme.

After several minutes of worrying about Karen, I stirred myself and made a cup of tea. I opened the wardrobe and looked at the array of clothing we had amassed. I knew Karen would expect me to use it.

On the dresser, in front of the large mirror, Karen's make-up, perfume and hairbrush sat beside my own. The soft slippers she'd bought herself the previous week 'to comfort her sore feet' lay discarded beside the bed. I took off my shoes and pushed my feet into the moccasin style slippers.

I drank the tea whilst sifting through the other things Karen had left behind. In a drawer of the other dresser I found a wallet. Inside, along with the several pounds Karen had kept, was a creased photograph of a smiling man. It must be her father, I thought, as I turned it over in my hands.

I didn't undress that night. Nor could I bear to get into bed. I curled up on the settee and watched the television until the programmes finished and the test card came on. I finally fell asleep as I stared unseeing at the windows, where a glimmer of mauve indicated dawn was fast approaching.

34. Hells Angels

I didn't wake, the next morning, when Carole let herself into my room. I opened bleary eyes and stared at her as she offered me a cup of tea.

"You didn't go to bed. Your poor girl. Were you lonely?"

I sat up and stretched. "A bit. It's just strange being here on my own without Karen. We used to talk a lot. She's my best friend, you know. I never really had many friends before."

"You had the best friend anyone could ever have," Carole replied. "Anyone that Mam feels so strongly about is blessed. She's a wonderful woman."

"Yes. She is. Without her, I'd never have met any of you."

"Well. Al explained a lot to me yesterday. Mam entrusted you into our care, so we'll all do whatever we can to look after you. I'm afraid you're going to have to get used to living here alone though. You can't go through your life sleeping on the sofa when there's a perfectly good bed just over there. Come on. Up you get and drink your tea. When you've been to the bathroom, we'll have some breakfast together and I can show you the things I brought with me."

Carole had brought a pair of spectacles. They had thick, pink frames. I turned my nose up at them, of course, but Carole insisted I try them on. The glass in them was perfectly clear and I could see well. I stared at myself in the mirror. I did look totally different. No-one would look at me twice. I also looked several years older.

"Now. I brought you some other small things as well," Carole said. She handed me a plain, gold ring. "Put that on. I hope it fits you."

I went to put the ring on my right hand, but Carole nudged me. "Not that hand! It's supposed to look like a wedding ring. No policeman is going to suspect you're only fifteen if you're wearing a wedding ring - and other things."

The ring was a little loose, but Carole insisted I could wedge something at the back of it so it stayed on my finger. Next, she gave me a silky, patterned scarf and showed me how to wear it around my shoulders.

"Those flat shoes you've got are really good. Teenagers always wear such high heels. I've never met any other girl your age who wore flat shoes."

"I did wear high heels for the first week," I admitted, "But my feet got really sore and sweaty so I got these for working in."

"Good idea. You've learned a valuable lesson there, Keri. Comfort always takes precedence over fashion in my book. Now. This is the hardest part. You're going to have to tone down your make-up. Maybe wear none at all."

"None at all?"

"Well, perhaps some mascara and a little lipstick. But you can't wear your 'kitty-kat' eyeliner. It marks you out straight away as young. Do you think you could do your make up so it looks like mine?"

I studied her face. She had a tiny amount of discreet eye shadow, some mascara and just a touch of blush. Her lipstick was pink rather than the red I favoured. I really didn't want to change my make-up, but Carole had a point. I always wore my eyeliner and eye shadow in such a distinctive way. It would be a dead give-away if the police were seriously searching for me.

"Now. We need to think of a surname for you. Something not suspicious. So nothing like 'Smith' or 'Jones'. And a new birth date that you'll have to memorise. Just in case the police come, asking questions. They always want to know your name, address and date of birth, see?"

We decided I would be Anna Stephenson. My date of birth would be February the first nineteen fifty two - making me twenty one. Carole seemed to think that would be enough for the time being. She warned me that I might need more of a story if there were any chance the police might call on me at the bed-sit. She suggested I claim to have run away from an unhappy marriage but added that we'd work on that over the next few days.

I arrived for work just a little after midday. Don opened his eyes wide when he saw me, but forbore to make any comment. Clara made an acid remark about my 'new' spectacles and added that she hoped it would enable me to 'see' dirt on plates and cutlery. This was a dig at some shoddy washing up I'd done the previous week. I didn't reply. I couldn't afford to get into any kind of argument. Clearly, Clara had not been apprised of my true situation.

The Hell's Angels came into the shop at about three that afternoon. The man called Tramp studied me for a moment before he placed his order. "You sure look different with those specs on, girl. Older too. I had you pinned for about seventeen but I guess you're getting on past twenty."

I smiled. "Looks can be deceiving," I replied. "Same as usual?"

"Yep. You guys do the best frothy coffee in town." He hesitated. The other Hells Angels went to sit down at their customary table. An elderly couple looked appalled at the leather jacketed men striding past them. I watched to see what they'd do. When they merely shook their heads at one another and the man leaned closer to murmur something to the lady, I turned back to Tramp. He looked kind of expectant ... almost like a dog waiting to go for a walk. I realised he'd spoken and I hadn't heard what he said.

"Pardon?"

Tramp dropped his eyes. "Not if you don't want to. I mean ... if you already have a boyfriend ..."

"Er ... are you asking me out?"

He looked up. His eyes really were very deep blue. "Yeah. If you want to."

"OK. Where are we going?"

He shrugged. "There's a gig on tonight at our local. Good bunch of lads. All bikers, but you don't seem to mind us lot."

I thought about spending another evening and night all alone at the bed-sit and found I didn't want to. Although surrounded by people all day long, I actually felt very isolated and lonely.

"All right. That sounds OK. No hanky-panky though. All right?"

Tramp grinned. His face lit up and I smiled too. "You drive a hard bargain, but I promise I'll behave. Where shall I pick you up? Have you got your own brain bucket?"

"I'll meet you outside here and no, I haven't got my own crash helmet."

"Right. I'll bring a spare. About half eight be all right with you?"

"Fine."

I watched him walk toward the others and noticed he was probably as tall at the one they called 'Tool'. On the back of his sleeveless denim jacket, which he wore over the top of his leather, the familiar skull in a crash helmet grinned at me between the legend 'Hells Angels - England'.

I found it quite difficult to concentrate for the rest of the day. Even after the Hells Angels had left, I kept thinking about Tramp. Part of me felt attracted toward him; another part of me was just as equally repelled. I didn't fully understand the way I felt and there was no-one I could discuss it with. I couldn't speak to Don; Clara was out of the question. Besides, she'd scolded me several times for my errors that day.

When I finished work at eight that evening, I barely said goodbye to anyone. I snatched up my jacket and bag and hurried back to the bed-sit.

I felt frustrated that I couldn't have a bath, because someone else had got there first - probably the girl from the room next door. I made do with a wash, using the sink in the kitchenette in my room. After thinking hard, I applied my make-up as I usually did. I really needed to feel 'myself'. After all, in the dark and amongst such a large group, I'd hardly be picked out.

I dressed carefully in tight jeans with wide flares and a black, lacy top Karen had left behind. It felt good to wear my high heeled shoes again too. I surveyed myself in the mirror before tucking the key safely into my bag with my cigarettes and purse.

I didn't hurry back to the ice-cream parlour. Although I didn't have a watch, I knew I was a little late because the alarm clock showed just after eight thirty when I left the bed-sit. Some part of me hoped that I'd be late enough that Tramp would have given up waiting; the other part of me felt full of anticipation and excitement. I rounded the corner onto the sea-front and saw a large motorbike at the side of the road. Tramp had his back to me, but I knew it was him.

I walked forward and touched his shoulder. He turned and looked me up and down.

"My, but you scrub up well, girl!" He passed me a crash helmet he'd been holding between his thighs. "Here. Stick this on and we'll get going. What is your name anyway? I've heard folks calling you Kitty and Anna and that bitch of a woman just calls you 'girl'."

"All of those names are mine," I replied, tugging the crash helmet on. "There's a lot in a name. You're called Tramp, but that's not your real name, is it?"

"Ooooh, you're a sharp one." He turned the key in the ignition and stood up to kick-start the bike, which throbbed into life with an almighty roar.

I climbed on the back and felt for the foot pegs with my feet. Without further pause, Tramp pulled out into the stream of traffic and we were off. I paid little attention to where we were going, revelling as I was in the fresh, sea-air and the thrill of being on a bike again. All too soon, Tramp steered the bike away from the sea-front and we travelled along a long, wide road.

After several more twists and turns, Tramp pulled up outside a large pub. Many other bikes were crowded into the car park. In fact, I saw no cars there at all. Using his feet to guide the large machine, Tramp manoeuvred the bike into a wide space between a gleaming red bike with a naked lady painted on the tank and a jet black, low machine.

I stepped off, undid the strap on the crash helmet and shook my hair out.

"Tell you what," Tramp said, putting his arm across my shoulders. "I reckon you do look like a cat, so that's what I'm gonna call you – 'Kat' with a 'K'. You don't have to tell me your real name. There's something about you I just can't put my finger on, but I guess we all have secrets."

Several leather-jacketed men were gathered outside the pub. Most of them had pint glasses in their hands. As we approached, Tramp leaned down to my ear and said, "Just so you know, I've got no big secrets. You're right. They all call me Tramp, but that's because I get about a lot and don't care where I lay my head. My real name is David. David Eastbrook."

I nodded, but I didn't reply. I'd need to know this 'David' an awful lot better before I told him who I really was. Anyway, I liked the name 'Kat' and I felt it suited me. Certainly better than 'Keri' ever had.

Tramp kept his arm around my shoulders as we approached the group of men. They all openly stared at me; one or two whistled. I kept my head up and did not react to their looks or the few remarks made.

"That's enough of that," Tramp snapped. "This is Kat and she's with me. So you can all keep your paws off her."

"Cool it, man," one of the men muttered.

"Just making sure you all know, that's all. Where's Johnny?"

"In there." An enormous man with a bushy, black beard indicated the pub doorway. "He was looking for you."

Tramp steered me between the men and on into the main saloon. Cigarette smoke hung in a haze in the mainly red lighting. As we pushed between crowds of leather-jacketed men and women in short skirts, I caught a glimpse of the main bar - the only source of normal light in the room.

A woman wearing a leather mini skirt and a see through top stepped in front of Tramp. "Hello, Tramp. Where you been, baby?" She had blonde hair which was so long it almost touched the hem of her skirt!

"All right, Jo-Jo? This here is Kat and she's with me. You make sure there's no bitching. I like this woman and I'll not have any crap thrown her way from the others."

Jo-Jo looked me up and down. I suddenly felt very young, rather stupid and totally out of my depth. Next to this beauty, I thought myself plain and dowdy. I did my best to smile.

"Hello, Kat," Jo-Jo said, after a too-long pause.

"Hi."

"You've got yourself the second best man in here, girl. How'd you manage to pull him?"

"Shut up, Jo-Jo," Tramp pushed past the woman and approached a table, where about twelve men were seated. The table held dozens of pint glasses, some full, others nearly empty. The smell of beer mixed with cigarette smoke, leather and various colognes and perfumes. I felt a little dizzy.

Several of the seated men greeted Tramp as he approached. I immediately noticed there was some kind of hierarchy here. They treated Tramp with deference, not just respect. One of the men stood up and offered his seat. Tramp immediately sat down and pulled me onto his knee.

The man seated next to us on the left had jet black hair which fell past his shoulders. Two braids hung down from his forehead, dangling next to trimmed, black sideburns. His eyes were dark under straight brows and he had a perfectly trimmed moustache and goatee beard. He stared at me.

Tramp grinned and gave me a slight hug. "Johnny, this here is Kat. Had to go pick her up. That's why I'm late."

The dark man winked at me before he spoke, in a severe tone to Tramp. "Women wait on us, you fool, not the other way around. You were supposed to be here at half past eight. Played hard-to-get, did she?"

"Actually, I didn't finish work until eight. It's not his fault." The words simply fell out of my mouth.

Johnny looked at me again. "So you work?"

I nodded.

"That's always good. Half of these lazy lumps don't work these days and there're only a handful of tarts with a job. Good on you."

I became aware that I'd probably spoken out of turn. Nobody said anything but their expressions conveyed more than words ever could. Johnny turned his attention to a short man who looked younger than most.

"Randy, get over to the bar and get Tramp and his lady a drink. She'll have cola."

I sat very still on Tramp's knee and stared at my own hands. The men began an earnest conversation, but I paid no attention. I looked up and noticed Jo-Jo, with a couple of other women. She beckoned to me. I stood up. I thought Tramp ignored me, but as I moved toward the women, he reached out and patted my behind.

The youth, Randy, pressed a tall glass of cola into my hand as I moved past the other seated men. It had ice and a slice of lemon in it.

"Thanks."

Randy did not reply. He stepped around me and placed a pint of beer in front of Tramp before moving round the table to stand behind Johnny.

Jo-Jo caught my arm and steered me deeper into the press of bodies. Three women stood with her; each held a glass of what I thought must either be whisky or something similar.

"You met Johnny." Jo-Jo said.

I nodded.

"You don't know anything about this lot, do you?" she added.

"I suppose not."

"Come outside with us for a while. We'll let you know what to expect, what to tolerate and from who - and what not to do or say."

Clutching my glass of cola like a talisman, I followed the women outside. The group of men had gone.

"You're not even eighteen, are you?" Jo-Jo snarled, as soon as we stepped into the car park.

A woman with heavy, green eye-make-up and short, dark hair laid a hand on Jo-Jo's arm. "Don't scare her, Jo." She turned to me. "I'm Sandie. I think you must be the girl from the ice-cream parlour, yes?"

I nodded.

Sandie smiled. "I thought so. I heard all about you and how Tramp's been mooning over you for a couple of weeks. This must be a bit of culture shock for you. The bikes and the men - everything. Is this the first time you've been on a bike?"

I shook my head. "No. I like bikes. I've never been to a place like this before though."

Jo-Jo tossed her head. Her hair swirled in the light breeze. "There's no place for you here, little girl."

Sandie scowled. "Leave her be, Jo! You can't just chase her away! Tramp would be furious - you'll never get him like that!"

That one remark told me I already had an enemy. Jo-Jo wanted to be with Tramp and I had arrived on the scene, spoiling her plans. I wanted to flee. Jo-Jo looked as if she might be very spiteful. I wished Karen were with me; she'd know how to deal with this situation.

Jo-Jo scowled at me. "Dump him. Tell him you changed your mind and don't want to be with him! Tell him you don't like this kind of lifestyle ..."

I drew myself up and sipped at the cola. "Actually, I think this lifestyle will suit me rather well. Why would I 'dump' Tramp? I haven't got to know him yet and I like him."

Jo-Jo glared at me, turned and marched back into the pub. Sandie giggled. "Phew! She won't forget that in a hurry! Watch your back, Kat."

"Why? What'll she do to me?"

One of the other women snorted with laughter. I turned to her. I noticed she was dressed in leather trousers and a tight, sparkly top. She had a round face with dimples in her cheeks and chin. She wore very little make up. "Reckon Jo's met her match with this one," she chuckled.

I spent probably an hour in the car park with the group of women. I learned that Jo-Jo had been Johnny's woman, but she'd been unfaithful to him. I listened as the women described how Johnny had beaten up the other Hell's Angel she'd been with and humiliated Jo-Jo publicly by denouncing her as a slut in front of the whole group.

I wondered why she hadn't simply left. Had it been me, I'd have crawled away in shame and never shown my face again. I said as much.

Chrissy, the woman who had laughed, nodded her head. "Yep. Me too. But Jo's got 'issues'. When she was with Johnny she was all self-important and lorded it over all of us, like she was our Pres. She's set her sights on Tramp now, but he loathes her."

The hierarchy of the group was quite simple. Johnny was the 'President' of the group; Tramp his second-in-command. Apparently, whenever Johnny went away - which he did frequently, the whole group deferred to Tramp. The men seated around the table were 'officers' of the club. The young man, Randy was a rookie, or 'on-trial' as a club member. As such, he was expected to do all the donkey work - fetch and carry, run errands. The proper term for this station, I learned, was 'a prospect'.

Although Jo-Jo had tried to lead the women, they really had no hierarchy of their own. Most of them were either married to one of the Hells Angels or had been with them for a long time. The emphasis was on 'family'. Apparently, it was very difficult to 'get into' the group from the outside - hence I was unusual.

I asked a great many questions, all of which the women answered candidly. Of those men who had jobs, they were very intelligent and highly qualified. A list of names and professions amazed me. Solicitor, architect, doctor, business manager, even an undertaker!

"Stop!" I giggled. "I'll never remember all of this!"

Chrissy grabbed my hand. "You will, after a surprisingly short time, you'll see. I'm a nurse ... and a mum as well. I don't get to half as many meetings and gigs as I used to. Always need to get a babysitter. You're welcome to visit my house any time you like though. If I'm not home, Gavin will welcome you as well."

"Thanks. Er ... Tramp doesn't work?"

"He doesn't need to, the lucky sod. He's a fully qualified electrical engineer, but he only works now and then - basically, when his dad pressures him because some of the guys are off sick or something."

"He fixed the fridge at the ice-cream parlour when it broke. Don was ever so pleased."

"That sounds just like him. Did you know he's wealthy?"

I shook my head. "I only know he's a Hells Angel and knows how to fix fridges ... and made sure everyone behaved themselves when I told them to."

The women laughed. Sandie hugged me. "Well, you've got quite a catch, Kat. He's a good bloke. Doesn't drink much, hates drugs and gets all over-protective of women. Hang on to him, if you can. There's not a woman among us wouldn't have dropped everything and rushed to his feet, had he asked or shown any interest. Not that we'd be unfaithful to our hubby's of course!"

We all laughed. The atmosphere had become friendly once Jo-Jo had left. None of the women questioned me; they simply accepted me as a new member of their 'family'. It was a humbling experience but one which also made me feel – for the first time, as if I actually 'fitted' somewhere.

We returned to the pub when the band started playing. The music was loud with a great beat. I loved it. I'd never heard anything like it before. It made me feel ... alive ... and full of energy.

Tramp found me amongst the women, swinging my hips and nodding my head to the beat.

"Like the music?" he bawled.

"Yeah."

I had several drinks of cola. No-one pressed me to drink alcohol. I noticed Tramp drinking cola as well for most of the evening. It never occurred to me that this might be unusual.

At the end of the evening, Tramp escorted me back to his bike.

"Best get you home, girl. You're working again tomorrow?"

"Yep. I work every day."

"What? Don't you ever get a day off?"

I hadn't had even one day off since I began work at the ice-cream parlour. I hadn't noticed. The place was equally as busy, if not more, on a Sunday.

"Never really thought about it," I admitted.

"Ask your boss for a day off and we'll go somewhere together for the day. How does that sound?"

"OK."

"Now. Are you gonna tell me where you live so I can take you home? You don't stay with your parents, do you?"

"No. I live on my own. I've got a bed-sit round the corner from the ice-cream parlour."

Tramp frowned. "It's none of my business, but ... how long have you lived on your own? You're not a student ... you'd be back in university by now if you were."

"It's complicated," I replied as I dragged the crash helmet onto my head. "Perhaps I'll tell you about it one day."

"Perhaps you will."

The ride back into the main town was even better than the ride out because there were fewer vehicles on the road. I felt perfectly safe and secure on the big bike with Tramp's broad shoulders in front of me. In fact, I felt disappointed when I recognised the street where I lived. Tramp pulled the bike up, right outside the door.

He switched the engine off and came to the door with me as I fumbled in my bag for the key.

"Thanks for coming out with me tonight, Kat. Will you come out with me again?"

I looked up, into his deep blue eyes. "Yes. If you really want me to. I enjoyed myself tonight."

He bent his head and kissed the end of my nose, light as a butterfly. I think I probably blushed. I'd hoped he might kiss me properly. To cover my embarrassment, I turned away and opened the door. I reached inside and flicked on the stairway light switch.

"Goodnight, Tramp. Thanks for a lovely evening."

I stepped inside, closed the door and leaned against it. I waited there for several minutes before I heard the engine of the bike roar into life and the sound of Tramp pulling away. I lingered to listen to the sound of the bike moving along the seafront, then climbed the stairs to my room.

Although it was late, I took a bath and made sure I'd cleaned off all my make-up. I made myself a cup of tea and wound up the alarm clock before plonking myself down on the settee, wrapped in a fluffy towel.

I thought about the group of people I'd met; the women who had been so friendly toward me; Jo-Jo, who I'd have to be careful of. That Johnny instinctively knew I was under eighteen bothered me. The fact that Tramp hadn't pressed me for answers - or anything else was another enigma. I considered all the horrible things people had said regarding bikers and Hells Angels.

The conclusion I came to was simple. What people didn't know about, they feared. It was the same with the gypsies. I'd fitted in with them too. I clambered into bed, checked the clock and curled up to go to sleep. For the first time since Karen had been caught, sleep came easily to me.

35. Tramp

Tramp was incredibly discreet. When the Hells Angels came into the shop, other than wink at me when I served their drinks, he gave no outward sign that we were anything other than acquaintances. For this, I felt relieved. I was pretty sure Don would pass no comment, but he might mention it to Al. Clara, I had no doubt, would have had a great deal to say on the matter.

I didn't ask Don for a day off. I couldn't bring myself to do so. The shop continued to be very busy and I had an inkling that if they managed without me for one day, they might then decide I was surplus to requirements. Anyway, as far as I knew, Don hadn't had a single day off in all the time I'd been there!

About three days after my evening out with Tramp, I found him sitting outside the main door of building where I lived. He sat on the pavement, leaning against the wall next to the door. I saw no sign of his bike. As I approached, he scrambled to his feet and grinned at me.

"I didn't like to hang about outside the ice-cream bar. That woman in there doesn't like you and I don't want to make any trouble."

"Where's your bike?"

"In the main car park down the road. It'll be all right. Do you want to come out for a while ... maybe get something to eat?"

I glanced up and down the street. There were plenty of people about, but I couldn't see anyone paying specific attention to me and Tramp. I stepped forward and opened the front door.

"Come in for a while. I'll make a cup of tea or something."

Tramp followed me through the door and up the stairs to my bed-sit. I felt a slight anxiety because I couldn't remember if I'd left the place tidy enough to receive visitors.

Once inside, Tramp looked around, taking note of the old, but serviceable, furniture and my meagre possessions scattered about. He walked to the big window and peered out.

"How long have you lived here?"

I hung my jacket in the wardrobe and moved to fill the kettle. "A few weeks now. I'm getting used to it. I have to share the bathroom and toilet with other people on this floor, although there is another one upstairs if I'm desperate."

"It's not a bad place. Close to where you work anyway. Mind if I sit down?"

I waved a hand. "Fine. I haven't got any coffee. Do you drink tea?"

Tramp grinned. "If it's hot and strong, I'll drink practically anything. No sugar please."

When I turned from making the tea, I saw he had taken off his leather jacket and put it on the end of my bed. He sat on the settee in his scruffy jeans and faded blue tee shirt. I noticed a tattoo on his forearm - the familiar Hells Angels insignia. I sat down on the other end of the settee and handed him a mug of strong tea, which he accepted.

"You're quite an enigma, Kat. You haven't told me anything about yourself; where you come from; why you're here in this dead-end town; nothing."

"I don't know much about you either. Only your real name and that you're the second in command of the club ... and you've got a really cool bike."

He sipped at the hot tea. "That's easily rectified. I'm twenty four; I've been a dutiful son and got a first class degree - just as Mummy and Daddy thought I should. I haven't got a place of my own; I stay with any one of the club who'll put me up. Now and then, I go home, wash up, tidy my hair and act as the folks think I should. I'm pretty good with anything electrical or mechanical, but I'm lazy and only work when my father starts begging! I don't smoke weed because it makes me sick; I hate politics and I like kittens, snowdrops and rainbows."

I think I successfully hid my reaction to his age by sipping at my tea. He was nine years older than me! Even so, my heart fluttered inside my chest as he smiled. His deep blue eyes twinkled.

"Your turn."

I hesitated. I worried that if I told him my true age, he'd leave and that would be that. What could I safely tell him?

Tramp leaned forward and put his half-empty cup on the floor. "Look ... Kat ... you don't have to tell me anything if you don't want to. After all, it's none of my business. Anyway, you didn't exactly throw yourself at me did you? I'm the one who's intrigued."

He leaned back and rummaged in his jeans pocket. "It is all right to smoke in here?"

I stood up and fetched the ash-tray. I accepted one of his cigarettes and for a few minutes, we sat quietly, simply enjoying the nicotine.

"Your ... President ... Johnny. He doesn't like me, does he?"

"Johnny? He's all right. He gets ideas and he's always suspicious when new faces arrive, particularly women."

I nodded. I already knew about his experience with Jo-Jo and felt I didn't need to touch on that subject.

Tramp stubbed out his cigarette and picked up his tea. "He thinks you're a runaway. Told me I'm biting off more than I can chew."

I choked on my tea. Tramp leaned across the gap between us to pat my back.

When I'd recovered my breath I hung my head and wondered what to say.

"It's all right." Tramp soothed. "I'm a grown up. I don't need Johnny - or anyone else - to tell me what to do or how to live my life. You need not tell me anything. I like you anyway. I'll go, if you want me to."

I swallowed. I had to take the chance. After all, so far in my life, bikers and gypsies had been the only ones who ever listened to me or accepted me for being myself. I looked into Tramp's face and made my decision.

"I am a runaway, Johnny's right. How did he know?"

Tramp shrugged. "I guess he's done enough running of his own to recognise one when he sees one. So where have you run from? Did you jump bail or something?"

I shook my head, not least because I didn't know what 'bail' meant. "I ran from a children's home with my best friend. She got caught a couple of weeks ago, so now I'm on my own."

"A children's home you say? So you're under eighteen then."

I nodded.

"I'd never have known it. You're very mature. Was it bad? At the children's home, I mean."

"Yep. But not as bad - for me, anyway - as being at home."

Tramp nodded. "Before you even tell me about 'home' I can tell you that parents can be an utter pain. Most folks would say that I had the most privileged of upbringings but I'd disagree. All right, so money was never a problem, but money isn't everything. When you've got a father with great expectations who hardly ever seems to be around and a mother who is more worried about what her friends and neighbours might think if her son doesn't look just like Little Lord Fauntleroy all the time ...."

I laughed. "Little Lord ...?"

Tramp grinned ruefully. "I really didn't fit the mould the old lady had in mind. She wanted the perfect little boy, you know; cute suit, beautifully groomed hair and perfect manners. She's still upset with me now. She wanted me to go into politics!"

I had a mental picture of the only politician I was familiar with ... Edward Heath ... the Prime Minister. I couldn't help but grin widely at the comparison I made in my mind between the stuffy old man and this long-haired Hells Angel.

I made more tea and several slices of toast. I told Tramp everything - except my true age. The evening passed all too quickly. He made no judgemental remarks, except for muttered curses about my step-father, my mother and the 'carers' at Garfield House.

"So you see," I finished, "I really don't know where I fit. I never want to go back to Garfield House. I can't ever go back home or back to the gypsies. So here I am."

"There's no 'never', Kat. If you can stay free until you reach eighteen, there's nothing any of them can do to you. You've got no prison sentence hanging over your head. Even if they pick you up, once you're eighteen, you can tell them to take a running jump. You'd be able to visit your Nana then as well and your old lady couldn't do anything about it."

"I know."

"Well. It seems to me you've done mighty well on your own. You've got a job and a place to stay - that's a lot more than most runaways could manage. You must have been lonely though, once your friend was caught?"

"Yeah. That was grim. I still worry about her. She's obviously not told them anything or they'd have been here right away to get me."

"She sounds like a real good friend." He stood up. "It's late. I have to go because I've gotta actually do some work tomorrow and the day after. You'll be needing to get up for work as well. Thanks for trusting me and telling me about yourself." He walked to the bed and picked up his leather jacket, shrugging it on in a practised movement.

I remained seated on the settee. "I guess I won't see you again."

Tramp stared at me. "Are you kidding? Of course you will! What? Did you think, once I knew about you that I wouldn't want to know you?" He sat down beside me and put his arms around me. "I'll be back tomorrow night, if you can bear to put up with me. I'll bring us a take-away to eat."

"OK. Just not fish and chips - please!"

Tramp laughed. I liked the sound. He released me from the hug and looked into my eyes. "Not fish and chips, I promise!" He leaned forward and kissed my cheek. "Get to bed, woman! You'll never get up in the morning if you don't! I'll see myself out. Night."

Before I could say anything, he'd crossed the room, opened the door and gone. Just like that. I touched my cheek where his lips had been. Already, the room seemed large and empty once again.

I washed up the cups and went to bed. However, I found sleep difficult. Every time I closed my eyes, I saw Tramp's handsome face. I wondered why he hadn't tried to kiss me properly or get me into bed. He was unlike any other male I'd ever met. I believed that he liked me; I simply couldn't understand why he behaved so differently.

I saw a lot of Tramp - and the other Hells Angels - over the next two weeks. I grew used to riding on the pillion of Tramp's bike, although I still felt exhilarated every time. I went to several pubs and visited three or four of the Hells Angels at home, always with Tramp. Everyone treated me well and welcomed me. Even Jo-Jo kept her distance, although I noticed her scowl every time she saw Tramp with his arm draped across my shoulders.

One Sunday afternoon, when the shop was unusually quiet and rain pelted down outside, Don approached me as I washed the cups and dishes.

"You can go home after you've done those. If you want. We won't have many more customers today, not with this weather. There are storms forecast tonight. You haven't had a day off since you've been here."

"Are you sure, Don? Only there'll be their cups to wash and the floor to do. Clara was angry with me yesterday because I went home before the floor had been done."

Don glanced at the group of Hells Angels chatting quietly at their customary table. "I'll do those. As for Clara, I'll deal with her. She's been picking on you unfairly for weeks. I don't know why she doesn't like you. In fact she's getting so spiteful lately I might even have a word with Al about it. Go on. You get yourself home in the warm."

"Thanks, Don." I dried my hands and went to fetch my jacket and bag.

As I left, stepping out into the wind and pouring rain, I saw Tramp stand up. I did not react, simply pulled the collar of my jacket tightly around my neck and ran through the deluge and the puddles.

My head bowed against the wind, I turned the corner into my street. For some reason, I looked up. A panda car was parked right outside my building and two policemen were standing at the front door, clearly speaking to someone. One of them was holding his hat on against the heavy gusts.

Appalled, I retreated to the corner where I could peer around the building to see what happened next. I watched the policemen enter through the doorway. It must be me they were looking for! I had all but forgotten that there would still be an ongoing search for me. My heart thundered in my chest and I shivered as raindrops dripped down my neck. I had no idea what to do.

I was about to turn and retrace my steps to the ice-cream parlour when a familiar arm draped across my shoulders.

"What you doing, Kat?"

I turned and saw Tramp with raindrops dripping off his eyelashes.

"It's the police, Tramp! They just went into my building! Oh, what am I going to do? They've found me!"

Tramp peered around the corner at the parked police car.

"Not yet, they haven't. Come on. You're coming with me!"

He grabbed my hand and we crossed the road, walking briskly through the rain until we came to the main car park. Several bikes were parked close together.

"Bugger. I haven't got your crash helmet here," Tramp cursed. "Never mind. You use mine. The Old Bill won't pull me. Anyway, I can outrun them if they do see us."

I tugged on his crash helmet whilst he kick-started the bike. When he'd manoeuvred the machine to face the other way, I clambered on, feeling the water on the seat seep through my jeans immediately. I didn't care. I simply wanted to be away from there and somewhere safe.

My first experience of bike-riding in pouring rain and a howling gale was one I shall never forget. I never felt afraid because I had every confidence in Tramp's riding ability, but it was not the most pleasant of experiences. The bike sped through the town and on out into the countryside. I wondered where he was taking me.

When Tramp steered the big machine through wrought iron gates which stood open to reveal a long, gravelled driveway, I knew. He'd taken me to his parents' house!

Tramp pulled the bike to a halt beside a gleaming Jaguar in front of the house. He stepped off the bike and grinned at me.

"We'll stop here a couple of days while we decide what to do." He snatched at my hand again. "Come on. Come and meet Mater and Pater!"

I allowed him to tow me up the five broad steps between a pair of ornamental pillars. He pushed a key into the lock and opened the door. An enormous vestibule with an expanse of tiled floor, surrounded by walls half panelled with oak greeted me. I looked up at a complex, glittering chandelier hanging above my head. Almost immediately, a man in a black suit with a stiff white-collared shirt and neat bow tie hurried forward.

"Master David! I shall go and inform your mother that you are here."

Tramp handed his Hells Angels jacket to the man and turned to me for the crash helmet.

"No hurry, man. We need to get cleaned up a bit. Tell her we'll be down in an hour or two."

The man inclined his head and turned away, holding the soaked leather jacket as if it were something vile. Tramp grinned. "Maybe I'd best take that upstairs with me, eh?" He retrieved the jacket.

"Come on. I'll have to take a bath and find some 'appropriate' clothes. Mother dear would have a fit if I turned up in the drawing room like this!"

I followed Tramp up a wide, oak-panelled staircase which had a beautiful, thick-piled carpet of green and gold. I stared at huge paintings hung on the creamy walls and noted expensive-looking vases and ornaments set on obviously antique tables.

Tramp marched along the broad landing and opened a door. "This is my room," he said. He seemed - almost embarrassed. I stepped over the threshold into a room I could scarcely believe.

A four poster bed dominated. It had curtains around it in a delicate shade of blue; they were tied to the bed-posts with navy blue cords. The walls were half-panelled, the upper half a pale blue. Yet more paintings graced the walls; some had small lamps over them.

Tramp closed the door and gently nudged me forward. "Bathroom's through there. If you want to go first, I'll see if I can find you something else to wear. I'm pretty sure there're a couple dresses stashed in the wardrobe - if you don't mind wearing one of my ex's cast-offs?"

I shook my head as I slipped off my flat, working shoes, which were soaked. I gazed down at them; they'd probably never be the same. "What shall I do with my jacket?"

Tramp peeled off his dripping tee shirt, revealing a broad, muscular chest. "Just chuck it on the chair in the bathroom. If we stay a couple days, Mrs. Wilson will get it cleaned and dried."

As I made my way across the room to the doorway Tramp had indicated, I wondered who Mrs. Wilson might be, but I forbore to ask.

The bathroom was huge, probably bigger than my bed-sit! I put the plug into the bath and turned the gold-coloured taps on. A wide mirror took up most of the far wall. I stood in front of it, staring at the wide-eyed girl. My face was rain-streaked, my complexion pale. My hair, from the ears down, dripped onto my sensible buttoned blouse. I felt very nervous indeed. If Tramp had told me he intended to take me to his family home, I'd have begged him not to.

I undressed and slipped into the hot water. On a shelf built into the tiled wall beside the bath, an array of soaps, bath products and face cloths were arranged. I took up a face cloth, soaked it in the hot water and used it to warm my face.

When I'd done bathing, I dragged my underwear back on, wrapped the biggest towel I'd ever seen around my body and opened the door. Tramp was sitting on the edge of the bed wearing only spotless white shorts.

"Better?"

I nodded. Tramp stood up and indicated a pile of clothes on a chair near the wide hearth. "There's more stuff than I thought. I hope you can find something to fit you. It's a darn good job my mother stays out of this room; she'd have taken them all down to her favourite charity shop if she knew they were there." He moved toward me. "I'll just have a quick bath, then we'll go down and meet the parents. Don't get nervous. They'll likely nag me for my wayward ways and bombard you with questions as well, but I'll deal with them. Make yourself at home." He stepped past me and closed the bathroom door.

I sorted through the clothes Tramp had left on the chair. All of them were clearly far more expensive than anything I'd ever worn. I tried on one or two skirts and dresses, settling eventually on a green, knee length dress which, although a little big in the bust, had a belt which reduced the obvious deficiency.

I rummaged in my bag for my lipstick and mascara. I found a small compact containing four different shades of eye shadow. I'd forgotten it was in there. I applied green and grey eye shadow, pale pink lipstick and a good coating of mascara. By the time I'd finished, Tramp had emerged from the bathroom wearing a fluffy white robe. He looked me up and down.

"You'll do," he commented. "You won't need to worry about shoes. If you haven't got slippers, you go barefoot in this house - the old lady won't make any comment on that. I'll put your shoes over here by the fire and get old Wilson to light it for us. They'll soon dry out."

I tried not to watch as Tramp dressed himself in smart trousers and a crisp shirt, which he left open at the neck. He looked totally different. It was hard to believe that the burly Hells Angel I'd ridden here with was the very same well-to-do young man carefully combing out his long, sandy hair.

"I always feel so uncomfortable in this get-up," Tramp complained, "But my old lady 'has standards' if you get my meaning. She can't live my life for me or stop me doing what I want, but when I'm here, I have to play at being the posh bloke!"

He fastened his hair into a pony tail and flashed me a smile. "It's not so bad. Dad's all right; he won't give you a hard time. Just don't get the old woman talking about politics, all right?"

"What sort of questions will she ask me?"

"Oh, insignificant, unimportant rubbish, as always. What school you went to, whether you know anyone with titles, what your father does for a living. If you look like you're in trouble, I'll intervene, don't worry. Come. We'd better go down or she'll be sending Wilson up to see where we got to."

With my heart in my mouth, I accepted the arm Tramp offered me and let him lead me out onto the landing and down the wide staircase. Everything had a dream-like quality. I couldn't quite believe any of it.

36. This Is How The Other Half Live

As it happened, Mrs. Eastbrook wasn't a problem for me. A slender, perfectly groomed lady, she treated me with cool politeness - not exactly unfriendly but certainly not warm.

I kept myself under tight control, making sure I didn't gawk at the richly appointed drawing room and its contents. For some reason, I thought about Great Uncle Bertie and Penelope as I sipped at weak tea served in thin china cups. I kept my back straight, as I'd been taught at All Hallows, sitting very correctly with my feet and knees together.

Tramp had introduced me as Kat. Mrs. Eastbrook assumed this was short for 'Katharine' and so that is what she called me. The only direct question she asked me was where I went to school. I told her truthfully that I'd attended All Hallows Convent in Ditchingham and she nodded approvingly.

When Mrs. Eastbrook eventually told us she intended to retire to bed early as she had a very busy schedule the next day, Tramp said he would take me to the small sitting room for a little while to watch the television. He added that he had an errand to run shortly after midnight but assured her he would return quickly. Mrs. Eastbrook folded her lips in disapproval but clearly knew better than to make protest.

When his mother had left the room, Tramp beckoned me to follow him. We crossed the enormous vestibule and went a little way down a corridor where we entered a much less formal room.

Tramp flung himself into an enormous armchair and gestured for me to sit.

"Well. That went OK, didn't it?"

"Did it? I don't think she approves of me."

Tramp waved a hand irritably. "That's nothing new. She wouldn't approve of anyone less than a princess! Don't worry about it. I'm sure you'll get on well with my father - whenever he finally puts in an appearance. Anyway, we've got other stuff to worry about at the moment."

I didn't relish the prospect of staying too long in this large, fancy house and said so.

Tramp shook his head. "We won't stop here long. Maybe just tonight, maybe tomorrow night as well. You give me your key and I'll go to your place with my rucksack and clear out all your stuff. The police won't have been in there yet - they wouldn't have a search warrant on the first visit. You write a letter to your boss at the ice-cream place, saying you had to go away for a week or something. I'll go deliver it in the morning."

"What? You mean I'll have to leave my bed-sit and my job?"

"You don't want to be caught, do you? I can't see how you could stay there."

"Where could I go?"

Tramp grinned. "I'll look after you, Kat. You just stay by me and we'll be fine. You do trust me, don't you?"

I nodded and tried to smile. However, deep inside, I'd already begun to mourn my loss. Once I'd become used to living alone and working every day, I'd come to enjoy it. I'd felt secure and unthreatened, despite being a little lonely now and then. I dreaded the upheaval of moving on and losing what little security I'd found.

Tramp stood up and crossed the room to a large, oak bureau. He opened it and riffled about amongst various pieces of stationery. He offered me a couple of sheets of plain, cream-coloured paper and a fountain pen.

"Here. I don't know how much your boss knows about you, but you'd better write him a letter. You'll know what you can and can't say. Obviously, don't mention this place or me. I'll go to the kitchen and make us a decent, strong cup of tea. That stuff my mother drinks is like dishwater!"

Resting on a small table beside the chair I'd sat in, I began to craft a letter for Don. It was difficult. I decided to tell the truth; Don would need to be able to tell Al what had happened. That Al might have to inform Mam worried me, but there was nothing for it but to let those who had helped me for so long know the reality.

I simply told Don how the police had been at the bed-sit when I left work and that I felt the need to vanish, yet again. Further, I thanked him and all the others for the risks they'd taken on my behalf. I assured them I was safe and with good people and expressed my regret at not being able to see any of them to say goodbye properly. By the time I'd finished writing, tears dripped off the end of my nose and I felt absolutely empty inside.

Tramp returned, bearing two steaming mugs of tea. He noticed my distress and set the cups down to enfold me in his arms.

"Don't cry, Kitten. It'll all work out all right, you'll see. I'm sorry you have to leave your work and your friends, but I promise I'll keep you safe."

I allowed myself to cry, my tears soaking into the fine fabric of Tramp's shirt. He said no more, simply held me until I'd cried myself out.

Eventually, I pointed to the letter and asked if he wanted to read it. He shook his head. "No. What you've put there is between you and those people. Here. Put it in an envelope, but don't seal it down. When I've cleared your bed-sit, I'll drop the key in the envelope. I'll give it to that bloke, Don when we go to the ice-cream place for coffee tomorrow afternoon. That way, none of us will arouse any suspicions."

We didn't watch television in the end. We sat in the comfortable chairs talking until nearly midnight. At last, Tramp stood up and took my hand.

"Come on. You get into bed and I'll get my gear on and go do what needs to be done. I'll be back before you know it. You'll be all right in my room on your own, won't you?"

I sat on the edge of the huge bed and watched Tramp change from his smart clothes back into his filthy jeans, scruffy tee shirt and still damp leather jacket. He tugged on his heavy motorcycle boots and stood up.

"There. That's more like it. I feel like me again! There's books and stuff to read over there if you can't sleep. I'll be as quick as I can. I'll make sure I leave the place clean and tidy." He leaned forward and planted a brief kiss on my forehead before leaving.

I didn't sleep. I wandered around the room, inspecting the paintings and expensive ornaments. In a glass case, near the window, a collection of model motorcycles were displayed. The nearby bookcase held a great many text books on subjects which varied from electrical engineering to astronomy. A small section contained paperback books. Amongst these, I found 'The Lord of The Rings' by JRR Tolkien.

I'd never read the book, so I took it from the shelf and curled up near the piled pillows on the bed to read. However, I couldn't concentrate. My mind wandered and I thought of Tramp, collecting all my belongings and clearing out the familiar room.

I began to worry. What if someone saw him? What if the police had already been into my room and taken everything? All manner of increasingly dreadful scenarios raced through my brain. Eventually, I could sit still no longer. I got up and paced the room, stopping every few minutes to stare out of the windows into the rain filled darkness.

It seemed like a very long time before Tramp returned, but in reality, it couldn't have been more than an hour and a half. Relief flooded me as he entered the room, a stuffed rucksack on his back. I tried to hold my composure but he immediately noticed my anxiety.

"It's OK. Everything's fine. No-one saw me." He took the rucksack off his back and placed it carefully beside the bed. "I got everything. Cleared all the drawers - even the kitchen stuff. I stripped off the bed and folded all the sheets and towels. You know, made it look like you'd taken your time and made a deliberate decision to leave."

Tramp sat down on a chair and began to unbuckle his boots. "We'd better try and get some shut-eye now. At least neither of us has to be up early."

I sat on the bed and watched as he took off his leather jacket. It suddenly occurred to me that I would be spending the night in this room with him - sharing his bed. My facial expression must have given away my thoughts. Tramp took his tee shirt off and looked my way.

"Don't worry, Kat. I won't touch you. I'll kip on the floor if it'll make you feel better?"

"But, it's your bed!" I protested.

He grinned. "I told you. That's why they call me Tramp. Reckon I could sleep standing up in a hole if I had to!"

I couldn't help but laugh a little. The decision not to make him sleep on his own bedroom floor arrived in my head immediately. He'd not tried to even kiss me in all the time we'd spent together. If I couldn't trust him now, I'd never be able to.

"No. It's all right. It's a big bed. I wouldn't be able to sleep at all if I knew you were on the floor - or standing up in a hole!"

"If you're sure?"

"I am sure," I replied, probably with more conviction than I actually felt.

"Right. I'll be back in a minute." He disappeared into the bathroom.

I peeled the green dress off and laid it on the chair next to his leather jacket before slipping between the crisp sheets wearing only my underwear. My heart thudded against my ribs; I could hear it in my ears as well. A vague knot of nausea swelled in my belly.

Tramp returned and clambered into bed beside me. He felt cold!

"Still raining a bit," he commented.

"You're cold."

"It'll pass. I'll soon get warm. There's an electric blanket. Want me to switch it on?"

I shook my head.

"Try to sleep, Kat. We'll get everything sorted out properly in the morning." He kissed the end of my nose, turned his back to me and pulled the covers up to his shoulders.

Within a few minutes, Tramp's breathing became slow and regular. I listened to the sound and found it soothing. He'd left the bedside light on; I picked up the Lord of The Rings and read a few pages.

I do not recall falling asleep. When I awoke, I found myself enfolded in Tramp's arms. His long, sandy hair spread on the pillow like heavy silk. I watched him sleeping; his body felt warm next to mine.

As if he felt me looking at him, Tramp opened his eyes. "Hello."

I giggled.

He drew me closer to him. "Did you sleep?"

"Yes. But I think I dropped your book. I read for a while."

He closed his eyes again. "Reading's always good. What book was it?"

"Lord of the Rings."

"Mmmm. Good book. Read it loads of times."

I thought he'd gone back to sleep because he said no more for several minutes. I lay, wrapped in his arms, feeling his breath against my neck. It was a pleasant sensation. I felt safe and relaxed. When Tramp spoke again, I had almost dozed off to sleep again myself.

"You hungry? My stomach thinks my throat's been cut!"

Again, I giggled at the expression he used. I found I did feel hungry. I also needed the toilet. "Yes. I could do with something to eat. I've got to go to the bathroom first though."

"Feel free. That's what it's for." His blue eyes snapped open and he smiled.

I felt all manner of confusing things. I fought the impulse to kiss him; it wouldn't be appropriate, I thought. To cover my embarrassment, I slid out of bed and rushed to the bathroom, where I leaned on the closed door.

When I emerged from the bathroom, Tramp had already dressed in his smart trousers and another shirt. As he headed for the bathroom, passing me, he indicated the rucksack. "All your stuff is in there. I folded everything up."

I selected a pair of jeans and one of the blouses I usually wore for work. By the time Tramp emerged, clean shaven and smelling of cologne, I'd applied a minimum of make-up and brushed my hair.

"You look great. Come on; let's get down to the kitchen and see if Mrs. Wilson will find the time to make us a big breakfast!"

"What about your mother?"

He glanced at his watch. "Nah. It's gone ten. She'll have left the house already. She said something about some charity 'do' she's helping to organise. She's hardly ever here in the mornings. Off with her snooty cronies, setting the world to rights I expect."

Mrs. Wilson turned out to be the cook and housekeeper. A petite woman with silvery hair swept back from her face and secured with pins. She clearly adored Tramp. She greeted us both warmly and had us sit at the wide kitchen table whilst she prepared bacon, eggs and toast for us to eat.

Mr. Wilson arrived whilst we were listening to Mrs. Wilson relate accounts of recent events at the house which included various parties and gatherings. Neither of the servants seemed to think it remotely strange that Tramp should have a female friend with him.

After we'd eaten and had several cups of the nicest tea I'd ever tasted, Tramp showed me around the house, which had so many rooms I feared I would easily get lost. We returned to 'The Games Room' when the tour had ended and Tramp tried his best to instruct me in the arts of playing snooker. I'd only ever played pool before and I thought the snooker table was as large as a tennis court. I was absolutely hopeless at the game - a source of some amusement to Tramp.

"I can tell you've played pool by the way you hold the cue. You'll find it easier to play snooker if you get down, right over the cue, so it's almost touching your chin. Hold the end of the cue as far back as you can, firmly but gently." He leaned over me to correct my grip. "Now. Look directly at the ball you want to hit. See. It's a straight line and you can see better now. Try it."

To my delight, the white ball struck exactly where I'd aimed and a red ball drifted neatly into a side pocket.

We played snooker for perhaps an hour before Tramp decided to ask Mrs. Wilson for sandwiches for our lunch. The little woman agreed and said she'd bring them to the small sitting room at about two o'clock.

Tramp took me walking in the extensive gardens surrounding the house. I goggled at a large swimming pool with an enormous patio area and summerhouse beside it. That this family was 'wealthy' seemed an understatement.

Tramp led me between some trees into a delightful flower garden. We walked the length of it until we came to a spot which remained clear of plants, save one. A small, marble headstone rested behind the plant.

"My dog, Norton. Lost him a few years back. This place has never seemed the same without him."

I swallowed. "I had a dog too. She was called Tammy ... but ... she died. My step-father bashed her so badly she had to be shot."

Tramp hugged me. "You must miss her. I know I miss Norton. He was a wonderful dog. A black Labrador. He used to wander around the house with shoes in his mouth. He nearly drove my mother mad."

I thought of Tammy and how she had spent long hours cringing in her basket in fear of the rows and both my step-father and mother's tempers. She'd never have dared to pick up a shoe.

"Tammy lived a miserable life, stuck in the house, scared of everyone except me. I loved her though."

Tramp kept his arm around me. "That's the important thing. She loved you and you loved her. Wherever dogs go, she'd have gone there knowing that."

We stood a while longer with bees buzzing and butterflies flitting between the bright flowers. The little flower garden was a peaceful place. It reminded me of Nana's garden at Mornington Road.

We ate sandwiches in the small sitting room and drank yet more of Mrs. Wilson's wonderful tea. At about a quarter to three, Tramp stood up.

"Right. I've gotta go and meet the lads and deliver that letter for you. Feel free to go where you like. If you're lonely, go in the kitchen and chat with Mrs. Wilson. I'll be a couple of hours. When I get back, we can decide what we're going to do."

I actually spent the time in Tramp's bedroom, curled on the bed reading some more of Lord of The Rings. I needed the distraction. I had no idea what would happen to me next; where I would go or in what direction life would lead me.

37. Moving On Again

Tramp managed to speak to Don under the pretence of looking at the fridge unit again. He told me how Clara had clicked her tongue and complained about the Hells Angels being in the shop and how much worse it looked to other customers seeing one on the serving side of the counter. Don had been stern with the woman and she'd gone off in a huff to take her break.

Police had not visited the ice-cream parlour in search of me. Tramp felt Don was genuinely concerned about me and where I might be staying. He'd done his best to convince Don that he was simply a messenger - that I'd approached him and asked him to give Don my letter because I'd hoped the Hells Angels would still go there for coffee.

"Do you think I could risk going back?" I asked.

Tramp shook his head. "Not if the police have been at the bed-sit. They could come back at any time and we don't want to have to go through all this again. I know you're upset about losing your job and your home, Kat, but I think it's safer not to go back."

"What will I do for money? I can't afford to live without working!"

"You need not worry about money, Kat. I'm loaded. I'll take care of you, I told you that. Anything you want or need, just ask."

This should have made me feel better, but it didn't. I found I had no desire to give up my independence. I couldn't find the right words to articulate this, so I didn't reply.

I think Tramp somehow knew how uncomfortable I felt. He hugged me. "If you really want to work, I'm sure we'll find something for you. You need somewhere a little less public than that ice-cream place, though. The police could have walked in there any time and seen you."

"Like what?"

"I dunno. Can you type?"

"No. At least, I've never tried."

"Well, don't you worry about it for now. We'll work on that after we've sorted out where we're gonna stay. I've had a couple of offers from the lads to put us up for a while."

"What?" I exclaimed. "Have you told them all about me?"

"Not everything. Just enough so they know to close ranks and make sure everyone looks out for you. Don't worry, Kat. All they know is that you're on the run. No-one knows from where or why, only that you need to remain hidden. You'd be surprised how common an occurrence this is!"

I relaxed a little. After all, Johnny had known instinctively that I was a runaway from somewhere. Maybe it was best if the club members knew.

"We're not gonna stay here for another night after all. I decided we'll go stay with Randy for a while. You know ... the prospect?"

"OK. Won't your mother be upset?"

Tramp scowled briefly. "No more than usual. Shame I didn't get to see the old man on this visit. Come on. Get your gear and we'll make a move. Randy lives on the far edge of town with his mother. She's a bit crippled so we have to help her out with stuff. You all right with that?"

I nodded.

I found the big rucksack difficult to get used to, seated on the pillion of the bike. It altered my weight and balance. I hoped it wouldn't affect Tramp's riding. The day was warm and the sun beat down as he drove through the lanes toward the town.

We entered an area where the houses were built in terraces. That it was run-down and poor was evident from the fact that several windows were boarded up and many of the tiny front yards had rubbish piled in them.

We drew up outside a tiny home in the middle of the terrace. A tatty motorcycle rested against the kerb. As we stepped off

Tramp's bike, the front door of the house opened and I recognised the short young man who had given me the drink on the first evening at the pub.

"Hey, Randy. You sure your mum is all right with this?" Tramp greeted the young man.

"Yeah. She's fine with it. She likes you. Ever since you rebuilt the shed and fixed up the back yard, she won't hear a word against you!"

We entered into a tiny, cramped hallway. A flight of stairs with threadbare carpet ran up the left hand side of the area. To the right, a door stood open a little.

Tramp headed straight for it and tapped lightly. "You decent, Mary?"

I heard a low chuckle. "Depends what you mean by decent. I'm soaking me feet so if that bothers you, you young scallywag, you can go fix me a cup of tea."

Tramp nudged Randy. "Come on. Let's fix her a nice cuppa. It's not polite to have a room full of men while you're soaking your feet!" He turned to me. "Take that rucksack off now, Kat. Leave it there by the door."

I followed the two men along the narrow passageway into another room. Several very tatty armchairs occupied the length of the far wall. A table, covered with clutter and used mugs faced me. Randy led the way across the room and through another doorway which opened onto a long, very narrow - and incredibly grubby kitchen.

"Ye gods, man! Don't you ever do any cleaning?" Tramp leaned across the sink and opened a window.

Randy shrugged. "Sometimes. I just never seem to get round to it."

Tramp snatched at the kettle, moved some dirty plates from the sink with one hand and turned on the cold tap. He filled and replaced the kettle and switched it on. "Right. Well, we're none of us doing anything right now, so we can crack on and get this place sorted. Kat'll help, won't you?" He turned to me, one eyebrow raised.

I glanced around. The place was grubby, but still nothing like as bad as Valerie's home had been. Mainly, it seemed to be dishwashing and taking out the trash.

"Yeah. I've seen worse. Got any hot water?"

Between the three of us, we cleared up the kitchen, washed, dried and put away all the dishes and cutlery and Tramp took the rubbish outside. When he came back, an orange and white cat followed him in. It wound round his legs and looked up at him, mewing.

"Hey, little kitty," Tramp bent and scooped the small creature up. Immediately it began to purr. I stroked its head as Tramp held it.

"Poor little thing," Tramp remarked. "I'd bet five quid you haven't fed it in a couple of days."

Randy rummaged in a cupboard and produced a can of cat food. "Wrong. I feed her every time she comes home, which isn't that often. She spends so much time out on the tiles."

Tramp made tea and I followed him through the now slightly less cluttered sitting room to the half-open door.

"Tea's up, Mary!" he called.

"Come on in," came the reply.

I followed Tramp into a small room which had been turned from a sitting room into a bedroom. A lady sat in a high backed chair beside an old fashioned hearth and mantelpiece. Her ankles and lower legs were swelled to enormous proportions, although she herself wasn't particularly fat. Beside her chair, I noticed a large, enamel bowl containing soapy water.

Tramp handed her the mug of tea he carried. "How've you been, Mary?"

The woman swept a strand of straight, gray hair away from her face and accepted the cup. "Oh, you know. I get by. Young Randy helps all he can. He's a good boy. I'm all the better for seeing you again. Who's your young lady friend?"

Tramp turned and beckoned me forward. "This is Kat. Randy said you were OK with us staying here for a while. Is that right?"

"Hello, Kat. It's nice to see David here with a young lady for a change. As for you staying, you know its fine by me, lad. You stop as long as you like. My, but this is a good cuppa." She smiled up at Tramp.

Tramp put his hand in his pocket and took out a wad of notes. "Even so, Mary. I don't expect to stay here for nothing. You still have bills to pay and my being here, using your electricity and watching your telly all costs money." He handed some money to the old lady, who pushed his hand away.

"Don't be daft! You keep your money, lad. You always help around the place whenever you're here. If you want to pay me, then you can have a go at fixing that old telly over there. Blessed thing keeps going all fuzzy."

Tramp set right to fixing the television. As he worked, Randy went into the hall and lifted the rucksack. He poked his head round the door and gestured for me to follow him up the stairs.

"You and Tramp can have this room," he said, opening a door.

I stepped inside and looked around. A very old fashioned iron bedstead took up most of the room. A massive old wardrobe, which had a folded piece of card under one side stood opposite the end of the bed. Crammed in a corner, I noticed a mismatched dressing table with a vanity mirror above it. Faded, floral curtains hung at the old sash window. The room smelled musty and disused.

"This was Mum's room. Before she got too poorly to get up the stairs. It hasn't been used for a while. Will it be all right?" Randy looked anxious.

I gave him my best smile. "Yeah. It's just great. Mind if I open the window and let some air in?"

Randy had to help with the window as it was stiff and clearly hadn't been opened in a very long time. I looked out on a neat yard with a wooden fence all around it. In fact, I could see into the yards on either side. Most were unkempt. I noticed a gate set in the back fence. The backs of the terrace in the next street faced me.

"Where does the gate lead to?" I asked, pointing.

"There's an alley. Comes out on the main road. Tramp and some of the lads cleared the garden for Mum. When Dad left, there was loads of crap out there. I never knew what to do with all the old iron and stuff."

"Your dad left?"

"Yeah. About five years ago when Mum got sick. It's no loss. He was a bastard; always drunk and clouting us. We've been happier since he went."

Interested, I sat on the edge of the bed, which creaked. "How long have you known Tramp ... and the others?"

"Met Johnny first. I was getting my head kicked in by skinheads and he came and gave them a taste of their own medicine. Must've been about a year after Dad left. Met up with him again couple of years back when there was a big fight on the beach. Skinheads again. I belted some bloke about to hit Johnny with a bit of pipe. That's when he invited me to prospect for the club."

"How long do you have to prospect for?"

"Till Johnny decides it's time for me to be a full member, I guess."

Leaving the rucksack unopened beside the bed, we went back downstairs to see how Tramp was doing with the television. He was explaining to Mary that he thought the problem might be the aerial. He promised to acquire a ladder and go up to the roof to adjust it just as soon as he could.

Randy made a simple meal ... and at urging from Tramp, washed up the dishes as well. We dried and put everything away. Once Mary had been made as comfortable as possible and given both a cup of tea and a jug of fresh water and a glass, we went out to meet the rest of the club.

That first evening, the club went for a bike run, deep into the countryside. It felt so good to be among the crowd with Tramp riding next to Johnny at the front. Johnny had no pillion passenger.

We stopped at a pub in a small village where most of the men had a pint of beer. The landlord didn't seem fazed by the appearance of two dozen or so leather jacketed men. I saw him chatting in a friendly manner with several club members. The few other patrons of the pub largely ignored us, although no-one was unpleasant.

This was the first of many evenings in company with the Hells Angels. I never saw any bad behaviour and no-one ever pressed me to drink alcohol. Whenever people began smoking 'funny fags' as Tramp called them, we took our leave. Now and then a few gentle, teasing remarks were made toward Tramp and his aversion to 'weed' but nothing offensive or serious.

Tool acquired a tattoo machine and made it known he needed 'skin' to practice on. One evening at the pub, I asked him to tattoo my name on my left forearm. I was so intent on sitting still and not twitching, despite the pain, I didn't notice he'd put 'Kitty' on my arm until he'd nearly finished. The letters were even enough but I was dismayed.

When returning from wherever he'd been with Johnny and a couple of others, Tramp raged at Tool, not just for getting the name wrong but for doing a tattoo on me in the first place. He didn't scold me though. When he'd finished telling Tool off in front of everyone, he simply bought me a glass of cola, sat beside me and talked of inconsequential things. I wondered if he'd shout at me when we returned home, but all he did was shake his head and tell me I'd live to regret it.

At night, after checking on Mary, Randy, Tramp and I watched the small television in the little back sitting room before Tramp and I went to bed together in the room which used to be Mary's.

Tramp always held me in his arms at night. Sometimes he kissed me, but he never once tried to go any further. I began to care for him deeply. Part of me almost wished he would go further; another part of me dreaded that if he did, it might spoil the relationship we'd developed.

Tramp was as good as his word to Mary. From somewhere, he got hold of an extendable ladder. Randy and I held it steady whilst he climbed up to the roof, where he spent a long time adjusting the aerial. I had to run back inside the house to see what difference, if any, his adjustments had made. When the picture was as good as perfect and Mary grinning with delight, I yelled up to Tramp and he slithered down the roof back to the top of the ladder.

The ladder couldn't be collected for a few days, so Tramp left it leaning against the back wall of the house, adjacent to our bedroom window. "No-one's gonna try burgling this place. Not with me and Randy here. I'll get Gav to come fetch it later in the week."

When we arrived at the pub that evening, Tramp was greeted by worried club members. There was no sign of Johnny, Gavin or Tool. Someone had already been to each of their houses and found no-one home and no sign of the motorcycles either.

Tramp shrugged. "I dunno where they are. Maybe they went off to do something, although it's strange, Johnny never mentioned anything to me. Hang on. I'll go phone his sister and see if she knows what's going on." He disappeared to the public phone booth in the lobby of the pub.

What happened next is a blur in my mind. That Johnny, Gavin and Tool had been set upon by a gang of skinheads I immediately understood. Gavin's bike had been smashed up and Tool was in the hospital with head injuries. Johnny and Gavin were with him.

The exodus from the pub was silent. Motorcycles roared into life and queued up behind Tramp. I sat on the back of the machine, wondering what exactly would happen. I felt afraid, but I had no idea of what or why.

We rode back toward the main town, on along the seafront and into another urban area I'd never been to before. To my surprise,

Tramp pulled the bike up outside a church. He switched the engine off and turned to me.

"Come on. I'm not having you involved in all this. Follow me."

I trailed behind him, into the churchyard, a thousand questions bubbling inside my mind, but somehow, unable to ask any of them. I turned and saw all the other Hells Angels sitting in a line behind Tramp's vacant bike. Jo-Jo caught my eye and smirked.

Tramp tried the door of the church, but it was locked. "Damn! Right. Wait here, all right? Don't smoke in this lobby. Go out into the graveyard if you want a fag. I'll be back to get you, no matter how long it takes. Don't go anywhere. Promise me?"

"Why? What's happening?"

Tramp grimaced. "It's best you don't know. We're settling an old score, shall we say. Now promise me you'll wait here for me?"

I nodded. He pecked me on the cheek and trotted back to his bike. I listened as the sound of the multiple motor cycles faded into the distance. It had just grown dark. I shivered; my thin jacket wasn't much protection against the cold.

Within about ten minutes, I edged out of the church porch toward the gravestones so I could have a cigarette. The headstones and statues glowed faintly in the last of the light. I squatted down behind a large tomb and tried not to imagine all the dead people around me. I'd never really worried about such things; on the other hand, I'd never been left alone in a graveyard at night!

I groped way back into the porch and sat on the bench with my legs drawn up beneath me. Now and again, I heard a car pass by, but other than that and the constant hooting of an owl, the night remained silent. It grew very cold indeed.

The third time I thought I'd have a cigarette and crept out of the porch, an icy wind blew. Overhead, the stars glittered in a clear sky. My hands were so cold I couldn't make them work the lighter! I'd stopped shivering, but I felt almost numb, save for the aching in my thighs and back. I stood up next to the tomb and jogged about on the spot for a few minutes. It did nothing to warm me. The wind whistled between the gravestones chilling me still further. I scuttled back to the relative warmth of the porch. At least it was out of the wind.

I have no idea how long I waited there, but it felt like several hours. I almost burst into tears with relief when I heard the sound of Tramp's motorcycle approaching. I tottered out of the porch to meet him as he walked into the churchyard.

"God, Kat. I'm so sorry. You're frozen! I'm such a fool. I should've taken you back to Mary's first."

He took off his leather jacket. "Put this on. I'll get us home as quick as I can."

I dragged the jacket on and followed him down the path back to the road and the bike. He rode fast all the way back to Yarmouth and the little terrace, probably breaking the speed limit. I marvelled that he didn't seem to be aware of the cold, riding as he was, in just a tee-shirt.

Randy's motorcycle was in its customary place. Tramp hurried to the door. Before he had a chance to knock, the door opened. The hallway was in darkness. We groped our way along to the back sitting room.

Once in the light, I could see the state of both men. Randy had a livid bruise on his cheek and a nasty looking gash just under his eye. His knuckles and hands were grazed and bloodied as well. My mouth dropped open. I turned toward Tramp and noticed he had his own share of injuries, although, apart from a split lip, his face was undamaged.

"What happened?" I breathed.

"What you don't know can't hurt you, Kat. Let's just say there was a bit of a punch up." Tramp answered quickly.

Randy turned away and went to make tea.

"But ... won't you get into trouble? I mean ..."

Tramp shrugged. "Doubt it. There's not many dare to make statements against us. I think we might have done the locals a favour. Those damned skinheads have been terrorizing the whole town recently."

We drank tea in silence. I could tell the men wanted to talk, so I told them I felt really tired and needed to go to bed. I retreated to the bedroom and sat on the bed, wondering just what had happened. I further worried about Tool; had he recovered or were his injuries serious? I didn't have long to wait before I could ask. Tramp appeared in the bedroom holding a pad of lint against his lip.

"Is Tool gonna be all right?"

He shrugged. "Haven't heard anything. I'll go out and ring Johnny's sister in the morning. He's a tough bloke; if anyone can handle being whacked round the ear-hole by a demented skinhead, it's him."

I undressed and got into bed. "Is your lip sore?"

"A bit. I've had a lot worse, believe you me. Are you getting warm now? I really am sorry I never thought to leave you a decent jacket or anything."

"It's OK," I lied. "I'm warm enough now." In fact, I still felt cold inside. Almost as if my bones themselves had frozen.

Tramp undressed and climbed into bed beside me. "Kat! You're frozen! Come here."

He wrapped me in his arms and I quickly fell asleep with my head on his chest, listening to his heart beating.

I awoke suddenly, a few hours later, to thunderous knocking at the front door downstairs. I sat up, panic overwhelming me. Tramp leapt out of the bed and dragged on his jeans and tee-shirt.

"Get up, Kat! Quick! Get dressed. That's the police!"

The knocking continued as I snatched up my jeans and shirt. I pulled on my shoes as Tramp buckled his boots.

"Tramp, what are we gonna do?"

I caught the flash of his white teeth as he grinned at me in the darkness. "Remember that ladder? Reckon you could make it down that all right? Come on. We'll have to be quick. If Randy doesn't go open the door to them, they'll kick it in. Poor Mary. I wonder what's made them come here."

He opened the window as wide as it would go and helped me to clamber over the sill. I groped for the side of the ladder with one hand and one foot.

"What if it slips? There's no-one to hold it!"

"It won't slip. Hurry!"

I caught hold of the ladder with my hand and eased my way across to the rungs. As I began to descend, Tramp followed me. Once down on the ground in the darkness of the yard, I had no idea what to do next. Tramp took hold of my hand and tugged me across the concrete to the back gate, which he opened just enough to peer out into the alleyway beyond.

We had to negotiate our way around all manner of dustbins and rubbish piled at intervals outside the other gates. More than once, I stumbled or stubbed my toe. I bit my lip so as not to cry out.

At one point, Tramp paused. In the very faint starlight, I saw him take his jacket off and peel away the denim cut-down, which he put back on. He handed the jacket to me. "Wear this," he whispered. "If I get caught, hide and stay hidden until its safe enough for you to move away from here. Get to the pub, if you can. Everyone there will see you're all right. I hope it won't come to that though. Our friends in blue aren't the brightest sparks on the bonfire; they might not even think of looking along here."

As he finished speaking, I heard men's voices and torchlight swept the alleyway.

"Get down!" hissed Tramp. "Don't move or make any noise."

The torchlight settled on his face and a stern voice called out, "Come on, lad. We've got the place surrounded."

Tramp put his hands in the air. "All right. I'm coming. Just get that light outta my face!"

I crouched beside a bin which smelled revolting; I fought the urge to gag. Terror surged through me. I heard Tramp move away and various men's voices as the police officers took hold of him. I strained to hear what they were saying.

"So, where's the girl?"

"What girl?" I heard Tramp answer.

"We had information that you were hiding a runaway here. A girl wanted by police."

"Really?" Tramp sounded genuinely surprised. "I don't think my girlfriend would take too kindly to that! What have you done with my girlfriend by the way?"

Another voice sounded in the darkness. "Oh. She's your girlfriend, is she? Long blonde hair and a bad attitude?"

"That'll be Jo. Where is she?"

"Down at the station. Right where you're going, sonny. Come on."

I heard another voice. "Sarge, you want us to have a look along this alleyway?"

"Nah. We've got who we came after. Him and the others. Leave it."

As soon as the voices diminished, I edged away from the foul smelling bin and heaved hard. I stood up, shaking with the fear that I might vomit. I wondered if the police had all gone. I leaned against a wall and as the shaking stilled, I thought about the things I'd managed to overhear. Tramp had spoken clearly enough for me to get the general idea that something had happened, regarding Jo-

Jo. Clearly, if she wasn't responsible for telling the police where we were, then she knew who was.

I shuffled further along the alleyway until I could see the road. Apart from several parked cars, all was silent. The street lights glowed orange, making everything look slightly tarnished. I tugged Tramp's leather jacket tight around my body, looked both ways and stepped out in the direction I thought I should go.

38. Lost and A Journey

I became hopelessly lost in the streets. When dawn arrived, I approached a milkman delivering door to door.

"Hello. Can you tell me how far I am from the town centre, please? I've ... er ... got a little bit lost."

The milkman looked me up and down. "I'll say! You look like you slept on the street! Are you all right, love? Had a barney with your boyfriend, have you?"

"Something like that," I mumbled.

"Right. Well you've got a tidy old walk ahead of you. I'd give you a lift, only I'm going the other way. Go straight down this road to the crossroads. Turn right and stay on that road until you get to the roundabout. You'll see a sign there for the town centre. You could get a bus, but there aren't any for an hour or more yet."

I murmured my thanks and set off. I felt reasonably safe amongst the houses but, once I'd stepped out onto the main road heading toward the roundabout, I felt very exposed. Every car which passed made me duck my head and hunch my shoulders; I dreaded that one might be a police car.

I stuffed my hands into the pockets of the leather jacket to warm them and felt a few coins. I drew them out. There looked to be probably a couple of pounds there in change. I stuffed the money back and kept walking.

As I came to the roundabout I happened to look up. A police car was approaching from the other direction. I glanced across the road and saw a business. Men were arriving for work. I crossed the road and mingled with them, watching from the corner of my eye until the police car had disappeared from sight.

Before any of the men had an opportunity to speak with me, I hurried away and stood looking toward the town. The road and roundabout looked very familiar to me. I thought the pub might be in the other direction, so I crossed two more roads and headed away from the town centre along a narrow footpath beside the road which became ever busier as time passed.

I walked for a very long time, passing areas where small rows of shops mingled with businesses, housing estates and even a school. None of it looked familiar. I found a children's play park and veered off the road to sit on a bench beside the swings and take stock of my situation.

I'd left Mary's house with nothing but the clothes I stood up in - and Tramp's jacket. I had only a small amount of money; I was lost; I was afraid. I considered trying to find a police station and hand myself in. Anything, even Garfield House, would be better than this aimless wandering. I'd never find that darned pub; I couldn't even remember what it was called!

The more I thought about it, the more stupid I felt. Fancy not taking any notice of the names of roads and pubs! I didn't even know the address of where I'd been staying. I wandered across the park to the public lavatories where I used the toilet, splashed my face with cold water and finger-combed my hair. I stared at myself in the mirror. What a fool, I thought. Now I had to decide what to do.

I have no idea how the idea popped into my head. Quite suddenly, more than anything else in the world, I wanted to see Nana. I thought I could maybe walk some of the way. Perhaps, if I could get to the next town, I could take a train and hide from the conductor when he came round checking tickets. I knew it was a very long way to Harlow, but I felt I could do it.

I set off, across the park, back to the main road, where I stuck my hands in my jeans pockets and began to walk briskly. After some fifteen minutes or so, I came upon a signpost. Apparently, the road I walked along was the A47 toward Norwich, some seventeen miles away.

The sun had become quite warm and I took off Tramp's leather jacket and slung it over my shoulder. Seventeen miles didn't seem very far, although I had no idea how long it would take me to walk. I knew, once I got to Norwich, I needed to find the A11 road and head toward Thetford, then Newmarket, then Bishops Stortford. Either that or go to Norwich station and try to get on a train without a ticket.

As I walked, I wondered what had happened to Tramp. Had he been arrested for his part in whatever had happened the previous night? What if he went to prison? I muttered and cursed under my breath for well over a mile. I had no telephone number on which to call him, no address at which to write to him. How could I have been so very foolish, ignoring such things?

I approached a lay-by where several trucks were pulled up. There was a very small cafe; not much more than a shed. I became aware that I hadn't eaten for a very long time, so I approached and studied the menu displayed in chalk on a black board by the doorway.

The aroma of cooking bacon and coffee lured me inside. A tiny kitchen, fronted by a counter not much bigger than a small desk occupied one end of the shed. The rest of it was crammed with tables and chairs. Several men sat, eating, drinking coffee or chatting.

I went to the counter and waited until the stout, male cook turned around.

"'Ello, love. Didn't see you there. What can I get you?"

"Um ... a bacon roll, please and a cup of tea."

"Ah. Only do tea in mugs here. Truck stop, see. That be all right for you?"

I nodded and fumbled in my pocket for the money. When I'd paid, I turned and looked about. All the tables were occupied. I moved toward one where one man sat alone, reading a newspaper.

"Mind if I sit here?" I asked, trying to keep my voice steady.

The man moved his paper and looked at me.

"Sure."

I sat down for only as long as it took for the cook to call over to me that my bacon roll was ready. I collected it and returned to my seat. I hadn't realised just how hungry I'd been. The roll barely filled the gap, but it was better than nothing. I drank half the tea and looked around.

The man opposite me folded his paper and put it down.

"Where you headed, love?"

"Harlow."

"Long way. I can give you a lift as far as Norwich, if that's any good? I turn off there. Hang on, maybe one of this lot are going further," he raised his voice. "Anyone going anywhere near Harlow?"

A very fat man looked up. He had eggs and bacon heaped on a fork in front of his mouth. "Going to Newmarket, why?"

The man opposite me jerked his thumb in my direction. "She's going to Harlow. I said I'd take her as far as Norwich, but if you're going on to Newmarket ..."

"Yeah. No problem. I'll just finish stuffing my face and we'll go."

"There you go, love. That's my good deed for the day. I'll leave the paper; you might want a read while you're waiting." He stood up, called a farewell to the cook, who raised a spatula by way of a wave, and left the cafe.

The fat man gestured to me. "Come sit over here, young 'un. I won't be long."

I picked up the mug containing the rest of my tea and moved to his table. The man shovelled more food into his mouth and took a big swig of his coffee. When he'd chewed and swallowed, he looked at me. "What's your name, lass?"

"Kat."

"Ah. That'll be short for Katharine, I 'spect. One o' my grand-daughter's called Katharine. What made you come in 'ere then? No luck hitch-hiking?"

"I was hungry."

The man grinned. "Good place to come then! You had enough to eat, have ya? You look like you'd snap in half if a strong wind came by. I'll stand you a breakfast if you're hungry."

"No. Thanks. I've had enough."

"Right then," he said, using a hunk of bread to wipe the plate clean. "I'll just pay me bill and we'll get on our way. You been in a big wagon afore?"

"No."

"You'll soon get used to it." He stood up and stuffed the bread into his mouth. I watched as he made his way to the counter and paid for his meal. He pointed at me once or twice as he chatted to the cook, but I couldn't hear what he said over the general conversation between the other men.

The lorry the man led me to was an immense, articulated thing with more wheels than a whole row of cars. He opened the driver's door and climbed into the cab before leaning over to open the passenger door.

"Hop up, chuck. 'Scuse the mess. I ain't used to 'aving female company on me travels. Usually, if I pick up hitchers, they're just young blokes what don't mind a bit of mess."

I scrambled up the steps and sat on the broad leather seat.

"I'm Alec, by the way. I'll have you in Newmarket in a couple of hours or so. If we're lucky, we might find someone else going on to Harlow, all right?"

"Thanks very much for the lift and it would be great if you could find me another one going on to Harlow."

Alec started the truck and pulled out of the lay-by onto the road. "That's all right, love. I get a bit nervous when I see young women hitchin'. There're some right unsavoury buggers about. You ought to be more careful; you could go an' get yourself bloody murdered. I s'pose you're a student and can't afford the train fare, yes?"

I nodded. It was easier than lying.

Throughout the journey, Alec talked a great deal - about anything and everything. He moaned at the price of fuel and what thieving wretches the government were. He had opinions about virtually everything and he didn't hesitate to share them. In fact, I spoke very little, but Alec didn't seem to mind. He practically chain smoked and offered his cigarettes freely. I accepted several, although I couldn't possibly have smoked as much as he did.

When, at last, Alec steered the huge vehicle into a large area full of other trucks and parked it up, he turned to me, a very serious expression on his face. "Right then. We'll go on over there to the cafe and see if we can't get you a lift for the rest of the way. Don't mind me. I make a lot of noise about this sort of thing. That way, if you should disappear, when it comes on the news, I'll know the bastard and tell the Old Bill. Safest way, believe me. Too many kids go missing every year. Come on. I'll buy you a buttie and a cuppa."

It didn't take Alec long to find a trucker who was headed toward Harlow and prepared to give me a lift. Alec took me to meet the man, a short, skinny fellow with dark hair and nicotine stains on his fingers, who he introduced as Dave.

"So you're one of them hard-up students are you, lass?" Dave asked, a wide grin splitting his deeply tanned face. "I been hard up enough times meself to know how hard travellin' can be. I've only just got 'ere, so I hope you're not in a hurry. I need to get meself some dinner and a couple of big mugs of coffee, then we're good to go."

"I'll be here a wee while myself," Alec added. "Gonna try and get some food inside this one. I swear these darned students starve theirselves."

Both men laughed. I followed Alec to a table and sat down. "You just wait there, Kat. I'll go fetch us a nice hot drink and summat to eat. I'll leave me fags. Help yourself."

I lit a cigarette and watched the crowd. There were very few women present. Mostly, the truckers wore open necked shirts and jeans, although one or two wore one-piece boiler-suits. Nearly all of them smoked. The air in the large cafeteria was hazy with the smoke of so many cigarettes.

Alec came back balancing two plates on one hand and two mugs in the other. He'd ordered me scrambled eggs on toast. My mouth watered and I realised I was actually extremely hungry. Alec beamed as I got stuck in. "That's more like it. Put some meat on your bones, lass."

All too soon, the man called Dave approached and said he was ready to leave. I thanked Alec for the lift, arranging me another and for feeding me. As I stood up to leave, Alec pressed half a pack of cigarettes into my hand.

"There you go, lass. You have these. I've got loads more. I did a run on the continent a few days back and got me some duty-frees. Been a pleasure havin' your company." He turned to Dave. "Just look out for her, all right? I don't like seeing girls hitchin' rides. You never know what might happen."

"Don't worry, mate. She'll be all right with me. I got a daughter about her age meself."

Once again, I found myself clambering the steps into another large cab. Dave was hauling a trailer full of metal machine parts. He was equally as talkative as Alec had been and the hour or so in his company passed very quickly. I began to recognise landmarks and knew there was not far for me to travel.

"Whereabouts in Harlow you want dropping, Kat?" Dave asked.

"It's actually Old Harlow where I'm going. I'm going to visit my Nana."

"Oh yeah? I'll turn off then and drop you there. No point going on into the big town if you'd have to make your way about three miles back is there?"

Dave pulled the truck to a stop at the top of the High Street in Old Harlow. I looked out the window at the familiar scene I hadn't seen for far too long and a lump rose in my throat. I thanked Dave profusely for going out of his way to get me safely to my destination.

"No problems, love. You just take care of yourself now. You need a lift, it's always best to ask a trucker. If one can't help you, he'll nearly always find you another who can. But it's best not to go hitch-hiking on your own. If you're determined to do it, bring a friend so there're two of you. Got it? There's safety in numbers. So long."

I jumped down from the seat and closed the door. I heard the air brakes hiss a little as Dave pulled away, heading back to the main road which would take him into the main town of Harlow.

At first, I simply stood at the end of the pedestrianised shopping area and stared at it, drinking in the familiar sights and smells. Then, my step feeling light, I walked down, between the shoppers, many of whom openly stared at me, heading toward Nana's home.

I paused outside Chestnut Cottage; I wished the dahlias were still in bloom, but in mid October, the garden looked strangely bare. I looked up at the thatched roof and noticed a couple of white doves sitting right near the chimney. It was a peaceful scene. The early afternoon sun warmed the black leather of Tramp's jacket, but I didn't take it off. I strolled along the streets, my mind full of nothing but Nana and how great it would be to see her again at last.

When at last, I turned into Old Road and saw the familiar pale blue door with its diamond shaped, leaded panel, my stomach knotted. I paused; I wondered what might happen if I couldn't stay here. Surely, Nana would never let the police take me away from her and return me to Garfield House?

Steeling myself, I approached the door and lifted the black, wrought iron knocker. I knocked three times and waited.

The door opened and there stood Nana. She wore a navy blue and beige tweed skirt and a matching navy blue light sweater. A single string of pearls hung at her neck.

I rushed forward, beaming, at the same moment as Nana cried out, "Oh! What are you doing? Who are you?" She stepped backward, holding her hands up in front of her face as if in fear of assault.

I stopped moving and stepped backward myself. "Nana. It's me, Keri. Why are you afraid of me?"

Nana peered at me closely and heaved a huge sigh of relief. "Why, so it is! You look so different with that black hair and the jacket thing. I thought you were one of those long-haired thugs come to burgle me!"

I rushed forward and hugged her. She began to cry and scold me all at once. "Where have you been all these months, you wicked girl? Oh, I'm so relieved you're all right!"

I began to cry as well. "Oh, Nana," I sobbed. "I thought you'd forgotten me - especially when you were so frightened of me."

Nana disentangled herself and held me at arms length. "You silly goat. To think I'd forget you! All these months I've been praying for you to be safe! When I got your letter, I was so worried. I didn't know what to do. In the end, I had to telephone your mother to let her know I'd heard from you. She went straight to the authorities of course, but they still couldn't find you!"

Paddy, the cat, arrived from wherever he'd been sleeping and wound around my legs. I wiped the tears from my eyes with my fingers.

"Please, Nana. Don't call Mother. She'll have them take me away again. Please, please, can I stay here with you? I'll be good. I'll help you. I can cook and clean and look after you."

Nana shook her head. "I'll have to call her, Keri. Then we'll see what might be done. A great deal has happened since you told Social Services to come and get you from Holly Cottage. In fact, so much has changed I can barely keep up with it all."

My mouth dropped open in amazement. "I didn't call the social workers, Nana. Mother did. She told dreadful lies about me and they dragged me away and put me in a children's home. Mother hasn't written or phoned once. She just wanted to get rid of me."

Nana looked thoughtful as she closed the front door. "Take that awful jacket off, Keri and sit down. I'll make us a cup of tea. I think you and I have a very great deal to talk about."

39. So Young For A Broken Heart

It was nothing like as easy as I'd thought to explain anything at all to Nana. Quite simply, she could not believe me!

I didn't go into any detail, but I told her my step-father, Terry, had been hurting me for years.

"Keri, you exaggerate so much! All parents have to 'hurt' their children sometimes! There has to be discipline, of course there does."

"Nana, I don't mean smacks for being naughty. I mean really, really hurting me. He ..."

Nana shook her head. "Yes, I'm sure he was heavy handed and often went too far, but ..."

"Nana! He used to punch me and kick me! He ... did other things ... really bad things to me as well."

"Oh, Keri, Keri, Keri. What am I going to do with you? How can anyone help you when you say such dreadful things? I know your mother would never let that happen. Of course not! I mean, there was that awful business recently when he tried to hit poor Russell ..."

I ground my teeth in frustration. "Nana. Please, please listen to me! I'm not lying! Mother didn't care! Sometimes, she asked him to thrash and beat me. The rest of the time, she did it herself! She used to punch and kick and scream at me, drag me about by my hair and ..."

"Is this what you told the authorities, Keri?" Nana interrupted, quietly.

"Mother called the social workers, Nana. I wouldn't know how to. She told them I was a liar and a thief; she said I was a slut and had sex with boys all the time and that she couldn't control me at all. They believed her and took me away."

Nana looked very stern. I'd never seen that expression on her face before. "Now listen to me," she began. I saw her hands firmly clasped together in her lap. "That's exactly what you were doing, isn't it? I've always loved you very much, Keri, but I had your poor mother on the telephone almost every day for weeks before you called out the social workers. She was so worried about you and the things you were doing!"

Tears sprang to my eyes. "Oh, Nana," I whispered. "Not you as well. I can't bear it!"

I put my hands to my face and began to sob. To have Nana think so badly of me broke my heart in two.

After a minute or two, I felt Nana's small hand on my shoulder. "Oh, Keri. I don't know what will become of you, dear. We all tried so hard, but ..."

I lifted my tear-stained face and looked into Nana's eyes. "I can't bear that you won't believe me, Nana. I didn't sleep around at all. I had no friends. Mother dressed me like an old woman and wouldn't let me do any of the normal things all the other girls did. Terry always hit me and then, when Mother got really nasty, he suddenly started being nice to me and started hitting her!"

Doubt filled Nana's eyes. "Yes, I know he was hitting your mother, dear. She told me."

"And his friend paid him money to have sex with me. That man got me drunk, Nana and I was sick. He did horrible things to me!"

Now, that's quite enough, Keri! You've let your imagination run too far! This won't do. No. It won't do at all!"

"But, Nana! It's all true!" I wailed, like a small child. Great sobs rose and shook my body and tears coursed down my cheeks and dripped off my nose and chin.

Nana moved away from me. I buried my face in my hands and began to sob. I actually felt as if my heart, deep inside me, was physically breaking in two. My head pounded; my nose ran and I could no longer think of anything but the pain my beloved Nana had caused by refusing to believe me.

At length, Nana returned with a cool face-cloth. She gently pulled my hands away from my face and smoothed the face cloth over my tear-streaked cheeks. I let her do it; in a way it felt comforting and took me back to my childhood, when Nana believed in me.

"That's better, dear. Please, don't get upset like that again. It breaks my heart."

I looked Nana straight in the eyes and said, very quietly. "You just broke my heart, Nana. I thought you believed in me. I've never lied to you; I wouldn't. I just never told you about what it was like at home. I don't know why I didn't. All the years Terry has been hurting me and all the time Mother hated me and screamed all those wicked things to me about my being born ruining her life, I always knew I had you."

Nana put her arm around me. "You still have me, Keri. I just think you're not very well, dear. Quite clearly, you believe what you're saying. I just know it cannot be true. Now. I'll make us a nice cup of tea and run you a warm bath. You'll feel better after a warm bath ... oh. I haven't got any clean clothes for you! Oh dear, oh dear!"

"It doesn't matter," I mumbled. "I like these clothes."

Nana went to the kitchen. I could hear her putting the kettle on and moving cups about. Paddy jumped on my knee and butted my chin with his head. I stroked the big cat in a distracted manner. I shouldn't have come here. It would have been better if I'd stayed in Yarmouth and somehow found the Hells Angels. I glanced at the door. If I grabbed Tramp's jacket and darted out the door, there was a reasonable chance I might manage to hitch a lift before the police picked me up; I had no doubt, if I vanished again, Nana would call the police.

I resisted the urge to run again. Nana returned with strong, hot tea and sat down in her usual armchair opposite me. She lit a cigarette.

I removed the pack of cigarettes from my pocket and lit one as well.

"Keri!" Nana exclaimed. "What are you doing?"

"I'm having a cigarette," I replied.

"But ... but ... you're only fifteen!"

I took a couple of long pulls from the cigarette and leaned forward to stub it out in Nana's ash-tray. "Sorry."

"How long have you been smoking?"

I thought back. "Quite a while now. No-one at the home minds. They sometimes give us cigarettes ... especially if they've been raping us or groping at us."

Nana's hand flew to her mouth as she gasped. "Keri! What an awful thing to say! Those people are chosen by the authorities; they're all qualified to care for children!"

I leaned forward and picked up the cigarette I'd just put out. I lit it again. "Really? Or are they trained in how to get whatever they want? Nana, they took us all to Jersey for a holiday."

"Yes. I heard you'd had a nice holiday."

"A nice holiday? Nana. I was raped. Several times. I was kept in a state of almost permanent drunkenness. Not just me. All of us. When we're not on holiday, the staff maul us about and sometimes sleep with us. They caught one of the men who raped me."

"Who caught what man? One of the carers?"

"No. The police on Jersey caught a man who raped me. He was going to kill me by drowning me in the sea - I wouldn't stop screaming. The police threw him off the island. There's an enquiry going on about it. The social workers want to know why I was left alone with a man like that ... and why I was so drunk as well."

Nana shook her head. She said no more, but I knew she still didn't believe me. I thought of Mam; how she'd not only believed me but gone to extreme lengths both to comfort and help me. An old gypsy woman had cared more than my own Nana.

"Why did you run away, Keri?"

"We were scared of what would happen when the social workers found out what's been going on at the home."

"We?"

"My friend, Karen. She came too. We ran away together."

Nana sipped at her tea. "And where is this Karen now?"

"She got caught a few weeks ago."

Nana shook her head again. "So, you've been all alone all this time?"

"No. I was with Tramp and his friends."

Nana spluttered into her cup. "A tramp? You've been living with a tramp? Good heavens! We must get you into the bath straight away!" She jumped up from her chair and struggled to haul me to my feet. "Come along, Keri. Quickly! You could have lice or fleas ... or something worse."

I stood up. "No, Nana. Not 'a tramp'. My friend's nickname is Tramp. His real name is David."

Nana let out a groan of dismay. "Oh no! That's even worse! You could even be pregnant if you've been living with a man! Come along. I can make more tea. I need you to get into the bath. Oh dear, oh dear!"

Protesting seemed useless. Anyway, I could use a bath, after all my walking and travelling. I followed Nana to her tiny bathroom. She set the taps running and turned to me.

"There. You jump in there and have a good scrub, dear. Give me your underwear and I'll rinse it out at the sink in the kitchen. I can put it on the radiators to dry. It won't take long. You can wear my dressing gown whilst you're waiting."

With a resigned sigh, I began to undress. Nana scooped up my socks, knickers, bra and blouse. "I'll wash all of these," she said as she left the bathroom.

I took my time in the warm water. There seemed no point in rushing. I had a very good idea that Nana would use the opportunity to telephone Mother and that shortly, either police or social workers or both would arrive to take me away. Tears slid from my eyes as I soaked.

After perhaps half an hour, Nana tapped on the door. "Are you all right, dear?"

"Yes, I'm fine," I mumbled.

Nana entered the bathroom. "I've washed out all your things. That's a very pretty blouse. Where did you get it?"

I looked up. "I bought it. I used to wear it to work."

Nana put the lid down on the lavatory. It had a fluffy cover on it. She sat down. "You've been working, Keri? Oh, my! What were you doing?"

"I worked in an ice-cream parlour, making desserts and serving people with drinks and ice-creams."

"I see. Did you enjoy it?"

"Yes, Nana. I did. It felt good to be working and earning my own wages. I had a lovely bed-sit too. I was happy there. I only ran away from there because the police were outside the door one afternoon when I finished work. I thought they'd found me."

"So what did you do?"

"That's when I went off with Tr ... I mean, David. He took me to his family's house. They're very well-to-do, Nana. David's mother reminded me of Penelope ... a bit."

"Oh. And these people. They simply let a strange, fifteen year old girl stay with them?"

I hung my head. The towel I'd twisted around my head like a turban began to come undone. I caught it before it fell in the bath. "They didn't know I was fifteen."

"So you lied to them?"

"No. Nana, they never asked how old I was. I suppose they just assumed I was older."

Nana caught sight of the tattoo on my arm. She stood up and took hold of my wrist to inspect it. "You'd better give that another wash, Keri."

I grinned. "Won't do any good, Nana. It's a tattoo."

I saw the look of shock on Nana's face. "It's all right," I added. "It's healed up now. It will be there forever."

Nana snatched up a face cloth, rubbed it on the bar of lavender soap and began to scrub at the tattoo. I had to pull my arm away.

"Nana, you're hurting me! It's a proper tattoo. It won't come off, no matter how hard you scrub."

Nana peered at the letters more closely. "'Kitty'?" she asked. "Why have you got 'kitty' marked on your arm?"

"It's my nick-name, Nana. That's all."

"Oh dear, my child. I really do not understand you at all. Come along, out you get. I'll make some more tea and get us something to eat." Nana handed me a large bath towel.

I dried myself quickly and put on Nana's towelling bath robe. It only came just past my knees. I rubbed at my hair and then inspected the pale towel to see if any dye had made marks. There were none.

Habit made me clean the bath out and leave the used face cloth on the side of the basin.

When I emerged from the bathroom, Nana was peeling potatoes. "I've got some lamb chops, dear. We'll have those with potatoes and beans."

"Can I do anything to help, Nana?"

"No. It's all right, dear. I'll just put these potatoes on and we'll sit and have a cup of tea."

I wandered through to the lounge and sat on the settee. I looked around the room. Nothing had changed since I'd last visited. Everything in the little house remained neat, clean and ordered. I noticed 'donkey' in his customary place on the shelf. I stood up and lifted the much-mended china ornament.

Nana brought fresh tea and put the cups on the small table next to her chair. She glanced at me.

"Ah. You're holding donkey. I cannot bring myself to throw him away, Keri, even though he's so broken. Every time I look at him, I think of you."

I replaced the ornament and sat down. "How long have I got, Nana?"

"Pardon?"

"Until they come for me? I know you rang Mother and told her I was here."

Nana looked flustered. "Oh. I didn't think you could hear me on the telephone when you were in the bath."

"I couldn't. I just knew that's what you'd do."

"Keri, I had to, dear! There are so many people who are worried about you. I had to let them know you're safe and that you're here with me. Can you not understand?"

I sighed. "Yes. I suppose so. Yet you don't seem to understand anything I've told you and what you did understand, you didn't believe. Mummy will make sure they take me back to that home, Nana and it will all carry on as before. No-one would think anything bad happens at Garfield House. They buy us pretty clothes and take us all on outings and stuff. To anyone looking in from the outside, everything looks just perfect."

"Perhaps that won't happen, Keri. If you tell the social workers the truth and let them know that your mother never really harmed you ..."

"But she did, Nana! All the time!"

"Look, Keri. It is not my place to say these things, but you must understand something. Your mother was so dreadfully unhappy with that awful man. Of course, she was often upset and I can imagine she shouted rather a lot and probably made mountains out of molehills. But I'm quite sure she'd never actually harm you, dear."

I stared at Nana in astonishment. "But ... you saw for yourself how she treated me! You knew how much she hated me, Nana."

"No, dear. I saw a very distressed and unhappy woman dealing with a violent, unpleasant man and a wilful daughter. I realise that now. You were good when you were with me because you were out of the stressful situation. It must have been awful for you with your mother and that vile man arguing all the time. No wonder you began to make up stories. They're splitting up now though. Your mother and Russell are going to come and stay with me here for a time until your mother can find another place to live."

"So there wouldn't be room for me as well?"

Nana hesitated. I think it may have been in that moment of hesitation that I decided I did not wish to stay around. I glanced at the radiator beside Nana's chair, where my underwear steamed gently.

Nana wrung her hands together. "Keri, it's not like that at all, dear."

"It will be though, when Mother gets here," I muttered. "Are my under-things dry yet?"

Nana put her hand on the clothes. "No. They'll be a couple of hours. I'm sure they'll be dry by the time ..."

"By the time Mother gets here." I finished the sentence for her. "Do you suppose she'll take me back to the home herself?"

Nana sniffled. "Oh dear, oh dear, Keri. I'm sure I don't know what to do for the best! I'm so sorry you're so unhappy. If things were different, I'd ask that you stay with me for a while, to get over your traumas. But you see it's all been arranged already. I was expecting your mother and Russell tomorrow anyway. They're just coming today instead now that I've let her know you're here."

"And I conveniently have no underwear or blouse to wear now."

"What? Surely, Keri, you cannot mean that I manipulated you?"

"Probably not, Nana. At least, not intentionally. It's true though, isn't it? I'm not going to run away from here in my jeans and your bath robe after all."

"Oh, Keri. I cannot believe I heard you say that! Why ever would you run away from me, dear? I've always loved you."

I tried to smile, but it didn't work very well. "Yes, Nana. You've always loved me. You always think the very best of everyone as well. Only now, you've heard so many stories about me and my wickedness you cannot believe the simple truth when I tell it to you. It's not you I need to run away from. It's everyone and everything else."

"Running away never solves anything, Keri. That much I know."

"It solved everything before I came here to you, Nana. I had a life. I was happy. I had a job, friends and freedom. Nobody hurt me anymore and no-one attacked me, raped me or called me a liar - or any other name either. Now I'll have to go back to that place and it'll all start all over again. But before that happens, I'll have to listen to Mother calling me names and pulling me to pieces, trying to make me feel as small and horrible as she can."

"Oh, Keri. Of course she won't do that! She'll be as relieved as I am that you're safe and well."

I leaned forward and picked up my cigarettes. Nana made no move to stop me as I lit one.

"I'll just sit here in your bath-robe and wait for her to get here, shall I?" I asked.

"We could watch the television if you like, dear. Or perhaps we could have a game of Scrabble, to pass the time. Those chops should be done by now. Let's have something to eat and then we can decide what to do until your mother arrives."

During the meal, Nana asked me how I'd managed to get to Old Harlow. When I told her I had hitch-hiked and accepted lifts from just two lorry drivers, her eyes grew round with horror. I endured a long lecture about the perils of accepting lifts from strangers. Of course, I knew Nana was right, but it didn't make it any easier to be told I'd risked my life to reach her, only to be handed straight back to Mother and ultimately, the authorities.

We did play Scrabble together. I won the game - that in itself was unusual. Perhaps I had very good letters; Maybe Nana didn't play to her full ability as she was so distracted.

My underwear and blouse dried nicely. I put them on and sat on the settee watching the BBC nine o'clock news without actually taking in any of it. I felt utterly bereft, as if there were no fight left in me. I found I really didn't care what happened at Garfield House when I went back there. After all, if I were determined enough, I could run away again and find Tramp.

When the door knocker rattled, Nana hurried to the door and opened it. Russell pushed into the room, pausing only to give Nana a peck on the cheek. He grinned at me, but his humour vanished when Mother spoke.

"Go straight upstairs, Russell. I'll call you when you can come down."

I watched dispassionately as Mother shrugged off her mackintosh and went to hang it up. She didn't greet me, simply scowled at me as she passed by the settee. Nana went to put the kettle on. I could hear her attempts at cheery conversation as she asked whether

Mother and Russell had enjoyed their journey. Mother stood in the kitchen doorway and answered her queries as if I didn't exist.

When Nana came back into the room bearing a tray with three cups of tea on it, Mother followed her and went to sit in the chair adjacent to Nana's. I watched as Mother lit a cigarette and took a long draw on it. I longed to light one of my own but didn't dare to.

"So," Mother began, blowing out a long plume of smoke. "Just what the bloody hell do you think you've been doing?"

Before I could reply, Mother added, "And to turn up here, of all places and worry the life out of Nana. You're just a selfish little bitch, never giving any thought to anyone but yourself."

"Milly!" Nana exclaimed.

"Be quiet, Mother. It has to be said. You don't know the half of it." Mother turned back to me. "Well?"

Here we go again, I thought to myself. *Here we go again.*

40. Traumatic Return To Garfield House

Two police officers attended to 'get' me from Nana's home. One of them was female.

Russell had been allowed downstairs but had been told he must not look at or speak to me. He sat at the dining table. When the male police officer put handcuffs on me, I saw Russell's eyes grow wide with disbelief.

I stood placidly in the handcuffs whilst Mother told the officers I was dangerous and likely to be aggressive. In the period of waiting, whilst Mother refused to listen to anything I tried to say, Nana had repeated most of what I'd told her – in a confused and somewhat inaccurate manner. Mother now relayed this - in her own way - to the attentive police officers.

"She's been hanging around with tramps, so I expect she'll need to be properly fumigated. She's been bathed and her clothes washed, but I doubt that will deal with the infestations she's likely to have. She's probably pregnant by now - she has a tendency to open her legs for anything remotely male. And when you discover exactly where she's been, with these tramps, you'll likely find a regular Aladdin's cave of stolen goods because she can't keep her sticky fingers to herself. I've no idea what else she's been involved with; drugs at the very least, I expect. I suppose the home will have to sort that out."

"And you are?" the male police officer asked.

"Why, I'm her mother of course! Now. I'd be obliged if you'd take her away. I've had an extremely trying day and a long journey to get here. As you can see," she indicated Nana, who sat in her armchair weeping, "My own mother has been greatly frightened and upset by this. No-one wants some leather-jacketed yob arriving on their doorstep."

After just a few more questions, the police officers led me out to the waiting panda car. I said nothing at all, not even 'goodbye' to Nana. Mother closed the door firmly behind us.

The female police officer sat in the back of the vehicle with me. She looked quite severe and stern but when she spoke, her voice was kind enough.

"It'll take us a little while, Keri, to process all your information. We'll need to make arrangements for you to be transferred to Dereham. You might have to spend the night with us."

I nodded and looked out the car window at the familiar streets.

When we arrived at Harlow police station, I was led through a back door, along a corridor and presented at a desk, where a stout policeman frowned at me.

"Ah. So here we have the runaway!" he exclaimed.

The handcuffs were removed. Some forms were filled in; I had to confirm my name and date of birth, then the female police officer led me into a small room with a table in it and three chairs.

"You'll have to be interviewed first, Keri, then I can take you down to the cells and you'll be able to have a cup of tea - if you want one."

An extremely bad tempered and harassed-looking detective entered the room. He had a folder with him. He sat down opposite me and read through it. The female police officer sat beside me.

"Right," the detective began. "So you ran away from Garfield House in Dereham some few of months ago. Is that correct?"

I nodded.

"Where have you been all this time and who has been caring for you?"

How could I possibly answer that question without getting Mam, Al, Don and so many others into trouble? I couldn't; so I didn't answer at all.

The detective sighed. "Look, I haven't got all night you know. I've got proper police work to do. Are you going to tell me where you've been and what you've been doing, girl?"

464

"No."

"Right then. That's all I needed. Let the bloody social workers sort it out. You'll be staying here over the night. I've already contacted the emergency social worker in Norfolk. They'll send someone to fetch you tomorrow." He turned to the female police officer. "Has she been searched?"

"Yes. She had a pack of cigarettes and a little over a pound in loose change. That's all."

"No drugs? A knife?"

The female police officer shook her head, negative.

"Well. That's something, I suppose. You see a leather jacket and usually it means one or the other - or both. I'm off; I've got some real work to do."

Without so much as another glance at me, the detective left the room. The female police officer stood and told me to go with her. I followed her out of the room, back to the desk. After a short wait, another police officer appeared. He had a large bunch of keys.

I was required to leave my jacket and shoes outside the cell door. I've no idea why. The female officer checked that I had no belt on my jeans then escorted me inside the stark room.

"I'll bring you a cup of tea in a moment, Keri. I expect you take loads of sugar?"

"No sugar, thanks," I replied as I gazed about at the grubby, cream walls, taking in the low bench fixed to one of them. A dark grey blanket and a pillow rested at one end. In the opposite corner, a stainless steel toilet, with no seat crouched like some beast. I could see no method of flushing that lavatory. The room smelled of old sweat, stale urine and disinfectant.

The female police officer withdrew and I heard the heavy door slam and a series of locks sliding into place. I sat down on the bench and stared at my hands. So now I was a true, hardened criminal, locked into a police cell! The ridiculousness of the situation suddenly occurred to me and I chuckled to myself.

I still had a smile on my face when the police officer returned with tea in a plastic cup and a slice of under-cooked toast on a paper plate.

"I must say," she began. "You look remarkably happy for someone locked in a cell."

"Just glad to get away from that cow who calls herself my mother," I replied.

The police officer shook her head and left the cell, locking the door behind her. I noticed a small peephole in the door and wondered if she was watching me. I shrugged and ate the toast, drank the tea down in a couple of gulps and stretched out on the bench with my hands behind my head.

I had no intention of going to sleep, but I awoke when there was a rattle at the door. I sat up. A tall police officer came in with a tray. It had several plastic cups of tea on it.

"Morning, love. You want sugar in your tea?"

"Morning?" I echoed. "Already?"

The policeman grinned. "You've been sleeping like a baby, love. I checked on you several times. Here y'are, a nice, hot cuppa. We've not got much for breakfast, I'm afraid. Just toast or a bowl of cornflakes. What'll you have?"

"Toast, please."

"Righty-ho. I'll be back with that in a few minutes." He left the room, expertly balancing the cups on the tray.

Although I hated the idea I might be watched, I used the revolting toilet. There was a button on the floor. I pressed it with my foot and the toilet flushed. I retreated to the bench, wishing I could wash my hands.

I'd drunk all the tea by the time the policeman came back with a slice of toast on another paper plate. He took the plate from the previous evening and the two plastic cups.

"You shouldn't have too long to wait now, love. There're a couple of social workers coming for you."

"May I have one of my cigarettes, please?" I asked.

"I'll bring you one in a moment, love. Got a few more breakfasts to dish out yet."

He locked the door again when he left.

Miss Partridge was one of the social workers who came for me. I'd never seen the other lady before. She had bouncing brown curls and merry eyes. She smiled at me.

"Well, young lady! You've certainly led us all a merry dance. Still, I'm very pleased to see you safe."

I followed the two women from the cell, grateful there would be no more handcuffs. I said as much and Miss Partridge turned to me in astonishment. "What do you mean? Were you handcuffed, Keri?"

I nodded. Miss Partridge spoke quietly to her colleague, who immediately turned to the police officer escorting us away from the cells.

"Is that correct, this child was handcuffed?"

The policeman shook his head. "I've no idea. I wasn't on duty last night. I shouldn't think so. I mean, she's just a kid. We'll ask the desk sergeant."

There was a significant delay whilst reports were sought and read. When it became apparent that I had been handcuffed, Miss Partridge's colleague remonstrated loudly with the desk sergeant. The unfortunate man raised his hands helplessly.

"According to this, the mother claimed she was violent and likely to be aggressive. What else could we do? It was only for the journey here."

"She is a child," the woman insisted. "Since when has this country clapped children in handcuffs 'for the journey'. I shall be contacting your superiors about this. Good day to you."

I never did learn that woman's name. She took me gently by the elbow and steered me away from the desk and out through a door which a policeman held open for us. Miss Partridge followed.

I sat in the back seat of the social workers car and stared out the window for the whole journey, looking at landmarks I'd seen only the day before, going in the other direction. The car travelled fast and it was only a matter of two hours or so until we reached East Dereham.

However, instead of going straight to Garfield House, the social workers took me first to a hospital, which came as some surprise to me.

"What are we doing here?"

"We have to get you examined by a doctor, Keri. To make sure you are healthy and there are no problems."

"Oh. Well, I'm fine, thank you. I don't want to see a doctor, there's nothing wrong with me."

"I daresay you don't, my dear, but it is what we have to do. Come along now, don't make a fuss."

Naive as I was, I had no idea why I was required to give a urine sample, nor why blood was taken from me. After a short wait, the social workers led me in to a consulting room.

An Asian doctor looked me up and down. He said something to me, but he was very heavily accented and I couldn't understand him. I stood there, between the two women, feeling helpless and not a little afraid. Miss Partridge whispered something to her colleague, who turned to me.

"Keri, the doctor needs to know if you have indulged in any sexual activity or taken any drugs whilst you've been away from Garfield House."

I shook my head. "No."

The doctor spoke quietly with the two women for a few moments. Miss Partridge turned to me. "The doctor wants to examine you, Keri. Can you strip to the waist and lie down on the couch? I'll stay with you. I know this is scary."

"It's not *scary*!" I retorted. "It's disgusting and vile ... and ... and ... humiliating. I've had all that done before when Mother said I was a slut and sleeping around. The only men who'd ever touched me were her filthy pig of a husband and his friend! You're not touching me!"

The following events were extremely traumatic for me. Apparently, the senior social worker had 'parental control' over me because I was less than sixteen years old. She signed a form giving permission for the examination to take place. I screamed and struggled and fought like a mad thing, all to no avail. The examination took place anyway with the two social workers and two nurses holding me down. Of course, it hurt as well because I was so tense and struggling so hard.

When it was done, I shook the people off me. "Get away from me, you vile perverts!" I shrieked. "I said no! You've as good as raped me - again!" I fell to weeping as I dragged on my underwear and jeans and groped for my shoes, which had been kicked away in the struggle. "I hate you! I hate you all!" I wept.

Miss Partridge laid a hand on my shoulder and tried to comfort me, but I shook her off, my face twisted into a snarl of utter outrage and fury. "Don't touch me!"

The social workers escorted me back to the car, the senior lady keeping a hand very firmly on my elbow. I had considered running again, but I knew I'd not get far, so I clambered back into the car and sat glaring at the two women.

The journey to Garfield House took no time at all. The car pulled into the driveway and Miss Partridge got out and opened the back door of the car for me. I looked up and saw Paul and Joss standing by the back door. Neither of them looked happy.

"So, the prodigal returns!" Paul boomed as I approached him with a social worker on either side of me. I made no reply.

"Come along, Keri," Joss urged. "I'll take you up to your room. Paul will speak with you later on."

I had no choice but to follow her. As we passed the kitchen, I saw Mrs. Webster and Mrs. Brown standing silently by the sink. Mrs. Brown smiled, but I turned away. It felt as if my heart had sunk right down into the pit of my stomach. Vaguely nauseated from the long journey and then the traumatic examination, I wanted nothing more than to lie down and sleep.

Joss led me right along the corridor upstairs to the room I'd originally had when I first came to Garfield House. She opened the door. Apart from a few personal items on the dressing table, there was nothing in the room except Lambie and a nightdress, which were laid out side by side on the bed.

"Get changed into your nightdress, Keri. If you're hungry, I'll have Mrs. Brown make you a sandwich."

I stared at Joss. "What? But it's only lunch-time!"

"Yes, it is," replied Joss. "That's why you can have a sandwich if you wish. You will get changed and give me your clothes, please."

I backed away. "No!"

Joss sighed. "Look, Keri. Please don't make this any more difficult than it already is. You'll have to get changed eventually, even if we have to undress you like a small child. You might as well be grown up about it."

"Why do I have to get changed? So you perverts can have another grope of me?" I yelled.

Joss paled slightly. "Don't be so foolish. You have to spend the rest of this week whilst you're not at school in your nightdress, that's all. To make sure you don't run away again. Those are the rules, I'm afraid."

"Fine!" I snapped, undoing my blouse. "Have the damned clothes, see if I care. But you damned well better make sure I get them back. I worked hard and paid good money for these!"

Joss removed all my clothes, even my knickers! When she'd left the room, I sat down on the bed and clutched Lambie to my chest.

"I might as well be dead, Lambie," I muttered. "At least if I were dead there'd be no more of this to live through."

With nothing better to do, I got into bed and hugged Lambie close to my chest. I fell asleep without tears and dreamed I was still at Randy's house with Tramp.

Joss came and woke me a couple of hours later and told me Paul wanted to speak with me. I sat up, bleary eyed, wondering if I were dreaming. Then the previous twenty-four hours came back to me and I remembered how I came to be back in Garfield House.

"Five minutes, Keri. That's time to go to the toilet and have a wash." Joss left the room.

When I came out of the toilet, I could hear children's voices downstairs. I felt a kind of anticipation; this meant the children were home from school. After I'd seen Paul and endured whatever he said to me, I'd be able to see Karen again.

I drifted down the stairs in my flimsy nightdress, feeling very vulnerable. If only Joss hadn't taken my knickers as well! I made my way to the office door and knocked.

"Come!"

I peered round the door. Paul sat on the chair at the desk; he had his back to me and did not look up from whatever he was doing. "Sit down, Keri."

I sat, perched on the edge of an armchair. Apart from the fact that I was wearing only my nightie, I didn't feel particularly afraid. After all, last time I ran away, the punishment had been almost non-existent.

Several minutes passed before Paul turned around in his chair and gave me his attention.

"I never thought I'd be having this conversation, Keri, not after last time. Did you learn nothing after your escapade with Valerie?"

I did not reply.

"Surely, you must have known you'd eventually be found, girl?"

I felt a sense of bold abandon. "But I wasn't found. I went to my Nana of my own accord. If I hadn't gone there, I'd still be free."

Paul scowled. "Don't be flippant with me, Keri."

I shrugged. "I'm not. It's true. If I hadn't gone to visit Nana, you'd never have found me."

"Where have you been?"

I looked away and said nothing.

"We'll find out eventually. You may as well tell me now."

I'll never tell you anything, I thought. Clearly, my face must have betrayed me because Paul leaned forward in his chair and shouted at me. "You will tell me where you have been!"

I stood up. "No!" I yelled back.

Paul stood up and reached toward me. I dodged away and darted toward the door. "Don't you touch me, you fat, perverted pig!" I bawled as I dashed out into the hall.

Paul flung the door wide and ran after me. I raced for the stairs. I heard him call out, "Joss! Joss! Quickly, I'm going to hit her!" I heard his heavy footsteps pounding up the stairs behind me.

I rushed into my bedroom and slammed the door, practically in Paul's face. He flung it open and entered the room. His face was deep red and I saw a thick vein on his forehead which I felt sure hadn't been there before. I backed away.

"You will not speak to me like that! I won't tolerate it!" Paul advanced toward me and slapped my face just as Joss appeared in the doorway.

Far from being cowed, I was furious. I stood my ground and glared at Paul. "That's right. What a big man you are! You can hit girls!"

"Why, you little ..." Paul lunged forward, but Joss stepped between us.

"That's enough!" she snapped. "We're not going to have children hospitalised because they've been battered. We've got more than enough troubles already."

"Why?" I sneered, "Because everyone knows you're all perverts?"

"Joss!" roared Paul.

Joss merely laid a hand on his arm and whispered something. Without another word, the two of them left the room. Joss closed the door quietly behind them.

I sank onto the edge of my bed and put a hand to my face, which stung. After a minute or two, I got up and crossed the room to peer in the mirror. Sure enough, a livid, raised hand-print showed on my cheek. I scowled at my own image.

On the off-chance, I checked the wardrobe and drawers for any sign of clothing. There was nothing. I sat down on the bed again and began to think about how I could escape. There had to be a way. Perhaps if I crept into someone else's room and took some clothes I could sneak out and run again.

Cautiously, I opened the door and peered out into the corridor. There seemed to be no-one about. Just as I opened the door properly, Mrs. Webster appeared at the other end of the corridor. She was carrying a tray. I stood perfectly still and watched her approach.

"It's more than you deserve, after all the trouble you've caused, Keri, but Joss insisted I bring you a cup of tea and a sandwich. Here you are."

For a second, I considered knocking the tray out of the woman's hands and fleeing past her. Then my common sense kicked in and I became aware that I hadn't eaten anything since the toast at the police station first thing in the morning. I accepted the tray.

"Thank you."

Mrs. Webster tossed her head. "Hmph! Well, at least your manners are reasonable enough. You're to stay in your room until you're called down, do you understand?"

I bit back a rude retort and nodded before retreating back into my room with the tray.

The holiday in Jersey of which I had such distorted and vague memories had made me so deeply suspicious I pulled the sandwich apart and inspected every part of it before eating. Likewise, I sniffed at the tea and sipped a tiny mouthful, swilling it around my mouth to see if I could detect any strange taste. Nothing seemed amiss and I gulped the tea down thirstily.

Having nothing to do at all, I paced the room, counting my steps in each direction. I almost missed the gentle tapping on my door. I rushed to open it, expecting to see Karen's face grinning at me. Instead, I saw Valerie. She looked pale and frightened.

"Are you OK?" she whispered. "Everyone's talking. Paul hit you, didn't he?"

"I'm all right," I whispered back. "I've had much worse than that from my step-father. At least it was only a slap."

"I can see the marks on your face."

"It doesn't matter. Why hasn't Karen been up to see me?"

"Karen? She's not here anymore. She only came back for three days. They made her stay in her nightie. She got in awful trouble because she wouldn't tell them where she'd been. They made her stay in her room all the time ... this room. Then I went to school one morning and when I came back, she'd gone. All her stuff as well."

I swallowed hard. "Where did she go?"

Valerie shrugged. "I dunno. I've tried to ask but they won't tell me anything. Everyone says it's none of my business." She glanced behind her, along the corridor. "I'm not supposed to be here. I told them I needed the toilet. Do you need anything?"

"A book. Any book will do, just so I've got something to read."

"I'll try." Valerie turned and crept away.

I closed the door and flung myself on the bed next to Lambie. "Oh, Lambie, Karen's gone! She was my best friend! I have to find out where she went. I must find her!" Even in my grief, no tears came. I think perhaps I'd cried all the tears I had when I was with Nana and she didn't believe what I told her. Even so, I'd never felt so entirely alone, not even just after Karen had been caught and I had the bed-sit to myself.

I've no idea exactly how long I sat there on my bed thinking about Karen, but it was a good hour or more. When I heard a sharp rapping at the door, I jumped.

"Come in!"

Little Mary stepped into the room. She walked solemnly over to me, stuck her hand up her jumper and pulled out a book, which she handed to me. "You've got to come down for your tea now," she said.

I tucked the book beneath my pillow and smiled at the small girl. "Thanks," I mouthed, then, raising my voice I said, "All right. I'm coming, although I don't want to come downstairs in my nightie."

Mary giggled and reached for my hand. "You've been naughty, haven't you, Keri?"

"Ever so naughty," I agreed as I let the small girl tow me along the corridor.

"Karen was naughty too, wasn't she?"

"I suppose she was."

Mary led me down the stairs. As we entered the dining room, the small girl turned and looked up at me. "Are you going away again, Keri? Like Karen did?"

Joss, standing close by, intervened. "No, Mary. Keri's going to stay right here with us for now. Go and sit down, there's a good girl. Thank you for telling Keri it's tea-time."

I glanced around the room. Valerie sat at the table in the window with a blonde-haired girl I'd never seen before. I began to move toward them, but Joss called me back.

"No, Keri. You're to sit here, please." She indicated a chair next to Mary at a table occupied only by the little children.

I sat, knowing protests would be useless. I felt incredibly self-conscious wearing my thin nightdress and my usually good appetite fled. I picked at the meal, willing time to pass quickly so I could run back to my room. It had not escaped my notice that John sat at a table behind me with an older boy I'd never seen before. I thought I could feel them staring at me.

Although only four days, the period of time I spent wearing only a nightdress and no underwear felt interminably long. After the first day, I was no longer required to stay in my room - even though I wanted to.

Valerie asked me many questions about where I'd been and how Karen and I managed to stay away from the police as they searched for us. I answered very few. I had a strong suspicion that Valerie had been asked to find out where I'd been and that she'd immediately pass this information to Paul and Joss.

I did tell her that I'd worked - but not where. I also said I'd found a boyfriend; I told her his name was David. It became harder and harder for me not to reveal anything at all about my time away; I learned to guard my tongue. In fact, I became far quieter and more self-possessed than I'd ever been in my life before. Valerie commented, more than once, that I'd changed a great deal during my absence.

The two new teenagers in the house largely avoided me. I wondered if they'd been told to, or whether they simply felt suspicious of me. The blonde girl, Sarah, now shared a bedroom with Valerie – the room I had previously shared with Karen. I think she must have been a little younger than me, probably about thirteen.

The other new teenager, Jake, spent all his time in company with John. The pair seemed to get along extremely well. I frequently saw them laughing and joking together. John no longer behaved strangely and I heard no-one call him 'weirdo' or anything else.

Several times, during those four days, I noticed Sally looking at me with an expression on her face I couldn't identify. She never spoke to me; if I smiled, she turned away. In fact, I began to notice that, apart from the occasional sarcastic or spiteful remark, she rarely spoke to anyone.

On Saturday, the fourth day of living in my nightdress, I retreated to my room to read when Neil gathered everyone else to take them out. I didn't ask where they were going and I knew better than to ask if I could go too. I curled up on the bed with Lambie in my lap and read more of the book little Mary had smuggled upstairs at Valerie's request: Swallows and Amazons.

Joss opened the door, without knocking. I didn't have time to hide the book, but Joss either didn't notice, or didn't care. She carried a very large box, which looked heavy.

"Keri, you have a visitor ... and I've brought your belongings. Put them away tidily, please."

Joss took two steps into the room and put the box down. She said something to the person just outside the door; I heard 'tea' mentioned, but I couldn't catch the whole sentence. I wondered who on earth would be visiting me.

I nearly dropped the book in shock as Mother stepped into the room. She glanced around before her gaze rested on me.

"Why are you still in your nightdress at two in the afternoon?"

I shrugged. "They took all my clothes away."

Mother nodded. She turned to regard the large box Joss had left on the floor. "Well, you could get dressed now."

"I bet they only gave them back because you came," I muttered as I stood up.

Mother sat on the end of the bed as I rummaged through the box. Everything appeared to be there. I ignored Mother as best I could as I dragged on some underwear. I found my favourite 'skinny' jumper and the embroidered jeans, which I pulled on, tossing my nightdress toward the bed. When I turned back, I saw Mother folding the nightdress.

"Why are you here?" The blunt question did not seem to disturb Mother in the least.

"So you think I shouldn't bother to visit my daughter?"

"You've never bothered before!"

Mother hesitated briefly. "A lot has been happening. I ... er ..." she looked around the room.

I sat down near the pillows to pull on my socks. "Nana told me you're splitting up with that pig and going to stay with her."

"Yes. That's part of it. I'll have to find a new job first and then save up to buy a house."

I didn't know a great deal about real estate or the details of house purchase. Even so, I thought Mother had owned the house in Swanton Abbot. Surely, I mused, if she'd now sold it, she could afford to buy another house. "Why can't you just buy another house straight away?"

"Holly Cottage was in his name. He sold it whilst I was with Nana. Not that it's anything to do with you, but I'll have to fight him through the Courts now to get my share."

"Oh."

"It could take months; maybe even years. He killed my two kittens as well."

"Kittens?"

"The place was so empty without any animals in it. I got a couple of kittens - for company."

It had never occurred to me that Mother needed 'company'. My stomach clenched at the thought of how the poor kittens might have suffered at Terry's hands. "He's a wicked man."

"Yes."

A long, awkward pause made me shift uncomfortably. Mother reached into her handbag and took out a pack of cigarettes. She took one out and made to light it; her lighter wouldn't spark.

"We're not allowed to smoke in our rooms," I murmured.

Mother continued, unsuccessfully, to light her cigarette. I reached over to my bedside drawer and tugged it open. After groping for a few seconds, my fingers closed on a book of matches stuck to the roof of the drawer space with sticky tape - an old trick of Karen's. I offered them to Mother.

To my amazement, Mother offered me a cigarette! I accepted it in silence and waited for Mother to strike the flimsy match.

For several minutes, we smoked, knocking the spent ash into our cupped hands. I studied Mother; she looked older. Deep lines had appeared on her forehead and at the side of her mouth. Her brassy hair had a smattering of fine, grey streaks.

"I think they're intending to move you to another home soon."

"Why? Because I ran away from here?" I didn't like the prospect of being moved. For all the problems at Garfield House, it was familiar and even though I'd only recently returned from running away, I felt settled enough.

Mother shook her head. "No. If I weren't moving, they'd leave you here. It's because I'm moving to Harlow. Something about having to be within so many miles of family. They asked if I wanted you back at home."

I stood up and moved to the wash-basin to run the end of my cigarette under the cold water before tossing it in the waste-bin. "And you said 'no'."

Mother copied what I'd done, pausing to look out the window before throwing the sodden dog-end away. "How could I say anything else? Even if there was room, I couldn't have you at Nana's. You'd drive her mad with worry, the way you behave. And then there's Russell. There'd be arguments and ..."

"And anyway, you hate me and can't bear the thought of having me anywhere near you," I interrupted.

Mother sat down on the bed again. "No! Oh, why is this so difficult?"

I stood by the window, looking out onto the concrete yard. "Yes, you do. You've told me enough times how you hate me and how I ruined your life, just by being born."

"That was temper ... frustration ... oh, I don't know."

I turned around. "When you arrived at Nana's house the other day, you didn't even say 'hello' to me! I might be only fifteen, but I'm not stupid. Nothing has changed at all! I don't understand why you've come here."

Mother scowled - a familiar expression. "Look, I'm trying to be ..."

"What? A normal mother? Why?" I turned back to the window so that Mother should not see the tears which had filled my eyes. I swallowed, before continuing, "I suppose they've started asking awkward questions or something. So you came to visit me. Other kids here sometimes get to see their parents, but most don't. You never visited me before ... you never even wrote to me or anything."

"I ... no. No, I didn't."

Quite suddenly, I knew why Mother had come. She was trying to say goodbye. Forever. She'd separated from her horrible husband, left her home and everything she'd worked so hard for, lost her precious kittens - which clearly meant more to her than I did. Now she intended to begin again. Just her and Russell - and Nana. I didn't figure in her plans at all. Perhaps she felt guilty. More likely, she was trying to convince the authorities that she was a good person and responsible mother.

I didn't know what to say. Part of me accepted the realisation and felt relief that I'd never have to lock horns with her again. Another part felt afraid, rejected and alone. I tried not to dwell on the latter as I turned and walked back to the bed.

"Can I have another cigarette, please?"

Mother handed me the packet and the book of matches. I lit a cigarette and blew a plume of smoke toward the ceiling.

"When I was ... on the run ... I had a good life. I had a job; nothing fancy, but it suited me and the wages were more than enough to live on. I had a place to live and I kept it clean and tidy. I had friends too," I paused and looked at Mother. "Not the sort of friends you'd approve of, but friends nonetheless. I was happy. If not for the fact that I knew the police and authorities were searching for me, life would have been perfect. I only went to Nana's because the police came to where I was living. I thought they had found me ... so I ran ... again."

Mother said nothing. Her cold blue eyes looked angry.

"I went to Nana because I thought she loved me. I had some stupid, childish notion that I'd be able to live with her."

"Impossible!"

"Yes. Even if you weren't going to stay with her, I know that now. Nana could never have had me there. She'd been told too many bad things about me by then."

Mother snorted derisively. "Hah! She'd only been told the truth!"

I looked directly into Mother's horrible eyes. "Was she told how your rotten husband raped and beat me?" I said, quietly.

Mother's eyes widened slightly.

"You were so convinced I was a slut and slept around and that you were the perfect mother, always doing your best for me and having it thrown back in your face. Yet you never once stopped him. You never protected me or stood up for me."

"Why, you little liar! How can you come out with such preposterous drivel?" Mother snatched up her cigarettes and lit one.

I moved to the hand basin and dropped my half smoked cigarette into it, leaving it to smoulder away. "So, you think I'm lying - as usual. You always accuse me of lying. It's hard you know, when you do your best to always be truthful and the person who is supposed to love you most, no matter what, always accuses you of lying." I stayed beside the basin. "Why do you think I would lie about something like that? How would I know about all the vile things I know, if it were all lies?"

Mother tossed her hair back from her face. "I've no idea what you 'know' or think you know ..."

"I know that little girls aren't supposed to have sex with their step-fathers - or be sold to their step-father's friends. I know what pain and humiliation are. I've known since I was five!"

"You really haven't changed at all, have you? You're still the lying, manipulative, attention-seeking little bitch you've always been!"

"I'm not arguing with you, Mother. You've never understood at all. It's normal for little girls to want attention from their mothers. The only attention I ever got from you was in the form of scoldings, thrashings and accusations. All I ever wanted from you was love and ..."

"Love? What do you know of love? You took me to hell and back dozens of times! That I didn't get rid of you sooner is the firmest proof that I loved you, stupid girl!"

"Yes. I'm stupid. Stupid enough to keep trying to get my mother to love me, want me, protect me. Nana always loved me, you know. Of course you know. It made you furious that she never had any problems with me, didn't it? There was never anyone there, at Nana's, who hurt me or called me names. No-one accused me of anything either." I moved toward the door. "And now, you've taken that from me as well. You came here to say goodbye - just so they think you're a nice person, not really because you wanted to see me."

Mother stood up. "I can see I've wasted my time."

"Yes," I agreed. "You have. You've always hated me and you hurt me for long enough to make me hate you right back."

Mother grimaced.

"But I don't hate you, Mother. I can't be bothered. You see, I know I'm none of the things you always told me I was," I paused, thinking about the way I'd raised the money to run away from Garfield House. *Perhaps I was a slut, after all.* I dismissed the intrusive thought and continued, "I know I'm not a horrible, bad person. I'm a teenager. Before that, I was a little girl - a very frightened and unhappy little girl. Soon, I'll be grown up ..."

"Yes, and you'll not last long! I expect you'll be on drugs within a year or two or be pregnant and riddled with sexually transmitted diseases."

The venom in Mother's tone did not surprise me.

"Maybe. But it won't matter to you, will it? You won't have to deal with me anymore. Goodbye, Mother. I hope you have a better life than you've had up to now. I certainly will."

I watched Mother's eyes fill with tears. I wondered how she felt. Was she furious because she couldn't strike me, here at Garfield House? Perhaps she was simply relieved that she'd never have to see me or talk to me again. I stood by the open door; Mother stood by the bed.

"I'm going downstairs now," I said, when Mother said no more. "I expect Joss or someone will make you a cup of tea."

I walked out of the room and along the corridor. I heard Mother close the door and knew she followed me but I didn't turn around. I walked down the stairs and saw Mrs. Webster on her way to the kitchen.

"Mrs. Webster," I called. "I think my mother would like a cup of tea before she leaves."

Mrs. Webster looked up and smiled. "I'll go and put the kettle on straight away."

I paused at the foot of the stairs and turned to Mother. "The kitchen's down there," I pointed along the passageway. "I expect Mrs. Webster will talk to you. She's got a very low opinion of all the kids here. You'll get on really well, I expect."

I turned away. Mother caught my arm. "Keri. It wasn't supposed to be like this. I wanted to ... I don't know. I wanted to be able to talk to you properly, just once."

I shook Mother's hand away with a shrug of my shoulder. "There's no point," I mumbled. "You'll never know who I really am or approve of me, no matter what I do. Just go. Give my love to Nana." I wandered into the play room and sat down on one of the settees.

I heard Mother's footsteps as she walked toward the kitchen. That she'd talk to Mrs. Webster about me I had no doubt. I found I really, genuinely, didn't care anymore. I stood up and switched the television on. Hopefully, Mother would leave and I wouldn't have to speak to her again.

41. A Huge Surprise

Mrs. Webster was the only person who mentioned Mother's visit at all. She spoke to me as she served the evening meal. "It was so nice to actually meet your mother, Keri. What a pleasant woman! I think it's such a shame that the two of you don't get along."

I didn't dare speak, for fear I'd say something awful. As usual, Mother had been perceived as a 'pleasant woman'. I had no doubt she'd painted a picture of me as the devil-child, probably with horns and a long, whippy tail as well!

"Did your mum come and visit you, Keri?" Mary piped up.

I nodded. "Yes, but she's gone home now, Mary."

"My mum never comes," Mary began. Her eyes filled with tears.

Mrs. Webster wrapped her arms around the little girl. "Now, now, Mary. Don't get upset, dear. Would you like to come and help me fetch the bread rolls from the kitchen?"

Mary sniffed and nodded her head. "I better wash my hands again first."

When Mrs. Webster had left the room, John called over to me. "Hey! Keri! What's it like to have your clothes back?"

I heard Jake snigger, but I ignored it. "Better than my nightdress all the time, John. I never thought I'd see proper clothes again!"

"At least you never stole anyone's clothes," John began. "Karen took ..." he stopped speaking as Mrs. Webster returned to the room with Mary.

I turned and glanced at John. I didn't speak, merely willed him to continue. As soon as Mrs. Webster had settled Mary and left the room to fetch soup, I whispered, "What did she take?"

"She took my jeans and Jake's shirt. In the middle of the night. She was gonna run again the next day I think, but they caught ..." Mrs. Webster returned, bearing a large tureen of soup.

I made a mental note to speak with John when the meal ended. Perhaps he knew more about what had happened to Karen. It hadn't occurred to me that John would know anything, but as I ate my soup, I pondered. Karen would also be suspicious of Valerie. Maybe she'd spoken to John instead; they'd never got along particularly well so the staff wouldn't think of asking John anything.

Later, I was allowed to go to the play barn with the other teenagers and Neil. John hovered by the record player whilst Neil supervised a game of darts. Once I'd been beaten, I drifted over to the record player and began looking through the discs in a large box.

"I'm putting the music on!" John spoke loudly.

"Can't I even look to see what there is?" I replied.

"You can look, but I probably won't play what you want me to."

I glanced at Neil. He didn't appear to be taking any notice of us. I bent my head over the box and muttered, "Did Karen give you a message for me?"

"She never thought you'd be caught," John replied, quietly. "But she told me if I ever saw you again, she's sorry she took your teddy. She wanted something to remember you by."

A lump formed in my throat. Of course! There should have been the little cat teddy I'd had for Christmas. Why hadn't I noticed Lambie was alone? I lifted out a record at random and shoved it under John's nose.

"Will you play that?" I spoke loudly.

"Nope. I told you, I'm choosing the music."

I dropped my voice. "What else did she say?"

"They sent her to a lock-up. She said 'run again if you can'. I don't think she wanted you to get sent to one as well."

I had a sensation, as if my heart had turned over in my chest. "Where?" I whispered.

John shrugged. "I'm not playing that, either. I always choose the music." He raised his voice, almost to a shout.

Neil looked over. "Come on, John. Let Keri choose one record, eh?"

"Oh, all right. But only one," John replied, putting a sulky expression on his face.

Neil turned back to the game of darts.

"Don't know the address," he whispered. "But it's in Norwich somewhere. I heard them talking about it. If I find out the name, I'll let you know. Will you run again?"

"Maybe. My mother said they're gonna move me away from here. I don't know how long I've got."

I selected 'He Ain't Heavy, He's My Brother' by the Hollies and handed the disc to John. "Play that one for me, please? I really miss Karen. She was like the sister I never had. Now I've lost her."

John accepted the record. "Yeah. This is a good tune. I'll play it." He hesitated, glancing at Neil before adding, "Good luck. I hope you get away. Don't get caught next time!"

I had no opportunity whatsoever to get away. There seemed to be a member of staff present every minute of every day. When Monday morning came, I learned I would be escorted to school and handed over to a member of school staff. I would also be met after school and escorted home.

Apart from the humiliation of having an adult walk to school with me - usually Neil or Joss, I writhed under the extra attention from teachers. I had to remain in full view at all times. If I went to the toilet during breaks, a teacher came with me and waited outside until I'd finished.

Gordon sympathised when we sat together and Valerie wasn't around. "I don't know how you stand it," he said. "It would drive me insane."

"It does drive me insane, but if I make a fuss, it'll just get worse. All I can do is keep my head down and put up with it. Maybe they'll let up after a week or so. Once they think I'm settled and won't run again. That's when I'll go."

"That Valerie told me to try and find out where you went," Gordon muttered. "She wants to tell the people at the home. She even offered to pay me for information. As if I'd tell on you! You were the first person to treat me like a human being."

An idea formed in my mind. "Tell you what," I whispered. "I'll make up a heap of rubbish for you to pass on. How's that? If you tell Valerie stuff so she can tell them at Garfield House, she'll tell you stuff as well."

Gordon grinned. "Yep. That'll do it. Whatever she 'pays' me, I'll split with you. How's that?"

Between us, we concocted a story which we thought sounded plausible enough. Gordon would tell Valerie I'd been in Norwich all the time I'd been away. I'd worked on the market, selling vegetables and rented a room in a big house near the city centre. Satisfied with the story we'd invented, we began to chatter about other things.

I told Gordon what had happened during the holiday on Jersey and my suspicions that perhaps we'd all been drugged. He shook his head.

"Why don't you tell someone? I mean, there must be someone in authority who'll listen to you, surely?"

"Gordon, I don't know who to trust! I thought Mrs. Webster was a really nice lady until I overheard her saying horrible things about us all. Mrs. Brown seems all right, but I can't bet on it. I trusted Joss when I first went to Garfield House because she seemed really nice. I thought she believed me when I told her about the way my mother and step-father treated me. Now, I know she must be in on it all as well! She must know what the men do to the girls at every opportunity. She certainly knew about me and Karen being out in night-clubs and pubs when we were on Jersey; she didn't do anything to stop it and she never said a word if we were away from the camp-site all night! They're all twisted, horrible, untrustworthy perverts!"

Gordon nodded. "Before you came, I often wondered what went on there. So many of the kids are ..."

"Strange?" I suggested.

"Sometimes strange," Gordon admitted. "But always unhappy and angry. What about the police? Could you go to the police and tell them?"

I shook my head. "I don't think so. When I told that policeman on Jersey what had happened to me, he took me back to the camp-site and all the staff convinced him I was a born liar, trouble-maker and a slut. I found out, while I was on the run, he should have taken me to the police station and had me make a statement - and get me examined by a doctor. But none of that happened. I think kids like me are never believed, Gordon."

"Hah!" Gordon snorted. "How handy that must be for your so-called 'carers'."

I settled back into the school routine relatively easily. I caught up quickly with what I'd missed and found the constant revision for the GCE examinations the following June to be easy. Teachers praised me frequently; in particular, the maths teacher, who thought my new-found ability to mentally manipulate numbers most impressive.

At Garfield House, I took great care to be polite to all staff members and not to get myself into any kind of altercation with anyone at all.

Very gradually, the supervision became less and less. By the end of November, I was permitted to walk to school with Valerie and Sarah. Valerie often tried to get me to talk about my time away, but I gave her little information. I constantly mentioned Norwich and pretended I'd made a mistake when, one day, I 'let slip' that I'd worked on a market stall. Valerie absorbed all this information. I knew she'd tell Joss or Paul at the earliest opportunity.

One Friday afternoon, after school, Valerie, Sarah and I were messing about together in the yard. We had coats on and sat on the bunker smoking and shivering. Something made me look up toward the gate. A man stood there.

The light was poor and I strained to see who it might be. He looked vaguely familiar. He took a step forward and light from the window of the kitchen caught the side of his face. My heart lurched.

Valerie noticed where my gaze was directed. "Who's that, I wonder?" she asked.

Still unsure, I slid off the bunker and took a couple of steps toward the gate. "I think it's someone I know," I replied.

"Well. He's tall, isn't he? Someone from your family?" Valerie came to stand beside me. Together we stared at the man.

"Hmmm. My family. Yes, you could say that."

Sure now that my eyes were not deceiving me, I raced along the short driveway and flung myself into Tramp's arms.

Neither of us spoke. Tramp held me tightly and pressed his face against my neck. All manner of emotions whirled and chased within me. I felt breathless, dizzy, elated and terrified, all at once.

Valerie and Sarah arrived at my shoulder.

"He's your boyfriend!" Valerie exclaimed. "I knew you had a boyfriend! That explains where you've been. There had to be someone looking after you." She turned and ran back to the house.

Keeping one arm draped across my shoulder, Tramp watched her go. "I guess that means trouble?"

Sarah hesitated, then followed Valerie into the house.

"I refused to tell them where I'd been or who with. I filled Valerie full of rubbish, telling her I'd been in Norwich, working a market stall and renting a room in a big house. I never mentioned you - or any of the others. Someone will be out here in a minute, to chase you away."

"They can try," Tramp muttered. "As far as I know, this place isn't a prison. I checked it out. You're allowed to have visitors."

He steered me toward the house. "Come on. Take me inside and introduce me to your wonderful social worker types. I can't wait to meet them."

I pulled back, hesitating. "Tramp. I never told you. I'm only fifteen."

He grinned and hugged me again. "That's all right, Kitten. I worked that out for myself - well, Johnny helped. As far as this lot are concerned, I'm only nineteen, all right? I'll say I met you in Norwich when you were working the market."

Joss came hurrying to the back door. She looked Tramp up and down, taking in his smart appearance. Before she could say anything at all, Tramp stepped forward, offering his hand.

"Hello. You must be Joss? I'm David. David King. I rang the social services department to see if it would be all right for me to visit and they said it would be fine."

Joss accepted Tramp's hand. "Er ... yes ... of course. Won't you come in?"

Tramp ushered me ahead of him as he stepped over the threshold. "Hey, this is quite a place; just as you described it."

Joss turned and gave Tramp a sharp look, which she quickly changed to an uncertain smile. "Keri, take your friend, David into the dining room for now. I'll ask Mrs. Webster to make a pot of tea. I'll be back in moment, I've just got to ... er ... I'll ..."

Tramp gave Joss his most winning smile. "Oh, don't worry about us. The dining room will be just fine. The offer of tea is most welcome too."

Joss actually blushed! She turned and hurried away. I had no doubt in my mind that she was running to Paul.

"Did you really ring the social services?" I whispered.

"Yep. I told them I met you while you were on the run. I had an awful job finding out your real name; I spoke to some social worker and said I wanted to see you, rekindle our acquaintance ... and check that you're all right."

"Oh." I stared at the floor.

Tramp grabbed my hand and squeezed it. "That's not really why I came, Kat. I'm gonna get you out of here."

We sat down at one of the dining tables - on opposite sides. "What happened ... that night, after the police took you?" I whispered.

"Ha! I knew Jo would cause trouble for the club. She was identified as a person who threw a brick through a window. Police picked her up and oh boy, did she squeal! She told them about you, although she didn't know your real name. I thought it would be easy enough to convince the police I wasn't hiding a runaway. One of Sandie's cousins turned up at the nick, pretending to be you - well, the girl I'd been staying at Randy's with anyway. She's about your size. I managed to convince the police I'd been seeing her and Jo and that Jo was out to cause trouble for me out of jealousy. They took all your stuff away from Randy's house. That wasn't the problem. I got well and truly nicked for being a part of the ... er ... trouble earlier on."

"Oh, no! What will happen to you now?"

Joss returned to the room with Mrs. Webster. Tramp stood up.

"Mr. King, my husband would like a word with you, if you don't mind. Keri, go and help Mrs. Webster to prepare some tea."

Tramp inclined his head respectfully and followed Joss from the dining room. Mrs. Webster watched him as he walked past her.

"He's a rather well-off and refined young man, if I'm any judge," Mrs. Webster began. "Goodness alone knows how you met him - and I'm not expecting you to tell me, either. You've been up to no good, young lady, and I'm pretty sure there's more trouble brewing."

"He's my friend," I mumbled.

"Yes, I'm sure he is. I wonder what lies you told him for that to have happened!" She turned and made for the kitchen. For a few seconds, I sat at the table, wondering what on earth would happen next. I stood, pushing my chair out of the way and hurried after Mrs. Webster.

"What do you mean?" I demanded. "Why do you think I would've told David lies?"

Mrs. Webster paused in her filling of the kettle. "Your mother told me all about you, Keri. To think, I used to believe you were actually quite a nice girl!"

I doubted that, very much. I could have argued, insisted Mother was the one who told lies, but it seemed pointless. In any event, I wanted to be allowed to see Tramp. I already had a knot of anxiety in the pit of my stomach, worrying about what might be being said in the office.

"Shall I get the cups out for you?" I asked.

Mrs. Webster stopped and stared at me. "Didn't you hear what I just said to you?" she asked, incredulous.

I nodded. "You don't like me because Mother told you things about me."

"I ... that's not what I meant, Keri. I ... didn't mean that I don't like you; of course not. I should just like to know how you met that young man, that's all."

"I expect Paul will tell you, later on. You probably wouldn't believe me if I told you anyway. You just said you think I tell lies."

Mrs. Webster pressed her lips together in a firm line. I knew she was irritated and I didn't want to exacerbate the situation any further.

"I'll go back to the dining room and wait."

I didn't need to wait long. Tramp returned, with Paul and Joss. Mrs. Webster brought a mug of tea each for me and Tramp, then the adults left us, although I felt certain they were close by, listening.

Neither of us spoke for several minutes; Tramp grinned. "I'm staying for tea, Keri! How about that?"

"Really? How come?"

"Paul invited me. He said I can stay until nine o'clock. Apparently, there's a 'play-barn' where we can go after tea."

I nodded. "There is. There's a record player and a dart board in there."

"Good. I can let you beat me at darts."

I laughed at his serious expression.

Mrs. Webster brought the cutlery and plates through and asked us if we'd set the tables for her. Of course, Tramp charmed her with his smile and wonderful manners. It pleased me to see the old woman obviously flustered.

"Joss said you and your friend can eat at the small table over there," Mrs. Webster said. "So don't forget to set that one as well."

During the meal, Tramp made an awful lot of small talk. He commented on everything, from the weather to politics. Absolutely nothing he said could have been misconstrued by anyone who was listening. I noticed Joss glance our way several times, although Paul resolutely refused to look away from his meal.

When the meal ended, Tramp winked at me and stood up. "May I help with the washing up?" he asked of Mrs. Webster.

"What? I mean ... no, of course you don't need to do that. Off you go to the play-barn now. We can manage the washing up."

"Well. If you're quite sure?"

Mrs. Webster smiled. "Yes, young man. I'm quite sure."

I led Tramp across the concrete courtyard to the play-barn. I fully expected that John, Jake, Sarah and Valerie would be in there, but it was empty.

"Listen," Tramp said. "This might be the only chance I get to tell you. The only statement against me - or any of the others - is Jo's. She's out to cause as much trouble as she can. I'm out on bail at the moment. I'm pretty certain it's not gonna come to court. There're a few strings being pulled, not least by my father. I'm going to Ireland, Kat and I want you to come with me."

"Ireland?" I echoed.

"Just for a while. We'll find a place to live over there and get it all done up how we want it. Then, we'll go across to Scotland and stay there for a month."

"Why?" I asked.

Tramp dropped to one knee and took my hand. "Because, you beautiful, strange and intriguing woman, I want you to marry me. If you'll have me that is?"

I gasped. I looked into Tramp's earnest, deep blue eyes and caught my breath. I don't believe I'd ever been so totally surprised in my life. My heart thundered in my ears and I felt my knees beginning to tremble. Tears welled up and filled my eyes. I sank to my knees in front of him.

"Oh, Tramp! Of course, I'd have you! But ... I'm only fifteen! I'm not old enough to get married ... to anybody."

He wiped a tear, trickling from the corner of my eye with his fingertips. "I know. That's why we go to Ireland. Then, when you're sixteen, we go over to Scotland, to Gretna Green. If we stay for a month or so, we can be married there. Once you're my wife, no-one will ever be able to hurt you again. After that, even if you decide you hate the sight of me, you'll be a married woman and able to make your own decisions. Even if you don't really like me enough to want to actually be with me - but I think you do – it'll get you out of here and to freedom. Will you come?"

"Like you? Of course I like you! Maybe I even ..." Tramp put his finger against my lips.

"Don't say it. I know how I feel. It's more than just being intrigued and fascinated. But ... as you said, you're only fifteen and I don't want or expect you to make any kind of commitment like swearing undying love for me. In a few months or years you might feel differently. I just want you to say that you'll come with me."

"How? I'm not allowed out of here without a member of staff. They've only just stopped taking me to and from school! They're so sure I'll run again."

"What about at night? Could you get out at night somehow?"

"I don't know! All the doors are locked at night. There's always one member of staff on duty, but I don't know if they stay awake or not."

Tramp drew me closer and hugged me. "Come on, Kat. Think! There has to be a way out of this place!"

I racked my brains. Suddenly, I recalled the fire escape door behind the curtain in my bedroom. I stood up and went to the window, setting my eye to the small hole in the wire-reinforced glass. I stared up at the end of the house. A metal platform stood outside the fire door. There were metal steps leading down to the ground.

"Come here, Tramp. Look!" I moved, so he could peer out of the hole himself.

"That fire door is in my bedroom! If only I'd thought of it before! I could have been gone as soon as I got my clothes back!"

Tramp moved away from the hole and switched on the record player. He snatched up a disc and put it on. "Someone's coming," he muttered. "Some bloke with a beard and two girls."

"That's Neil," I replied.

Tramp's lip curled in a snarl. "The one who ...?"

I nodded. "Please, Tramp, don't say anything or start a fight."

"Don't worry. My biggest problem is getting you out of here. I won't do anything to jeopardise that."

The door opened. Valerie and Sarah came into the play-barn with Neil following immediately behind them.

"Hello," said Neil, grinning widely. "You're Keri's friend, David, aren't you? Hasn't she thrashed you at darts yet?"

"I'd like to see her try," Tramp replied. He shook Neil's hand but when Neil turned away, I saw Tramp wipe his hand against his trousers as if disgusted.

We spent two hours or so playing darts, listening to music and generally chatting. Tramp seemed to mix in with my care home 'friends' just as easily as he mixed in everywhere else! Eventually, Neil looked at his watch and announced that it was half past eight and I should take Tramp back to the house for a warm drink before he left.

We walked across the concrete yard slowly. Tramp looked up at the fire door and hugged me. "I'll come for you tonight, all right? Don't worry, I won't let you down. I'll wait by the front gate, in the shadow of the gatepost."

"How will we get away?"

"It's all right. I've got my bike - and your crash helmet too. We'll be long gone before they even know you've run again. By this time tomorrow, we'll be safe in Ireland."

"What time shall I meet you?"

"Not too early. Make it between two and three. Anyone who is awake then will likely be dozing around that time."

"Tramp! I haven't got a watch!"

Tramp slipped the expensive watch from his own wrist. "You have now," he joked. "Still got my leather, or did they take it off you?"

"I've still got it. I haven't had a chance to wear it though. I'd have to creep downstairs to the cloakroom to get it ... and that might mean I'm caught. There's no way I could take it upstairs with me."

We paused outside the back door. Inside, I could hear Mrs. Webster or someone else, in the kitchen. Tramp shuffled us into the shadow at the side of the house and very gently, kissed me.

My heart raced and I knew then that nothing would keep me from leaving Garfield House with this extraordinary man.

"How about I ask for my jacket back and take it with me when I leave? After all, it is mine and they can hardly say no, especially if you agree."

"Yes. That would work. You'll need your leather jacket anyway."

"It's all right, Kat. I've got another one. It just gets that one away from here for you to wear later. Come on, let's go inside. I'm sure there's someone watching us through the hole in the window of the play-barn."

Once again, we sat in the dining room. Mrs. Webster supplied us with cocoa and chocolate biscuits. I could barely drink the cocoa; certainly, I couldn't eat anything as I felt far too excited.

We chatted about inconsequential things - the darts we'd played and how Tramp had managed to beat me twice; the record collection and how it could do with some improvement. When Mrs. Webster came back for the empty cups and to tell us we had just five minutes left, Tramp asked if he could bring some records with him on his next visit and donate them to the collection.

"Why, yes. I don't see why not. That would be a very kind thing to do, young man." Mrs. Webster smiled as she left the room.

Joss came along at nine o'clock. She behaved very politely, but I could see she still felt suspicious. As Tramp headed toward the door, he turned and looked at Joss.

"I just remembered! Have you got my leather jacket here? I lent it to Keri," he looked down at me, "Sorry, Keri, but I really need it. Leather jackets are expensive."

Joss frowned. "Yes. I think Keri came back with a leather jacket. If you just wait there a moment, I'll pop to the cloakroom and find it."

As Joss moved away, so Mrs. Webster reappeared. The home rarely had so many adults about in the evenings. Even when I'd still been forced to wear only my nightdress, it would have been one member of staff, perhaps two. When Paul ambled along the passageway, I realised they thought I might try to leave with Tramp. I'm pretty sure Tramp cottoned on to their suspicions too.

"Thanks so much for letting me visit Keri, Paul," Tramp said. "I've enjoyed seeing her and I'm pleased she's settled down again so well. Would it be all right if I visit again? Perhaps next week?"

"Well," Paul began. "That very much depends on how Keri behaves. So long as she doesn't do anything stupid and keeps behaving well, yes, you can visit again next week."

Joss came back with Tramp's leather jacket. She handed it to him and he flashed her a dazzling smile. "Thanks very much." He turned to me. "It's been really good to see you, Keri. I'm glad you're safe. Didn't I tell you everything would work out all right for you if you just came back here? It looks like a nice place and everyone's been very kind to me. Sorry, I have to take my leather jacket. I'm sure you understand?"

I nodded. "I suppose so. You will come back next week, won't you?"

Tramp ruffled my hair. "Sure I will. I said I would. Now, I have to go. Work tomorrow so I need to get home. See you."

"Goodbye, Mr. King," Paul said as Joss opened the door to let Tramp out.

Tramp raised a hand. "Thanks for the meal, it was delicious. See you next week!"

Joss closed the door. Feeling I should say something 'normal', I turned to Joss and said, "Next time we go shopping, can I have a leather jacket, Joss? Please?"

"We'll see. Now, go and have your bath and get ready for bed."

I left the three adults and raced up the stairs. Only when I got into my room did I grin widely. I lifted my sleeve and stared at the watch Tramp had given me. Only five past nine! I had a whole six hours to wait until I was free. I gathered up my nightdress and wash things and rushed to the bathroom.

I lay in the warm water staring up at the light, thinking about Tramp, down on his knee in front of me. In less than twenty four hours, I'd not only be free, I'd be miles away, in another country. And in about four months, I'd be married! I began to sing a song, very quietly to myself ... "The first time ever I saw your face, I thought the sun rose in your eyes ..."

42. Escape!

Although sorely tempted, I went nowhere near the fire door in my room. I lay reading Swallows and Amazons, even though I couldn't concentrate on the story. I kept glancing at the time.

When Joss put her head around the door at about half past ten and told me to put my book down, turn out the light and go to sleep, I begged to be allowed to finish the chapter.

"No. I know what that means! You'll be up half the night reading like you've been in the past. Put the book down now. It will still be there tomorrow."

I made a show of grumbling to myself, but I put the book down on the bedside cabinet and switched off the light.

"That's better. Good night, Keri."

"Night."

Joss closed the door. I sat up and looked at the light shining through the gap under the door. It remained partially blocked. I lay down again, guessing that Joss would remain outside the door for several minutes before peeking to see if I had put my light on again.

Sure enough, after some few minutes, during which time I listened to the steady 'tick-tick' of Tramp's watch, I heard the door open very quietly. I kept my eyes closed and tried to make my breathing even. The slight 'click' the door made on closing told me Joss had checked and been satisfied I hadn't defied her.

I sat up. All I had to do now was to somehow stay awake for around four hours! I didn't dare open the curtains or switch the light back on. I had no idea how many times, if at all, Joss or any other member of staff checked the rooms during the night. I began to worry. What if staff checked every hour or so?

Eventually, common sense prevailed. I thought back to how Karen and I had sat up, sometimes very late, with nothing but torch-light. No-one ever caught us. In fact, one night when little Mary had been ill, Sally ventured into the staff quarters to wake someone up to come help.

I gathered my clothing in the dark. The only bag I had in the room was the tasselled shoulder bag I'd not used for ages. It wouldn't hold much. I carefully rolled up some underwear and a couple of pairs of socks. I shoved Lambie in next. Since I never intended to come back, I couldn't leave my floppy, woolly friend; I'd had him from birth. There was just enough room in the bag for a spare pair of jeans but nothing else. I sat down on the bed, keeping the bag close. There was not enough of a gap beneath the divan for me to cram it under the bed. If anyone came in, they'd see it.

I got back into bed and hugged the bag close to me before checking the time - again. The little dial had luminous figures and hands so I could easily see it. 'Packing' had taken precisely nine minutes! I sighed. My most pressing concern was that I'd fall asleep.

Fortunately, a mixture of worry and excitement kept me wide awake. Close to one o'clock, I had to leave my room to go to the toilet. The corridor, lit by the dim night-light, remained silent and empty. When I came out of the lavatory, I edged toward the top of the stairs and stood listening, straining my eyes to see if there might be any glimmer of light coming from beneath the office door.

Satisfied, I crept back to my room and closed the door. Not long to wait now. I bent to pick up my clothes, which I'd left on the floor and noticed an unmistakeable shadow move against the faint light coming through the gap under my door.

Heart thundering, I crept to my bed and got into it, curling myself around the stuffed bag of belongings. No sooner had I done so, than my door opened. I lifted my head.

"Who's that?"

"Why were you out of bed, Keri?" It was Neil speaking. "You're not ill, are you?"

"No. I had a bad dream and got up to go to the toilet," I lied.

"All right. So long as you're not ill or anything. Try to go back to sleep now. Goodnight."

"Night, Neil."

The door closed. I cursed under my breath. How had he known? Had he seen me creep toward the top of the stairs? I slid out of bed and lay flat on the floor, close to the door, trying to see under the gap. What if he were just standing in the corridor? Maybe they knew my plans!

I chided myself for foolishness. How could anyone possibly know, or even guess? Tramp had asked permission to visit next week - he'd even promised to bring some records for the collection in the play barn.

I sat on the floor beneath the window, where I could clearly see the lit gap under the door. Minutes dragged by until I became convinced the watch was faulty. When, at last, the watch showed ten to two, I lay down to try and peer under the door one last time before getting dressed. Only then did I realise I had no shoes! How stupid of me not to have somehow brought some shoes upstairs! I considered going down the darkened stairs to the cloakroom, where shoes were kept, but dismissed it, almost as soon as I thought it. Nothing for it, I would have to leave either in my bedroom slippers or barefoot. I tugged on another pair of socks; I would leave without shoes. I knew Tramp would soon get me some. I pulled the bag from under the bed-covers and put it across my shoulder and body.

Moving the curtain slightly, I peered out the window. I could see little. The concrete courtyard beneath seemed utterly black. A street light cast a little illumination from the front of the house; just enough for me to be able to make out the bulking shapes of the minibus and Paul's car. I focused on the one gate post I could partially see beyond the shrub at the side of the drive. I noticed no movement; nothing unusual at all - not that I knew what it generally looked like in the middle of the night. I wondered where Tramp would wait for me.

I waited until the watch showed ten past two and groped my way toward the curtain in the corner of the room. I remembered how the school fire door worked. There was a wide bar across the middle - very similar to one I'd noticed on this door. I knew I had to push and lift the bar to open the door.

Shoving my bag behind me so it hung down at the back of my thighs, I set my hands to the cold metal bar. This was it! This would be the last I'd ever see of Garfield House, social workers or any kind of abuse or restriction. My heart lurched in my chest as I pushed down on the bar and lifted it upward.

I heard the lock mechanism disengage and gave the door a hefty shove with my shoulder. It wouldn't budge! Confused, I let go of the bar and using my fingertips, felt all around the door edge in case there were some other lock. Nothing. With panic and frustration building, I tried the bar again. Why wouldn't the door open?

I spent perhaps ten minutes struggling with the fire door, to no avail. Stifling a sob, I crept away from the curtain. Somehow, the fire door had been secured. Why this hadn't occurred to me I have no idea. I sat down on the edge of my bed and thought about it.

At school, all the fire doors worked; there were regular fire drills and students were required to file quietly out of the nearest exit - often a fire door. I knew how important it was that these doors should never be obstructed or prevented from being opened, in case of emergency. That this door in my room either did not work or had been secured in some way infuriated me. Of course! They'd never have put me in this room alone if there'd been any chance I could get out of the fire door! Why on earth hadn't I checked it earlier?

I padded across to the window and peeped out again. This time, I thought I saw a shadow that hadn't been there before. Once again, my heart lurched. It must be Tramp, waiting patiently for me to come out and climb down the steps of the fire escape. I had to get out somehow!

I tried to picture the outside of the building in my mind. If I climbed out the window and hung by my fingertips, how far would I have to drop? The answer came to me very quickly; too far for me to achieve it without serious injury. I couldn't call to Tramp either. Any unusual noise, the sound of someone calling out, Might bring Neil or someone else straight away.

It seemed I had no choice other than to leave via a downstairs window. I thought I could escape from the window in the laundry room, next to the cloakroom. If I went down there, I could also get a pair of shoes on my way through.

I opened the door as silently as possible and peered out into the dimly lit corridor. Although fear made my hands clammy and my heart felt as if it were in my mouth, I slipped out of the door and pulled it closed with a barely audible click. Moving slowly, I edged along the corridor until I came to the first bathroom door, where I paused to listen.

I heard nothing at all; it seemed everyone was sleeping soundly. I crept forward until I came to the junction which led to the staff quarters, nearly at the top of the stairs. Here, I listened again, straining my ears for any slight sound which might indicate someone was awake. Again, only silence.

At the top of the stairs I suddenly wondered if they creaked. I'd never taken any notice because I'd never before had to employ stealth on these stairs. I stepped forward and grasped the hand-rail with my right hand, setting my foot delicately on the first stair. No creak gave me away, so I continued, down the stairs and into the large, dark hallway.

The dim night-light in the corridor above did not reach all the way down the stairs. I had to pause again, to let my eyes adjust. Holding my hands in front of me, I crossed the hall and found the wall on the right, which I used to guide me to the corridor which led to the cloakroom and laundry room.

The blackness in that corridor was absolute! I could see nothing at all. With my heart thudding, I let my fingers trail along the wall on the right until I found the doorway into the cloakroom. Fortunately, it stood open, as usual. However, I knew, without going in there, I'd never be able to find my own shoes in the blackness. Besides, I might knock something over and make a noise; several things lived in the cloakroom as well as coats and shoes, including the small children's scooters and various other large, outdoor toys.

I managed to cross the gap and continued down the corridor, still trailing my fingers along the wall. I passed two closed doors; I knew these were store-rooms. Finally, I came to the end of the corridor and felt solid wall in front of me. All I had to do was edge along it to the door.

A very faint light coming in through the un-curtained windows illuminated the laundry room. Just enough for me to see the vague shapes of the two washing machines and the giant dryer on the far side of the room. I made straight for the window and reached across the double sink unit to open it.

The handle was stiff, but eventually, I managed to force it up and open the window. Glad that I wasn't wearing shoes after all, I clambered onto the sink unit and straddled the windowsill.

The gap was only just wide enough for me to wriggle and twist my way through it. Even so, I pulled a muscle in my groin as I dragged the other leg up and over the sill. I dropped down, landing on all fours. I stood up, wiped grit off my hands and turned around to push the window almost closed.

I stood still and listened again. I'd made it! Everything remained still and silent. Just a few yards away, Tramp waited to whirl me away to a new life. All I had to do now was reach the gate and freedom. Feeling very pleased with myself I crossed the concrete courtyard, wincing every now and then as my feet landed on small stones. Reaching the corner of the building, I peered around it toward the street. There was definitely someone standing there, leaning against the gate post.

I stepped out and jogged the last few yards down the driveway and onto the street. I rushed toward the shadow I'd seen, a wide smile on my face.

"Hello, Keri," said Neil, conversationally. "Going somewhere, were you?"

43. Leaving

How Neil had managed to lie in wait for me outside the gates of Garfield House at gone two in the morning mystified me ... but not for long. Neil grabbed my arms firmly and marched me into the house - the back door was unlocked!

I fumed silently to myself at my struggle to make my way through the corridor, cloakroom and laundry when all the time I could have simply opened the door and left! Neil shoved me, quite roughly, toward the door of the office, which he leaned forward to open.

Inside, sitting by the fireplace in armchairs, were Paul and Joss. Both were wearing their night attire. A very small and dim lamp glowed on the mantelpiece. On seeing me, Joss shook her head and Paul scowled. Neil followed me into the room, switching on the main light as he did so.

"Exactly as George reported," Neil crowed. "I told you she'd get out, even if we locked the fire-door."

I said nothing at all. Inside my mind, I was already away and free, travelling on Tramp's motorbike toward a new life, free of all this. I wondered if he'd seen Neil and hidden somewhere else. Did he watch my capture?

"I expect you're wondering where your Mr. 'King' is, Keri?" Paul sounded smug.

I shrugged.

"He's been arrested. We're not entirely stupid, you know. You're not the first determined runaway we've dealt with here and I doubt you'll be the last. Did you think we wouldn't check up on unexpected visitors? The false name didn't help in the least."

My heart lurched in my chest. Tramp had been arrested? How? More importantly, why? I opened my mouth, intending to demand answers, but Joss spoke before me.

"I'm so disappointed in you, Keri. Don't you know how dangerous Hells Angels are? When I think about you mixing with such undesirable men, getting involved with alcohol and drugs and heavens alone knows what else, I ..."

"I've never got involved in those things!" I blurted. "And they're not 'undesirable men'! At least none of them got me drunk or raped me - or sold me to the highest bidder like you did!"

"You shut your mouth!" Paul snapped. "We'll have none of that!"

"No. You want me to keep my mouth shut so you don't get into trouble! I'm going to tell the whole world about you - all of you!"

Paul actually laughed at me! "Go ahead. No-one will listen and those who do will not believe you. You're leaving here in a few hours anyway and I can assure you, you'll not find it so easy to simply 'walk out' of the place you're being sent to." He turned to Joss. "I think we'll have a cup of tea now, Joss, if you wouldn't mind making it."

I edged toward the door, but Neil stepped between it and me and I knew I couldn't escape. Besides, even if I got out of the door - out of the house, I couldn't run far or fast without shoes. Frustration and anger gave me a false courage.

I snarled at Paul, "How did you know? Were you listening at doors to what we said? I'll bet you were, you pervert! I expect you were hoping to see some kind of sex ..."

"Oh deary me, what an active imagination you have, Keri!" Paul grinned. "None of us need to go listening at doors! If we did that, we'd be misled all the time. No. It's just as I said, we made enquiries when your friend - 'Tramp' I think he's known as - arrived. He spun a convincing enough yarn, but you see, your belongings were recovered from a house in Great Yarmouth a day or so before you arrived at your grandmother's. You had Karen's things too, didn't you?"

I refused to reply. Paul continued. "When your friend turned up, we already had a pretty good idea of who he might be. He didn't fit the description of the man known as Johnny King, so we had the police run some more checks. How you can say that man is not 'undesirable' I have no idea. He's already out on bail for a charge of Grievous Bodily Harm!"

I recalled the night I'd waited so long in the cold churchyard whilst Tramp and the rest of the club had gone off to 'settle a score'. He'd made sure I was not involved in any way.

"The police were very interested in the information we gave them."

"What information?" I mumbled.

"We had George follow your friend - at a distance of course - when he left here. He went straight to a pub where he met up with a crowd of those Hells Angels. Did you really think you could run away to Ireland and get married?"

"It would be better than being here!" I snapped.

"Yes, I'm sure you think it would be. Yet, before you go back to bed, let me tell you something, Keri. That man would never have married you - anyway, you're far too young. You're not telling me you are naive and silly enough to believe you'd live happily ever after with some grubby man nearly ten years older than you?"

"He's not grubby!"

"Not when he came here, perhaps. If it hadn't been for the information we'd already received from the police when they brought your things back here, we might have believed him. After all, he's well spoken and looked presentable."

I didn't dare tell Paul and Neil anything at all about Tramp. I felt sure they'd only run to the police with it. That they had no idea of the true bond Tramp and I had formed whilst I'd been away was obvious. I trusted Tramp. Having seen his family and spent so much time in his company, I knew he was decent. I certainly did believe I'd live happily ever after with him.

Joss arrived with a tray. I noticed there were four cups on it.

"You can have a quick cup of tea, Keri, and then you must go back to bed. You'll be up quite early and you have a long journey to make." Joss poured the tea and handed me a mug.

"Where am I going? I suppose you're having me sent to prison as well?" I couldn't muster much more of a fight as I already battled tears which threatened to overwhelm me. My heart felt as if it had shrivelled inside me and once again, fear and panic were building in my belly.

"Don't be silly, Keri! Girls of fifteen don't get sent to prison! Of course not." Joss sat down, pulling her dressing gown over her knees.

"Where then?" I persisted.

"A new home, for girls only. We waited quite some time for them to find a place for you. You have to leave here, Keri, since your family has moved so far away. We actually only finalised the arrangements earlier yesterday afternoon." Paul answered my question.

I ground my teeth. Why hadn't I fled when Tramp left? If we'd gone, straight from the play-barn, we'd have had a few minutes start at least and a chance.

"Hurry up and drink that tea, girl," Paul added. "We've all spent half the night up and chasing about after you already. You need to get to bed and to sleep and so do I. I'll not be sorry to see the back of you; you're trouble, with a capital 'T'."

As I drank the tea, my mind raced. I had no intention whatever of going to sleep! I fully intended to climb out the window as soon as I'd been left alone in my room, never mind that I Might injure myself. I had to get away!

Joss escorted me to my room. I almost expected her to remove all my clothing and belongings, but she didn't. I sat down on my bed and pulled the jeans out of the small bag, tossing them to the floor. Beneath, lay Lambie, all squashed in with my socks and underwear. I tugged him out and held him against my chest.

"Come along, Keri. Get back into your nightdress. I'm so tired. I think we've all had quite enough excitement for one night, don't you?" Joss sounded weary.

I got undressed and pulled on the nightdress I'd left discarded on the bed just a couple of hours earlier. I switched on the bedside lamp, expecting Joss to tell me to switch it off. Again, she made no remark upon it.

"Goodnight, Keri. I'll see you in the morning and help you pack your things."

Joss left the room and closed the door. Immediately, I stood up and went to the window, where I opened the curtains and struggled with the window catch. It had been locked! I rushed to the fire-door and swept the curtain aside. I tried the bar again and again. Nothing would budge that door.

Frantic, I opened my bedroom door and saw Neil, sitting on a chair at the end of the corridor. He gave me a cheery wave.

Utterly defeated, I closed the door, flung myself onto the bed and sobbed bitter tears into Lambie's tatty, woollen body. I wept for the freedom I'd so nearly had; for Tramp, having been arrested; for all the vileness I'd endured in my life and the injustice of everything.

I woke, bleary eyed and with the kind of headache prolonged weeping always leaves. Joss had entered my room with some cardboard boxes.

"Good morning, Keri. You'd better get yourself washed and dressed and hurry down to breakfast. Your social worker will be here at half past nine." She put the boxes on the floor under the window and left the room before I could think of anything to say.

Mrs. Webster made me sit with the little ones at breakfast, ensuring I had no chance whatever to speak with either Valerie or John. I felt very much aware of Valerie and Sarah staring at me, but I didn't turn round to look at them. What could I say, after all?

I ate very little; my stomach was knotted with anxiety and the headache didn't help at all.

"Come along, Keri!" Mrs. Webster chided me. "You're not setting a very good example to the young ones by not eating."

"Sorry. I've got a headache and I feel a bit sick."

"I'll get you an aspirin then. Lack of sleep does that to a person." Mrs. Webster left the table and headed toward the office.

I took the opportunity to glance at Valerie. Her eyes were wide. "What's happening? Did you do something?"

"I got caught trying to run last night. They're sending me somewhere else today."

"Oh, no! Keri, I'm so ..."

Valerie stopped speaking as Mrs. Webster returned with two aspirin and a glass of water, which I accepted. It still didn't help my appetite though. I nibbled at a piece of toast, anxiety building by the minute.

As the meal ended, Joss came to the dining room to fetch me. I had no choice but to follow her, acutely aware of the many eyes that watched in silence. As we reached the corridor, I heard little Mary's voice, "Mrs. Webster, has Keri been naughty again?"

"Never you mind, dear," Mrs. Webster replied. "It's time for Keri to move on from here, that's all."

When we reached my room, I immediately noticed several full bags standing next to the boxes Joss had left earlier.

"These are the things we recovered from the house in Great Yarmouth. You'll have to sort through them. I expect some of the clothes belong to Karen - not that she'll need them now."

I pounced on that statement immediately. "Why won't she need clothes?" I asked, obvious alarm sounding in my voice.

"Because she has to wear a uniform in her new place, Keri. When she finally leaves there, I'm sure she'll be given new clothes. Now, we need to sort all these things out quite quickly. Apparently, you'll be limited as to what you can and cannot have at this new home."

This sounded peculiar too, although I couldn't bear to ask any more questions; I felt too afraid of what the answer might be.

Joss left me sorting through the clothes Karen and I had shared. I wanted to keep all of them, but Joss tersely informed me I could only keep what would fit into three boxes. She'd gone down to collect my footwear and coats from the cloakroom.

When Joss returned, she found me on my knees, clothing scattered all around and weeping again. She placed a hand on my shoulder.

"Come on, Keri. You can't cry for ever. You brought all this upon yourself. If you'd only behaved properly, we might have been able to keep you here for longer. Yet you've made so many problems for us, we now have no choice - especially since your mother has moved away and insists you need to be closer to her."

I sniffed. "I don't believe that! My mother hates me."

Joss began to pick up and fold the clothes. "So you've said before, Keri, but when I met with her, she seemed to me like a perfectly nice lady who cannot understand why her only daughter should behave the way she does."

"If she hadn't let her foul husband rape me, I wouldn't have got into any trouble at all! She even hated me before she married him. She told me enough times."

Joss paused and looked at me. "Listen, Keri. You keep making allegations of rape and abuse. You're like the boy who called 'wolf' when there was no wolf. One day, it will really happen to you and by that time, no-one will believe you at all."

I gaped at Joss. "What? You know I was raped on Jersey! They caught him and threw him off the island! You know what Paul and Neil do to me - to all of us! Why can't you tell the truth?"

Joss shook her head. "I don't know anything, Keri, only that you're very promiscuous and have a very violent and unpredictable temper – and a tendency to make up incredible stories. The sad thing is, sometimes, you're so convincing, people nearly believe you. I did, at first."

I scowled. "How do you explain those X-Rays then? The ones that showed all my ribs had been broken in the past? Did I make that up as well?"

Joss continued packing my clothes into a box. "I expect there was a mix-up with medical records or something. There is bound to be a reasonable explanation, Keri."

Briefly, I considered slapping this woman. Her words were all the more hurtful because, when first I arrived at Garfield House, she had appeared to believe me and had been so kind. Yet somehow, despite all the frustration, the injustice and the anxiety, I could not find it in me to fight any more, not even verbally.

I let Joss choose which clothes I would keep and which I'd leave behind. I sat on the bed, clutching Lambie, only half paying attention. I did leap up and snatch the handkerchief Mam had given me from Joss's hand. "That's mine! It was a present and it means a lot to me!"

Joss shook her head. "Very well, but it should really be washed; it's very grubby."

I tucked the handkerchief into my pocket. "I don't care."

Neil arrived at my bedroom door to tell Joss that Miss Partridge had arrived. He lifted one of the boxes and Joss lifted another. "Can you manage that last box, Keri? If not, I'll come back and fetch it."

I shook my head. Lifting the box would mean letting go of Lambie and I had no intention of doing that. I followed Joss and Neil along the corridor, down the stairs and into the office.

Miss Partridge looked up as we entered. She'd been speaking with Paul. Clearly, he'd told her of my attempted escape the night before.

"Hello, Keri. Are you looking forward to moving?"

"No."

Miss Partridge smiled, in a vague, distracted manner. "How very strange. You don't seem to like it here very much. I thought you'd be eager to move."

"No."

Miss Partridge turned back to Paul and began speaking about money and valuables - of which I thought I had neither. However, it turned out that not only did I have some savings of which I'd been unaware; there was also the matter of a 'Leaving Grant' since I would be moving to another authority. I paid little attention to the details.

Actually, leaving happened all of a sudden. I hadn't known that Joss and Neil already stowed the boxes into Miss Partridge's car. When Miss Partridge stood up and shook Paul's hand and he wished her a pleasant journey, I felt surprised.

"Goodbye, Keri," Paul held out his hand to me.

I turned away. Paul might have thought me rude but the truth was I had such a lump in my throat I couldn't speak.

I followed Miss Partridge out the front door, down the steps and around to where her car was parked. Joss and Neil stood nearby. I refused to look at either of them as I got into the passenger seat.

The last I saw of Garfield House and everything that had ever been familiar - if painful for me – as Miss Partridge edged her car out onto the Norwich Road, was Joss waving as the young children ran about in the courtyard behind her.

Epilogue

This ends the second part of my long-winded biography. I should like to be able to report that I went on to a new life and found happiness and peace. Unfortunately, that is not the case. My life took on an even darker and more sinister aspect as I found myself transported to a completely new area of the country and incarcerated behind the locked doors of a Home Office Approved School for 'Intelligent but Maladjusted and Emotionally Disturbed Girls'.

My story continues in the next volume which will be entitled Keri-Karin.

Printed in Great Britain
by Amazon.co.uk, Ltd.,
Marston Gate.